The Sixth Amendment in Modern American Jurisprudence

Recent Titles in
Contributions in Legal Studies

Equal Separation: Understanding the Religion Clauses of the First Amendment
Paul J. Weber, editor

Common Law in Southern Africa: Conflict of Laws and Torts Precedents
Peter B Kutner

A History of the Anglo-American Common Law of Contract
Kevin M. Teeven

"We Have a Duty": The Supreme Court and the Watergate Tapes Litigation
Howard Ball

The Shaping of Ninteenth-Century Law: John Appleton and Responsible Individualism
David M. Gold

Comparative Constitutional Federalism: Europe and America
Mark Tushnet, editor

Church-State Constitutional Issues: Making Sense of the Establishment Clause
Donald L. Drakeman

The Politics of Obscenity: Group Litigation in a Time of Legal Change
Joseph F. Kobylka

An Essential Safeguard: Essays on the United States Supreme Court and Its Justices
D. Grier Stephenson, Jr., editor

A "Representative" Supreme Court? The Impact of Race, Religion, and Gender on Appointments
Barbara A. Perry

State Constitutions and Criminal Justice
Barry Latzer

The Sixth Amendment in Modern American Jurisprudence

A CRITICAL PERSPECTIVE

Alfredo Garcia

Contributions in Legal Studies, Number 67

GREENWOOD PRESS
NEW YORK • WESTPORT, CONNECTICUT • LONDON

Library of Congress Cataloging-in-Publication Data

Garcia, Alfredo.
The Sixth Amendment in modern American jurisprudence : a critical perspective / Alfredo Garcia.
p. cm.—(Contributions in legal studies, ISSN 0147–1074 ; no. 67)
Includes bibliographical references and index.
ISBN 0–313–27877–6 (alk. paper)
1. Criminal procedure—United States. 2. Right to counsel—United States. 3. United States—Constitutional law—Amendments—6th.
I. Title. II. Series.
KF9625.Z9G37 1992
345.73′05—dc20
[347.3055] 91–44047

British Library Cataloguing in Publication Data is available.

Library of Congress Catalog Card Number: 91–44047
ISBN: 0–313–27877–6
ISSN: 0147–1074

First published in 1992

Greenwood Press, 88 Post Road West, Westport, CT 06881
An imprint of Greenwood Publishing Group, Inc.

Printed in the United States of America

The paper used in this book complies with the Permanent Paper Standard issued by the National Information Standards Organization (Z39.48–1984).

P

In order to keep this title in print and available to the academic community, this edition was produced using digital reprint technology in a relatively short print run. This would not have been attainable using traditional methods. Although the cover has been changed from its original appearance, the text remains the same and all materials and methods used still conform to the highest book-making standards.

To Cindy, whose wisdom far exceeds mine and without whose unswerving support this book would not have been possible; to James and Christina, who provided a constant source of joy; and to my mother, Rosalina, whose courage, dignity, and perseverance in the face of adversity furnished inspiration.

Contents

Preface

The bicentennial of the Bill of Rights in 1991 provides an apt occasion for a book focusing on the Sixth Amendment. In comparison to the inordinate amount of scholarly attention devoted to the Fourth and Fifth Amendments, the Sixth Amendment has not generated as much concern.[1] This text represents a modest attempt to fill that void in the literature, because the last significant work on the topic is Francis Heller's historical analysis of the amendment, published in 1951.[2] Heller's work is historically important but has been rendered obsolete by the jurisprudential developments of the last few decades. During that time, the Sixth Amendment has undergone significant change pursuant to its incorporation into the Fourteenth Amendment.

I do not endeavor to furnish a comprehensive treatise on the Sixth Amendment. Rather, I offer an interpretive analysis of the doctrinal development of the amendment by concentrating on the United States Supreme Court's interpretation of the amendment since the 1960s. My perspective is colored by almost a decade of experience in the criminal process, both as a prosecutor and as a defense attorney, in Miami, Florida. Although theory plays a role in the analysis, experience in the ''real world'' of criminal law informs a large part of the text.

The principal thesis of the book is that the Supreme Court's recent interpretation of the amendment has been marked by doctrinal inconsistency and by a failure to adhere to the functional and symbolic values that are inherent in the amendment. A corollary to this thesis is that the Court has adopted a ''crime control'' ideology, stressing efficiency rather than the core ideal of a fair trial that the amendment is designed to safeguard. Moreover, my approach differs from the conventional treatment of the topic, which maintains that the recent doctrinal development of the Sixth Amendment has deviated from the Court's interpretation of the Fourth and Fifth amendments.

The book is divided into six chapters, covering the rights to counsel, to confrontation, to compulsory process, to a speedy trial, and to a jury trial, as well as the clash between the right to a free press and the right to a fair trial. The first chapter provides the thematic and structural framework of the book through the lens of the right to counsel, which may be viewed as the touchstone of the Sixth Amendment. The remaining chapters deal with the other discrete, but related, components of the amendment within the context of the adversary system of adjudication. The conclusion assesses how the Court's interpretation of the amendment has advanced or detracted from the interests fostered by the amendment, which is the cornerstone of the criminal adversary process.

I have incurred numerous debts during the course of writing this book. My colleague Don Lively encouraged me to pursue the project, and he read and commented upon most of the manuscript. Similarly, Ellen Podgor reviewed parts of the work and offered helpful suggestions. Dean Jacqueline Allee generously provided financial support during the summer of 1991. Dean Leigh Taylor and his staff furnished technical assistance and an atmosphere conducive to legal research and writing. Mike Bloom (class of 1991) and Gaston Cantens (class of 1993) were invaluable research assistants.

Parts of this book have appeared in the *American Criminal Law Review*, *Duquesne Law Review*, and *Southwestern University Law Review*. I am grateful to the editors of those journals for giving me a forum in which to express my views.

Finally, and most importantly, this book would never have reached fruition without the wonderful and dedicated support of my wife, Cindy. Her love and inspiration were a constant source of strength.

NOTES

1. The only exception to lack of scholarly focus on the Sixth Amendment is the confrontation clause.

2. Heller, THE SIXTH AMENDMENT TO THE CONSTITUTION OF THE UNITED STATES (1951).

The Sixth Amendment in Modern American Jurisprudence

1

The Right to Counsel under Siege: Requiem for an Endangered Right?

The Sixth Amendment[1] occupies a pivotal role in the panoply of rights accorded criminal defendants through the Bill of Rights to the U.S. Constitution. This distinction flows from the amendment's prescriptive, symbolic, and practical value to the adversary system of adjudication. The inherent significance of the amendment within the context of the American criminal justice system rests upon the fact that it fosters and promotes the functional and normative purpose of affording a criminal defendant a fair trial.[2] To a large extent, the amendment embodies the paradigm of a system of justice that furnishes the individual with the pertinent tools with which to defend against the organized power of the state. The complex of rights delineated in the amendment are meant to equalize the balance of power in the criminal process by granting the defendant an indispensable shield against the natural advantage the prosecution enjoys in a criminal trial.[3]

With a few notable exceptions,[4] the Supreme Court's recent Sixth Amendment jurisprudence has been marked by doctrinal inconsistency and by a failure of the Court to adhere to the core values embedded in the amendment.[5] The promise of an expansive interpretation of the amendment engendered by the Warren Court has given way to a fundamentally different conception. As a result, both the functional and symbolic roles of the amendment have been steadily eroded. This trend is particularly evident in three of the clauses that provide criminal defendants with the means to counter the natural advantage the prosecution enjoys and that ensure ''fair process'' norms.[6] These three clauses encompass a defendant's rights to counsel, to confrontation, and to compulsory process.[7] By diminishing the Sixth Amendment rights of criminal defendants, the Court has emphasized a ''crime control'' ideology. Such an ideology conflicts with the values ingrained in the amendment.[8]

My perspective is at variance with the orthodox notion advanced by legal scholars that the recent doctrinal development of the Sixth Amendment has deviated from the Court's restrictive interpretation of the Fourth and Fifth amendment rights of criminal defendants. According to the conventional scholarly approach, the Burger Court fashioned a "hierarchy" of rights in which the protections accorded to criminal defendants under the Sixth Amendment were given precedence over comparable Fourth and Fifth amendment claims.[9] Although this characterization of the Court's doctrinal approach to the Sixth Amendment might have been accurate during the 1970s, it is inapt for the 1980s and 1990s. The new course the Court has chosen was dramatically illustrated in the 1988 Term, in which seven out of eight cases involving Sixth Amendment claims were decided against the interests of the defendants.[10]

Similarly, both the Burger and Rehnquist Courts have indulged in the rhetoric that trial-related rights of criminal defendants deserve greater respect than those not associated with the trial stage.[11] Consequently, the Burger Court rationalized its narrow construction of the exclusionary rule by labelling it a "judicially-created" structural remedy protective of Fourth Amendment rights through its deterrent effect.[12] This depiction of the exclusionary remedy was employed to distinguish it from a criminal defendant's "personal" constitutional rights.[13]

A useful way to understand this "hierarchy" thesis is by dissecting the Court's jurisprudence with respect to the right to counsel. Among the rights enumerated in the Sixth Amendment, the right to counsel may be regarded as the touchstone of the amendment.[14] In the 1960s and 1970s, the Court construed the right to counsel as the mechanism to ensure a criminal defendant a fair trial.[15] As previously suggested, a distinct countertrend has emerged, however, in which the efficiency, "crime control," rationale has significantly abridged a defendant's right to counsel. This outlook has been evident in decisions that have limited the defendant's right to select private counsel of choice[16] and that have also infringed upon this right by allowing the government to strip defendants of the right to choose private counsel through the pretrial forfeiture of allegedly "tainted" (i.e., drug-related) assets.[17] The "efficiency" perspective is also conspicuous in the narrow construction of the applicable criteria employed to resolve ineffective assistance of counsel claims.[18]

Several discrete themes surface from the Court's current treatment of the right to counsel. As the foregoing discussion indicates, the Court has demonstrated a perceptible concern for efficiency and, correspondingly, "crime control," in determining the suitable parameters of the right to counsel. Moreover, the Court has denigrated the dignitary values that are deeply rooted, both historically and functionally, in the Sixth Amendment and, particularly, in the right to counsel.[19] Finally, the Court has improperly relied upon ethical standards to thwart claims propounded by criminal defendants based on the right to counsel.[20]

The purpose of this chapter is to analyze these related themes within the context of the symbolic, functional, and practical values served by the Sixth Amendment's guarantee of the right to counsel. The chapter does not purport to furnish an exhaustive or comprehensive analysis of the manifold facets of the right to counsel; rather, it aims to identify and critique broad yet significant trends that have adversely impinged upon the right to counsel. This will be accomplished by examining the historical foundation of the right and by probing the functions of the right in light of the conflicting objectives of our adversary process. Therefore, the second part of this chapter will examine the historical background of the right to counsel; the third part will analyze the functional and normative aspects of the right in the context of our adversary system of adjudication; the fourth part will explore the themes that have emerged in the Court's recent jurisprudence on the right to counsel; and the final part will set forth the thesis that the Court's recent doctrinal approach to the right to counsel is based upon ideological and administrative expediency and reflects a myopic view of the practical and symbolic purposes the right fosters in our criminal justice system. In essence, the Court has adopted the tenet that defendants possess a revocable privilege to counsel rather than a fundamental constitutional right.

HISTORICAL FOUNDATION: ENGLISH AND COLONIAL BACKGROUND

The history of the right to counsel is inextricably tied to the English and colonial jurisprudence that led to the genesis of the Sixth Amendment. In examining the historical background, it is evident that the right to counsel did not receive favorable treatment in either English or early colonial jurisprudence; instead, the right was ultimately accepted, especially in the colonies, as a response to political exigencies. In fact, the grudging recognition of the right to counsel in England is betrayed by the fact that defendants accused of felonies other than treason were not entitled to lawyers until 1836.[21]

This antipathy that the British common law displayed toward the assistance of counsel derived from the weakness of the government vis-à-vis its enemies.[22] A historian of British law noted that this refusal to extend the help of counsel to the accused was approved by the public principally "because the government was so weak and its enemies so strong that it was felt, not without reason, that it must take every advantage of its enemies."[23] The Glorious Revolution in 1688, however, led to a more stable political situation and thus to the extension of the help of counsel to defendants accused of treason.[24] In fact, the Treason Act of 1695 ushered in a series of reforms in English criminal procedure that granted accused persons the right to notice and to compulsory process.[25] Despite the progress brought about by these revisions, however, the right to counsel was extended only to defendants charged with misdemeanors or treason.[26]

Given this hostility of the English system toward counsel, it was inevitable that such distrust would be carried over to the colonies. Moreover, to the extent that British criminal procedure was riddled with abuse of power, the "professional" lawyer was bound to become the symbol of oppression. In fact, this aversion to the profession is manifest in the West New Jersey Charter of 1676, which gave litigants the right to defend their cases and, concomitantly, freed them of the compulsion to hire counsel.[27]

Eventually, a shift in this attitude occurred in the American colonies because, unlike the mother country, they employed the inquisitorial institution of the public prosecutor. The prosecutor wielded great power due to his familiarity with procedural niceties, the "idiosyncrasies" of juries, and the personnel of the court.[28] As a consequence, the assistance of counsel and the allied rights ultimately enumerated in the Sixth Amendment became essential to counter the prosecutor's advantage. Ultimately, the denial of these rights formed part of the grievances listed in the Declaration of Independence.[29]

The right to counsel, therefore, found its way into most state constitutions after the colonies declared their independence.[30] The assistance of counsel, in turn, complemented the correlative right to self-representation.[31] Accordingly, it was natural that opposition to the Federal Constitution arose in part because the procedural protections accorded the accused in state constitutions, with the exception of the jury trial, were conspicuously missing from the new document.[32] This antagonism directed at the Constitution was allayed through the adoption and passage of the Bill of Rights, which included the trial-related safeguards outlined in the Sixth Amendment.

A look at the historical record reveals the extent to which the need for a proper equilibrium of forces between the prosecution and the accused led to the forging of the protections embodied in the Sixth Amendment. As one thoughtful commentator has remarked, the call for a Bill of Rights reflected the American public's insistence upon "the maintenance of a fair balance in criminal trials, and to that end the protection of the rights of the accused."[33] Preserving the rights of the accused, moreover, necessarily implied a repudiation of the English proscription of counsel in serious criminal cases.

Although the American safeguards designed to redress the imbalance of power that existed in English procedure included the right of the accused "to have the Assistance of counsel for his defense,"[34] the Sixth Amendment did not embrace the right to appointed counsel.[35] Rather, what the amendment connoted at the time of its enactment was that "the right to counsel meant the right to retain counsel of one's own choice and at one's expense."[36] Nearly two centuries later, the Supreme Court took into account the transformation and evolution of American jurisprudence and progressively implied the right to appointed counsel as essential to the structure of the Sixth Amendment. The logical culmination of this interpretation was the Warren Court's landmark ruling in *Gideon v. Wainwright.*[37] It is instructive, therefore, to scrutinize this jurisprudential development as a means of distilling the "modern" meaning of the right to counsel.

Modern Historical Evolution

The emergence of an expansive approach toward the right to counsel may be traced to the Supreme Court's seminal decision in *Powell v. Alabama.*[38] In

Powell, the Court determined that the assistance of counsel was "fundamental" in nature, and hence essential to ensure a defendant a fair trial.[39] Moreover, the *Powell* Court decided that the right comprehends "effective" assistance, rather than the mere perfunctory appearance of counsel.[40] Finally, the majority held that the due process clause of the Fourteenth Amendment required the appointment of counsel in a capital case.[41] Even though the *Powell* decision was carefully limited to its particular facts, it contained the seeds of a fundamental metamorphosis in the Court's conception of an attorney's role in a criminal proceeding. Implicit in this new understanding was the notion that the criminal process should strive to attain a modicum of equity by affording both sides the opportunity of vigorously asserting their positions.

In *Powell*, the Court expanded the scope of the Sixth Amendment by going beyond the original intent of the right to counsel clause. What the clause contemplated was the right of the defendant to choose private counsel; it did not envision the provision of appointed counsel.[42] The *Powell* Court recognized that a "defendant should be afforded a fair opportunity to secure counsel of his own choice."[43] Whether counsel was appointed or selected, however, is not the sole calculus in assessing the right to counsel; what the right necessarily implicates in an "effective," "zealous" advocate rather than the mere "*pro forma*," passive appearance of a defense attorney.[44]

The factual predicate of *Powell* illustrates the Court's concern for effective advocacy as integral to the assistance of counsel. In that case, the famous "Scottsboro" black defendants were charged with the rape of two white women.[45] The cases of the nine youthful defendants were severed, and three separate arraignments and trials were conducted in a single day.[46] More important, counsel appointed to represent the defendants were ill-prepared to represent them; their appearance amounted to a sham.[47] Given the emotionally charged atmosphere in which the trial occurred, a lack of effective counsel inevitably ensured a conviction.

It is within this framework that *Powell* must be viewed. The majority not only abhorred the sham nature of proceedings, but it also condemned the trial court for preventing the defendants from consulting with counsel and preparing their defense.[48] The egregious circumstances out of which *Powell* arose led the Court to reaffirm the "fundamental character" of the right to counsel in our adversary system of adjudication.[49] In an oft-quoted passage, the *Powell* Court acknowledged that counsel is indispensable to the balance of power requisite to an adversary system of adjudication, especially when the individual does not have the means to hire an attorney. The majority cogently wrote:

> [T]he right to be heard would be, in many cases, of little avail if it did not comprehend the right to be heard by counsel. Even the intelligent and educated layman has small and sometimes no skill in the science of law. If charged with a crime, he is incapable, generally, of determining for himself whether the indictment is good or bad. He is unfamiliar with the rules of evidence. Left without the aid of counsel, he may be put to

> trial without a proper charge, and convicted upon incompetent evidence, or evidence irrelevant to the issue or otherwise inadmissible. . . . He requires the hand of counsel at every step of the proceedings against him. . . . If that be true of men of intelligence, how much more true is it of the ignorant or illiterate, or those of feeble intellect.[50]

A "logical corollary" of this rationale was that the "right to be heard" by counsel implied "the right to have counsel appointed."[51] Although the *Powell* Court narrowly crafted its holding to apply solely to the factual circumstances of the case,[52] it foreshadowed a broader application of its holding by emphasizing the widespread acceptance of appointed counsel in all criminal prosecutions by most states.[53]

Aside from professing the importance of appointed counsel to the equipoise implied within the adversary process, the *Powell* Court tacitly identified another intrinsic, nonfunctional value: the right of the individual defendant to be treated with a measure of dignity.[54] As the foregoing discussion suggests, the majority was concerned with sustaining the defendants' inestimable self-worth, regardless of financial condition, when faced with the intricacies of the criminal process. At one point in its analysis, the *Powell* Court intimated that, even assuming the absence of a viable defense, the defendants were entitled to the assistance of effective counsel.[55] When confronting the organized force of the government, therefore, the individual defendant, according to the *Powell* decision, deserves a robust advocate who will preserve her right to contest the charges and, at the same time, safeguard her dignity.

The logical extension of the dignitary and adversarial benefits conferred on criminal defendants by *Powell* occurred six years later when the Court decided *Johnson v. Zerbst*.[56] In *Zerbst*, the majority broadened the reach of *Powell* at the federal level by holding that the Sixth Amendment compels the assistance of counsel in all prosecutions, absent waiver by the accused.[57] The *Zerbst* Court reaffirmed the underlying rationale espoused in *Powell* by stressing that, without an attorney, the typical defendant suffers a marked disadvantage against the government.[58] Furthermore, the majority acknowledged that court proceedings present an impenetrable barrier to an unskilled layman, who may see the process as "intricate, complex, and mysterious."[59]

Significantly, *Zerbst* also enlarged the parameters set forth in *Powell* by establishing stringent criteria for a valid waiver of counsel. Rejecting the proposition that failure to assert the constitutional right to counsel because of ignorance may constitute a valid waiver, the *Zerbst* Court instead created a presumption against waiver of the assistance of counsel.[60] A valid waiver entails an "intentional relinquishment of a known right or privilege."[61] Accordingly, an unrepresented defendant must competently and intelligently waive her right to counsel; in turn, the validity of the waiver is to be measured in conformity with the facts of each case, "including the background, experience, and conduct of the accused."[62]

The vitality infused into the right to counsel clause by *Powell* and *Zerbst* continued unabated in the early 1940s. In *Glasser v. United States*,[63] the Court lent substance to the meaning of effective assistance of counsel and reaffirmed the rigorous waiver standards enunciated in *Zerbst*. *Glasser* dealt with the thorny issue of defining the contours of effective assistance of counsel when a single defense attorney represents multiple defendants charged with the same crime. Such representation leads to a substantial likelihood that counsel will be confronted with the dilemma of protecting conflicting interests. A defense attorney who faces this quandary should decline multiple representation, lest he deprive one of the parties of the right to an effective and zealous defense.

Consistent with this rationale, the *Glasser* Court held that when a trial court is informed that conflicting interests might arise from multiple representation and ignores the potential conflict, the affected defendant is stripped of her right to effective assistance of counsel.[64] Moreover, the majority explicitly declared that such error is not deemed harmless but requires reversal of the conviction.[65]

Further, mere silence by the defendant in the face of the conflict is not tantamount to a waiver of effective assistance of ''conflict-free'' counsel.[66] Despite the fact that the defendant was a prosecutor who presumably was intimately acquainted with the criminal trial process, the *Glasser* Court refused to construe his silence when the conflict arose as a waiver. Rather, the Court viewed Glasser's experience as one factor to be considered ''in determining whether he waived his right to the assistance of counsel.''[67] Citing the strict criterion for a valid waiver of counsel established in *Zerbst*, the majority in *Glasser* charged the trial court with the duty of ensuring effective representation for the accused by obtaining an intelligent and competent waiver from the defendant.[68]

Finally, the *Glasser* Court evinced its solicitude for meaningful, effective assistance by maintaining that a defendant should be afforded the ''undivided assistance of counsel of choice'' regardless of the possibility of a conflict of interest.[69] In addition, the majority disavowed a prejudice-based test for determining ineffective assistance due to a conflict of interest; instead, it noted that ''[t]he right to have the assistance of counsel is too fundamental and absolute to allow the courts to indulge in nice calculations as to the amount of prejudice arising from its denial.''[70]

Despite the vitality with which the Court interpreted the right to counsel, it was reluctant to tread upon the prerogative of the states to determine the appropriate boundaries of the right. Consequently, in *Avery v. Alabama*[71] the majority reiterated the fundamental character of the assistance of counsel,[72] characterizing it as ''sacred,''[73] while simultaneously deferring to the judgment of state courts. *Avery* implicitly endorsed the ''fundamental fairness'' doctrine, according to which the specific guarantees of the Bill of Rights are deemed to be applicable to the states only if those precepts are essential to the ''concept of ordered liberty.''[74] In accordance with this perspective, the *Avery* Court held that the defendant was not deprived of the effective assistance of counsel because the trial court denied a continuance, even though defense counsel had been given only three days to prepare for a first-degree murder trial.[75]

Carrying the fundamental fairness doctrine to its ultimate conclusion, the Court in *Betts v. Brady*[76] held that the Fourteenth Amendment's due process clause did not mandate counsel for an indigent defendant charged with a felony offense.[77] The majority deemed such a requirement unnecessary to safeguard fundamental principles of fairness. Instead, the *Betts* Court undertook a survey of state constitutions, which yielded the conclusion that most states did not consider appointment of counsel for indigents a "fundamental right, essential to a fair trial."[78] Comity, in effect, took precedence over constitutional imperatives.

Even though the holding in *Betts* is counterintuitive,[79] the majority sought to justify its position by relying on the particular facts out of which *Betts* arose. The defendant was charged with robbery, demanded and was refused appointed counsel, and proceeded to trial without the benefit of counsel.[80] Betts unsuccessfully relied upon an alibi defense. He was forty-three years old, familiar with the criminal process, and "of ordinary intelligence." Given these circumstances, the majority reasoned that Betts had the "ability" to defend himself on the narrow alibi issue on which the outcome of the trial hinged.[81]

As Yale Kamisar has observed, the *Betts* Court devised a "prejudice" or "special circumstances" standard. Such a test required a defendant in a noncapital case to show that he had suffered prejudice by proceeding without counsel or that special circumstances based on his intelligence level, lack of education, or complexity of the charge or defense made the proceedings "fundamentally unfair."[82]

The problem with the prejudice–special circumstances test is that it presents an insurmountable barrier for the defendant. In essence, the absence of defense counsel creates the distinct impression that "no lawyer could have saved the defendant anyway, and thus the lack of counsel often serves as a justification for the lack of counsel."[83] As Justice Black pointed out in dissent, one cannot reasonably determine whether counsel could have affected the outcome of the trial when no counsel was furnished to the indigent defendant.[84] Further, a careful review of the trial transcript in *Betts* reveals that competent defense counsel could have exposed serious problems with the prosecution's case, such as a questionable pretrial identification of Betts.[85]

Ultimately, the *Betts* majority was guided by the pragmatic implications of affording counsel to indigent defendants in serious criminal cases. What would preclude the extension of the rule to misdemeanor or other petty criminal charges? For that matter, an extreme interpretation of such a rationale would result in having to provide the protections of due process to civil cases involving property.[86] Therefore, the majority avoided the outcome dictated by its precedent in *Powell*, *Zerbst*, and *Glasser* by employing a worst-case scenario argument and by submitting to the states' authority in defining the proper scope of the right to counsel.

The Paradigm: *Gideon v. Wainwright*

The formidable task faced by Abe Fortas when he was appointed by the United States Supreme Court to represent Earl Clarence Gideon was to blunt the rationale undergirding *Betts*; that is, he had to convince the Court that providing counsel in all criminal cases was not a "radical" step, and he had to deflate the "federalism" issue.[87] Fortas accomplished this feat by persuading the Court that the "special circumstances" standard was anti-federalist because it fostered federal review of state court rulings; and he swayed the Court to the belief that providing counsel in all state felony prosecutions was not revolutionary but "evolutionary."[88]

Gideon constituted a powerful affirmation of the fundamental nature of the right to counsel. Endorsing the essential character of the right, a unanimous Court adhered to the rationale underlying *Powell* and rejected the flawed reasoning of *Betts*.[89] More important, the opinion acknowledged the reality of not affording an indigent defendant counsel: an "unequal" contest in which the defendant's interests are slighted.[90] It is axiomatic that such a proceeding is antithetical to the values and policies upon which the adversary system is based.

Accordingly, the underpinning of *Gideon* rests on the notion that a fair trial requires a certain balance of power between the prosecution and the defense. To the extent that the government has and spends the resources necessary to secure a conviction, so must the defendant have a lawyer to combat the prosecution. Since "there are few defendants charged with a crime . . . who fail to hire the best lawyers they can get to prepare their defenses," equal protection dictates that an indigent defendant should have the assistance of counsel.[91]

Few decisions have evoked as much popular support as *Gideon*. Indeed, Kamisar characterized *Gideon* as "one of the most popular decisions ever handed down by the United States Supreme Court."[92] The popularity of *Gideon* is attributable to its simplicity and to its grounding in common sense. As one commentator has remarked, the opinion is a landmark because "it affirmed a right that is now fundamentally accepted in our society."[93] Furthermore, *Gideon*'s approval stems from its validation of the adversary process; that is, the decision provided legitimacy to a system founded on an adversarial clash between two relatively equal sides whose conflicting interests allegedly produce an accurate result.[94] Given the natural imbalance promoted by a proceeding in which the defendant lacked an attorney, it was inevitable that the *Betts* special circumstances–prejudice test would give way to *Gideon*'s formula. The legitimacy of the criminal adversary process, on which the accused's liberty depends, demanded such an outcome.

Admittedly, the symmetry advanced by a fair balance of power between the prosecution and the defendant is a normative construct rather than a real prospect.[95] A perfect equilibrium has not been attained, especially with regard to indigent defendants. "Resource deprivation" hampers defense attorneys who represent indigent clients. Their ability effectively to counter the prosecution's natural advantage is impaired by a combination of excessive workloads, lack of adequate funds for investigation and expert witnesses, and nominal support staff.[96] Although the promise of *Gideon* has not been practically fulfilled, its normative aspect is nonetheless viable.

Despite the lack of a perfect correspondence between the ideal and the reality, one can discern circumstances under which the availability of counsel to an indigent defendant may decisively affect the outcome of a criminal proceeding. The example *par excellence* of this phenomenon is *Gideon*. Gideon was convicted principally because he lacked the acumen and experience of a seasoned criminal trial attorney. Upon retrial of the case, Gideon obtained the services of an able attorney, Fred Turner, who made the "difference." Turner's skills contributed to Gideon's acquittal not because of his knowledge of the nuances of criminal law or evidence; rather, Turner's perspicacity enabled him to argue a fundamental point that created a reasonable doubt. The elementary detail Turner stressed was the lack of evidence relating to the proceeds of the burglary Gideon was alleged to have committed.[97]

In sum, the *Gideon* decision represents the apex, both normatively and functionally, of an adversary process that accords indigent defendants a measure of equality in a criminal proceeding. Even if this equality has turned out to be somewhat illusory, the adversary system was legitimated by the *Gideon* Court to the degree that the decision contributed to the public perception that the system was "fair" and that "fairness" was not a function of a defendant's financial ability.

The Due Process–Equal Protection Approach

Consistent with the egalitarian premise underlying *Gideon*, the Court simultaneously extended its breadth to the appellate realm in *Douglas v. California*.[98] Utilizing the equal protection analysis implicit in *Gideon*, the majority held that an indigent defendant is entitled to appointed counsel for his first appeal as a matter of right.[99] The *Douglas* Court thereby invalidated a California procedure under which counsel was denied to indigent appellants whose appeal was deemed "frivolous" by the appellate court upon review of the trial record.[100]

Douglas is significant because it enlarged the boundaries of *Gideon* by relying upon either the equal protection or the due process clause[101] of the Fourteenth Amendment rather than the right to counsel provision of the Sixth Amendment. As Justice Harlan's dissenting opinion emphasized, *Gideon*'s foundation did not prescribe the majority's holding in *Douglas*.[102] Despite *Gideon*'s rejection of invidious financial classifications to deprive an indigent defendant of counsel at trial, the opinion rested upon the Sixth Amendment's right to counsel clause rather than on equal protection grounds rooted in the Fourteenth Amendment.[103] Nevertheless, the majority in *Douglas* sought to bolster its holding by quoting the adage in *Griffin v. Illinois*[104] that equal justice is denied "where the kind of appeal a man enjoys 'depends on the amount of money he has.' "[105] Therefore, the *Douglas* majority concluded, "an unconstitutional line between rich and poor" is drawn when an indigent defendant is refused appellate counsel on her first appeal as a matter of right.[106]

If one approaches *Douglas* from a due process rather than an equal protection perspective, the majority opinion resonates the reasoning upon which *Gideon* rests: fundamental fairness. In effect, access to an attorney for appellate purposes should not be predicated on the financial ability of the defendant. Rather, a fair procedure requires, at least on the first nondiscretionary appeal,[107] that the defendant have the means to challenge effectively her conviction.

In conjunction with *Gideon*, which was handed down the same day, *Douglas* served a legitimating function.[108] Not only did *Douglas* ratify the normative and practical principles advanced in *Gideon*, but it also augmented the animating force behind *Gideon*: that indigency should not constitute a barrier to the fair procedures integral to an adversary process of adjudication. Further, *Douglas* broadened the parameters of the Court's criminal jurisprudence by affording indigent defendants significant procedural safeguards outside the ambit of Sixth Amendment protections.

The Aftermath: *Argersinger*, *Scott*, and *Ross*

What Justice Clark called the Court's "new fetish for indigency"[109] underlying *Gideon* and *Douglas* continued unabated in the early 1970s. The watershed occurred in 1972, when the Court expanded the scope of the Sixth Amendment by requiring the appointment of counsel for indigent persons charged with misdemeanors and facing jail terms. In *Argersinger v. Hamlin*,[110] the Court held that, "absent a knowing and intelligent waiver, no person may be imprisoned for any offense, whether classified as petty, misdemeanor, or felony, unless he was represented by counsel at his trial."[111] This holding represented the rational culmination of the attempt to achieve a reasonable balance of forces between prosecution and defense in a criminal trial.

Principles of fairness outlined in the Court's evolutionary approach toward the right to counsel dictated *Argersinger*'s outcome. Quoting from *Powell v. Alabama*, the *Argersinger* Court underscored the necessity of counsel for a fair trial.[112] Moreover, the distinction between misdemeanors or petty offenses and felonies was inconsequential; indeed, the "assembly-line" justice meted out in lower courts compelled the assistance of counsel to ensure the accused a fair trial.[113] Therefore, this rationale entailed the rejection of the limiting approach to the right to a jury trial, based on the distinction between major and minor or "petty" offenses, followed by the Court in *Duncan v. Louisiana*.[114]

In spite of its far-reaching effect, the *Argersinger* decision skirted the issue of whether counsel should be provided indigent defendants absent the prospect of imprisonment.[115] In his concurring opinion, Justice Powell criticized the "mechanistic" approach taken by the majority.[116] From his vantage point, the majority's solution would lead to perverse, unfair results. Due to the fortuity of circumstances, an "accused indigent would be entitled in some courts to counsel while in other courts in the same jurisdiction an indigent accused of the same offense would have no counsel."[117] Instead, he envisioned an ad hoc, case-by-case approach that would give the trial judge substantial latitude in determining whether counsel is required.[118]

More importantly, Justice Powell took the majority to task for failing to apply its logic to all petty offenses, rather than circumscribing it to cases in which some imprisonment is imposed. It is anomalous, he cogently argued, to deny counsel in some circumstances wherein the penalty, though not involving prison, is harsher than brief imprisonment. Thus, although both the Fifth and Fourteenth amendments protect property as well as life and liberty, the majority's perspective was based on an untenable distinction.[119]

Finally, Justice Powell accentuated the practical repercussions of *Argersinger*: that is, the opinion's imposition of a potentially intolerable burden on an overtaxed state criminal justice system.[120] This argument was reminiscent of the hurdle Abe Fortas had to overcome when he convinced the Court to overturn *Betts*; in effect, Justice Powell believed such an extension of *Gideon* constituted a "radical" step that would entail adverse systemic effects.[121] What Justice Powell failed to recognize, however, was *Argersinger*'s salutary symbolic and normative impact.

Given the *Argersinger* majority's repudiation of Justice Powell's perspective, it is ironic that the Court endorsed its rationale in *Scott v. Illinois*.[122] In that case, the majority curtailed *Argersinger*'s reach by holding that an indigent defendant is entitled to counsel only when imprisonment occurs and not when imprisonment is merely authorized but not imposed.[123] In drawing the line at actual imprisonment, the majority subscribed to the reasoning espoused by Justice Powell in *Argersinger*: an expansion of *Argersinger* "would create confusion and impose unpredictable, but necessarily substantial, costs on fifty quite diverse states."[124] The adoption of this reasoning in *Scott* is paradoxical in light of its disapproval by the *Argersinger* majority.[125]

Furthermore, the *Scott* Court's concern about the systemic effects of extending *Argersinger*'s scope lacked empirical foundation. Indeed, the majority in *Scott* acknowledged that its conclusion rested on shaky grounds.[126] As Justice Brennan pointed out in dissent, an "authorized imprisonment" standard would not have an adverse impact on the criminal justice system. Indeed, a majority of states at the time *Scott* was issued had implemented the "authorized" imprisonment criterion without detrimental results.[127] In fact, Scott would have been entitled to counsel under the existing laws of thirty-three states.[128]

The flawed "systemic effect" rationale underlying *Scott* was complemented by the majority's deprecation of the devastating implications attaching to a criminal conviction. As Justice Powell noted in his concurring opinion in *Argersinger*,[129] significant deprivations other than imprisonment accompany a criminal conviction. The negative consequences stemming from a conviction may preclude the defendant from performing civic duties, such as the right to serve on a jury, and prevent her from obtaining licenses required for certain occupations.[130] Moreover, the stigma and moral opprobrium that accompany a conviction for theft, the applicable offense in *Scott*, are not inconsequential.

If one accepts the premise that a hierarchy of rights is enumerated in the Sixth Amendment, the foremost of which is the right to counsel, the crabbed logic sustaining *Scott* emerges in bold relief. In *Lakeside v. Oregon*, the Court accepted such a hierarchy by stating that, "[i]n an adversary system of criminal justice, there is no right more essential than the right to the assistance of counsel."[131] The *Argersinger* Court, moreover, had implicitly supported the primacy of the right to counsel when it reasoned that the assistance of counsel was more fundamental to a fair proceeding than the right to a jury trial.[132] Therefore, *Scott* denigrated the right to counsel because, as long as no imprisonment occurred, a defendant would not be allowed counsel even if the offense was "nonpetty."[133] In fact, the theft offense for which Scott was convicted was not "petty": it carried a maximum potential punishment of one year in jail.[134]

Furthermore, it is ironic that the practical implications of *Scott* would pose more serious systemic problems than the alternative "authorized imprisonment" standard it rejected. As Justice Powell pointed out in *Argersinger*, and Justice Brennan reiterated in his *Scott* dissent, the "actual imprisonment" test presents numerous administrative difficulties, which include time-consuming decisions before trial of the likely sentence, inaccurate predictions, discretionary abuse and attendant "unequal treatment," and "apparent and actual" bias.[135]

From a normative, symbolic, and functional viewpoint, *Scott* represents a considerable retreat from the progressively expansive interpretation of the right to counsel which characterized the Court's previous jurisprudence. The vast majority of criminal prosecutions in this country are for misdemeanor offenses.[136] Since *Scott* denies appointed counsel for indigent defendants charged with misdemeanor offenses in which a jail term is not imposed, it distinctly conveys the impression to defendants that the system lacks "fairness." To the extent, moreover, that most of the public is exposed to the criminal justice system at the misdemeanor or "petty offense" level, the *Scott* opinion undermines confidence in the equity and fairness of the process. The *Scott* Court conveniently ignored the maxim embraced in *Argersinger* that "[t]he requirement of counsel may well be necessary for a fair trial even in a petty-offense prosecution."[137] Given the "assembly-line" nature of misdemeanor prosecutions, counsel may, in fact, make as much, if not more, of a difference in the misdemeanor context as at the felony level.

The deleterious ramifications flowing from *Scott* were somewhat ameliorated in *Baldasar v. Illinois*.[138] This decision proscribes the use of an uncounseled conviction for the purpose of sentence enhancement. Specifically, the *Baldasar* Court, in a *per curiam* opinion, held that an uncounseled misdemeanor conviction may not be employed to transform a misdemeanor offense into a felony for which a prison term may be imposed under an enhancement statute. Despite *Baldasar*'s mitigating effect, the opinion fails to remove the bulk of the pernicious effects fostered by *Scott*.

Congruent with *Scott*'s limitation upon *Argersinger*, the Court in the mid-1970s narrowed the reach of *Douglas v. California*.[139] In *Ross v. Moffit*,[140] the majority held that neither the equal protection nor the due process clause of the Fourteenth Amendment required the appointment of counsel for discretionary appeals.[141] *Ross* represents a strained construction of the precept enunciated in *Douglas*. The *Ross* majority unsuccessfully sought to distinguish *Douglas*, on both a due process and an equal protection basis.

The *Ross* Court attempted to justify its holding on due process grounds by maintaining that the appellate process differs from the trial stage because an appeal is initiated by the defendant to overturn his conviction. Conversely, at trial the defendant needs an attorney as "a shield to protect him from being 'haled into court' by the State and stripped of his presumption of innocence."[142] The rationale underlying this contention is fundamentally flawed. If the *Douglas* Court had adhered to this reasoning, it would have not provided counsel to indigent defendants for the first appeal as a matter of right. In effect, what the defendant attempts to achieve in her appeal, regardless of whether the appeal is discretionary or not, is to "upset the prior determination of guilt."

The equal protection argument that the majority in *Ross* relied upon is equally deficient. Recognizing that a lawyer well-versed in the intricacies of discretionary review would be immensely helpful to any litigant, the majority sought to downplay such an advantage. Any disadvantage suffered by the indigent appellant because he lacked counsel for a discretionary appeal, the majority argued, was "relative" compared with the considerable handicap confronted by the defendant in *Douglas*.[143] In turn, the "handicap" was minor because the defendant had the benefit of the brief filed on his behalf and, in some cases, an opinion by the intermediate court of appeals.[144]

It is instructive to juxtapose this rationale with the justification for denying counsel to an indigent litigant in the first appeal as a matter of right. Indeed, the *Douglas* Court rebuffed the notion that a dispassionate appraisal of the record by an appellate court to determine the validity of an appeal dispensed with the need for counsel. The "evil" fostered by such a procedure was discrimination against the indigent defendant.[145] Similarly, *Ross*'s discriminatory impact is undeniable.

As Justice Harlan pointed out in his *Douglas* dissent, one must stretch the imagination to accept the notion that "the requirements of fair procedure are exhausted once an indigent has been given one appellate review."[146] Counsel is as "necessary to the fair administration of justice" in a discretionary appeal involving a substantial constitutional claim as she is in an initial appeal taken as a matter of right.[147] The distinction the *Ross* majority sought to invoke, therefore, was spurious.

Emerging from the logic event in both *Scott* and *Ross* is the Court's preoccupation with order and efficiency to the detriment of constitutional imperatives. Although the Court eschewed the conceivably "radical" systemic implications of both *Argersinger* and *Douglas*, explicitly in *Scott* and implicitly in *Ross*, it weighed the impact of its ruling on the criminal justice system. Accordingly, the course charted by the Court in the mid-1970s and the 1980s differed from the compass followed by *Gideon*, *Douglas*, and *Argersinger*. "Practical" concerns suddenly loomed large against the ideal of fairness *Gideon* and its progeny sought to promote. Those pragmatic considerations, however, were chiefly imaginary[148] and masked the policy shift that had occurred due to the changing composition of the Court.[149]

CLASH OF VALUES, THE ADVERSARY PROCESS, AND THE RIGHT TO COUNSEL

> Our system of criminal law must serve two masters: ideally, it strives toward the goal of a fair trial; practical needs demand that it should secure strict enforcement of the law. The guarantees of the Sixth Amendment were intended to assure the former; modern conditions have evoked doubts lest law enforcement be defeated under the guise of safeguards intended for the furtherance of fairness in the criminal trial.[150]

Nearly four decades ago, a student of the Sixth Amendment expressed the basic antinomy that underlies our criminal adversary process.[151] In viewing the tension between the competing goals of ''crime control'' and ''due process,'' Herbert Packer devised a polar model representing the two extremes of the spectrum.[152] Peter Arenella, in turn, constructed a refined, more sophisticated version of Packer's typology.[153] Given its greater utility, it is worthwhile to explore Arenella's construct within the context of the conflicting objectives served by the criminal justice system. In particular, the dichotomy manifest in the model must be viewed through the prism of the interests advanced and safeguarded by the right to counsel.

Comparing the policy objectives apparent in the jurisprudence of the Warren Court and that of the Burger Court, Arenella contends that both Courts strove to ''accommodate the tension between efficient crime control and protection of individual rights.''[154] Consequently, he believes that, in comparing differing policy emphases pursued by distinct Courts, the proper frame of reference is not the tension between due process or crime control; rather, it is the Court's perception of the functions served by American criminal procedure.[155]

Elaborating upon and illuminating those functions, Arenella identifies three primary purposes underlying American criminal procedure: to provide a means of vindicating substantive criminal law goals; to furnish a dispute mechanism that efficiently allocates scarce resources and diffuses power among state officials; and to perform a ''legitimation function by resolving state-citizen disputes in a manner that commands the community's respect for the fairness of its process as well as the reliability of its outcomes.''[156]

In assaying these three purposes, the legitimation role is inextricably tied to the Sixth Amendment's right to counsel clause. Principally, the clause fosters respect for the system by guaranteeing ''procedural fairness'' and by ''ensuring formal equality of access to the system.''[157] Additionally, the assistance of counsel promotes aims other than accuracy in the outcome of the process by encouraging the defendant's meaningful participation in the inner workings of the system; that is, the defendant is treated not as a mere object of the process but is accorded dignity and respect through representation by counsel intimately acquainted with the operation of the criminal adversary mechanism.[158] Accordingly, the Supreme Court has acknowledged the obverse of the coin; that is, a defendant has the right to waive the assistance of counsel and conduct her own defense.[159]

Therefore, the right to counsel significantly advances "fair process" and "dignitary" norms that serve to legitimate the operation of the criminal justice system. Moreover, these norms are not necessarily consonant with achieving an accurate result. Indeed, from a result-oriented perspective, both norms may hinder the determination of factual guilt because they reflect the policy values of a system premised upon suspicion of unlimited governmental power. Consequently, both substantive and procedural barriers serve as checks against the unbridled exercise of the state's coercive monopoly.[160]

Further, the fair-process and dignitary norms incorporated in the right to counsel retain their relevance even assuming a failure to implement them. The system's viability depends to a certain extent on the public perception that the criminal process operates fairly, rather than solely on the system's scrupulous adherence to fair procedure and process. Even though reality and perception must to some extent coincide, the criminal process is validated if it produces the "appearance" of subscribing to and respecting the safeguards embodied in the Bill of Rights and, specifically, in the Sixth Amendment's provision of counsel.[161]

It is plausible to downgrade the ability of the Supreme Court's criminal procedure jurisprudence to affect the administration of criminal justice in the United States.[162] Nevertheless, conceding the soundness of such a view does not detract from the practical and functional impact of the assistance of counsel on the everyday world of criminal justice. A lawyer does make a difference, as the Court has repeatedly acknowledged; the system would be drastically different without the effect of *Gideon* and, to a lesser extent, *Argersinger*. Although the ideal behind *Gideon* has not been fully realized, its prescriptive force and widespread acceptance by the public cannot be gainsaid.

In fact, the Supreme Court has recognized the vital symbolic function played by the assistance of counsel. In *Kimmelman v. Morrison*,[163] the Court remarked that the right to counsel is a fundamental right which "assures the fairness, and thus the legitimacy, of our adversary process."[164] Deviation from the norms embodied in the right to counsel and from the rights enumerated in the Sixth Amendment subverts public confidence in the fairness of our criminal justice process.[165] A strong correlation between ideal and reality, moreover, is necessary to give life to the protections embedded in the Sixth Amendment. Rather than being treated as mere disembodied abstractions, the safeguards built into the Sixth Amendment, including the right to counsel, must be vigorously enforced. In Justice Frankfurter's words, "[p]rocedural devices rooted in history were written into the Bill of Rights not as abstract rubrics in an elegant code but in order to assure fairness and justice before any person could be deprived of 'life, liberty, and property.' "[166] Thus, although a system may arguably survive by creating the perception of adherence to fair process norms, in an adversary system, where Sixth Amendment rights are at the fulcrum of the process, mere "perception" is not sufficient.

The recent travails experienced by General Manuel Noriega, the former director of Panama, epitomize the need for convergence of perception and reality. Ironically, a dictator supposedly brought to face justice in a quintessentially democratic society denounced the American criminal justice system because, in his view, it failed to provide him with energetic, untrammeled legal representation. Addressing the United States District Court for the Southern District of Florida, Noriega in bold terms assailed the government for stripping him of his fundamental right to a fair trial. He described his plight in the following fashion: "They [the government] have taken my money, deprived me of my lawyers, videotaped me in my cell, wiretapped my telephone calls with my lawyers and even given them to the [Guillermo] Endara government [of Panama] and to the press."[167]

Moreover, Noriega expressed skepticism at the professed inability of the "powerful" American government to unfreeze his overseas bank accounts to enable him to pay his attorneys.[168] As a consequence, Noriega faced the prospect of being relegated to the role of a "pauper," and his attorneys confronted the dilemma of not being able to continue representation at the rates allowed for court-appointed criminal lawyers.[169]

Noriega's predicament vividly illustrates the important symbolic role of the right to counsel. The impression conveyed to the public by Noriega's indictment regarding the ability and willingness of the criminal justice process to afford him the opportunity to employ the "best counsel money can buy" detracts from the legitimacy of the system. In effect, a layperson who reads Noriega's statements in the media senses that perhaps the right to counsel and, more broadly, the right to a fair trial embodied in constitutional protections accorded criminal defendants are merely, in Justice Frankfurter's words, "abstract rubrics in elegant code."[170]

In addition, the United States's justice system must ensure the conflation of symbol and function in Noriega's case. A failure to secure adequate legal representation in such a complex case would seriously cast doubt on the commitment of the system to both fair process and a just result. Although the notoriety surrounding the Noriega case is certainly atypical, his situation is a telling example of the leading role played by the Sixth Amendment and, in particular, the right to counsel in the imagery and reality of the American criminal justice process. To the degree, moreover, that the public gleans information about the criminal justice system through the atypical case reported by the media, the symbolic role of the right to counsel merges with the necessity of vigorously implementing its safeguards.

Finally, the dignitary values undergirding the right to counsel assume heightened importance in such an aberrational context. Noriega, the deposed supreme leader of a foreign nation, stood without the wherewithal to contest the powerful prosecutorial forces marshalled by the U.S. government. Therefore, he not only explicitly contested his ability to receive a fair trial but also tacitly called into question the government's willingness to accord him the dignity befitting his status by allowing him the ability to hire counsel with the resources and skills to conduct a dynamic defense.

Depicting the challenge posed by Noriega's indictment of the criminal justice system, the *New York Times* editorialized that the general's "impassioned complaint hits home."[171] More important, the *Times* captured the essence of the normative and functional objectives the Sixth Amendment fosters by noting that Noriega's prosecution is not sullied by "branding [the general] a betrayer of his country's election, accusing him of crime or even for forcibly taking him into court."[172] Rather, the editorial incisively observes, what the government "owed" Noriega, and the American public, "is a prosecution governed by America's highest standards. If a jury decrees his guilt, that verdict should not be tainted by ours."[173] In short, the legitimacy of the general's prosecution rested upon scrupulous adherence to the "fair process" norms delineated in the Sixth Amendment.

DOMINANT THEMES IN RIGHT TO COUNSEL JURISPRUDENCE

Having established the theoretical and pragmatic bases underlying the right to counsel, it is worthwhile to identify the prevailing themes of the United States Supreme Court's modern jurisprudence in this critical area. Accordingly, three prominent motifs will be illuminated: the dichotomy between crime control and efficiency versus the "fair process" values advanced by the right to counsel; the extent to which the Court has promoted the dignitary values inherent in the right to counsel; and the Court's use of ethical prescriptions to constrict the breadth of the right to counsel.

Crime Control and Efficiency Versus Fair Process

As the preceding section illustrated, the Sixth Amendment's guarantee of counsel conflicts with society's need for effective law enforcement.[174] To the extent the right to counsel leads to a conflict between efficient crime control and individual rights designed to inject fairness into the process even at the cost of an accurate result, it typifies a fundamental controversy at the root of the adversary system. This dichotomy forcefully emerges in two spheres: the clash between the right to counsel and undercover government efforts to obtain incriminating statements from criminal suspects; and the degree to which the effective assistance of defendant's counsel interferes not only with the prosecution's ability to secure a conviction but also with the efficiency of the criminal justice system.

The Right to Counsel, Informants, and the Attachment of the Right to Counsel

The right to counsel is critically implicated in cases where the government employs informants to elicit incriminating statements from criminal suspects in the absence of counsel. An analysis of these cases underscores the difficulty of balancing the competing interests of the government's need to investigate crime versus the suspect's right to counsel at critical stages of the criminal process. Deceptive tactics used by law enforcement to extract confessions from criminal suspects offend the fair-trial norms protected by the right to counsel. Moreover, the informant cases raise the decisive question of when the right to counsel attaches and what safeguards attend the triggering of the right. Before undertaking a broader analysis of the Court's doctrinal propensities in this area, however, it is essential to provide a thorough description of the pertinent cases.

In the seminal case of *Massiah v. United States*,[175] the Court defined the parameters within which it would apply the right to counsel when the government employs informants to elicit information from criminal suspects. In *Massiah*, the government surreptitiously interrogated an indicted defendant, who had retained an attorney, through the use of a codefendant who had decided to cooperate with the authorities. The defendant, during a conversation with the codefendant-turned-informant, made several incriminating statements. These statements were overheard by a government agent through a radio transmitter that had been installed in the codefendant's car, where the conversation took place. The government introduced Massiah's inculpatory declarations at trial, despite the strenuous objection of defense counsel.[176]

The *Massiah* Court cited the concurring opinion in *Spano v. New York*,[177] which provided the doctrinal underpinning for its decision. In *Spano*, four justices adhered to the proposition that an indicted defendant could not be interrogated by the police without the presence of counsel.[178] This precept stemmed from the rationale that allowing such a practice might deny a defendant "effective representation by counsel at the only stage when legal aid and advice would help him."[179] Therefore the Court in *Massiah* held that "the petitioner was denied the basic protections of that guarantee [the right to counsel] when there was used against him at his trial evidence of his own incriminating words, which federal agents had elicited from him after he had been indicted and in the absence of counsel."[180]

Underlying this reasoning was the primary norm promoted by the right to counsel: a fair trial. The *Massiah* Court, therefore, buttressed its position by quoting from *Powell v. Alabama* the proposition that from arraignment to trial, when trial preparation and investigation are vital, the assistance of counsel is as crucial as at the trial itself.[181]

Furthermore, though *Massiah* was distinguishable from *Spano* because it did not involve "direct" interrogation of the defendant, the Court stressed that the vitality of the right to counsel depended on its application to indirect and "surreptitious'' interrogation as well as to questioning conducted in the jailhouse. Quoting the lower court dissenting opinion in the case, the majority noted that ''[i]n this case Massiah was more seriously imposed upon . . . because he did not even know that he was under interrogation by a government agent.''[182] Consequently, the Court formulated the ''deliberate elicitation'' standard as the proper means for safeguarding the right to counsel when a defendant formally charged with a crime becomes the target of an undercover investigation by the government.

It is important to note that in *Massiah* the Court added a crucial caveat. The majority sought to attain the delicate balance between effective law enforcement and the defendant's right to a fair trial. In attempting to reach this accommodation, the Court concluded that the government would not have been precluded from continuing to investigate the alleged criminal activities of the defendant or his accomplices, although he had already been indicted. Its holding, the Court emphasized, merely prohibited the introduction of the defendant's own incriminating statements, obtained in the absence of counsel, by the prosecution at his trial.[183]

In fact, the principle embodied in this dictum was affirmed in *Hoffa v. United States*.[184] In *Hoffa*, the defendant was on trial for a violation of the Taft-Hartley Act. An informer who had secured Jimmy Hoffa's confidence recorded several conversations that revealed Hoffa's efforts to bribe the jurors in the trial. The Court in *Hoffa* assumed that the defendant's *Massiah* rights were not violated since the rights involved the Taft-Hartley charge, and the undercover investigation concerned only the unrelated bribery charges.[185]

Despite its far-reaching impact, however, *Massiah* lay dormant, largely obscured by *Miranda*[186] and its progeny, until the Court revived it thirteen years later in *Brewer v. Williams*.[187] The facts of that case were particularly gruesome, involving the murder of a ten-year-old girl by an escaped mental patient. The defendant voluntarily surrendered to the police upon the advice of counsel and was arraigned on an arrest warrant by a judge in Davenport, Iowa. Detectives from Des Moines, where the crime had occurred, transported the defendant from Davenport to Des Moines. During the trip, Detective Leaming delivered the ''Christian burial speech,'' appealing to the defendant's religious sensibilities so that the defendant would lead detectives to the girl's body. The defendant ''responded'' to the speech by directing the detectives to the body.[188]

The ''speech'' was delivered despite the repeated requests of the defendant's counsel that Williams not be questioned about the crime until he arrived in Des Moines and consulted with counsel, and in spite of the detectives' assurance to Williams's attorneys that they would not question him.[189]

Circumventing the delicate Fifth Amendment issue of whether the ''speech'' was tantamount to interrogation,[190] the *Brewer* Court instead decided the case on Sixth Amendment grounds. In essence, the Court ruled that *Massiah* was violated because adversary proceedings had begun against Williams and he had the right to legal representation when the government elicited incriminating statements from him.[191]

Although *Brewer* did not involve undercover activities by the authorities, it is noteworthy for two principal reasons: it reaffirmed and broadened the deliberate-elicitation standard set forth in *Massiah*, and it clarified a crucial issue left unresolved in *Massiah*: the precise point at which the right to counsel attaches and the suspect is thereby entitled to the services of an attorney.

Brewer significantly expanded the protections decreed in *Massiah* by extending them regardless of the covert nature of the investigation. The majority noted that the distinction between the surreptitious interrogation in *Massiah* and the open "questioning" in *Brewer* was "constitutionally irrelevant."[192] Thus, *Brewer* presaged the Court's pronouncement in *Maine v. Moulton*[193] that "[t]he Sixth Amendment guarantees the accused, at least after the initiation of formal charges, the right to rely on counsel as a 'medium' between him and the State."[194] In conjunction with *Massiah*, therefore, *Brewer* strongly intimates that, after the commencement of formal charges against the accused, law enforcement personnel must communicate with the accused through counsel.[195]

The second important issue elucidated in *Brewer* concerns the point at which the right to counsel attaches and thereby compels the police to deal with the accused through counsel. The *Brewer* Court determined that the defendant's right to counsel had attached before Detective Leaming delivered the "Christian burial speech" since the defendant had been arraigned in open court in Davenport on an arrest warrant. Reiterating the criteria delineated in *Kirby v. Illinois*,[196] the Court noted that "a person is entitled to the help of a lawyer at or after the time that judicial proceedings have begun against him—'whether by way of formal charge, preliminary hearing, indictment, information, or arraignment.' "[197] Therefore, though *Massiah* prohibited questioning of an indicted defendant by undercover government agents about a crime for which he was under indictment, *Brewer* made clear that the prohibition extended to questioning of an unindicted defendant who has been formally charged with a crime.

If *Brewer* breathed life into *Massiah*, *United States v. Henry*[198] continued the resuscitation. In *Henry*, an informant who shared the same jail cell with the defendant had been requested by a government agent to be attentive to any statements made by the defendant but not to initiate conversations with or question him about the charge for which he had been indicted. Eventually, the defendant, during the course of conversations that took place in the cell he shared with the informant, admitted his participation in the crime to the informant. The informant testified at trial regarding the substance of Henry's incriminating statements.[199]

Applying the "deliberate elicitation" criterion adopted in *Massiah*, the Court reversed Henry's conviction on the ground that his right to counsel had been violated by the government's actions. The *Henry* Court stressed three factors as crucial to its analysis of the case: the fact that the informant was paid by and acting under the instructions of the government, that he was a "fellow inmate" of the defendant, and that the defendant was under indictment and in custody when the conversations with the informant occurred.[200]

Although the government argued that the incriminating statements were not "deliberately elicited" from Henry because the informant was explicitly instructed not to initiate any conversations with him, the majority discounted this reasoning. The informant's contingency fee arrangement with the government and his accessibility to the defendant, Chief Justice Burger emphasized, must have led the agent working with the informant to believe that Henry would "likely" reveal his involvement in the bank robbery.[201]

The holding of the *Henry* Court appeared to foreshadow a significant broadening of the "deliberate elicitation" standard, given the phrasing employed by the majority. The Court stated that "by intentionally creating a situation likely to induce Henry to make incriminating statements without the assistance of counsel, the Government violated Henry's Sixth Amendment right to counsel."[202] As Justice Blackmun remarked in dissent, the majority opinion seemed to distort the meaning of the "deliberate elicitation" test by extending the rationale of *Massiah* to "cover even a negligent triggering of events resulting in reception of disclosures."[203]

Shortly thereafter, however, the Court dispelled any notions that it was expanding the applicability of the "deliberate elicitation" standard, though it affirmed the basic dictates of *Massiah*. It will be instructive, therefore, to examine two decisions handed down in the 1985–86 Term which directly construed *Massiah* as well as *Henry*.

In *Kuhlmann v. Wilson*,[204] the Court elaborated upon the underlying rationale of *Henry*: It resolved the question, specifically left unanswered in *Henry*, of whether a defendant's right to counsel is violated when a government informant plays the role of a passive listener, without actively attempting to obtain from the defendant incriminating statements about the crime with which he is formally charged.

The factual pattern in *Kuhlmann* was remarkably similar to that of *Henry*. After the defendant, Wilson, was arraigned on murder and armed robbery charges, an informant was placed in the same jail cell with him. The detective with whom the informant was cooperating told him not to ask any questions but merely to listen to what the accused might have to say. The ostensible purpose of the detective's instructions was to determine the identities of the defendant's accomplices.[205] Ultimately, the defendant disclosed his participation in the crimes to the informant.[206]

Reversing the appellate court decision, the Court affirmed Wilson's conviction and held that the "deliberate elicitation" criterion had not been contravened by the government's tactics. The majority opinion deferred to the state court's findings that the informant followed the detective's instructions, asked the accused no questions regarding the pending charges, and "only listened" to the defendant's "spontaneous" and "unsolicited" statements.[207]

Therefore, the majority concluded that the right to counsel is not automatically violated when an informant reveals to the authorities incriminating statements made by a defendant; rather, the defendant must show that "the police and their informant took some action beyond merely listening, that was designed deliberately to elicit incriminating remarks."[208]

The *Kuhlmann* majority did not place great weight on the fact that the informant, after listening to the accused's initial denial of his participation in the crimes with which he was charged, noted that his story "didn't sound too good."[209] Furthermore, it failed to mention that the government assigned the defendant to a cell overlooking the scene of the crime.[210]

Justice Brennan's dissent highlighted these two factors, as well as the considerations stressed by the majority in *Henry*; that is, as in *Henry*, the informant in *Kuhlmann* was paid by and following the instructions of the government, he was a cellmate of the defendant, and the accused was in custody at the time he made the incriminating remarks.[211] Given these circumstances, Justice Brennan observed, "the State intentionally created a situation in which it was foreseeable that the respondent would make incriminating statements without the assistance of counsel."[212] Thus, the state in essence deliberately elicited Wilson's admission of guilt.

One must stretch the imagination in order to reconcile the holdings in *Henry* and *Kuhlmann*. The Court's characterization of the informant in *Kuhlmann* as a "passive listener" requires a suspension of disbelief. A government informant who develops a relationship with the defendant, "happens" to share the same cell, and engages the defendant in conversation about the crime is hardly a "passive listener." Although the defendant's conversation with his brother about the crime might have been the triggering event for the confession, "the groundwork for [the defendant's] confession was laid by the State."[213]

Despite the Court's restrictive interpretation of the "deliberate elicitation" standard in *Kuhlmann*, it nonetheless reaffirmed its underlying rationale in *Massiah* in *Maine v. Moulton*.[214] In that case, the defendant and a codefendant were indicted by a grand jury, retained private counsel, and entered pleas of not guilty at the arraignment. Subsequently, codefendant Colson received threatening phone calls and purportedly met with defendant Moulton, who according to Colson discussed the possibility of killing one of the state's key witnesses. Eventually, with the advice of counsel, Colson decided to cooperate with the police and agreed to assist the authorities in the pending prosecution of Moulton. In exchange for his cooperation and possible testimony, the police promised to file no further charges against Colson.[215]

Pursuant to this agreement, officers placed a recording device on Colson's telephone to monitor the alleged threats against him and any calls from Moulton. Three conversations between Colson and Moulton were recorded, none of which yielded incriminating statements by Moulton.[216] In the final conversation, however, Moulton suggested a meeting with Colson to plan their defense to the pending charges. This information prompted the police to supply Colson with a body wire transmitter to record the contents of the meeting.[217]

At the meeting, Colson and Moulton not only intricately concocted their trial strategy but Colson also prodded Moulton to make inculpatory remarks about the pending charges by claiming to have a faulty memory.[218] During the course of the conversation, moreover, Moulton developed a chimerical scheme to eliminate a crucial state witness by means of poison darts.[219]

In upholding Moulton's contention that the government violated his Sixth Amendment right to counsel, the majority invoked *Massiah* and *Henry*; it held that "the Sixth Amendment is violated when the State obtains incriminating statements by knowingly circumventing the accused's right to have counsel present in a confrontation between the accused and a state agent."[220] Proof of the government's knowledge, the Court asserted, could be established through circumstantial evidence, as in *Henry*, that the government "must have known" that its agent was likely to elicit incriminating statements from the defendant without counsel.[221]

Accordingly, the majority imputed such knowledge to the state in *Moulton* because the purpose of the meeting between Colson and Moulton was to discuss their pending trial and, concomitantly, possible defenses to the charges against them.[222] In addition, the Court reiterated the dictum established in *Massiah*; that is, the government is not prevented from continuing an investigation of an accused person who has been charged with a crime; but it is barred from introducing statements obtained from the accused relating to pending formal charges and secretly elicited through the use of an undercover agent or informant in the absence of counsel.[223]

This reasoning refuted the government's contention in *Moulton* that the conversations between Moulton and Colson should have been admissible because the police were investigating unrelated crimes when Colson recorded the conversations with Moulton: to wit, the threats to Colson and Moulton's alleged plan to kill a key state witness. Consequently, the majority precluded resort to the pretext of a pending investigation of unrelated charges as a means for the government to violate the Sixth Amendment "by knowingly circumventing the accused's right to the assistance of counsel."[224]

The *Moulton* Court sought to strike a balance between the interest of the government in ferreting out crime and the rights of criminal defendants by reaffirming the chief premise of *Massiah*. As a counterbalance to the limitations imposed by *Massiah* and *Brewer*, however, the government is not constrained by the Sixth Amendment in using agents to obtain evidence from criminal suspects as long as adversary proceedings have not been initiated against them. This prevents the use of the right to counsel as a barrier to governmental encroachment. Alternatively, the government does not violate the right to counsel, even though adversary proceedings have begun, if it does not "deliberately elicit" incriminating information from the suspect in the absence of counsel.[225]

Furthermore, the crucial importance of the point attachment of the right to counsel for the analysis of Sixth Amendment issues arises in a series of decisions in which the Court reached inconsistent results. In *Moran v. Burbine*,[226] the majority refused to extend the benefits of the right to counsel to a suspect deceived by police who failed to tell the suspect about the attempts of a lawyer to contact him and despite the assurances of the police to the lawyer that they would not question him. The suspect made incriminating statements to detectives after *Miranda* warnings were properly administered. Since formal adversarial proceedings had not been instituted when the suspect was interrogated, the majority concluded that the defendant could not rely on the Sixth Amendment right-to-counsel guarantee to suppress the incriminating statements he made during the interrogation.[227] This holding was, of course, consistent with the teachings of *Moulton*.

By contrast, in *Michigan v. Jackson*[228] the Court invalidated confessions made by two suspects although they signed a waiver of rights form after detectives administered *Miranda* warnings. The critical difference in *Jackson* was that the suspects had been arraigned and had invoked their right to counsel before the interrogation that yielded the incriminating statements.[229] The *Jackson* Court held that, "[I]f police initiate interrogation after a defendant's assertion, at an arraignment or similar proceeding, of his right to counsel, any waiver of the defendant's right to counsel for that police-initiated interrogation is invalid."[230] Moreover, the majority nullified the waiver, although the law firm appointed to represent the defendant had not yet received notice of the appointment and the defendant had not been told that a law firm had been appointed to represent him.[231]

Basing its holding on the reasoning of *Edwards v. Arizona*,[232] the *Jackson* majority appeared willing to establish a bright-line approach with respect to police-initiated questioning of a suspect formally charged with a crime. Even though *Edwards* was predicated upon the Fifth Amendment proscription against self-incrimination, the *Jackson* Court observed that the prohibition prescribed by *Edwards* was even more compelling when a suspect is formally charged with an offense.[233] Of course, the holdings in *Moulton*, *Henry*, *Brewer*, and *Massiah* buttressed the majority holding in *Jackson*, since the initiation of adversary proceedings made it more imperative that the suspect be afforded the safeguards inherent in the Sixth Amendment's guarantee of counsel.[234]

The *Jackson* majority strongly intimated that it wished to institute a bright-line rule by quoting from *Moulton* for the proposition that the Sixth Amendment assures the accused, after formal charges have been lodged against him, "the right to rely on counsel as a 'medium' between him and the State."[235] Further, the fact that Jackson and his lawyers had been unaware of the appointment of counsel seemed to indicate that neither the invocation nor the appointment of counsel was required to trigger the prohibition of police-initiated interrogation. As the *Jackson* Court noted, "after a formal accusation has been made—and a person who had previously been just a 'suspect' has become the accused within the meaning of the Sixth Amendment—[the right to counsel] is of such importance that the police may no longer employ techniques for eliciting information from uncounseled defendants that might have been proper at an earlier stage of their investigation.''[236]

Indeed, *McLeod v. Ohio*[237] lent authority to the argument for a bright-line rule regardless of the appointment of counsel. In *McLeod*, the Court affirmed a decision that the police could not elicit information after indictment even though counsel had not been appointed. Furthermore, in *Henry*, the Court invoked *Massiah* although the government arranged for the use of an undercover agent before counsel was appointed.[238]

In a crabbed reading of *Jackson*, however, the Court slighted the bright-line approach and instead opted for a formalistic interpretation of *Jackson*'s teachings. *Patterson v. Illinois*[239] presented the Court with an opportunity to definitely establish a clear rule paralleling the standard set forth in *Edwards*.[240] Rejecting this opportunity, the majority in *Patterson* held that police-initiated interrogation after the attachment of the right to counsel and the commencement of formal proceedings against the suspect does not violate the Sixth Amendment provided the accused does not invoke his right to counsel and properly executes a *Miranda* waiver.[241]

In effect, the *Patterson* Court equated the situation confronting a suspect who has been formally indicted with that of a ''preindictment'' interrogatee whose right to counsel is in existence and available for his exercise while he is questioned.''[242] To justify this result, the majority reasoned that *Miranda* warnings were sufficient to apprise an indicted suspect of his Sixth Amendment right to counsel and thereby to waive such a right by submitting to interrogation prompted by the police.[243]

Ignoring the distinction resting on the commencement of formal proceedings against the accused, the *Patterson* majority disingenuously maintained that this factor ''does not substantially increase the value of counsel to the accused at questioning.''[244] The Court conveniently dismissed *Kirby*'s important lesson that the initiation of formal criminal proceedings is not a ''mere formalism'' but, rather, signals the government's commitment to prosecute; it also ''solidifies'' the parties' adverse positions.[245] Therefore, permitting the government to bolster its case once it has decided to prosecute the accused detracts from the fair-process norms the Sixth Amendment advances. The adversary system's underlying theme of a relatively balanced contest between parties is significantly undermined when the prosecution can seal the defendant's fate by depriving her of an attorney before the contest begins.[246] Under *Patterson*'s reasoning, the government may circumvent the rules underlying the adversarial process ''by confronting the defendant behind counsel's back.''[247]

The fine distinction on which *Patterson* rests shows the majority's flawed reasoning. In essence, the *Patterson* Court bases the right to counsel on chance: whether the accused has requested counsel or counsel has been appointed on his behalf. This rationale is at variance with the principles espoused by the Sixth Amendment; those precepts interpose counsel as a ''medium'' between the prosecution and the accused once formal proceedings begin, and do not turn on illusory distinctions. As Justice Blackmun reminded his colleagues, once the Constitution affords the accused an attorney, "counsel must be furnished whether or not the accused requested the appointment of counsel."[248] The fortuitous circumstances on which *Patterson* rests give the prosecution an opening to take advantage of a "gap" between the initiation of the adversary process and the appointment of counsel for the defendant.[249]

Not totally content with its restrictive interpretation of the Sixth Amendment in *Patterson*, the Court continued to dilute its impact in *Michigan v. Harvey*.[250] In that case, the majority held that statements taken in violation of *Jackson*'s "prophylactic" rule are admissible to impeach a defendant's false or inconsistent testimony at trial.[251] Likening *Jackson*'s teachings to *Miranda*'s protection of Fifth Amendment values, the majority in *Harvey* deduced that, since a confession given in violation of *Miranda* may be used for impeachment purposes, so must an inculpatory statement that transgresses *Jackson*.[252] Exception to *Miranda* is founded on the view that a defendant ought not to subvert the integrity of the trial by using a "prophylactic" rule to testify untruthfully. As a result, the *Jackson* Court found such a rationale compelling in the context of the Sixth Amendment.[253]

The problem with this justification lies with its amalgamation of Fifth and Sixth amendment tenets. The questioning at issue in the *Miranda* cases occurred before the government had gathered enough evidence to charge the suspect formally with a crime. However, where the prosecution has initiated formal proceedings against the accused, the government's role has markedly changed, since its proper focus is accusatory rather than investigatory. As Justice Stevens put it, the government "is no longer merely engaged in the task of determining who committed an unsolved crime; rather, it is preparing to convict the defendant of the crime he allegedly committed."[254]

Because the Sixth Amendment promotes fair process trial norms that differ from the values the Fifth Amendment fosters, the reasoning supporting *Harvey* is suspect. More concretely, the right to counsel is designed to assist the accused when he is "confronted with both the intricacies of the law and the advocacy of the public prosecutor."[255] This guarantee should therefore not be circumscribed; rather, it is necessary in all parts of a trial, not just in the prosecution's case-in-chief.[256] Again, the restriction outlined in *Harvey* weakens the adversary system to the extent that it prevents the defendant from relying on counsel as a "medium between him and the State."[257]

One may contrast the Court's refusal to adopt a bright-line approach in *Patterson* and *Harvey* with the Court's fidelity to such a perspective with respect to the *Edwards* standard.[258] In *Edwards*, the Court prescribed a bright-line rule that once a suspect is given *Miranda* warnings and invokes his right to counsel, police-initiated interrogation is prohibited.[259] In subsequent decisions construing the scope of *Edwards*, the Court has declined opportunities to limit its reach. Thus, the Court has held that *Edwards* applies even when the interrogation deals with a different crime,[260] and despite the fact that counsel is provided to the accused but is not present at time interrogation takes place.[261] It is ironic that, although the majority in both *Patterson* and *Harvey* resorted to *Edwards*,[262] it has failed to embrace *Jackson*'s mandate with the same fervor.

Indeed, the Court's niggardly reading of *Jackson* culminated with its decision in *McNeil v. Wisconsin*.[263] Construing *Jackson* as "offense-specific," the *McNeil* majority sanctioned custodial interrogation of a suspect whose right to counsel had attached with respect to the crime of armed robbery; however, the questioning and purported *Miranda* waiver involved unrelated charges. The majority's rationale rested on the proposition that *Jackson* is offense-specific while *Edwards* is not.[264] Further, *McNeil* rests on the distinction between the Fifth and Sixth amendments' guarantees of counsel: that is, the Fifth Amendment protection against the pressures inherent in custodial interrogation through provision of counsel and the Sixth Amendment safeguard of the adversary process by interposing defense counsel between the government and the accused once adversary proceedings have begun.[265]

At bottom, however, *McNeil* is predicated upon the Court's interest in furthering crime-control objectives. The majority explained that if custodial interrogation were prohibited for any offense once the right to counsel attaches, the police would be precluded from securing "uncoerced confessions," thereby "seriously [impeding] effective law enforcement."[266] That *McNeil* rests on this policy objective is underlined by its counterintuitive nature; as the Court noted in *Jackson*, "[i]t makes little sense to afford relief from further interrogation to a defendant who asks a police officer for an attorney, but permit further interrogation of a defendant who makes an identical request to a judge."[267] The Sixth Amendment, in short, must take a back seat to the Court's desire to further law enforcement interests.

Analysis of the Right to Counsel, Informants, and the Attachment of the Right to Counsel

An analysis of the Court's definition of the right to counsel in the context of cases involving undercover government agents reveals the complexities of attempting to simultaneously protect the rights of criminal suspects and society's interest in preventing crime. The Court has striven to balance these conflicting demands by affording the suspect absolute protection from active government attempts to secure incriminating information through the use of undercover informants after formal adversary proceedings have begun against the suspect. The reasoning behind this solution to the problem is that, after the initiation of adversary proceedings, "the government has committed itself to prosecute, and . . . the adverse positions of [the] government and [the] defendant have solidified."[268]

Conversely, the Court has noted that "[t]o exclude evidence pertaining to charges as to which the Sixth Amendment right to counsel had not attached at the time the evidence was obtained, simply because other charges were pending at the time, would unnecessarily frustrate the public's interest in the investigation of criminal activities.''[269]

This perspective has generated criticism by scholars who believe that it is too formalistic, not adequate to protect the suspect's right to counsel, and subject to abuse and manipulation by the police. Instead, they suggest that the prohibition against surreptitious interrogation be extended to conduct that occurs after formal arrest.[270] The gist of this thesis is the seeming anomaly of treating identical, deceptive police tactics differently based on arguably nonsensical distinctions.[271]

Others suggest that this interpretation misapprehends the nature of the Sixth Amendment and, specifically, *Massiah*; that is, it blurs the distinction between the Fifth and the Sixth amendments and construes *Massiah* as merely an ''extension of and an alternative to'' *Miranda*.[272]

Although one may find merit in both of these opposing viewpoints, the focus of this section is the degree to which the Court has reconciled the opposing objectives of efficiency and fair process to the detriment of the right to counsel. In viewing the informant cases through this perspective, it is plausible to conclude that the Court has, in the main, carefully limited *Massiah*'s dictates and has tilted the scale in favor of crime control. The three noteworthy exceptions to this trend are, of course, *Henry*, *Brewer*, and *Jackson*. However, as we have seen, *Henry*'s impact was considerably weakened by *Kuhlmann*, and *Jackson*'s as well as *Brewer*'s force was diminished by both *Patterson* and *Harvey*. *Kuhlmann*, moreover, merely ratified *Massiah* in what could only be construed as a patent violation of the *Massiah* doctrine.

The Court's recent preoccupation with efficiency adversely affects a defendant's right to a fair trial and is not warranted in light of the objectives served by the adversary process. Once the government determines it has sufficient evidence to formally charge a suspect with a crime, any attempts to secure inculpatory statements from the accused are superfluous. For example, in *Kuhlmann*, the purported reason for placing an informant in the same jail cell with the defendant was to secure information about his accomplices.[273] The police had ''solid evidence'' of the defendant's participation in the crimes he was indicted for before engaging the services of the informant.[274] If the authorities only sought information concerning the defendant's accomplices, then the admission at trial of any evidence of Henry's involvement in the crimes was unnecessary. Similarly, in *Harvey* the government had ample evidence, including a statement by Harvey, with which to prosecute the defendant.[275] A distressing implication stemming from the Court's undue emphasis on the crime control rationale is the denigration of the focal role played by the right to counsel in the adversary process. In associating Fifth and Sixth amendment values, the majority of the Court slights the more profound significance attending the right to counsel. As the Court has stressed on other occasions, the right to counsel is the linchpin of the criminal justice system for the accused because it ''affects his ability to assert any other rights he may have.''[276] In essence, if the government is allowed to engage in what amounts to pretrial discovery or deposition of the accused after it has decided to prosecute, the trial rights of the defendant are hollow indeed.[277]

In addition, both *Patterson* and *Harvey* give short shrift to the egalitarian values served by the right to counsel. The rules announced in those cases punish the ignorant and the poor. *Patterson* allows the government to take advantage of an ignorant or naive defendant who fails to invoke the right to counsel after she is formally charged with a crime. Furthermore, *Harvey*, as well as *Patterson*, discriminates against indigent defendants who are unable to post bond and thereby run the risk of being subjected to governmental interrogation.[278]

To the extent that the Court has pursued a narrow, highly circumscribed approach to the proper scope and application of the right to counsel in this arena, it has depreciated the fair process and legitimation functions inherent in the Sixth Amendment. Since the Sixth Amendment is designed "to assure fairness in the adversary criminal process,"[279] permitting the government to amass more evidence than it needs, at the defendant's expense, to mount a successful prosecution hardly advances that noble ideal. Rather, such a rule ignores the heightened importance of the defense attorney once the government has marshalled its vast and powerful resources against the accused by initiating formal proceedings.

Effective Assistance of Counsel Versus Efficiency

The right to counsel necessarily encompasses effective assistance by an attorney rather than merely "pro forma" representation. This concept was elucidated by Justice Sutherland in *Powell v. Alabama*.[280] Vigorous representation by effective counsel is central to the legitimacy and premises of the adversary system. Because the theory upon which the adversary systems rests is that the "truth" is "best discovered by powerful statements on both sides of the question,"[281] the Court has on numerous occasions underscored the importance of effective counsel in the criminal process.[282]

Assuming the indispensability of effective counsel in an adversary system, the issue is joined as to what constitutes effective assistance of counsel. To be sure, egregious instances occur in which effective assistance is conspicuously missing from the process. *Powell* is an excellent illustration of such an occurrence. When a flagrant conflict of interest emerges from multiple representation, it is logical to presume that effective representation of the defendant's interests does not exist. A more difficult question to answer is what parameters define "effective assistance" and what criteria the trial and appellate courts should apply in determining whether to upset a judgment because effective assistance was not rendered.

These problems pose a thorny dilemma for the courts to resolve. On the one hand, adherence to strict rules defining effective assistance could infringe upon tactical decisions by defense counsel and discourage representation of criminal defendants.[283] Further, such stringent standards could potentially lead to a flood of appellate challenges based on ineffective assistance of counsel.[284] Conversely, applying a loose, fluid definition of effective assistance and imposing requirements which make it difficult to reverse convictions or pleas based on ineffective assistance threaten to render illusory the promise of the right to effective assistance of counsel.

In striking the proper balance between efficiency and fair process, it seems clear that, for normative and functional purposes, a dynamic, forceful view of effective assistance is critical. If we are to accept the notion that the adversary process requires a meaningful contest in which the defendant can test the government's case, then the defendant must be afforded an effective sword to pierce the prosecution's heavy armor.

Unfortunately, the Court has shrunk from its task in this area, opting instead for a narrow conception of effective assistance. Furthermore, the Court has constrained the ability of criminal defendants to choose counsel who will assiduously contest the prosecution's case. This trend runs counter to the essence of the adversary process, whose ideal is an evenly matched battle between skilled opponents.

Effective assistance of counsel clashes with the goal of efficiency and, more importantly, with the ability of the prosecution to obtain a conviction. *Wheat v. United States*[285] illustrates effective defense counsel thwarting the successful prosecution of an alleged kingpin of a major drug distribution enterprise. *Wheat*, moreover, reflects the phenomenon William Genego called the advent of the "new adversary."[286] This refers to the emergence of powerful defense counsel able to give the prosecution a run for its money. Changes in the criminal defense bar deriving from the government's recent emphasis on white-collar and drug-related offenses produced this development. The prosecution confronted different, more powerful adversaries who were paid well by their clients and therefore possessed the resources with which to effectively counter the prosecution's natural advantage. The "new adversaries" faced none of the resource constraints appointed attorneys had to contend with.[287]

In addition, the "increased pool of rich defendants [affected] not only the manner in which individual cases [were] defended, but the criminal defense bar in general," by making the practice of criminal law more remunerative, and thereby, more attractive.[288] Unfortunately, the emergence of this powerful defense bar provoked a defensive response by the government. It has attempted to deter such vigorous defense attorneys through various intimidating tactics. For example, the prosecution has sought to chill effective representation by the "new adversary" through statutory means (e.g., forfeiture provisions), disqualification of counsel, law office searches, electronic surveillance of attorneys, the use of informants at defense meetings, and required reporting of cash payments that defense attorneys receive from clients to the Internal Revenue Service.[289]

Genego describes these tactics as a "natural competitive response to the changes in defense representation," which "impose burdens or costs on those who represent criminal defendants."[290] Such coercive methods employed by the government to hamper effective defense advocacy lead to virtually unfettered prosecutorial power and discretion.[291] More important, Genego's survey of defense attorneys vulnerable to these practices demonstrates that the prosecutorial attack on the "new adversary" has been successful because defense counsel are behaving differently as a result of the governmental offensive. Further, the more experienced and highly paid defense lawyers are the most frequent targets of the new prosecutorial tactics.[292]

Although the assault launched by the government on the "new adversary" appears to be working, it subverts the legitimacy of the adversary system. The adversary model rests on the ideal of evenly matched opponents battling to advocate their clients' interests and, simultaneously, weakening their opponents' case.[293] It appears, however, that the government does not welcome an even contest; rather, it has sought to preserve its competitive edge by forestalling the development of a strong adversary capable of fighting on even terms. The United States Supreme Court, moreover, has assisted the government in its efforts to blunt the "new adversary" by allowing the government to disqualify effective defense counsel and by permitting the prosecution to strip criminal defendants charged with drug-related offenses of their counsel of choice.[294]

Given the competing interests of effective representation and efficient prosecution of criminal defendants, it is essential to probe the Court's definition of effective assistance in light of the underlying goals advanced by the adversary process. Furthermore, because a criminal defendant's ability to choose counsel directly bears upon effective representation, it is necessary to delve into the Court's jurisprudence in this domain.

Effective Assistance of Counsel: What Does It Really Mean?

After the United States handed down its opinion in the landmark case of *Gideon v. Wainwright*,[295] courts strove to determine what constituted effective representation of criminal defendants. At the time *Gideon* was decided, courts employed a criterion under which defense lawyers rendered adequate representation if their performance did not cause the trial to be a "farce and mockery."[296] In response to invitations by commentators and defendants to give meaning to *Gideon*'s promise through a more demanding standard of competency, courts fashioned the "objective, reasonably competent" criterion.[297] A consensus favoring the "objective standard of reasonable competency" evolved among federal appellate courts by the early 1980s.[298]

The problem with the new standard was two-fold: defining "reasonably competent" representation and determining when deficient performance warranted reversal of a conviction due to ineffective assistance of counsel.[299] Reasonably competent representation was largely defined on a case-by-case basis, and most courts required that the defendant claiming ineffective assistance establish prejudice to secure a reversal of the judgment of conviction.[300] Consequently, the new criterion did not appreciably alter the success rate of ineffective assistance claims, but it did enhance the legitimacy of the criminal process by alerting the public and the legal community that defense counsel would be required to fulfill "minimal standards of conduct."[301]

In *Strickland v. Washington*,[302] the United States Supreme Court addressed the issue of ineffective assistance of counsel. The standard adopted by the Court did not differ from the "objective reasonably competent" norm accepted by the bulk of appellate courts. The Court's principal, overriding concern in *Strickland* was the potential adverse systemic effect of a broadening of the reasonably competent model. As the majority stressed, "[t]he availability of intrusive post-trial inquiry into attorney performance or of detailed guidelines for its evaluation would encourage the proliferation of ineffectiveness challenges."[303] Indeed, the *Strickland* Court raised the specter of pervasive "second trials" in which defense counsel's unsuccessful defense would be assailed.[304]

As a consequence of this ordinate emphasis on efficiency, the *Strickland* Court crafted a nearly insurmountable, "highly demanding" standard of competency.[305] The *Strickland* criterion consists of a two-pronged test: to prove ineffective representation warranting reversal of the judgment of conviction, the defendant must establish that counsel's performance was deficient and that the deficient performance prejudiced the defense.[306] In turn, the majority concluded that great deference must be accorded to counsel's performance. Indeed, the reviewing court "must indulge a strong presumption that counsel's conduct falls within the wide range of reasonable professional assistance."[307] Moreover, even if the defendant proves deficient performance, she must establish "a reasonable probability" that the performance affected the outcome.[308]

The formidable barrier erected by the *Strickland* test is glaringly apparent in *Kimmelman v. Morrison*.[309] Defense counsel in that case failed to request discovery from the state and hence missed the deadline for filing a timely suppression motion.[310] Although the *Kimmelman* Court characterized the defense attorney's decision as unreasonable and outside the range of "prevailing professional norms,"[311] it remanded the case to the trial court to ascertain whether the defendant could establish the prejudice prong of the *Strickland* standard. The Court observed that the conviction would stand if the state could prove that the search fell within an exception to the Fourth Amendment's prohibition against warrantless searches. In the alternative, if the state failed on this count, the defendant would still have to establish that the factfinder would have had a reasonable doubt about defendant's guilt absent the evidence counsel failed to suppress.[312]

Viewed objectively, the insuperable threshold erected by *Strickland* stems from the Court's result-oriented perspective. Though the majority in *Strickland* endeavored to clothe its opinion in language suggesting concern for "fair-process" precepts, the overarching theme of the Court was efficiency and, correspondingly, "just results." While the majority spoke of the need to focus on the "fundamental fairness of the proceeding," it emphasized ensuring against an unreliable, unjust result due to a "breakdown" in the adversarial process.[313] The extremely deferential criterion delineated by the *Strickland* Court does not entitle the defendant to a dynamic, strong defense, but merely provides him with the guarantee of "minimally effective assistance of counsel."[314] This minimal requirement, moreover, reflects the *Strickland* Court's preoccupation with administrative efficiency: by fashioning a demanding ineffectiveness standard, the Court tried to avert a flood of potentially successful ineffectiveness challenges.[315]

United States v. Cronic[316] provides another illustration of the Court's emphasis on result rather than process. The rhetoric employed by the Court in *Cronic* resounds with "fair process" while the substance is redolent of result. Underlying the Sixth Amendment right to effective counsel, according to the *Cronic* Court, is "the right of the accused to require the prosecution's case to survive the crucible of meaningful adversarial testing."[317] Despite the fact that such "testing" does not compel a confrontation between evenly matched adversaries, a criminal trial should not be "a sacrifice of unarmed prisoners to gladiators."[318]

Ironically, *Cronic* exemplifies a contest pitting an "unarmed prisoner" against a gladiator. The defendant in *Cronic* was charged with a complex "check-kiting" scheme involving over nine million dollars.[319] Before trial, the defendant's retained counsel withdrew and the trial judge appointed an inexperienced, young lawyer with a real estate practice to represent Cronic.[320] The trial court, moreover, gave this young counsel only twenty-five days to prepare the case, though the government spent more than four and one-half years investigating and preparing its case.[321]

In reversing the appellate court decision, which concluded that Cronic did not receive assistance of counsel because his counsel was hampered in preparing the case, the Court concluded that the defendant was not deprived of effective counsel.[322] The *Cronic* Court reasoned that defense counsel was not hindered in his preparation because the only "bona fide" jury issue centered on the defendant's intent to defraud.[323] Further, the Court disingenuously maintained that the fact that Cronic's lawyer's practice was in real estate and that he was conducting his first jury trial did not adversely affect his performance.[324]

In sum, the Court legitimized an uneven contest between a fully armored, powerful government (i.e., Goliath) against an inexperienced, harried defense counsel (i.e., David) lacking the intricate skills necessary for successful criminal trial practice. Furthermore, the *Cronic* Court acknowledged that it was neither wise nor proper for the trial court to appoint such inexperienced defense counsel in such a complex case.[325] However, it deemed such an issue beyond the bounds of its power by noting that its only concern was to address what was constitutionally compelled.[326] Therefore, the possibility arises that a trial judge who wishes to ensure a conviction in a criminal case can appoint totally inexperienced defense counsel, afford her minimal time to prepare, and still comply with the commands of the Sixth Amendment's right to counsel.

From a fairness perspective, the *Cronic* opinion falls short of the mark. The perception of fairness that forms an integral part of the adversary system is conspicuously missing in *Cronic*. As the Court remarked in *Wheat*, federal courts have "an independent interest . . . in ensuring that legal proceedings appear fair to all who observe them."[327] It is obvious that such an imperative did not guide the trial court in *Cronic*. Further, the United States Supreme Court, while paying homage to the principle of fairness in the criminal adversary process,[328] instead focused on the result by accentuating the reliability of the conviction. This reliability derived from the absence of a "breakdown in the adversarial process."[329]

Because the Court judged that this "breakdown" did not occur, it left the defendant with the unenviable task of establishing an ineffective assistance claim pursuant to *Strickland*; that is, Cronic had to point to "specific errors or omissions" of his defense attorney and thus satisfy the stringent two-step test outlined in *Strickland*.[330]

The indelible mark imprinted by the Court's tightly circumscribed definition of the scope and the parameters of effective assistance in *Strickland* contrasts sharply with the Court's bold pronouncement in *Gideon*. Thus, although the *Gideon* Court deemed the right to counsel to be fundamental and "essential to fair trials,"[331] the contours of that fundamental right were severely constricted by the Court's concern with efficiency and the systemic impact of a meaningful standard of effective assistance of counsel. Although the adversary system does not require perfect balance between competing forces, its legitimacy stems from assuring "a modicum of equality between the Government and those it chooses to prosecute."[332]

It is difficult to validate the "fair-process" norms undergirding the criminal adversary process and the Sixth Amendment when the Court interprets the fundamental right to counsel in such a narrow fashion. In fact, viewed from the perspective of the public, the Court's definition of effective counsel hardly comports with notions or perceptions of fairness. It is difficult to contend that there existed a "modicum of equality" between the prosecution and the defendant in *Cronic*. The public would not perceive such equality if it were given an opportunity to witness a trial in which defense counsel was clearly not at ease, told the jury it was his first trial, and used notes in opening statement.[333] Further, the perception created by the Court's delineation of a "minimally effective" counsel model in *Strickland* hardly inspires confidence in the promise fostered by *Gideon*.

Nexus Between the Right to Select Counsel and Effectiveness

Closely linked to the ability of the defendant to procure effective counsel is the means to choose an attorney in whom she has confidence and whom she trusts. The right of the defendant to obtain counsel of choice is historically rooted in the Sixth Amendment.[334] Indeed, the Sixth Amendment was initially construed as embracing only the right of the defendant to choose and secure counsel and not the right to appointed counsel.[335] The Court, moreover, has buttressed this principle on several occasions.[336] This right to retain private counsel is crucial to the validity of the adversary process because it ensures somewhat of an equilibrium between the prosecution and the defense.[337] Furthermore, allowing the defendant to choose counsel furthers the "fairness and integrity of criminal trials."[338]

Of course, this right to choose counsel is not absolute. For example, an indigent defendant does not have the right to select his own attorney, provided that counsel appointed in his behalf is competent.[339] Nor is the defendant free to choose counsel whose representation of other co-defendants will significantly impair the lawyer's ability to advocate the defendant's cause.[340] Absent these strictures, however, a criminal defendant ought to have the opportunity of securing an attorney who she believes will be an effective advocate and forcefully challenge the government's case.

The Court's jurisprudence in this sphere is seriously flawed, reflecting its strong preference for crime control and efficiency imperatives and its corresponding deprecation of the critical role of the defense attorney in the criminal process. Juxtaposing the Court's narrow definition of the right to effective assistance of counsel with the ease with which it has confined the ability of defendants to obtain counsel of choice is revealing. In two bold strokes, the Court has managed to undermine the primary avenue for most indigent defendants to assert their right to the effective assistance of counsel through the restrictive test adopted in *Strickland*; at the same time, it has also weakened the ability of defendants to retain private counsel by endorsing the legislative attempt to deprive those accused of drug offenses from choosing private attorneys and by permitting the government to advance imaginary, spurious reasons to disqualify effective defense attorneys. Therefore, the two major Supreme Court opinions restricting the defendant's right to choose private counsel deserve close scrutiny.

An unabashed interest in advancing law enforcement interests informs the Court's majority opinion in *Caplin & Drysdale v. United States*.[341] Rejecting the notion that the federal drug forfeiture statute[342] should be construed as exempting assets a defendant would use to retain private counsel, the *Caplin* majority held that the pretrial forfeiture of assets a defendant would use to pay her attorney violated neither the Sixth Amendment right to counsel of choice nor the due process clause of the Fifth Amendment.[343]

Embracing the legislative concern with the baneful influence of drugs on American society, the *Caplin* Court succumbed to such blandishments and thus shunned its role as a bulwark against legislative endeavors to curtail fundamental rights.

The Court's flagrant crime control outlook is evident in its rejection of Caplin's contention that allowing a drug defendant to use assets to pay an attorney serves the same ends as forfeiture; that is, it "dispossesses a drug dealer or racketeer of the proceeds of his wrong doing."[344] Rather, the *Caplin* majority avowed that another important government objective was to use the funds seized from criminal defendants pursuant to the statute to fund "law enforcement activities."[345] In addition, the Court noted that another goal of the statute was to strip the economic power of "organized crime and drug enterprises."[346] This aim, according to the majority, encompassed the right to preclude the use of such financial means to secure private counsel.[347]

Acknowledging the troubling aspects of its opinion, the *Caplin* majority sought to assuage its qualms by resorting to pragmatic considerations. In fact, the majority was unable to discard flippantly the argument that it was "somewhat unsettling" to accept the tenet that the government has a "legitimate interest in depriving criminals of economic power, even . . . [if] that power is used to retain counsel of choice."[348] Rather, it merely trumpeted the truism that "the quality of a criminal defendant's representation may turn on his ability to retain the best counsel money can buy."[349] Thus the *Caplin* Court left no doubt about its predilections: It thoroughly concurred with legislative efforts to deprive defendants charged with major drug offenses of their ability to hire private attorneys. Consequently, the majority gave a strong boost to the prosecution's attack on the "new adversary." In doing so, the Court bared its crime control bias and extolled the virtue of an "ends justifies the means," result-oriented policy perspective.

Justice White, who spoke for a bare majority in *Caplin*, repudiated the due process contention that the application of the forfeiture statute would seriously impair the balance of power between the prosecution and the defense.[350] Instead, the *Caplin* majority maintained that although the Constitution affords the defendant a fair trial through the "due process clauses," the components of a fair trial are delineated in the Sixth Amendment. Consequently, a defendant stripped of the means to hire an attorney under the forfeiture statute must satisfy the stringent criterion to establish ineffective assistance of counsel enunciated in *Strickland*.[351]

Finally, the *Caplin* majority's rank endorsement of a law enforcement mentality emerges in its dauntless approval of forfeiture provisions as "powerful weapons in the war on crime."[352] In response to the cogent argument that such provisions created boundless opportunities for prosecutorial abuse, Justice White entrusted the task of circumventing potential misuse to the wisdom of the trial courts.[353]

In *Caplin* the Court profoundly altered the balance of forces between the government and the accused in the criminal process. As the dissent pointed out, the *Caplin* majority succeeded not only in undermining the essence of the adversary system but it also gave the government virtually unfettered discretion to deter and disqualify talented or aggressive defense counsel from representing defendants in complex drug-related cases.[354] In effect, the *Caplin* opinion demonstrates the Court's cavalier disregard for the premises underpinning the adversary process of adjudication. In its attempt to join the legislative and executive branches in battling the scourge of drugs in American society, the Court has ignored its role as the guardian of fundamental freedoms. Among those freedoms, the right to be represented by chosen counsel is deeply embedded in our jurisprudence.

Furthermore, the *Caplin* decision detracts from the perception of fairness integral to the American adversary process. The defendant who is denied private counsel will perceive the process as unfair and will question the legitimacy of her conviction.[355] From a broader standpoint, though the public may perceive the exclusionary rule as an unwarranted "technicality" that permits criminal defendants to deflect their "just deserts," its view of the role of defense counsel in the criminal process is without doubt markedly different. A layperson will concur with the assessment that vigorous representation is largely a function of the ability to "retain the best counsel money can buy."[356] Thus, a member of the public familiar with the *Caplin* opinion will see it for what it is worth: an attempt by the Court to preclude defendants in complex drug cases from buying legal talent to combat the prosecution's vast resources. Whether or not the public agrees with this result-oriented outlook, its perception of the fairness of the system will be substantially transformed.

Though atypical because of the notoriety of the defendant, the prosecution of General Noriega illuminates the extent to which the *Caplin* Court overlooked the adverse implications of its holding. Although the defense attorneys retained by Noriega agreed to remain in his case, they did so only after the Austrian government released $1.6 million of his assets from a frozen bank account.[357] Nevertheless, the unfrozen assets covered only expenses previously incurred by the defense. Thus, Noriega's lawyers agreed to accept the trial judge's offer to become court-appointed attorneys at the special rate of seventy-five dollars an hour. Significantly, given the complexity of Noriega's drug-related case, his defense team suffered a serious setback because it was forced to dismiss its specialist in classified documents, which were central to the general's defense. Ultimately, the task of analyzing the classified documents fell to a "novice."[358]

Noriega's difficulty in obtaining sufficient funds to retain a full-fledged defense team cast him in the role of the "underdog."[359] Even though not all of the general's assets were frozen, the predicament Noriega confronted in mounting an effective defense in his complex drug case evinces the imbalance created by the defendant's lack of access to funds with which to retain private counsel.

The complexities of drug-enterprise cases highlight the disparity between the resources available to the government and those accessible to a defendant deprived of the wherewithal to contest dynamically the prosecution's case. Such a discrepancy is inconsistent with the criminal justice system's goal of affording at least a "modicum of equality" between the government and the defendant. Certainly the imbalance fostered by pretrial drug forfeiture is at odds with the edifice supporting the criminal adversary process: "a truly equal and adversarial presentation of the case."[360] It is hard to accept the *Caplin* majority's position that "if appointed counsel is ineffective in a particular case, a defendant has resort to the remedies discussed in *Strickland*."[361] As we have seen, those "remedies" are largely illusory.

Consistent with the underlying policy rationale animating *Caplin*, the Court sought to elevate administrative efficiency to new heights in *Wheat v. United*

States.[362] *Wheat* reflects the Court's alignment with governmental objectives to deprive drug defendants of effective counsel. In that case, the defendant, an alleged intermediary in a wide-scale drug enterprise, attempted to retain a private attorney who had successfully defended the leader of the conspiracy.[363] However, the prosecution objected to the defendant's substitution of counsel on the grounds that it created "a serious conflict of interest," since the attorney represented two other codefendants allegedly involved in the same conspiracy.[364]

Although Wheat was willing to waive his right to conflict-free representation,[365] and the government's concern with a conflict of interest was completely unfounded,[366] the *Wheat* majority held that trial courts ought to be accorded wide discretion in refusing defendants' waiver of conflicts of interest even when a mere potential of conflict exists, "which may or may not burgeon into an actual conflict as the trial progresses."[367] Therefore, the *Wheat* Court held that, although trial courts must accord the defendant a presumption in favor of her counsel of choice, such a presumption "may be overcome not only by a demonstration of actual conflict but by a showing of a serious potential for conflict."[368]

The effect of the Court's manifest crime-control perspective and its disparagement of the vital role of counsel in the criminal process is evident when one contrasts *Wheat*'s weak presumption in favor of the defendant's counsel of choice with the almost insurmountable presumption of effective assistance of counsel outlined in *Strickland*.[369] While the defendant faces an imposing hurdle in overcoming the presumption that counsel was effective, the government may easily defeat the presumption of defendant's right to counsel of choice by showing a mere "potential" for conflict.

Moreover, the *Wheat* majority placed greater emphasis on administrative efficiency than it did on the defendant's right to counsel of choice. By suggesting that trial courts be afforded "broad latitude" to accept or reject defendant's choice of counsel, the *Wheat* Court asserted its interest in ensuring that judgments entered by trial courts "remain intact on appeal."[370] This concern derives from the Court's belief that if trial courts agree to the defendant's waiver of conflict-free representation, the defendant may later assert he did not receive effective assistance of counsel.[371] Such a fear is obviated by a *Faretta*-type inquiry which assures that a defendant's waiver is knowing and voluntary.[372] In essence, the majority in *Wheat* seemed to agree with the proposition that the right to counsel does not supersede societal interests in the "effective administration of justice."[373] In *Wheat*, the Court put great faith in the ability of judges to determine when a potential conflict of interest flowing from multiple representation of codefendants jeopardizes a defendant's right to a fair trial. More important, the *Wheat* majority deferred to the trial court's ability to discern when the prosecution is manufacturing a conflict to deprive the defendant of "particularly able counsel."[374] Indeed, by giving such discretion to trial judges and by suggesting that decisions made by trial judges in this area should be expected to withstand appellate scrutiny, the *Wheat* Court has apparently foreclosed the defendant from appealing an abuse of discretion by the trial judge. Therefore, the defendant would have scant likelihood of success in appealing the government's manufacture of a conflict to deprive him of counsel of choice if the trial judge agreed with the prosecutor's contention that a serious potential for conflict existed. In fact, this is precisely what occurred in *Wheat*.[375] The defendant, therefore, confronts a similar insuperable obstacle in appealing a deprivation of her counsel of choice as she does in demonstrating that her trial counsel was ineffective.

One must view the crime-control penchant exhibited by both the Burger and Rehnquist courts with a certain amount of foreboding. In pursuing an outcome-oriented, law-enforcement path, the Court has lost sight of, indeed ignored, "the function of the independent lawyer as a guardian of our freedom."[376] As a consequence, the Court has overlooked the normative and functional value attending the right to counsel in the adversary process. In its zeal to promote and facilitate law enforcement objectives and, particularly, the fight against the pervasive influence of drugs in American society, a majority of the Court has slighted the importance of the balance required for the smooth functioning of the criminal adversary system of adjudication. Fair process norms central to the system have yielded to a crime-control policy in conflict with the adversarial system of adjudication. In addition, the Court seems unperturbed about the lack of a perception of fairness engendered by its inordinate focus on administrative efficiency and governmental interests.

Dignitary Values and the Right to Counsel

A distinguishing feature of the American adversary process is its zealous protection of the litigants' dignity. Bostjan Zupancic has pointed out that, "In societies which believe that the individual is the ultimate repository of existential values, his status vis-à-vis the majority will remain uncontested even when he is accused of a crime. He will not be the object of purposes and policies, but an equal partner in a legal dispute."[377] The lawyer plays a key role in ensuring this dignitary interest in the American system of criminal adjudication. What sets the American criminal process apart from that of a totalitarian society is the fact that the defendant is not an object to be acted upon but rather an autonomous individual. A corollary of this precept is that the defense lawyer is not the agent or a servant of the state; instead, the attorney is the defendant's "champion against a hostile world."[378]

Though the attorney serves to protect the defendant's dignity against the forces arrayed against him, the Supreme Court exalted the autonomy of the defendant in *Faretta v. California*[379] by holding that a lawyer may not be foisted on a defendant against his wishes. *Faretta* represents the apotheosis of the Court's support for dignitary norms underlying the American adversary system. Since rendering its opinion in *Faretta*, however, the Court has been loath to recognize the crucial dignitary norms promoted by the right to counsel. Rather, the Court has devalued the critical link between the defendant's dignity and the attorney's role in preserving and safeguarding the client's autonomy against the government. Using *Faretta* as a point of departure, we will examine the Court's direction in this important realm.

Faretta and Dignitary Values

The *Faretta* Court encountered a fundamental dichotomy: the right to self-representation versus the necessity of an attorney "to assure the defendant a fair trial."[380] The majority sought to resolve this conundrum by relying on the historical record and by attempting to discern the intent of the Framers.[381] From this framework, the *Faretta* majority drew the conclusion that the right to self-representation was implied within the structure of the Sixth Amendment.[382]

Dealing with the inherent contradiction between the right to representation and its decisions holding that defense counsel ensures the accused a fair trial,[383] the *Faretta* Court emphasized the dignitary norms underlying the adversary process. In essence, the majority stressed that imposing counsel on the defendant against her will is contrary to the beliefs of the Founding Fathers and of the framers of the Bill of Rights. In fact, such an idea was alien to the Founders because it conflicted with the "inestimable worth of free choice," deeply ingrained in our value system and the Constitution.[384] Furthermore, the *Faretta* Court underscored the crucial nexus that exists between effective representation and the quality of the defendant's relationship with his attorney. As Justice Stewart, writing for the majority, remarked, the effectiveness of defense counsel will be diminished by the defendant's reluctance to accept the attorney's services.[385]

Profound respect for the defendant's dignity and autonomy are enshrined in *Faretta*. The majority opinion affirms the primacy of the individual as a hallmark of the American adversary system. The preeminence of the defendant emerges from the Court's depiction of the right to defend as "personal" and its stress upon the corresponding right of the defendant to opt for self-representation, even against his interests.[386] Evidencing its deep regard for the defendant's dignity and autonomy, the *Faretta* Court enjoined trial courts to scrupulously honor the defendant's choice because "respect for the individual . . . is the lifeblood of the law."[387]

Even though *Faretta* represents the apex of the Court's respect for the accused's dignity and autonomy, the majority in *Faretta* had to grapple with the tension between self-representation and the crucial role played by an attorney in a criminal proceeding. Accordingly, the Court recognized that "[i]n most criminal prosecutions defendants could better defend with counsel's guidance than by their own unskilled efforts."[388] Therefore, the majority resolved this predicament by requiring a knowing and intelligent waiver of the right to counsel as a precondition to self-representation.[389]

Faretta's Aftermath: The Decline of Dignitary Values and the Right to Counsel

If *Faretta* marks the zenith of the Court's efforts in safeguarding the individual's dignity, developments in the Court's subsequent jurisprudence diverge significantly from the dignitary norms advanced in *Faretta*. Rather, the Court has depreciated the dignitary and autonomous decision-making by the criminal defendant that is critical to the adversary process as well as to the effective assistance of counsel. One would not indulge in hyperbole by portraying *Faretta* as a mere aberration. Several decisions documenting this ominous trend typify the Court's devaluation of the dignitary values championed in *Faretta*.

Faretta Misconstrued: *McKaskle v. Wiggins*

The only case in which the Supreme Court has directly construed the contours of *Faretta* is *McKaskle v. Wiggins*.[390] The Court in that case sought to define the breadth of self-representation when the trial court appoints standby counsel to assist the defendant over the accused's objection. Interpreting *Faretta* not to preclude standby counsel's unsolicited participation, the *McKaskle* Court devised a clumsy two-pronged test to determine whether a defendant's right to representation has been breached by standby counsel's unwarranted interference. This standard judges a *Faretta* violation by asking whether (1) the defendant was allowed to control his defense by making all critical tactical decisions and controlling the questioning of witnesses; and (2) whether the unwanted participation by standby counsel "destroys" the jury's perception that the defendant is defending himself.[391]

In effect, the *McKaskle* Court betrayed its true intentions when it pointed out that *Faretta* is not transgressed by the appointment of standby counsel over the defendant's objections "even in the unlikely event that [standby counsel] somewhat undermines the *pro se* defendant's appearance of control over his own defense."[392] What concerned the majority in *McKaskle* was the potential for disruption produced by a defendant who conducts his defense without the assistance of standby counsel. Therefore, the Court asserted that when a judge appoints standby counsel against the defendant's wishes, that procedure comports with *Faretta*'s mandate because it "relieves the judge of the need to explain and enforce basic rules of courtroom protocol" while simultaneously helping the accused to surmount "routine obstacles that stand in the way of the defendant's achievement of his own clearly indicated goals."[393]

The contradictions inherent in the majority opinion are manifest when the Court vainly attempts to reconcile the principle that "excessive" involvement by standby counsel undermines the perception of self-representation and weakens the dignitary values underlying the right to proceed *pro se* with the notion that a proscription of participation by standby counsel in the presence of the jury is "unnecessary."[394] Although the majority sought to settle this inconsistency by formulating its two-part test, the test fails to correct the impression conveyed by *McKaskle* that standby counsel can participate in a criminal trial against the defendant's wishes "until the clients renew their objections and trial courts draw the line."[395] Indeed, as Justice White observed in dissent, the *McKaskle* majority embraced the "result-oriented, harmless-error standard" it allegedly repudiated.[396]

Ironically, the *McKaskle* Court achieved the result it sought to avert: an erosion of the dignitary norms that the right to self-representation advances and the weakening of the autonomous decision-making that lies at the heart of *Faretta*. The reason for the Court's approach may be discerned in its preoccupation with "efficiency" to the extent that standby counsel facilitates the trial court's task while simultaneously ensuring the unassailability of the trial verdict. This rationale is evident in the majority's conclusion that deference be accorded to the trial court's rulings regarding the conflict between standby counsel's participation and the defendant's objection thereto.[397] In sum, the *McKaskle* decision misconstrues the chief import of *Faretta*: the safeguarding of the defendant's dignity and autonomy even if such interests militate against her right to a fair trial.

The Link Between Dignitary Values and Effective Assistance of Counsel

An inextricable link exists between the confidence and trust a criminal defendant has in his lawyer and the effectiveness of the defense attorney. In fact, the American Bar Association Standards for Criminal Justice note that "[d]efense counsel should seek to establish a relationship of trust and confidence with the accused."[398] As another court has put it, "[b]asic trust between counsel and defendant is the cornerstone of the adversary system and effective assistance of counsel."[399] Of course, this nexus derives naturally from the adversary system's regard for the dignity and autonomy of individual litigants as active participants in the process rather than mere interested observers.[400] One of the principal objectives of the adversary system is to give the parties to a dispute "a sense of involvement and control in the decision-making procedure."[401] That "involvement and control," in turn, are predicated upon a smooth relationship between the litigant and her attorney.

Despite the heightened importance of the relationship between the client and the attorney in our adjudicatory process, the Supreme Court has recently minimized this vital association in the criminal realm. Given the severity of sanctions a criminal defendant confronts if he is convicted, the inherent distrust the accused may have toward the criminal process is ameliorated by his faith in his lawyer's capacity to advocate his cause zealously. In fact, a defendant may be willing to accept an unfavorable result if she believes the outcome reflects a fair process.[402] The defendant's attitude, in turn, will be a function of her confidence and trust in her attorney. Notwithstanding these self-evident propositions, the Court has rejected this critical component of the criminal adversary process.

In *Morris v. Slappy*,[403] the Court gratuitously affirmed in dicta that the Sixth

Amendment did not encompass the "right to a meaningful attorney–client relationship."[404] In that case, the defendant was represented by the public defender, who was replaced with another member of the office six days before his trial began.[405] However, in seeking a midtrial continuance so that he could be represented by his original attorney, Slappy neither expressed dissatisfaction with substitute counsel nor, obviously, did he make a timely motion to be represented by his original attorney.[406] Therefore, the Court did not have to render its opinion that the Sixth Amendment does not guarantee a meaningful relationship with counsel.[407]

By categorically renouncing this tenet in an inapt context, however, the Court chose to disregard the fundamental nature of the attorney–client relationship to the criminal process. In reversing the Ninth Circuit's recognition of the right to a meaningful attorney-client relationship, the Court raised unfounded concerns.[408] Thus, the Court asserted that it was impossible to assure the "rapport" between the defendant and her attorney implied by the appellate court's pronouncement.[409] The Court, however, misconstrued the import of a right to a meaningful nexus between the attorney and the defendant. The appellate court did not decree an "unqualified" right by an indigent defendant to an attorney of choice; rather, it merely acknowledged the link between the attorney–client relationship and both the "quality of representation" and "the defendant's ability to present an effective defense."[410]

Indeed, the *Slappy* Court evinced a certain bias against indigent defendants by rejecting out of hand the notion that an indigent defendant, much like his wealthy counterpart, has "an interest in continued representation by a particular attorney who has been appointed to represent him and with whom the defendant has developed a relationship."[411]

In sum, the dignitary values *Faretta* safeguarded were scorned in *Slappy*. Central to the adversary process of adjudication is a relationship of trust and confidence between the defendant and her attorney.[412] To a large degree, the willingness and ability of the defendant to acquiesce in the outcome of the criminal process hinges upon his confidence and belief in the efficacy of trial counsel. Since the Court refuses to acknowledge at least a "qualified" right of an indigent defendant to continue an existing relationship with appointed counsel, it further undermines, if it does not obliterate, any belief in the legitimacy of the system that the accused may have had.

Carrying the logic behind *Slappy* to absurd lengths, the Court in *Wheat v. United States*[413] denied Wheat the right to choose private counsel. Contradicting the premise of individual autonomy upon which *Faretta* rests, the *Wheat* majority opted for a "paternalistic view of the citizen's right to select his or her own attorney."[414] With its "paternalistic" perspective, the *Wheat* Court reached the quintessential counterintuitive result: protecting the defendant from her own folly by preventing the defendant from waiving her right to conflict-free counsel. Sound logic dictates that if a defendant can waive the right to counsel and defend herself, "a fortiori [she] can choose to have a conflicted lawyer."[415] Rather, the

Wheat Court conveniently ignored *Faretta*'s teachings by valuing administrative efficiency over individual autonomy. As Bruce Green correctly notes, however, the *Faretta* Court refused to place concerns over the finality of judgments above the defendant's interest in dignity and autonomy.[416]

Not only did the *Wheat* majority disregard the dignitary norms underlying the criminal process, but it also slighted the right of the defendant to secure the counsel of his choice. In doing so, the majority failed to acknowledge the vital trust and confidence between attorney and client which serves to legitimize the outcome of the proceeding as well as to enhance the effectiveness of counsel.[417]

In a similar vein, the Court in *Caplin & Drysdale v. United States*[418] neglected the critical connection between the defendant's confidence in his lawyer's "dedication, loyalty, and ability," and his view of the legitimacy and fairness of the criminal justice system.[419] When the prosecution strips the defendant of the right to choose counsel through pretrial forfeiture of allegedly "tainted" funds, it destroys the defendant's faith in the validity of the process.[420] In effect, if the government selects defendant's attorney by resorting to pretrial forfeiture of his assets, the accused will view such counsel "as the [g]overnment's agent rather than his own."[421] This concept impugns the dignitary values supporting the adversary system by perpetuating a feeling of helplessness and lack of participation on the part of the defendant. *Caplin* is at cross-purposes with the fundamental premise of the adversary process that the litigants ought to feel a sense of participation and independence rather than a sense of futility to affect the outcome of the litigation.

The cumulative impact of *Slappy*, *Wheat*, and *Caplin* is unmistakable: a significant abridgment of the defendant's dignitary interests in counsel who will be perceived as effective and who will foster the defendant's belief in the legitimacy of the criminal process. More important, these cases espouse a philosophy which demeans the dignity and autonomy of the criminal defendant. Since the defense attorney represents the accused's "champion against a hostile world,"[422] one hardly expects such an ideal to be realized when counsel is forced upon an unwilling defendant. The Court has launched an assault on a major underpinning of the adversary system by degrading the significance of dignitary norms. *Faretta* stands as an anomaly that is readily jettisoned when pitted against the efficiency, crime-control rationale advocated by a majority of the Court.

Ethical Norms and the Right to Counsel

Another ill-advised facet of the Court's recent jurisprudence is its propensity to employ ethical standards as a means of reducing the scope of the right to counsel. Two cases illustrate the Court's misuse of ethical prescriptions to contract a criminal defendant's right to the effective assistance of counsel. Both *Nix v. Whiteside*[423] and *Wheat v. United States*[424] reflect this disturbing trend. On the other hand, the Court does not seem to be as concerned with questionable ethical practices by prosecutors that impinge on a defendant's right to counsel, as *Patterson v. Illinois*[425] demonstrates. It is instructive, therefore, to analyze these cases with a view to discerning whether the Court's reliance on ethical norms is warranted.

In *Nix v. Whiteside*,[426] a majority of the Court improperly relied upon ethical canons in deciding a Sixth Amendment right to effective assistance of counsel issue. The central question in *Nix* was whether defense counsel deprived his client of effective assistance by threatening to expose the defendant's intention to commit perjury at his trial for first-degree murder.[427] Although Chief Justice Burger, speaking for the majority, attempted to eschew the constitutionalization of particular ethical prescriptions, he failed miserably in that task. In essence, while purporting to decide the case solely by the two-pronged ineffective assistance of counsel test set forth in *Strickland v. Washington*,[428] the chief justice conducted an exegesis on the appropriate response by a criminal defense attorney to her client's suggestion that he will commit perjury at trial. In fact, the majority in *Nix* issued the broad imperative that both the Model Code of Professional Responsibility as well as the Model Rules of Professional Conduct require disclosure by the attorney of client perjury.[429]

As Justice Brennan observed in his concurring opinion, the majority's digression into the proper approach to client perjury was "pure discourse without force of law."[430] Further, as scholars have pointed out, the chief justice's ruminations on the proper course of conduct by a defense attorney when a client proposes to perjure himself is rife with inaccuracies and misstatements of the law relating to client perjury.[431]

Properly framed, the issue the Court faced in *Nix* was whether Whiteside's lawyer deprived him of effective assistance, not whether counsel's "behavior conformed to any particular code of legal ethics."[432] In applying the first prong of the *Strickland* standard, however, the *Nix* Court relied upon ethical prescriptions in determining that Whiteside's conduct "fell within the wide range of professional responses to threatened client perjury acceptable under the Sixth Amendment."[433] This analysis was superfluous because the *Strickland* Court held that in reviewing ineffective assistance claims, both prongs (performance and prejudice) need not be analyzed; rather, if the prejudice threshold was met, a determination of counsel's performance was unnecessary.[434] Consequently, the *Nix* Court could have disposed of the case without gratuitously rendering its views on the appropriate response to threatened client perjury.

By issuing its skewed perspective on the problem of client perjury, the *Nix* majority seemed to suggest that whenever a defense attorney threatens to expose what she perceives is her client's plan to commit perjury, the lawyer's conduct would not conflict with the defendant's right to effective assistance of counsel. While the facts of *Nix* appeared to indicate Whiteside's desire to perjure himself, other situations would suggest a different analysis. For example, if the attorney at midtrial threatens to withdraw on the basis of his unfounded belief that his client intends to commit perjury, such an action would undermine the client's right to effective assistance of counsel.[435] Moreover, Whiteside's attorney did not expose his client's plan to commit perjury until post-conviction proceedings began; if the foregoing situation had arisen, the Sixth Amendment issue would have come into play.[436]

Rather than recognizing the complex nature of the problem relating to client perjury, the *Nix* majority indulged in a far-ranging excursion of ethical canons that was unnecessary to resolve the case. As Justice Blackmun noted, the defense attorney's response to her client's attempt to commit perjury depends on a multiplicity of variables: for example, "how certain the attorney is that the proposed testimony is false, the stage of the proceedings at which the attorney discovers the plan, or the ways in which the attorney may be able to dissuade his client."[437] Since *Nix* represents an exception to the rule in that counsel was quite certain that his client intended to commit perjury, it does not contradict the precept that attorneys who "adopt the role of judge and jury to determine the facts . . . pose a danger of depriving their clients of the zealous and loyal advocacy required by the Sixth Amendment."[438]

Similarly, the Court in *Wheat v. United States*[439] raised unfounded ethical apprehensions regarding multiple representation of criminal defendants in order to justify the denial to the accused of his counsel of choice.[440] In refusing to accept Wheat's motion to substitute counsel and his corresponding waiver of the right to conflict-free representation, the Court adduced the possibility that the substitution could have led to counsel's violation of the ethical "limitations on multiple representation."[441] The purported rationale of the *Wheat* majority was that disqualification of Wheat's counsel protected the courts' "independent interest in ensuring that criminal trials are conducted within the ethical standards of the [legal] profession."[442]

As Bruce Green has ably shown, however, the ethical standards did not preclude Wheat's substitution of Iredale as his counsel.[443] The conflict which might have arisen from the substitution of counsel in *Wheat* was different from that created by representation of multiple defendants at joint or successive trials. Rather, "it was a case in which, at worst, defense counsel would simultaneously represent a defendant and a government witness, since the government's case against two of attorney Iredale's three clients was essentially over and only Wheat was awaiting trial."[444] Therefore, the only potential conflict emerging from Wheat's proposed substitution of Iredale as his attorney would occur because of Iredale's need to cross-examine a former client. Such a potential conflict is not deemed serious enough to warrant attention by the drafters of the Model Code.[445] Finally, Wheat's waiver of the right to conflict-free counsel "would have eliminated not only the ethical barrier, but the conflict itself."[446]

Comparison of *Nix* and *Wheat*

In juxtaposing the use of ethical norms by the Court in both *Nix* and *Wheat*, a result-oriented jurisprudence emerges in bold relief. *Nix* represents the Court's superfluous reliance on ethical prescriptions to intimate that defense lawyers are always justified in exposing what they correctly or incorrectly perceive to be attempts by their clients to commit perjury. Such a broad dictum, of course, not only is unwarranted but is potentially at odds with the right to counsel.[447] In similar fashion, the *Wheat* majority improperly relied on ethical norms to deprive the defendant of the right to select his counsel of choice.[448] Thus, the Court's misplaced use of ethical norms to restrict the right to counsel reveals its bias toward the government's position and a concomitant depreciation of the vital role of defense counsel in the criminal adversary process.

Indeed, this outcome-driven perspective is evident when one compares the Court's inordinate emphasis on ethical standards for criminal defense counsel in both *Wheat* and *Nix* with its apparent apathy toward the ethical norms of prosecutors in *Patterson v. Illinois*.[449] In that case, the prosecutor interviewed the defendant after he had been indicted and the right to counsel had attached, securing a second confession from Patterson.[450] As Justice Stevens remarked in dissent, this behavior by the prosecutor was ethically improper, for in the civil realm it is unethical for an attorney to obtain evidence from an opponent's client without notice or permission from the trial court.[451] Not only is such conduct a "breach of professional ethics" in the criminal context but it also contravenes notions of fairness inherent in the adversary process.[452]

The *Patterson* Court sanctioned this flagrant breach of ethics and fairness by holding that postindictment questioning by either the police or the prosecution is consistent with the right to counsel and the adversarial process as long as the defendant does not explicitly invoke her right to counsel and the government obtains a proper *Miranda* waiver from the accused.[453] Paradoxically, as the facts of *Patterson* amply demonstrate, neither the prosecutor nor the police had a compelling need to obtain confessions from the defendant after he had been indicted for murder by a grand jury. In fact, police had secured a statement from the defendant before he was indicted.[454] Moreover, the prosecutor engaged in overkill when he sought a second confession from Patterson after the police had already obtained a postindictment confession from the defendant.

In conclusion, the pattern one may discern from the Court's misreliance upon ethical norms to constrain the breadth and scope of the right to counsel bodes ill for the normative and functional aspects of the Sixth Amendment. While making bold pronouncements on the need for ethical norms and integrity in the criminal justice system, the Court has manifested a certain disdain for the integral role the defense attorney plays in ensuring the perception and reality of fairness that should mark the adversary process. The excessive concern for adherence to ethical standards, moreover, is not only misplaced, but it also betrays the Court's policy orientation against the rights conferred on criminal defendants in the United States Constitution.

THE RIGHT TO COUNSEL: FUNDAMENTAL RIGHT OR REVOCABLE PRIVILEGE?

Since the seminal decision in *Gideon*, the Court has proclaimed and reaffirmed the proposition that the "right of an accused to counsel is a fundamental right."[455]

In *Gideon*, the Court stressed the salient role of the defense attorney in our criminal process by noting that the right to counsel "may not be deemed fundamental and essential to fair trials in some countries, but it is in ours."[456] The concept of fairness, of course, pervades the criminal adversary system. In effect, the ultimate goal of the criminal justice system is not to convict the guilty; rather, it is to ensure a fair proceeding which "results in a just judgment."[457]

Though professing fidelity to the "fundamental right" to counsel, the Court's recent jurisprudence reflects a different understanding of the function of counsel in the criminal process. In fact, one may posit that the Court has at times construed the right of the defendant to counsel as a revocable privilege rather than a fundamental right. Several examples shed light on this proposition.

Through its exceedingly narrow interpretation of when the defendant is entitled to deal with the government only with the assistance of counsel, the Court has disparaged the importance of counsel once the government has committed itself to prosecute. Thus, while holding in *Michigan v. Jackson*[458] that once a defendant has been indicted and invoked the right to counsel the government may not interrogate him, the Court retreated from fashioning a bright-line rule in *Patterson v. Illinois*.[459] As a consequence, the right to counsel is revocable after adversary proceedings have begun if the defendant does not invoke it. Further, statements taken from the accused in violation of *Jackson* do not warrant exclusion if they are used for impeachment purposes.[460] In effect, the "right" to counsel, though attaching at the commencement of adversary proceedings against the accused, is revocable if not asserted by the defendant.

Furthermore, the time-honored right to choose private counsel has become revocable at the whim of the government. The gist of both *Caplin* and *Wheat* is that the government may disqualify the defendant's counsel of choice by seeking pretrial forfeiture of his assets or by "manufacturing" a conflict of interest; both weapons serve to preclude dynamic, skillful defense counsel from vigorously contesting the prosecution's case. Such tactics are inimical to the basic thrust and ideal of the adversary system of adjudication: an even "fight" between two skillful opponents.

In addition, the "fundamental right to counsel" necessarily entails the right to the effective assistance of counsel. By fashioning a standard that, at best, guarantees criminal defendants "minimally effective" assistance of counsel, the Court has made the right to counsel ring hollow. In essence, the "fundamental right" to counsel becomes a revocable privilege in the face of the insurmountable odds a defendant faces in establishing the ineffectiveness of her counsel.

Finally, to the extent the Court has failed to recognize the nexus between the attorney–client relationship and the effectiveness of counsel, it has detracted from the fundamental nature of the right to an attorney. In slighting the dignitary values underpinning the right to counsel and the adversary system, the Court has stripped the right to counsel of its "fundamental" character and has thereby turned it into a rather empty privilege.

The effect of the Court's treatment of the right to counsel as a revocable privilege rather than a fundamental right signals an ominous erosion of the minimal balance required to legitimize the criminal adversary process. The criminal justice system's viability depends upon a rough equivalence of ability and resources between the prosecution and the defense.[461] Although the system does not require a perfect equilibrium, "because only in rare cases will the parties be equal in their presentational ability,"[462] it does command at least a modicum of balance in order to comport with the adversary framework. That minimal balance is related to the overarching goal promoted by the adversary process: fairness.

Some scholars and courts have argued, however, that fairness in the criminal sphere is not contingent upon symmetry because the superior resources enjoyed by the prosecution are counterbalanced by the constitutional safeguards afforded to the defendant.[463] Further, Jay Silver has posited the construct of "equality of arms," through which procedural rights to present the case must be equally accorded to both sides.[464] One may accept these arguments and still view the Court's curtailment of the right to counsel as adversely affecting the legitimacy of the criminal adversarial process. Without an attorney to vigorously assert the constitutional rights to which defendants are entitled, those rights may not be properly safeguarded. Similarly, without counsel conversant with the nuances of the criminal justice system, the defendant may not be able to effectively utilize the "arms" allegedly at his disposal.

Ultimately, the Court's drift toward a crime-control perspective with respect to the right to counsel detracts from the fair-process norms embodied in the Sixth Amendment, for the attorney is the repository of those rights for the criminal defendant. Moreover, the symbolic, normative function performed by the Sixth Amendment and, particularly, the right to counsel, is equally restricted by the Court's shortsighted perspective. The perception of fairness necessary for the system's legitimation suffers when a "fundamental right" is construed as a revocable privilege.

CONCLUSION

As one of our foremost constitutional legal scholars has reminded us, an overarching theme of our emergence as an independent nation was the "triumph of individual liberties against government power . . . epitomized by the Bill of Rights."[465] In fact, the enactment of the Bill of Rights was greatly attributable to the perceived need to afford safeguards to criminal defendants.[466] In countering the arguments against the passage of a bill of rights, moreover, the Founding Fathers and the architect of the Bill of Rights, James Madison, stressed the didactic purpose such rights might serve.[467] Indeed, Madison was acutely aware that "mere paper barriers" against governmental excesses might prove futile in times of hysteria, but he recognized that the barriers "raised a standard that might educate the majority against acts to which they might be inclined."[468] In short, what Madison sought to accomplish through the Bill of Rights was to forestall legislative and executive abuse.[469]

It appears that the U.S. Supreme Court has lost sight of Madison's goal in securing the enactment of the Bill of Rights. In particular, the right to counsel, a cherished protection firmly embedded in the document, has foundered on the shoals of political expediency. Neither the war on drugs nor the fight against the pernicious effects of crime in American society will be won by the denudation of vital constitutional safeguards that undergird the criminal adversarial process. Judge Posner is correct when he points out that logic "doesn't enter into the law's cycling between generous and niggardly protection of criminal defendants' rights."[470] What does "enter" into the protection of defendants' rights is the notion fostered by those who secured the enactment of the Bill of Rights that "paper barriers" would remind the judiciary of its commitment to shield fundamental rights against majoritarian impulses.[471] The Court has shirked its responsibility in this regard by forgetting the "function of the independent lawyer as [the] guardian of our freedom."[472]

NOTES

1. The Sixth Amendment provides that: "In all criminal prosecutions, the accused shall enjoy the right to a speedy and public trial, by an impartial jury of the State and district wherein the crime shall have been committed, which district shall have previously been ascertained by law, and to be informed of the nature and cause of the accusation; to be confronted with the witnesses against him; to have compulsory process for obtaining witnesses in his favor, and to have the Assistance of Counsel for his defense," U.S. CONST. Amend. VI. Of course, the provisions of the Sixth Amendment have been extended to the states through the Fourteenth Amendment's due process clause. *See*, e.g., *Gideon v. Wainwright*, 372 U.S. 335 (1963) (right to counsel); *Duncan v. Louisiana*, 391 U.S. 145 (1968) (right to an impartial jury); *Washington v. Texas*, 388 U.S. 14 (1967) (right to compulsory process); *Pointer v. Texas*, 380 U.S. 400 (1965) (right to confrontation); *Klopfer v. North Carolina*, 386 U.S. 213 (1967) (right to a speedy trial).

2. The Supreme Court has categorized the criminal defendant's right to a fair trial as "the most fundamental of all freedoms," *Estes v. Texas*, 381 U.S. 532, 540 (1965). The Court, however, disavowed the notion that the Sixth Amendment takes precedence over other provisions of the Bill of Rights. *See*, e.g., *Nebraska Press Ass'n v. Stuart*, 427 U.S. 539, 561 (1976) ("The authors of the Bill of Rights did not undertake to assign priorities as between the First Amendment and Sixth Amendment rights, ranking one as superior to the other.")

3. Of course, the largely trial-related rights afforded criminal defendants in the Sixth Amendment, and in other provisions of the Bill of Rights (e.g., the Fifth Amendment privilege against self-incrimination), "[do] not envision an adversary proceeding between two equal parties." Rather, those rights recognize the "awesome power of indictment and the virtually limitless resources of government investigators," *Wardius v. Oregon*, 412 U.S. 470, 480 (Douglas, J., concurring). In effect, the rights the U.S. Constitution confers on criminal defendants are "designed to redress the advantage that inheres in a government prosecution," Id.

4. *See*, e.g., *Brewer v. Williams*, 430 U.S. 387 (1977) (police violated defendant's right to counsel by eliciting information from the defendant in the absence and against

the wishes of defendant's attorneys after the initiation of adversary proceedings); *Michigan v. Jackson*, 475 U.S. 625 (1986) (once the right to counsel attaches and is invoked by the defendant in open court, any waiver of that right by the suspect in response to "police-initiated" interrogation is nullified).

5. *See*, e.g., Garcia, *The Winding Path of* Bruton v. United States: *A Case of Doctrinal Inconsistency*, 26 AMER. CRIM. L. REV. 401 (1988) (Court's interpretation of the *Bruton* doctrine and Sixth Amendment's confrontation clause marked by inconsistency and failure to adhere to fundamental values underlying Sixth Amendment's confrontation clause); Garcia, *The Compulsory Process Clause and the "Sporting Theory of Justice": The Supreme Court Evens the Score*, 28 DUQ. L. REV. 619 (1990) (Court's construction of Sixth Amendment compulsory process clause denies criminal defendant right to present critical evidence and runs counter to precedent).

6. This is the term employed by Arenella in an incisive article on the functions of criminal procedure. *See*, Arenella, *Rethinking the Functions of Criminal Procedure*, 72 GEO. L. J. 185 (1983).

7. For a critique of the Court's doctrinal interpretation of the confrontation clause, *see*, e.g., Jonakait, *Restoring the Confrontation Clause to the Sixth Amendment*, 35 UCLA L. REV. 557 (1988) (Court has subsumed the basic premise of the confrontation clause under evidentiary principles); Garcia, *Winding Path*, *supra* note 5 (Court's restrictive and inconsistent application of *Bruton* doctrine denies criminal defendants right to confrontation); Garcia, *Compulsory Process, supra* note 5 (Court's interpretation of compulsory process clause denies defendant right to present exculpatory evidence).

8. Of course, Packer posited two "models" of the criminal justice system—the "due process" and "crime control" models—in his influential book. *See* Packer, THE LIMITS OF THE CRIMINAL SANCTION 153 (1968). Arenella has constructed a more sophisticated version of Packer's models based on the purposes served by criminal procedure. *See* Arenella, *supra* note 6 at 213–28.

9. Whitebread & Slobogin, CRIMINAL PROCEDURE (2nd ed.) 4–5 (1986).

10. As two commentators have observed, in the 1987–88 Term, in all but one case decided the Court held that the Sixth Amendment right involved was "either outweighed by the Court's interests in ensuring the 'integrity' of the trial, or that a violation of the right could be considered harmless." The sole exception, *Coy v. Iowa*, 108 S.Ct. 2798 (1988), stemmed from the Court's belief that the right of face-to-face confrontation was essential to a fair trial. *See* Rosenthal & Rice, *Whittling Away the Right to Counsel: The Supreme Court's New Approach to the Sixth Amendment*, 3 CRIM. JUST. 2 (1989).

11. *See*, e.g., *Kimmelman v. Morrison*, 477 U.S. 363, 374 (1986) (distinguishing Fourth Amendment as not implicating trial rights from the "fundamental" right to counsel).

12. *United States v. Calandra*, 414 U.S. 338, 348 (1974).

13. *Stone v. Powell*, 428 U.S. 465, 486 (1976).

14. The fundamental character of the right was highlighted in *Gideon v. Wainwright*, 372 U.S. 335 (1963). The *Gideon* Court noted that: "The right of one charged with a crime may not be deemed fundamental and essential to fair trials in some countries, but it is in ours," id. at 344.

15. Most notably in the seminal cases of *Gideon v. Wainwright*, 372 U.S. 335 (1963) (right to appointed counsel for indigent defendants applicable to the states through operation of the Fourteenth Amendment's due process clause); and *Argersinger v. Hamlin*,

407 U.S. 25 (1972) (indigent defendant may not be incarcerated for misdemeanor offense without assistance of counsel).

16. *Wheat v. United States*, 486 U.S. 153 (1988).

17. *Caplin & Drysdale v. United States*, 109 S.Ct. 2646 (1989).

18. *Strickland v. Washington*, 466 U.S. 668 (1984).

19. *See*, e.g., *Faretta v. California*, 422 U.S. 806 (1975) (criminal defendant has the right to self-representation provided that she knowingly and intelligently waives the right to counsel).

20. The most egregious example of this approach is *Wheat v. United States*, 486 U.S. 153 (1988).

21. Heller, THE SIXTH AMENDMENT TO THE CONSTITUTION OF THE UNITED STATES 10 (1951); *see* also, *Faretta v. California*, 422 U.S. 806, 825 (1975).

22. Heller, *supra* note 21, at 10.

23. Id. (citing 5 Holdsworth, A HISTORY OF ENGLISH LAW, 196 (1927)). It is ironic that counsel was required by the infamous "Star Chamber," primarily as a means of stripping the defendant of the ability to defend against the charges. The defendant's answer to the indictment had to be signed by counsel. If it was not endorsed by counsel, then the defendant was deemed to have confessed to the allegation. In turn, counsel were dissuaded from signing such indictments by threats of sanctions if "frivolous" defenses were interposed. *See Faretta v. California*, 422 U.S. at 821–22 (citing Holdsworth, *supra* at 178–79 and 1 Stephen, A HISTORY OF THE CRIMINAL LAW OF ENGLAND, 340–41 (1883)).

24. Heller, *supra* note 21, at 10.

25. *Faretta v. California*, 422 U.S. at 824.

26. *See supra* note 21 and accompanying text.

27. Heller, *supra* note 21 at 17. In fact, self-representation was the norm under the English common law. Self-representation was required of every litigant at one time in the history of the common law. *Faretta v. California*, 422 U.S. at 823 (citing 1 Pollock & Maitland, THE HISTORY OF THE ENGLISH LAW 211 (2nd ed. 1909).

28. Id. at 21.

29. Id.

30. *Faretta v. California*, 422 U.S. at 828–29.

31. Id. at 828–30.

32. Even the jury trial clause of Article III of the Constitution was criticized as narrowly circumscribing the right to a jury trial. *See* Heller, *supra* note 21 at 25.

33. Heller, *supra* note 21, at 27.

34. U.S. CONST. Amend. VI.

35. *Bute v. Illinois*, 333 U.S. 640, 660–66 (1948) ("[T]he right guaranteed [by the Sixth Amendment] is one of employing counsel, not of having counsel provided by the Government" (quoting National Commission on Law Observance and Enforcement (Wickersham Commission), REPORT ON PROSECUTION 30 (1931))).

36. Beany, THE RIGHT TO COUNSEL IN AMERICAN COURTS 21 (1955). That the Sixth Amendment did not entail the right to appointed counsel is buttressed by Section 35 of the Judiciary Act of 1789, passed by the first Congress and signed by President Washington one day before the Sixth Amendment was proposed. The act stipulated that "in all the Courts of the United States, the parties may plead and manage their own causes personally or by the assistance of . . . counsel," 1 Stat. 73, 92 (1789). *See Faretta v. California*, 422 U.S. at 805–06; Beany, *supra* at 28. As one commentator noted,

"That the constitutional guarantee [of the right to counsel] did not comprise the right of a prisoner to have counsel assigned to him by the court if, for financial or other reasons, he was unable to retain counsel appears to have been generally understood," Heller, *supra* note 21, at 110.

37. 372 U.S. 335 (1963).

38. 287 U.S. 45 (1932).

39. Id. at 68–70.

40. Id. at 58, 73.

41. Id. at 71. Of course, the Court's holding was predicated upon the due process clause of the Fourteenth Amendment because it involved a state prosecution and the right to counsel had not been "incorporated" into the Fourteenth Amendment's due process clause. The Court eventually incorporated the clause in *Gideon v. Wainwright*, 372 U.S. 335 (1963).

42. *See supra* notes 34–36 and accompanying text.

43. *Powell*, 287 U.S. at 53.

44. Id. at 53, 58, 71.

45. Id. at 49.

46. Id. at 49–50.

47. Id. at 56–58. In fact, as the Court noted, "until the very morning of the trial no lawyer had been named or definitely designated to represent the defendants," Id. at 56.

48. Id. at 59.

49. Id. at 68–70.

50. Id. at 68–69.

51. Id. at 72.

52. Id. at 71. The Court held that, given the particular situation in *Powell*, "the necessity of counsel was so vital and imperative that the failure of the trial court to make an effective appointment of counsel . . . was a denial of due process within the meaning of the Fourteenth Amendment," id.

53. Id. at 73.

54. This value was explicitly recognized by the Court in *Faretta v. California*, 422 U.S. 806 (1975). (Right to self-representation "implied within the structure of the Sixth Amendment"; preservation of individual autonomy worthy of constitutional protection.) For an application of this value to the confrontation clause of the Sixth Amendment, *see* Massaro, *The Dignity Value of Face-to-Face Confrontations*, 40 U. FLA. L. REV. 863, 897–917 (1988).

55. *Powell*, 287 U.S. at 58.

56. 304 U.S. 458 (1938).

57. Id. at 463. The Court held that "The Sixth Amendment withholds from federal courts, in all criminal proceedings, the power and authority to deprive an accused of his life or liberty unless he has or waives the assistance of counsel."

58. Id. at 462–63.

59. Id. at 463.

60. Id. at 464–65.

61. Id. at 464.

62. Id.

63. 315 U.S. 60 (1942).

64. Id. at 76. As the Court put it, "[T]he Sixth Amendment contemplates that [the

assistance of counsel] be untrammeled and unimpaired by a court order requiring that one lawyer shall simultaneously represent conflicting interests,'' id. at 70.

65. Id.

66. Id. at 70–71.

67. Id. at 70.

68. Id. at 70–71. The majority remarked that a court must ''indulge every reasonable presumption against the waiver of fundamental rights,'' id. at 70 (*citing Aetna Ins. Co. v. Kennedy*, 301 U.S. 389, 393 (1937); *Ohio Bell Telephone Co. v. Public Utilities Comm'n*, 301 U.S. 292 (1937)). The *Zerbst* decision had adopted this waiver standard, *Johnson v. Zerbst*, 304 U.S. at 464. Further, the *Glasser* Court chastised the trial judge for ignoring the possibility of conflicting interests. It noted that the trial judge shoulders the responsibility of conducting the trial ''with the solicitude for the essential rights of the accused,'' id. The conflict became evident at trial when defense counsel refused to cross-examine a witness and failed to object to certain allegedly inadmissible, hearsay testimony in order to protect the interests of the codefendant, id. at 73–75.

69. Id. at 75. The majority observed that, ''Irrespective of any conflict of interest, the additional burden of representing another party may conceivably impair counsel's effectiveness,'' id.

70. Id. at 76.

71. 308 U.S. 444 (1940).

72. Id. at 446.

73. Id. at 447.

74. *See*, e.g., *Palko v. Connecticut*, 302 U.S. 319 (1937). During the 1960s, of course, the Court adopted the ''selective incorporation'' approach to assess the scope of the due process clause of the Fourteenth Amendment in relation to the specific guarantees of the Bill of Rights. *See*, generally, Lafave & Israel, CRIMINAL PROCEDURE, Sec. 2.4–2.5 (1985).

75. Id. at 450–53.

76. 316 U.S. 355 (1942), overruled by *Gideon v. Wainwright*, 372 U.S. 335 (1963).

77. Id. at 473.

78. Id. at 467–71.

79. As Justice Black pointed out in dissent, depriving a defendant of counsel because of his indigent status is at odds with ''common and fundamental ideas of fairness and right.'' Moreover, ''[w]hether a man is innocent cannot be determined from a trial in which, as here, denial of counsel has made it impossible to conclude . . . that the defendant's case was adequately presented,'' id. at 476 (Black, J., dissenting).

80. Id. at 457. Betts did not waive his right to counsel, though he did relinquish his right to a jury trial.

81. Id. at 472.

82. Id. *See*, Kamisar, *Gideon v. Wainwright*: A Quarter-Century Later, 10 PACE L. REV. 343, 348 (1990). The Court had suggested in *Bute v. Illinois*, 333 U.S. 640, 660 (1948), and reaffirmed in *Hamilton v. Alabama*, 368 U.S. 52, 54–55 (1961), that there was an absolute requirement of appointed counsel in capital cases. It should be emphasized that the special-circumstances category was subject to frequent modification and expansion. *See*, e.g., *Williams v. Kaiser*, 323 U.S. 471, 474–77 (1944); *Chewning v. Cunningham*, 368 U.S. 443, 446–47 (1962); *Hudson v. North Carolina*, 363 U.S. 697, 701–04 (1960).

83. Kamisar, *supra* note 82, at 350.

84. *Betts*, 316 U.S. at 476 (Black, J., dissenting).

85. Kamisar, *supra* note 82, at 351–52.

86. *Betts*, 316 U.S. at 473. The majority remarked that, ''[A]s the Fourteenth Amendment extends the protection of due process to property as well as to life and liberty, if we hold with the petitioner, logic would require the furnishing of counsel in civil cases involving property,'' id.

87. Krash & Lewis, *The History of* Gideon v. Wainwright, 10 PACE L. REV. 379, 380–82 (1990).

88. Id. The ''antifederalist'' argument convinced Justice Harlan, who did not wish to embrace the ''incorporation'' doctrine, id. at 382. *See*, *Gideon v. Wainwright*, 372 U.S. 335, 349–52 (Harlan, J., concurring).

89. *Gideon v. Wainwright*, 372 U.S. 335, 342–44 (1963).

90. Id. at 344.

91. Id.

92. Kamisar, *The Gideon Case 25 Years Later*, N.Y. TIMES, Mar. 10, 1988, at A27, col. 1.

93. Krash & Lewis, *supra* note 87, at 382.

94. The culmination of the adversarial process is, of course, a trial in which both sides present their version of the ''truth.'' Some commentators contend that the adversarial system is ''misdescribed as a search for truth.'' *See*, e.g., Saltzburg, *Lawyers, Clients, and the Adversary System*, 37 MERCER L. REV. 1 (1984). Others, however, maintain that ''truth should be the reigning objective of every trial.'' *See*, e.g., Steffen, *Truth as Second Fiddle: Reevaluating the Place of Truth in the Adversarial Trial Ensemble*, 1988 UTAH L. REV. 799.

95. White, *Evidentiary Privileges and the Defendant's Constitutional Right to Introduce Evidence*, 80 J. CRIM. L. & CRIMINOLOGY 377, 387 (1989).

96. *See* generally, Margulies, *Resource Deprivation and the Right to Counsel*, 80 J. CRIM. L. & CRIMINOLOGY 673 (1989).

97. *See* Kaye, Gideon v. Wainwright: *A Lesson in the Obvious*, 10 PACE L. REV. 419, 420–21 (1990).

98. 372 U.S. 353 (1963).

99. Id. at 355–58.

100. Id. at 354–55.

101. The majority did not explicitly avow whether it was basing its ruling on due process or equal protection grounds. The tone of the majority opinion relies heavily upon equal protection analysis. However, one could construe the decision based on equal protection or due process. *See* Harlan's dissenting opinion, *Douglas*, 372 U.S. at 360–67 (Harlan, J., dissenting).

102. Id. at 363 (Harlan, J., dissenting).

103. Id. Justice Harlan observed that: ''[I]f the present problem may be viewed as one of equal protection, so may the question of the right to appointed counsel at trial, and the Court's analysis of that right in *Gideon v. Wainwright* . . . is wholly unnecessary. The short way to dispose of *Gideon* . . . would be simply to say that the State deprives the indigent of equal protection whenever it fails to furnish him with legal services, and perhaps with other services as well, equivalent to those that the affluent defendant can obtain,'' id.

104. 351 U.S. 12 (1956). In *Griffin*, the Court struck a procedure that denied an indigent defendant access to a free trial transcript for the purposes of appellate review.

105. *Douglas*, 372 U.S. at 355 (quoting from *Griffin v. Illinois*, 372 U.S. at 19).

106. Id. at 357.

107. It should be stressed that the *Douglas* Court limited its holding to first appeals as a matter of right and declined to extend this logic to discretionary appeals, *Douglas*, 372 U.S. at 356.

108. *See supra* notes 92–98 and accompanying text.

109. *Douglas v. California*, 372 U.S. at 359 (Clark, J., dissenting).

110. 407 U.S. 25 (1972).

111. Id. at 37.

112. Id. at 31.

113. Id. at 34–37.

114. 391 U.S. 145, 159 (1968) (right to jury trial applied only to non-petty offenses punishable by more than six months' imprisonment). This six-month standard was also endorsed by the Court in *Baldwin v. New York*, 399 U.S. 66 (1970). Recently, in *Blanton v. City of Las Vegas*, 489 U.S. 538 (1989), the Court held that a defendant is entitled to a jury trial for an offense punishable by a jail term of less than six months "only if he can demonstrate that any additional statutory penalties, viewed in conjunction with the maximum authorized period of incarceration, are so severe that they clearly reflect a legislative determination that the offense in question is a 'serious' one."

115. *Argersinger*, 407 U.S. at 37.

116. Id. at 44–66 (Powell, J., concurring). Justice Powell was joined by Justice Rehnquist in his concurring opinion.

117. Id. at 54.

118. Id. at 63–66. Justice Powell delineated three criteria to provide guidance to trial courts: (1) the complexity of the offense; (2) the probable sentence upon conviction; (3) the idiosyncracies of the case, id. at 64.

119. Id. at 51–52.

120. Id. at 58–62.

121. *See supra* notes 87–88 and accompanying text.

122. 440 U.S. 367 (1979).

123. Id. at 373–74.

124. Id. at 373.

125. *Argersinger*, 407 U.S. at 37 n. 7. In fact, the majority stated in that footnote that, "We do not share MR. POWELL's doubt that the Nation's legal resources are sufficient to implement the rule we announce today."

126. Id. at 373–74 n. 5.

127. Id. at 385–86 (Brennan, J., dissenting) (citations omitted).

128. Id. at 388.

129. *See supra* note 119 and accompanying text. Ironically, although Powell criticized the majority in *Argersinger* for not extending the right to counsel to indigents in all criminal cases, he concurred in *Scott*'s outcome because of his "reservations about the *Argersinger* rule," *Scott*, 440 U.S. at 374 (Powell, J., concurring).

130. *Scott v. Illinois*, 440 U.S. at 380–381 (Brennan, J., dissenting). Scott was convicted of petty theft and fined $50 after a bench trial. The maximum penalty for the offense in Illinois was a $500 fine or one year in jail, or both, id. at 368.

131. 435 U.S. 333, 341 (1978).

132. *Argersinger*, 407 U.S. at 30. The Court noted that, "While there is historical support for limiting the 'deep commitment' to trial by jury to "serious criminal cases,"

there is no such support for a similar limitation on the right to the assistance of counsel,'' id. (footnotes omitted).

133. *Scott*, 440 U.S. at 380 (Brennan, J., dissenting).

134. Id. at 368.

135. *Argersinger*, 407 U.S. at 52–55 (Powell, J., concurring); *Scott*, 440 U.S. at 383 (Brennan, J., dissenting).

136. *See*, e.g., Lafave & Israel, CRIMINAL PROCEDURE 9 (1985) (roughly 20 to 30 percent of all arrests are for felonies; the rest are for misdemeanors).

137. *Argersinger*, 407 U.S. at 33.

138. 446 U.S. 222 (1980).

139. *See infra*.

140. 417 U.S. 600 (1974).

141. Id. at 610–18.

142. Id. at 610–11.

143. Id. at 616.

144. Id. at 615.

145. *Douglas*, 372 U.S. at 355.

146. Id. at 366 (Harlan, J., dissenting).

147. Id.

148. *See supra* notes 123–26 and accompanying text.

149. This phenomenon is corroborated by the Court's decisions extending the ''logic'' upon which *Ross* is based. In *Pennsylvania v. Finley*, 481 U.S. 551 (1987), the Court held that prisoners do not have a constitutional right to counsel for collateral attacks on their convictions, id. at 555. In fact, the *Finley* majority argued that the ''analysis'' of the *Ross* Court ''foreclosed'' Finley's constitutional claim, id. at 556. Further, in *Murray v. Giarratano*, 109 S.Ct. 2765 (1989), the Court applied *Finley*'s rationale in holding that death row inmates are not entitled to counsel for postconviction relief. *Giarratano*'s precedential value, however, was diluted by fact that it was a plurality opinion.

150. Heller, *supra* note 21, at 143.

151. Id.

152. *See* Packer, *supra* note 8.

153. *See* Arenella, *supra* note 6, at 213–28.

154. Id. at 195.

155. Id.

156. Id. at 188.

157. Id. at 201.

158. Id. at 200.

159. *Faretta v. California*, 442 U.S. 806 (1975).

160. Arenella, *supra* note 6, at 202.

161. Id.

162. Weisberg, *Criminal Procedure Doctrine: Some Versions of the Skeptical*, 76 J. CRIM L. & CRIMINOLOGY 832 (1985).

163. 477 U.S. 365 (1986).

164. Id. at 374 (citing *Gideon v. Wainwright*, 372 U.S. at 344).

165. In the broader context of the Sixth Amendment trial-related rights, *see*, e.g., *Batson v. Kentucky*, 476 U.S. 79, 87 (1986) (discriminatory jury selection procedures undermine public confidence in the system).

166. *Adams v. United States ex rel. McCann*, 317 U.S. 269, 276 (1942).

167. MIAMI HERALD, Nov. 17, 1990, at 1A, col. 1.

168. Id. Noriega forcefully asserted that when he was heading the Panamanian government, the United States would "ask me to arrest people, to allow the search of Panamanian flag vessels, to send people to the United States for trial and to freeze bank accounts. I know that when the United States seriously requests something of a foreign government, they get it," id.

169. Id., Nov. 14, 1990, at 1–2B, column 2.

170. *See* note 165, *supra* and accompanying text.

171. NEW YORK TIMES, Nov. 20, 1990, at A20, col. 2. The general's complaint was that he was "at the mercy of a totally unfair and unjust system" of American justice.

172. Id.

173. Id.

174. *See supra*.

175. 377 U.S. 201 (1964).

176. Id. at 202–203.

177. 360 U.S. 315 (1959).

178. Id. at 326–27.

179. Id. at 326 (Douglas, J., concurring).

180. *Massiah*, 377 U.S. at 206.

181. Id. at 205, quoting from *Powell*, 287 U.S. at 57. The pertinent quotation reads as follows: "during perhaps the most critical period of the proceedings . . . that is to say, from the time of the arraignment until the beginning of the trial, when consultation, thorough-going investigation and preparation [are] vitally important, the defendants . . . [are] as much entitled to such aid [of counsel] during that period as at the trial itself."

182. *Massiah*, 377 U.S. at 206.

183. Id. at 207.

184. 385 U.S. 293 (1966), *reh. den.*, 386 U.S. 940.

185. Id. at 304–09.

186. 384 U.S. 436 (1966) (custodial interrogation of suspects requires certain prophylactic safeguards to protect the suspect's right against self-incrimination).

187. 430 U.S. 387 (1977).

188. Id. at 389–93.

189. Id. at 391.

190. In *Rhode Island v. Innis*, 446 U.S. 291 (1980), the Court resolved this issue by holding that *Miranda* applies to conduct by the police that constitutes the "functional equivalent" of interrogation.

191. Id. at 401.

192. Id. at 400.

193. 474 U.S. 159 (1985).

194. Id. at 176.

195. As Justice Stevens subsequently stated in *Patterson v. Illinois*, 487 U.S. 287 (1988), *Massiah*, *Brewer*, *Moulton*, and *United States v. Henry*, 447 U.S. 264 (1980), "suggest that law enforcement personnel may not bypass counsel in favor of direct communications with an accused," *Patterson*, 487 U.S. at 302, n.2. (Stevens, J., dissenting).

196. 406 U.S. 682 (1972). *See* also, e.g., *United States v. Gouveia*, 467 U.S. 180 (1984).

197. *Brewer*, 420 U.S. at 387.

198. 447 U.S. 264 (1980).
199. Id. at 266–67.
200. Id. at 270–71.
201. Id. at 271.
202. Id. at 274.
203. Id. at 279.
204. 477 U.S. 436 (1986).
205. Id. at 439, 460.
206. Id. at 440.
207. Id. at 459–60.
208. Id. at 459.
209. Id. at 439–40.
210. Id. at 476 (Brennan, J., dissenting).
211. Id. at 475.
212. Id. at 476 (citing *United States v. Henry*, 447 U.S. at 274). The dissent acknowledged that, unlike the situation in *Henry*, what eventually prompted the defendant's admission of guilt seems to have been a visit from his brother. Nevertheless, Justice Brennan stated that the "State's actions had a sufficient nexus with respondent's admission of guilt to constitute deliberate elicitation within the meaning of *Henry*," id.
213. Id.
214. 474 U.S. 159 (1985).
215. Id. at 162–63. Colson also gave a full confession to the crimes for which he and Moulton had been indicted.
216. Id. at 163–64.
217. Id. at 164.
218. Id. at 165–66.
219. Id. at 165, n.4.
220. Id. at 176.
221. Id. at 176, n.12.
222. Id. at 176–77.
223. Id. at 179.
224. Id. at 180.
225. Id. at 176. The majority observed that "[t]he Sixth Amendment is not violated whenever—by luck or happenstance—the State obtains incriminating statements from the accused after the right to counsel has attached," id. (citing *United States v. Henry*, 447 U.S. at 276).
226. 475 U.S. 412 (1986).
227. Id. at 430–31.
228. 475 U.S. 625 (1986).
229. Id. at 628.
230. Id. at 636.
231. Id. at 627.
232. 451 U.S. 477 (1981). In *Edwards*, the Court delineated a bright-line rule in which a suspect in custody, who has "expressed his desire to deal with the police through counsel, is not subject to further investigation by the authorities until counsel has been made available to him, unless the accused himself initiates further communication, exchanges, or conversations with the police," id. at 484–85.
233. *Michigan v. Jackson*, 475 U.S. at 631.

234. Id. at 629–30.
235. Id. at 632, quoting from *Maine v. Moulton*, 474 U.S. at 176.
236. Id. at 632.
237. 381 U.S. 356 (1965).
238. *United States v. Henry*, 447 U.S. at 265.
239. 487 U.S. 285 (1988).
240. *See* note 231, *supra* and accompanying text.
241. Id. at 300.
242. Id. at 290–91.
243. Id. at 292–97.
244. Id. at 298–99. As Justice Stevens argued in dissent, the *Miranda* warnings do not impart sufficient information to warrant this conclusion. The warnings fail to inform the accused about the nature of the charges or the legal status of the indictment, nor do they indicate to the accused that she may be hampering her attorney's ability to negotiate a plea bargain, id. at 308 (Stevens, J., dissenting).
245. *Kirby v. Illinois*, 406 U.S. at 689.
246. It should be stressed that in *Patterson* the prosecutor conducted a full-fledged interrogation of the accused which resulted in the defendant's second confession to the murder he was charged with, *Patterson v. Illinois*, 487 U.S. at 288–89.
247. *Michigan v. Harvey*, 110 S.Ct. 1176, 1186 (1990) (Stevens, J., dissenting).
248. *Patterson v. Illinois*, 487 U.S. at 300–301 (Blackmun, J., dissenting) (citing and quoting from *Carnley v. Cochran*, 369 U.S. 506, 513 (1962)).
249. Id. at 301.
250. 110. S.Ct. 1176 (1990).
251. Id. at 1178.
252. Id. at 1180–81. In construing the reach of *Miranda*, the Court has held that voluntary statements which violate *Miranda* are admissible to impeach the defendant's testimony. *See*, e.g., *Harris v. New York*, 401 U.S. 222 (1971); *Oregon v. Hass*, 420 U.S. 714 (1975).
253. Id. at 1181.
254. Id. at 1188 (Stevens, J., dissenting).
255. *United States v. Ash*, 413 U.S. 300, 309 (1973).
256. *Michigan v. Harvey*, 110 S.Ct. at 1184 (Stevens, J., dissenting).
257. Id. at 1185 (quoting from *Maine v. Moulton*, 474 U.S. at 176).
258. *See* note 231, *supra*.
259. *Edwards v. Arizona*, 477 U.S. at 484–85.
260. *Arizona v. Roberson*, 486 U.S. 675 (1988).
261. *Minnick v. Mississippi*, 111 S.Ct. 486 (1990).
262. *Patterson v. Illinois*, 487 U.S. at 291; *Michigan v. Harvey*, 110 S.Ct. at 1180. Indeed, the *Harvey* majority asserted that "*Jackson* merely superimposed the Fifth Amendment analysis of *Edwards* onto the Sixth Amendment," id.
263. 111 S.Ct. 2204 (1991).
264. Id. at 2208.
265. Id. at 2208–09.
266. Id. at 2210.
267. *Michigan v. Jackson*, 475 U.S. at 633–34, n.7 (1986) (quoting *Michigan v. Bladel*, 421 Mich. 39, 63–64, 365 N.W.2d 56, 67 (1984), *see McNeil v. Wisconsin*, 111 S.Ct. 2210, n.1 (1991)). The majority vainly attempts to explain away this commonsense

observation by asserting that it does not apply to a "desire never to undergo custodial interrogation, about anything, without counsel present," id. *See* also Justice Stevens's dissent, id. at 2213 (Stevens, J., dissenting).

268. *Kirby v. Illinois*, 406 U.S. at 689.

269. *Maine v. Moulton*, 474 U.S. at 180.

270. *See*, e.g., White, *Police Trickery in Inducing Confessions*, 127 U. PA. L. REV., 581, 603 (1979); Whitebread & Slobogin, CRIMINAL PROCEDURE (2nd ed.) 409 (1986).

271. *See* Stuntz, *Waiving Rights in Criminal Procedure*, 75 VA. L. REV. 769, 835–37.

272. 1 Lafave & Israel, CRIMINAL PROCEDURE Sec. 6.4 477 (1984).

273. *Kuhlmann v. Wilson*, 477 U.S. at 439.

274. Id. at 460. Eyewitness testimony linked the defendant to the crimes, id. at 460, n.22.

275. *Michigan v. Harvey*, 110 S.Ct. at 1178.

276. *United States v. Cronic*, 466 U.S. 648, 653–54 (1984).

277. *Michigan v. Harvey*, 110 S.Ct. at 1190 (Stevens, J., dissenting).

278. Id. at 1188 n.11. "Those who are not held in custody after the attorney–client relationship has been formed are not exposed to daily contact with the police and therefore have little stake in the rule announced in this case. Because the indigent defendant has only occasional contact with his lawyer but is under the constant control of the prosecutor, it is he whose interests are more affected by the Court's ruling," id.

279. *United States v. Morrison*, 449 U.S. 361, 364 (1981).

280. *Powell v. Alabama*, 287 U.S. at 53.

281. *Penson v. Ohio*, 488 U.S. 75, 84 (1988), quoting Kaufmann, *Does the Judge Have a Right to Qualified Counsel?*, 61 ABAJ 569, 569 (1975) (quoting Lord Eldon).

282. *See*, e.g., *Evitts v. Lucey*, 469 U.S. 387 (1985); *Strickland v. Washington*, 466 U.S. 668 (1984); *Wainwright v. Torna*, 455 U.S. 586 (1982) (*per curiam*); *Penson v. Ohio*, 488 U.S. 75 (1988); *United States v. Cronic*, 466 U.S. 648 (1984).

283. *Strickland v. Washington*, 466 U.S. at 690.

284. Id.

285. 486 U.S. 153 (1988).

286. Genego, *The New Adversary*, 54 BROOKLYN L. REV. 781 (1988).

287. Id. at 786–787.

288. Id. at 787.

289. Id. at 788.

290. Id. at 803.

291. Id. at 853.

292. Id. at 814–819.

293. *See* Babcock, *Fair Play: Evidence Favorable to an Accused and Effective Assistance of Counsel*, 34 STAN. L. REV. 1133, 1163–74 (1982) (arguing that effective assistance at trial is indispensable in the United States "adversary game" model of adjudication). The Court has remarked that "The system assumes that adversarial testing will ultimately advance the public interest in truth and fairness," *Polk County v. Dodson*, 454 U.S. 312, 318 (1981). Although the adversarial model does not require a perfectly even match, presumably such an idea represents the quintessential goal of the system. Thus, Judge Wyzanski notes that: "While a criminal trial is not a game in which the participants are expected to enter the ring with a near match in skills, neither is it a

sacrifice of unarmed prisoners to gladiators,'' *United States ex rel. Williams v. Twomey*, 510 F.2d 634, 640 (7th Cir.), *cert. denied, sub nom. Sielaff v. Williams*, 423 U.S. 876 (1975).

294. *Wheat v. United States*, 486 U.S. 153 (1988) (allowing the prosecution to raise a dubious potential conflict of interest to disqualify effective defense counsel); and, *Caplin & Drysdale v. United States*, 109 S.Ct. 2646 (1989) (holding that pretrial forfeiture of defendant's allegedly ''drug-tainted'' assets not violative of Sixth Amendment right to counsel or Fifth Amendment's due process clause).

295. 372 U.S. 335 (1963).

296. This phrase was first used by the court in *Diggs v. Welch*, 148 F.2d 667 (D.C. Cir.), *cert. denied*, 325 U.S. 889 (1945). *See Trapnell v. United States*, 725 F.2d 149, 151 (2d Cir. 1983) for a compendium of cases applying the farce and mockery standard.

297. *See*, e.g., *United States v. DeCoster*, 624 F.2d 196 (D.C. Cir. 1979) (en banc); Genego, *The Future of Effective Assistance of Counsel: Performance Standards and Competent Representation*, 22 AM. CRIM. L. REV. 181, 186–89 (1984).

298. Genego, *supra* note 282 at 190.

299. Id.

300. Id. at 190–91. The Sixth Circuit deviated from this trend, holding that incompetent representation warranted automatic reversal. *Beasly v. United States*, 491 F.2d 687 (6th Cir. 1974).

301. Id. at 192.

302. 466 U.S. 668 (1984).

303. Id. at 690.

304. Id.

305. This is Justice Brennan's description of the standard in *Kimmelman v. Morrison*, 477 U.S. at 382. He asserted that ''*Strickland*'s standard, although by no means insurmountable, is highly demanding.''

306. Id. at 687.

307. Id. at 689.

308. Id. at 695. The Court characterized a ''reasonable probability'' as a ''probability sufficient to undermine confidence in the outcome,'' id.

309. 477 U.S. 363 (1986).

310. Id. at 368–69, 385.

311. Id. *Strickland* requires a reviewing court to decide whether counsel's ''identified acts or omissions were outside the wide range of professionally competent assistance,'' *Strickland v. Washington*, 466 U.S. at 690.

312. Id. at 391–92. Defendant was charged with the rape of an employee. The item the defendant's lawyer failed to suppress was a bedsheet seized from the suspect's home without a warrant. The bedsheet was analyzed by the state; the analysis yielded evidence that linked the defendant to the crime (i.e., the bedsheet contained semen from a man matching the defendant's blood type, and hairs removed from the sheet were similar to head hair of both the defendant and the victim), id. at 368–70.

313. *Strickland v. Washington*, 466 U.S. at 686, 696.

314. *See Caplin & Drysdale v. United States*, 109 S.Ct. at 2672 (Blackmun, J., dissenting).

315. Id. at 690.

316. 466 U.S. 648.

317. Id. at 656.

318. Id. at 657 (quoting from *United States ex rel. Williams v. Twomey*, 510 F.2d 634, 640 (7th Cir.), *cert. denied* sub nom. *Sielaff v. Williams*, 423 U.S. 876 (1975).

319. Id. at 649–51.

320. Id. at 649, 665.

321. Id.

322. Id. at 664–66.

323. Id. at 664–65.

324. Id. at 665. In fact, the court suggested that the defense lawyer's expertise in real estate law would be an asset because the case against Cronic dealt with a financial transaction rather than a predatory crime, such as armed robbery. This statement reflects the Court's total ignorance of the realities of criminal practice. Indeed, criminal trials are markedly different from civil ones: for example, the burden of proof is different (beyond a reasonable doubt versus the preponderance of the evidence); constitutional procedural issues are exceedingly intricate (i.e., would a real estate lawyer be well versed in Fourth, Fifth, and Sixth amendment jurisprudence?); and evidentiary issues are also complex (would a real estate lawyer be conversant with the rules regarding permissible impeachment of a defendant or the circumstances under which the government could use "bad acts" evidence pursuant to Federal Rule of Evidence 404 (b)?).

What makes the Court's spurious rationalization preposterous is that Cronic's attorney not only lacked civil trial experience but was engaging in his first jury trial.

325. Id. at 665, n.38.

326. Id.

327. *Wheat v. United States*, 486 U.S. at 160.

328. Id. at 656.

329. Id. at 662.

330. Id. at 666.

331. *Gideon v. Wainwright*, 372 U.S. at 344.

332. *Caplin & Drysdale v. United States*, 109 S.Ct. at 2673 (Blackmun, J., dissenting).

333. *United States v. Cronic*, 466 U.S. at 666, n.40. The Court dismissed the importance of such factors, maintaining that they did not conflict with a "reasonably effective defense" and might have been the "product of a reasonable tactical judgment." I doubt that counsel was comfortable with his first jury trial, especially since he was not familiar with the criminal process. In essence, he probably had no choice but to reveal to the jury his thorough unfamiliarity with jury trials and the criminal process in general.

334. *See* notes 34–37 and accompanying text.

335. Id.

336. *See*, e.g., *Chandler v. Freytag*, 348 U.S. 3, 9 (1954); *Powell v. Alabama*, 287 U.S. at 53; *Glasser v. United States*, 315 U.S. at 70.

337. *Caplin & Drysdale v. United States*, 109 S.Ct. at 2673 (Blackmun, J., dissenting).

338. *Wheat v. United States*, 486 U.S. at 166 (Marshall, J., dissenting).

339. *See*, *Morris v. Slappy*, 461 U.S. 1, 13–14 (1982); *Wheat v. United States*, 486 U.S. at 159, in which the majority stated that "[A] defendant may not insist on representation by an attorney he cannot afford."

340. *See*, e.g., *Cuyler v. Sullivan*, 446 U.S. 335 (1980); *Holloway v. Arkansas*, 435 U.S. 475 (1978).

341. 109 S.Ct. 2646. In the companion case to *Caplin*, *United States v. Monsanto*, 109 S.Ct. 2657 (1989), the Court held that the language of the Comprehensive Forfeiture

Act of 1984, 21 U.S.C. Sec. 853, unequivocally demonstrated congressional intent not to exempt attorneys' fees from its purview.

342. The statute at issue in *Caplin* was 21 U.S.C. Sec. 848 (1982 ed., Supp V) (defining a Continuing Criminal Enterprise), and specifically the portion of the statute which authorizes forfeiture to the government of "property constituting, or derived from . . . proceeds . . . obtained" from drug-law offenses. *See Caplin*, 109 S.Ct. at 2649.

343. *Caplin & Drysdale v. United States*, 109 S.Ct. at 2649.

344. Id. at 2654.

345. Id.

346. Id.

347. Id. at 2655.

348. Id.

349. Id. (quoting from *Morris v. Slappy*, 461 U.S. 1, 23 (1983)).

350. Id. at 2656–57, citing *Wardius v. Oregon*, 412 U.S. 470, 474 (1973).

351. Id. at 2656, n.10.

352. Id. at 2657.

353. Id.

354. Id. at 2674–75 (Blackmun, J., dissenting).

355. *Caplin & Drysdale v. United States*, 109 S.Ct. at 2673 (Blackmun, J., dissenting).

356. This is the phrase employed by the Court in *Morris v. Slappy*, 451 U.S. at 23, and endorsed by the *Caplin* majority in *Caplin & Drysdale v. United States*, 109 S.Ct. at 2655.

357. MIAMI HERALD, Jan. 29, 1991, at B1, col. 2.

358. Id. at 3B, col. 3.

359. Id.

360. *Caplin & Drysdale v. United States*, 109 S.Ct. at 2674 (Blackmun, J., dissenting).

361. Id. at 2655, n.7. The majority rejected the contention that a type of *per se* ineffective assistance of counsel exists when criminal defendants in complex drug cases are deprived of the right to retained counsel through pretrial forfeiture. The majority refused to embrace that argument because, in its opinion, it "would bar the trial of indigents charged with such offenses."

362. 486 U.S. 153 (1988).

363. Id. at 154–55.

364. Id. at 155.

365. Id. at 156.

366. The government's objection centered on the fact that counsel Wheat sought to retain Eugene Iredale, represented the ring leader, Juvenal Gomez-Barajas, and another minor player, Javier Bravo. Iredale secured an acquittal for Gomez-Barajas, but, to avoid a second trial on different charges, Gomez-Barajas decided to plead guilty to those charges (i.e., tax evasion and illegal importation of merchandise), id. at 155. The potential conflict, according to the prosecution, stemmed from the fact that, at the time of Wheat's trial, Gomez-Barajas was free to withdraw his guilty plea and opt for a trial, and that Bravo could be called as a witness in Wheat's trial, id.

As Justice Marshall's dissent shows, conclusive evidence demonstrates that the government manufactured the conflict to prevent Iredale, obviously a very capable criminal defense attorney, from representing Wheat. Proof of the prosecution's motives is gleaned from its eleventh-hour decision to call Bravo as a witness in Wheat's trial. Only after the prosecutor became aware of Wheat's attempt to substitute Iredale as his counsel did he arrange for Bravo's testimony at Wheat's trial by offering to recommend to the trial court a reduction in Bravo's sentence, id. at 170, n.3 (Marshall, J., dissenting). Moreover, the District Court readily acknowledged that Wheat's decision to retain Iredale was eminently sound, given the acquittal Iredale secured for Gomez-Barajas. Thus, the "prosecutor's decision to call Bravo as a witness may well have stemmed from a concern that Iredale would do an equally fantastic job at [Wheat's] trial," id.

367. Id. at 163.

368. Id. at 164.

369. *See supra* notes 297–328 and accompanying text.

370. Id. at 161.

371. Id.

372. In *Faretta*, of course, the Supreme Court held that a defendant has a right to self-representation as long as the trial court makes sure her waiver of counsel is knowing and voluntary, *Faretta v. California*, 422 U.S. at 834–35.

373. *See*, e.g., *In re Paradyne Corp.*, 803 F.2d 604, 611 (11th Cir. 1986), cited in *Wheat v. United States*, 486 U.S. at 158.

374. *Wheat v. United States*, 486 U.S. at 163.

375. As Justice Marshall indicated, "absent deference, a decision upholding the District Court's ruling would be inconceivable," id. at 168 (Marshall, J., dissenting).

376. *Walters v. National Assn. of Radiation Survivors*, 473 U.S. 305, 371 (1985) (Stevens, J., dissenting) (footnote omitted).

377. Zupancic, *Truth and Impartiality in Criminal Process*, 7 J. Contemp. L. 39, 133 (1982).

378. *See* Freedman, UNDERSTANDING LAWYERS' ETHICS 15–16 (1990) (quoting in part from ABA, *Standards Relating to the Defense Function*, 145–146 (Approved Draft, 1971)).

379. 422 U.S. 806 (1975).

380. Id. at 832–33.

381. Id. at 812–34.

382. Id. at 819.

383. Id. at 832–33 (citing *Powell*, *Johnson v. Zerbst*, *Argersinger* and *Gideon*).

384. Id. at 833–34 (footnotes omitted).

385. Id. at 834. In Justice Stewart's words, "[W]here the defendant will not voluntarily accept representation by counsel, the potential advantage of a lawyer's training and experience can be realized, if at all, only imperfectly," id.

386. Id.

387. Id. (quoting *Illinois v. Allen*, 397 U.S. 337, 350–51 (1970) (Brennan, J., concurring)).

388. Id.

389. Id. at 835.

390. 465 U.S. 168 (1983).

391. Id. at 178.

392. Id. at 184.

393. Id.

394. Id. at 181–82.

395. Id. at 195 (White, J., dissenting).

396. Id. at 194. Justice White was referring to the majority's assertion that the right to self-representation is not subject to harmless error analysis because of the dangers

associated with self-representation and the distinct probability of an ''unfavorable result'' to the defendant who invokes the right, id. at 177–178, n.8.

397. Id. at 177–78, n.8. In the Court's words, ''The trial judge may be required to make numerous rulings reconciling the participation of standby counsel with a *pro se* defendant's objection to that participation; nothing in the nature of the *Faretta* right suggests that the usual deference to 'judgment calls' on these issues by the trial judge should not obtain here as elsewhere.''

398. ABA Standards for Criminal Justice 4–3.1(a) (2d ed. 1980). The commentary to the Standards also state that ''[n]othing is more fundamental to the lawyer–client relationship than the establishment of trust and confidence,'' id. at 4–29 (commentary).

399. *Linton v. Perini*, 656 F.2d 207, 212 (6th Cir. 1981).

400. *See supra* notes 372–73 and accompanying text.

401. Hazard, ETHICS IN THE PRACTICE OF LAW 121–22 (1978).

402. *See* generally, Wolfram, MODERN LEGAL ETHICS Sec. 10.1, at 565, 568 (1986).

403. 461 U.S. 1 (1982).

404. Id. at 13–14. The Court did not have to issue this gratuitous dictum because it found that the trial court was correct in rejecting the defendant's ''midtrial motion'' for a continuance to substitute counsel, id. at 13. *See* also, Justice Brennan's concurring opinion, id. at 19 (Brennan, J., concurring).

405. Id. at 5.

406. Id. at 13. In fact, Slappy made his request eleven days after his original counsel had been replaced by another member of the public defender's office, id.

407. *See* note 397, *supra*.

408. The Ninth Circuit held that the Sixth Amendment right to counsel entails a meaningful relationship between the defendant and his lawyer. *Slappy v. Morris*, 649 F.2d 718, 720 (9th Cir. 1981).

409. *Morris v. Slappy*, 461 U.S. at 13–14.

410. Id. at 16 (Brennan, J., concurring).

411. Id. at 22. As Justice Brennan observed, ''Nothing about indigent defendants makes their relationships with their attorneys less important, or less deserving of protection, than those of wealthy defendants.''

412. Id. at 21–25.

413. 486 U.S. 153 (1988). For a discussion of *Wheat*'s factual predicate and its crime-control bent, *see* notes 357–70 and accompanying text.

414. Id. at 172 (Stevens, J., dissenting).

415. Green, *''Through a Glass, Darkly'': How the Court Sees Motions to Disqualify Criminal Defense Lawyers*, 89 COLUM. L. REV. 1201, 1237 (1989).

416. Id. at 1239.

417. *Wheat v. United States*, 468 U.S. at 168 (Marshall, J., dissenting). As Justice Marshall pointed out in dissent, the interest at stake in *Wheat* ''is nothing less than a criminal defendant's Sixth Amendment right to counsel of choice. The trial court simply does not have 'broad latitude' . . . to vitiate this right,'' id.

418. 109 S.Ct. 2646 (1989).

419. Id. at 2673 (Blackmun, J., dissenting).

420. Id.

421. Id.

422. *See* note 373, *supra*.

423. 475 U.S. 157 (1986).
424. 486 U.S. 153 (1988).
425. 487 U.S. 285 (1988).
426. 475 U.S. 157 (1986).
427. Id. at 159–62.
428. *See supra* notes 297–303 for a discussion of *Strickland.*
429. Id. at 168.
430. Id. at 177.
431. *See* Freedman *supra* note 373, at 133, n.114.
432. *Nix v. Whiteside*, 475 U.S. at 188 (Brennan, J., concurring).
433. Id. at 166–71.
434. *Strickland v. Washington*, 486 U.S. at 997. This point is made by Justice Blackmun's concurring opinion in *Nix, Nix v. Whiteside*, 475 U.S. at 184–89.
435. This scenario occurred in *United States ex rel. Wilcox v. Johnson*, 555 F.2d 115 (3rd Cir. 1977).
436. Freedman, *Client Confidences and Client Perjury: Some Unanswered Questions*, 136 U. PA. L. REV. 1939, 1954–55 (1988).
437. *Nix v. Whiteside*, 475 U.S. at 188–89 (Blackmun, J., concurring).
438. Id. at 189 (citations omitted).
439. 486 U.S. 153 (1988).
440. For a discussion of *Wheat, see supra* notes 357–70 and accompanying text.
441. Id. at 160.
442. Id.
443. *See* Green *supra* note 410, at 1215–22.
444. Id. at 1215.
445. Id. at 1216 (citations omitted).
446. Id. at 1221.
447. *See supra* notes 421–33 and accompanying text.
448. *See supra* notes 435–41 and accompanying text.
449. 487 U.S. 285 (1988).
450. Id. at 288–89.
451. Id. at 301 (Stevens, J., dissenting). Disciplinary Rule 7–104 of the ABA Code of Professional Responsibility (1982) states that:

> (A) During the course of his representation of a client a lawyer shall not:
> (A) Communicate or cause another to communicate on the subject of the representation with a party he knows to be represented by a lawyer in that matter unless he has the prior consent of the lawyer representing such other party or is authorized by law to do so.

In addition, Rule 4.2 of the ABA Model Rules of Professional Conduct (1984) stipulates that:

> In representing a client, a lawyer shall not communicate about the subject of the representation with a party the lawyer knows to be represented by another lawyer in the matter, unless the lawyer has the consent of the other lawyer or is authorized by law to do so.

452. *Patterson v. Illinois*, 487 U.S. at 301 (Stevens, J., dissenting).
453. Id. at 290–96.
454. Id. at 287.
455. *Kimmelman v. Morrison*, 477 U.S. at 377 (citing and quoting from *Gideon v. Wainwright*, 372 U.S. at 344).

456. *Gideon v. Wainwright*, 372 U.S. at 344.

457. *Oregon v. Kennedy*, 456 U.S. 667, 682 n.7 (1982).

458. 475 U.S. 625 (1986).

459. 487 U.S. 285 (1988).

460. *Michigan v. Harvey*, 110 S.Ct. 1176 (1990).

461. *See*, e.g., Schwartz, *The Zeal of the Civil Advocate*, 1983 AM. B. FOUND. RES. J. 543, 547, 549–50 (opposing counsel "should be roughly equal in their ability to perform their professional functions"; however, imbalance of resources in the criminal realm precludes proper functioning of adversary system); Frankel, *From Private Rights to Public Justice*, 51 N.Y.U. L. REV. 516, 518 (1976) (inequity of resources between the parties makes the system fail).

462. Schwartz, *supra* note 456, at 547.

463. *See*, e.g., Goldwasser, *Limiting a Criminal Defendant's Use of Peremptory Challenges: On Symmetry and the Jury in a Criminal Trial*, 102 HARV. L. REV., 808, 825–26 (1989); *United States v. Turkish*, 623 F.2d 769, 774–75 (2d Cir. 1980).

464. Silver, *Equality of Arms and the Adversarial Process*, 1990 WIS. L. REV. 1007, 1037–39 (equality of arms does not require equal skills or resources but the ability of both sides to present their cases by having the same rights to subpoena witnesses and records, introduce evidence, cross-examine witnesses, etc.).

465. Levy, ORIGINAL INTENT AND THE FRAMERS OF THE CONSTITUTION at 146 (1988).

466. Id. at 160.

467. Id. at 161–66.

468. Id. at 166.

469. Id.

470. Posner, THE PROBLEMS OF JURISPRUDENCE at 54 (1990).

471. Levy, *supra* note 460 at 164.

472. *Walters v. National Assn. of Radiation Survivors*, 473 U.S. 305, 371 (1985) (Stevens, J., dissenting) (footnote omitted).

2

The Confrontation Clause, the Hearsay Rule, and the *Bruton* Doctrine

The right to a defense rests upon two critical parts of the Sixth Amendment: the confrontation and compulsory process clauses. Together, these rights allow the defendant to test the prosecution's case and to call witnesses in her behalf. In effect, these clauses "constitutionalize the right to a defense as we know it."[1] The right to confrontation and to compulsory process are two sides of the same coin: They represent the crux of the adversary system of adjudication.[2] Therefore, the next two chapters will discuss these rights through the vehicle of two specific cases that elucidate the meaning and the current doctrinal development of these components of the adversary process.

INTRODUCTION

A basic goal of our adversary system of justice is to afford both parties to a controversy the opportunity to challenge and rebut the evidence presented by their opponents.[3] If the process reaches the trial stage, this objective is accomplished in large part through effective cross-examination of the witnesses offered by the opposing parties.[4] A constitutional dimension underlying this precept is embodied in the Sixth Amendment's confrontation clause,[5] which grants criminal defendants the right to confront their accusers.[6] Consequently, the denial of effective confrontation, especially at trial, abridges significantly a defendant's rights under the Sixth Amendment and thereby casts doubt on the fairness of the proceeding.[7]

Given the sheer complexity and diversity of the Supreme Court's confrontation jurisprudence, it is worthwhile to examine the confrontation clause through a representative doctrine. The *Bruton* doctrine reflects the values fostered by the confrontation clause and is a microcosm of the Court's interpretation of the clause. Therefore, we will examine the defendant's right to confront his accusers through the lens of this doctrine.

A special problem that infringes directly upon the right to confrontation could arise at joint trials, when the prosecution introduces into evidence the confession of a nontestifying codefendant that implicates the defendant in the crime charged. In such situations, the defendant may effectively be denied the opportunity to confront a potentially devastating accuser: his alleged partner in crime. The Supreme Court first dealt with this vexing question by holding that a limiting instruction issued by the trial judge directing the jury to consider the codefendant's confession in assessing only the codefendant's, rather than the defendant's, guilt was sufficient to protect the defendant's right to confrontation.[8] However, the Court reversed itself in *Bruton v. United States*[9] by holding that, despite the issuance of limiting instructions to the jury, the introduction at a criminal trial of the confession of a nontestifying codefendant that implicates the defendant violates the defendant's Sixth Amendment right to confrontation.[10]

This chapter traces the origins and development of the *Bruton* doctrine, placing particular emphasis on the Supreme Court's interpretation and application of the rule. The chapter argues that the Court's decisions issued since *Bruton* have been marked by a lack of doctrinal consistency and by a steady erosion of the fundamental values supporting the Sixth Amendment's confrontation clause. As commentators have suggested, the Court has subsumed the basic premise of the confrontation clause under evidentiary principles, essentially equating the clause with the principles governing the hearsay rule and its exceptions.[11]

Furthermore, this chapter advances the thesis that the Court's narrow interpretation of *Bruton* has the practical effect of undermining a criminal defendant's privilege against self-incrimination under the Fifth Amendment.[12] By denying effective confrontation, the Court's restrictive reading of *Bruton* places a criminal defendant in an unenviable position. He can either remain silent, and risk having the jury draw an adverse inference from the uncontested out-of-court statements of the codefendant that inculpate him, or take the stand to rebut the codefendant's prejudicial assertions, and thereby waive his privilege against self-incrimination.

This chapter first sets forth the doctrinal basis of the *Bruton* rule, with an extensive analysis of *Bruton v. United States*.[13] Next, it examines how well the remedies available to prevent a *Bruton* violation safeguard a criminal defendant from the prejudice *Bruton* intended to eradicate, expounds the exceptions to the *Bruton* doctrine established by the Supreme Court, and questions the proper scope of those exceptions. Then it explores whether and to what degree the constitutional protections afforded by the confrontation clause are at variance with the hearsay rule and its exceptions. Finally, it endeavors to show the conflict between a criminal defendant's Fifth Amendment privilege against self-incrimination and the denial of adequate confrontation under the *Bruton* doctrine.

THE DOCTRINAL BASIS OF THE *BRUTON* RULE

As a backdrop to the emergence of the *Bruton* doctrine, an analysis of the doctrinal underpinnings of the confrontation clause is warranted. Accordingly, this section will trace the decisions of the Supreme Court that shed light on the fundamental purposes of the clause[14] and then proceed to the specific question posed by the factual pattern presented in *Bruton*.

The Origins and Early History of the Confrontation Clause

As Justice Harlan's concurring opinion in *California v. Green*[15] notes, the origins of the confrontation clause are obscure.[16] The historical circumstances that led to its development are a matter of debate. Heller observes that the right to confrontation was recognized by the common law as a consequence of the violations of the right in the trial of Sir Walter Raleigh.[17] Raleigh was convicted solely on the basis of an affidavit of questionable reliability given by an alleged coconspirator who was not produced in court by the prosecution.[18] On the other hand, Kenneth Graham is convinced that the trial of Raleigh did not contribute to the passage of the Sixth Amendment but merely provides a "convenient but highly romantic myth."[19]

Whether the nexus between the Raleigh case and the Sixth Amendment is fact or myth, the early Supreme Court cases interpreting the confrontation clause primarily addressed the issue posed by the Raleigh trial: whether a "trial by affidavit" withstands constitutional scrutiny under the Sixth Amendment. In these cases the Court answered the question in the negative, but not without certain qualifications. The decisions are instructive because the Court dealt with the proper balance between the defendant's right to confrontation and the government's need to introduce out-of-court statements into evidence to secure a conviction.

In *Reynolds v. United States*,[20] the Court upheld the admission of the former trial testimony of a prosecution witness because the defendant was largely responsible for the witness's absence.[21] The Court noted that at a former trial of the defendant for the same offense the defendant enjoyed the "full opportunity" to cross-examine the now missing witness.[22]

By contrast, in *Motes v. United States*,[23] the introduction of the preliminary hearing testimony of a prosecution witness at the defendant's trial was deemed to be in contravention of the confrontation clause.[24] The critical fact in *Motes* was that the government's negligence, rather than the defendant's successful attempt to prevent the witness from testifying, accounted for the absence of the witness.[25] The Court concluded that it was inconsistent with the confrontation clause

> to permit the deposition or statement of an absent witness (taken at an examining trial) to be read at the final trial when it does not appear that the witness was absent by the suggestion, connivance, or procurement of the accused, but does appear that his absence was due to the negligence of the prosecution.[26]

The third case in this triad, and perhaps the most important, given its focus on the underlying objectives of the confrontation clause, is *Mattox v. United*

States.[27] The crux of *Mattox* involved the admissibility of the transcript of the defendant's former trial. The transcript was crucial to the prosecution because it contained the testimony of the two government witnesses who had since died. The Court undertook an analysis of the confrontation clause and reached the conclusion that:

> The primary object of [the confrontation clause] was to prevent depositions or ex parte affidavits, such as were sometimes admitted in civil cases, being used against the prisoner in lieu of a personal examination and cross-examination of the witness in which the accused has an opportunity, not only of testing the recollection and sifting the conscience of the witness, but of compelling him to stand face to face with the jury in order that they may look at him, and judge by his demeanor upon the stand and the manner in which he gives his testimony whether he is worthy of belief.[28]

Proceeding from that premise, the Court nevertheless held that the former trial testimony of the two deceased witnesses was admissible because of "considerations of public policy and the necessities of the case."[29] The Court recognized the accepted principle of evidentiary law allowing the introduction into evidence of dying declarations; combined with the opportunity the defendant had to cross-examine the witness at the former trial, it justified the introduction of the transcript "to prevent a manifest failure of justice."[30]

If a pattern may be discerned from the interpretative analysis of the confrontation doctrine by the Court in these early cases, it is that the critical right to confrontation accorded to a defendant under the Sixth Amendment is constrained by a rule of "availability."[31] This doctrine, in turn, was chiefly meant to prevent manifest injustice in the sense of tying the prosecutor's hand when events beyond the control of the government affected adversely the prosecution's case.

Delli Paoli v. United States

The criterion of availability as an essential adjunct to the right of confrontation was disregarded by the Court in *Delli Paoli v. United States*.[32] In that case, the trial court admitted into evidence the confession of a codefendant implicating the defendant in a conspiracy with which five codefendants were charged.[33] Although the opinion by the Court did not mention whether the confessing codefendant testified at the trial, presumably the confession was admitted in spite of the failure of the confessing codefendant to take the stand. Thus, for practical purposes, the defendant was "unavailable" at the trial through no fault or deliberate wrongdoing of the codefendant, who was prejudiced by the admission of the defendant's confession.

The prejudicial impact of the codefendant's confession was diminished, according to the Court, by the trial judge's instruction to the jury not to consider the confession of the one defendant in assessing the guilt of the other four defendants. This theory rested on the assumption that the jury had indeed followed the limiting instruction.[34] To buttress its holding, the Court literally engaged in a "leap of faith" predicated on the belief that the viability of the jury system rests on the notion that the "jury will endeavor to follow the court's instructions."[35]

Despite the Court's failure to acknowledge the weakness of its rationale, it did provide a logical solution to the problem presented by the facts of *Delli Paoli*: a separate trial at which the confession would not be admitted.[36] However, leaving the use of that remedy to the discretion of the trial judge signaled that severance in this particular context was not mandated by the confrontation clause.[37] Indeed, one factor stressed by the Court in assuming that the jury adhered to the limiting instructions was that no defendant requested a separate trial.[38]

In a vigorous dissent, Justice Frankfurter exposed the faulty logic of the majority opinion. In particular, he assailed the unwarranted assumption that juries would follow an instruction to ignore a confession by a defendant implicating a codefendant in determining the nonconfessing codefendants' guilt as a legal fiction requiring the jury to perform an impossible "psychological feat."[39] Justice Frankfurter advocated the logical solution in this instance that would have prevented unfairness to the nonconfessing defendants: severance.[40]

Pointer v. Texas

The *Delli Paoli* decision's force as precedent was destined to be eroded with the changing composition of the Supreme Court under the leadership of Chief Justice Earl Warren. Hints of *Delli Paoli*'s eventual demise can be gleaned from the Court's decision in *Pointer v. Texas*.[41] In *Pointer* the Court held that the Sixth Amendment was applicable to the states by virtue of the due process clause of the Fourteenth Amendment.[42] More important, the Court delineated the fundamental values underlying the confrontation clause.

In effect, the value the Court emphasized as the basis for the clause was the need to ensure a criminal defendant a fair trial. Reflecting on the possible value the Framers of the Bill of Rights sought to protect, the Court concluded that the inclusion of the right to confrontation within the Sixth Amendment manifested the conviction of the Framers that confrontation "was a fundamental right essential to a fair trial in a criminal prosecution."[43] According to the *Pointer* Court, cross-examination is the principal means of preserving a criminal defendant's right to confrontation and a fair trial.[44] Together, the Court noted, confrontation and cross-examination constitute the indispensable elements "for the kind of fair trial which is this country's constitutional goal."[45]

This forceful affirmation by the Court in *Pointer* laid the groundwork for the eventual overruling of *Delli Paoli*. If *Pointer* sounded *Delli Paoli*'s death knell, however, *Douglas v. Alabama*[46] sealed its fate.

Douglas v. Alabama

In *Douglas*, the defendant was charged with assault with intent to commit murder. His codefendant had been tried separately and convicted of the same charge. At Douglas's trial, the prosecution called the convicted codefendant as a witness to elicit corroboration of the codefendant's confession implicating the defendant in the crime charged. The codefendant, however, invoked his privilege against self-incrimination and refused to answer any of the prosecutor's questions, despite the trial judge's admonition that, given his conviction, he no longer enjoyed the privilege.[47] The prosecutor then sought successfully to have the codefendant declared a hostile witness so that he could have the privilege of cross-examination.[48]

Relying on a clever strategy, the prosecutor managed to convey the entire contents of the codefendant's confession to the jury by pretending to ''refresh'' the codefendant's recollection through reading the entire document aloud in court.[49] The prosecutor attained his main goal through this device because the confession of the codefendant was critical to the state. In the confession, the codefendant alleged that Douglas had fired the shotgun, the only direct evidence available to show that the defendant committed the act in question and had the requisite intent to murder.[50]

The *Douglas* Court held that, given these circumstances, the defendant was denied his right of confrontation under the Sixth Amendment.[51] The Court reasoned that Douglas was not able to cross-examine his codefendant regarding the confession, and that the right to cross-examination inhered in the confrontation clause of the Sixth Amendment.[52] The Court, moreover, buttressed its holding by pointing to two crucial factors: that the codefendant's invocation of the privilege against self-incrimination precluded effective cross-examination and possibly led the jury to conclude that the confession was true,[53] and that effective confrontation would have been possible only if the codefendant had affirmed that the confession was his.[54]

Douglas paved the way for the reversal of *Delli Paoli* by establishing the rule that when a prosecution witness is present in court but invokes the privilege against self-incrimination (and thus precludes the defendant from effective confrontation), the declarant's out-of-court statements are inadmissible. This situation is different from the previous line of cases decided by the Court in which out-of-court statements were deemed inadmissible due to violation of the confrontation clause. These previous cases involved a denial of confrontation because the prosecution introduced the out-of-court statements of witnesses who could not be cross-examined because they were not present in the courtroom.[55]

The most novel feature of *Douglas* is that the Court held that the mere physical presence of a witness at trial is not per se sufficient to satisfy the requirements of the confrontation clause. This, of course, was the situation in *Bruton v. United States*.[56]

Bruton v. United States

The reversal of *Delli Paoli* in *Bruton* could be construed as a significant expansion of a defendant's right to confrontation pursuant to the Sixth Amendment. However, as discussed below,[57] the Court has limited the scope of *Bruton* by restricting the force of its rationale and by applying inconsistently the doctrine which it so clearly enunciated in the case. It is essential, therefore, to examine thoroughly the Court's analysis in *Bruton* as a basis for judging the fidelity (or lack thereof) with which the Court has approached the *Bruton* doctrine.

The facts of *Bruton* are relatively straightforward. Bruton and his codefendant Evans were tried jointly before a jury on the federal charge of armed postal robbery. At the trial, a postal inspector testified that Evans had confessed to the robbery and had implicated Bruton in his confession.[58] The judge instructed the jury that it should consider Evans's confession solely in determining Evans' guilt, and that it should disregard the confession with regard to Bruton's involvement because in that regard the confession constituted inadmissible hearsay.[59]

The *Bruton* majority reversed the defendant's conviction and expressly overruled *Delli Paoli*, holding that the introduction of a nontestifying codefendant's confession inculpating the defendant violates the accused's "right to cross-examination secured by the Confrontation Clause of the Sixth Amendment."[60] Adhering to the rationale expressed in *Douglas*, the Court noted that the denial of confrontation in the instant case was more serious than that in *Douglas* because the confession was actually introduced into evidence, and the danger that the jury would consider the confession an accurate and truthful statement was therefore greater than in the case of the unofficial admission of the codefendant's confession in *Douglas*.[61]

Significantly, the *Bruton* majority opinion emphasized the importance of the confession in bolstering the prosecution's case against Bruton. The Court observed that "Evans' confession added substantial, perhaps even critical, weight to the Government's case in a form not subject to cross-examination, since Evans did not take the stand. Petitioner thus was denied his constitutional right of confrontation."[62] Hence, as in *Douglas*, the introduction of the confession denied the defendant the right to confrontation because it prevented cross-examination of a witness who provided a "crucial link" in the chain of evidence necessary for the prosecution to obtain a conviction.[63]

Furthermore, the majority opinion rejected the premise posited in *Delli Paoli* that curative limiting instructions to the jury would cure the prejudicial impact of a nontestifying codefendant's confession. The *Bruton* Court drew an analogy to *Jackson v. Denno*[64] as a basis for discarding the notion that a jury could be trusted to follow the limiting instructions.[65] Accordingly, the majority opinion adopted the reasoning of Justice Frankfurter's dissenting opinion in *Delli Paoli* that it is unrealistic to expect a jury to perform the "mental gymnastics" of disregarding evidence that clearly bears on the guilt of the defendant. More importantly, the Court dismissed the alleged advantages of reliance on limiting instructions by pointing out that the protection of constitutional rights far outweighs the supposed efficiencies of joint trials.[66] The *Bruton* Court recognized that the solution to the confrontation issue set forth in *Delli Paoli* conserved judicial resources, diminished inconvenience to witnesses, and prevented delays in trial by allowing a joint trial of codefendants. Nevertheless, the majority opinion quoted approvingly from Judge Lehman's dissenting opinion in *People v. Fisher*[67] the proposition that considerations of administrative convenience must give way to "fundamental principles of constitutional liberty."[68]

The majority opinion concluded by stating succinctly its rationale for overruling *Delli Paoli* as follows:

> [T]here are some contexts in which the risk that the jury will not, or cannot follow instructions is so great, and the consequences of the failure so vital to the defendant, that the practical and human limitations of the jury system cannot be ignored. Such a context is presented here, where the powerfully incriminating extrajudicial statements of a co-defendant, who stands accused side-by-side with the defendant, are deliberately spread before a jury in a joint trial. Not only are the incriminations devastating to the defendant but their credibility is inevitably suspect. . . . The unreliability of such evidence is intolerably compounded when the alleged accomplice, as here, does not testify and cannot be tested by cross-examination. It was against such threats to a fair trial that the Confrontation Clause was directed.[69]

Thus, the Court returned to the principle clearly established in *Pointer v. Texas*[70] that the confrontation clause is primarily intended to ensure a criminal defendant a fair trial, if not necessarily a "perfect one."[71] A joint trial is manifestly unfair when the defendant is precluded from cross-examining effectively a codefendant whose confession implicates the defendant and is admitted into evidence. Such a trial deprives a defendant of the right to confront his accusers.

Justice White's dissent in *Bruton* argued that the rule established by the majority would impair severely the prosecution's ability to try codefendants jointly.[72] Requiring severance in most circumstances when the *Bruton* question arose would impede the orderly administration of the criminal process. Because the majority had not specified what remedies would be available to deal effectively with the problem posed by *Bruton*,[73] Justice White attempted to fill the gaps. He assumed that the existence of a *Bruton* issue at trial would require the effective deletion from a codefendant's confession of all direct and indirect references inculpating other defendants, as well as any statement that could be used against a defendant once his "identity is otherwise established."[74] Justice White cautioned that these deletions must not alter the substance of the confession nor prejudice either the prosecution or the declarant.[75] These stark choices, Justice White reasoned, would leave the prosecution in a precarious situation: Barring the possibility of an effective deletion, the government would have the options of severance or of forgoing the use of the confession.[76]

REMEDIES

The degree to which the *Bruton* doctrine safeguards a criminal defendant's right to confrontation under the Sixth Amendment depends upon the availability of effective remedies for the confrontation problem presented in *Bruton*. Because the majority opinion did not provide sufficient guidance for lower courts regarding what solution addressed adequately the concerns raised in the decision, much confusion arose over the precise requirements *Bruton* established. The ultimate objective sought by the Court was to further compliance with the confrontation clause in order to give a criminal defendant a fair trial. In general, four remedies to the *Bruton* confrontation issue exist. However, the validity of these remedies must be judged according to their ability to provide a criminal defendant with effective confrontation pursuant to the Sixth Amendment and thereby provide him with a fair trial.

Severance

The best corrective measure available to a trial court when a *Bruton* issue surfaces is severance—that is, a separate trial in which the confession implicating the affected defendant is not introduced into evidence. This remedy is usually anathema to the prosecution because of the advantages prosecutors derive from joint trials. As Graham remarks, the prosecution derives tremendous benefit from shifting the burden of proof to the defense in a joint trial. This results from the fact that a joint trial often leads to conflict among defendants, "making the trial a three-sided controversy in which the defendants are pitted against each other as well as the state."[77] The alternative scenario also favors the prosecution in that codefendants will be reticent to testify for fear of implicating the other defendants under pressure of cross-examination.[78]

The argument favoring joint trials points to the alleged "efficiencies" inherent in the practice[78]: conservation of judicial resources, convenience for witnesses, and avoidance of trial delays.[80] Joint trials are also said to promote consistent verdicts or results and prevent unfairness to codefendants.[81]

The alleged advantages of joint trials for the efficient administration of the criminal justice process are, by and large, illusory.[82] The arguments favoring them are premised on the belief that severance will necessarily prompt all defendants to undergo jury trials, thereby taxing an already overburdened criminal justice system.[83] In most instances severance will result in only one trial, because the results of the first trial will encourage codefendants to plead guilty or to waive the right to a jury trial.[84]

Despite its simplicity and advantages, severance is often relied upon only as a last resort,[85] largely because of the prosecution's unwillingness to forgo the advantages of a joint trial and the trial judges' reluctance to conduct multiple trials in a case involving defendants charged with the same offense.

Forgoing Use of Codefendant Confessions at Joint Trials

A *Bruton* problem would be remedied easily by a promise from the government not to employ codefendant confessions implicating other defendants at trial. The problem with this apparently uncomplicated answer to a *Bruton* issue is twofold. In the first place, the prosecution will be reluctant to surrender the benefits of introducing the confession into evidence. Moreover, assuming the prosecution agrees to withhold the use of the confession, the temptation to introduce the evidence despite the promise will lead the prosecutor, either deliberately or inadvertently, to renege on the pledge and convey the substance of the confession to the jury.[86]

The possibility that the prosecution will bring the confession to the attention of the jury despite an agreement to the contrary was dramatically illustrated by analogy in the case of *Richardson v. Marsh.*[87] The *Marsh* case did not involve a direct promise by the prosecution not to use a nontestifying codefendant's confession against the defendant, but rather dealt with the redaction[88] of all references to the involvement of the defendant in the crime from the nontestifying codefendant's confession. Other evidence, however, linked the defendant to the crime.[89] The prosecutor was aware that the confession by the nontestifying codefendant was not to be used by the jury in determining the defendant's guilt.[90] Nevertheless, during closing argument, the prosecutor effectively nullified the limiting instructions given by openly prodding the jury to consider the confession in assessing the defendant's guilt.[91]

The ostensible advantage of this solution to the *Bruton* issue disappears in the light of practical difficulties attending its successful implementation. When compared with the conceptual simplicity and ease of implementing severance, the prosecution's forgoing the use of the codefendant's confession is not an efficient means of safeguarding a defendant's right to confrontation when a *Bruton* problem arises before trial.

Bifurcated Trial or Multiple Juries

Another alternative widely perceived as an effective antidote to *Bruton*-related problems is the use of either multiple juries or a bifurcated trial.[92] By conducting a bifurcated trial, the prosecution avoids the problems that arose in *Bruton* by trying both defendants jointly but withholding the codefendant's confession from the jury until it reaches a verdict with regard to the defendant. After this occurs, the jury is permitted to hear the confession of the codefendant and other evidence relevant to the codefendant's case.

Similarly, multiple juries may be used at a joint trial. A separate jury would be selected for each codefendant. Each jury would then be exposed only to evidence relevant to the codefendant whose fate it will decide. In a *Bruton*-type situation, the jury for a defendant who has been implicated by another codefendant's confession would be excused when the confession is introduced into evidence at trial. Each jury would hear separate closing arguments and render separate verdicts.

Although these alternatives address the interests of both the prosecution and the defense by allowing the prosecution to use the confession while protecting the defendant's Sixth Amendment right to confrontation, they suffer from serious flaws.[93] In *United States v. Sidman*,[94] the trial court chose to use multiple juries. Unfortunately, the juries were not separated when a government witness testified that the codefendant confessed to the crime and inculpated the defendant. As a result, the appellate court reversed the defendant's conviction.[95]

Similar problems could emerge when a court relies on the bifurcated trial to avoid infringing on a defendant's right to confrontation while simultaneously holding a joint trial. The Sixth Circuit Court of Appeals has noted that if a jury returned a guilty verdict on the first defendant in a bifurcated trial, "there could be a serious question whether the same jury could later give his co-defendant the dispassionate and unprejudiced hearing required by due process and the Sixth Amendment."[96]

The deficiencies associated with the use of either multiple juries or bifurcated trials point to the dearth of practical alternatives, other than severance, that preserve a criminal defendant's right to confrontation when a *Bruton* issue arises.

Redaction

The flaws associated with the remedies discussed previously are enhanced considerably when redaction—the deletion from the confession of references to any other defendant—is relied upon by the trial court. The trial court must consider whether the redaction will distort the confession to the detriment of the confessing defendant. It is possible that the deletion of parts of the confession could exclude a portion of the document that either exculpates or mitigates the guilt of the confessor.[97]

In addition, the trial court must undertake a close analysis of the confession to ensure that all language that refers directly or inferentially to the defendant be excised from the confession. This is difficult because the jury will likely infer that the confession refers to the defendant if the court merely substitutes a symbol or a blank for his or her name. This alleged remedy amounts to a "sham deletion."[98] Some appellate courts, however, engage in the fiction that such a deletion adequately protects a defendant's right to confrontation under *Bruton*.[99]

The critical question whether redaction effectively complies with *Bruton*'s mandate emerges in bold relief when a confession is edited to delete all references to the defendant. Such a confession presumably does not, on its face, incriminate the defendant. The issue resolved in *Bruton*, or course, was that the admission of a confession by a nontestifying codefendant implicating a defendant at a joint trial contravened the Sixth Amendment's confrontation clause. As a corollary to this principle, most appellate courts adhere rigidly to the theory that a confession must clearly inculpate the defendant to trigger *Bruton*'s protection.[100]

Assuming that a confession with all references to the defendant omitted has been admitted into evidence, the *Bruton* rationale apparently does not apply in the absence of a statement inculpatory on its face within the confession. This facile interpretation vanishes when the confession, linked to other evidence introduced at trial, clearly implicates the defendant in the crime. Courts have distinguished this situation from the typical *Bruton* scenario by pointing out that the inculpatory evidence against the defendant, rather than being established within the confines of the confession, is provided instead through "evidentiary linkage" or "contextual implication."[101]

Before the Supreme Court decided *Richard v. Marsh*,[102] most appellate courts adhered to the proposition that when a confession was redacted to delete all references to the defendant, and thus did not incriminate her in the crime charged, *Bruton* did not apply. Hence, such courts adopted the Procrustean notion that it was not necessary to examine any evidence other than the confession itself in determining its incriminatory value.[103] Unfortunately, the Supreme Court embraced this restrictive reading of *Bruton* in *Marsh*. It is instructive, therefore, to delve into the Court's analysis of the "evidentiary linkage" aspect of redaction in *Marsh*.

The defendant in *Marsh*, Clarissa Marsh, was tried with one of her codefendants,[104] Benjamin Williams, in spite of her contention that such a joint trial violated her right to confrontation under the Sixth Amendment.[105] Marsh and Williams were charged with two counts of felony murder committed during an armed robbery and with assault with intent to commit murder.[106] During the trial, the prosecution introduced Williams's confession, which was edited to exclude all references to Marsh.[107] Coupled with the testimony of the surviving victim, however, the confession demonstrated that Marsh had the requisite intent: She knew her codefendants planned to kill the victims after the conclusion of the robbery.[108] In fact, as Justice Stevens observed in dissent, when the prosecutor introduced Williams's confession in presenting his case-in-chief, he clearly indicated that the confession would incriminate both Williams and Marsh.[109] Williams did not take the stand at the trial.

Marsh then faced a Hobson's choice:[110] If she exercised her Fifth Amendment right not to testify, she would risk the very strong probability that the jury would find her guilty chiefly on the contents of Williams's confession. Nevertheless, she did not have the opportunity of confronting Williams to establish her lack of intent to kill the victims, since Williams exercised his privilege not to testify. Consequently, Marsh took the stand and testified that "she had possessed no prior knowledge that Martin and Williams were armed, had heard no conversation about [anybody] being harmed, and had not intended to rob or kill anyone."[111] The jury convicted Marsh of two counts of felony murder and one count of assault with the intent to commit murder.[112]

The majority opinion, written by Justice Scalia, held that no confrontation clause violation occurred in *Marsh*, because Marsh's Sixth Amendment rights were protected sufficiently by the limiting instructions issued to the jury not to consider Williams's confession in assessing Marsh's guilt.[113] This conclusion stemmed from the fact that the confession had been redacted to eliminate not only Marsh's name, but also any reference to her existence.[114]

Justice Scalia's opinion readily acknowledged that Williams's confession prejudiced the defendant.[115] Distinguishing *Bruton*, however, the majority espoused the dubious premise that because the confession was not on its face incriminating, but became incriminating when linked to other evidence introduced at trial (the defendant's own testimony), "it is a less valid generalization that the jury will not likely obey the instruction to disregard the evidence."[116]

The contradictions in Justice Scalia's conclusion are clear. First, the majority opinion acknowledges that the confession prejudiced the defendant by incriminating her in the crimes with which she was charged.[117] Indeed, given the prosecutor's admission at the time he sought to introduce the confession that it would powerfully incriminate Marsh as well as Williams, it would have been sheer hypocrisy for the majority to ignore the extent to which the confession harmed Marsh. However, Justice Scalia makes the unwarranted deduction that the confession was not incriminating on its face but only in conjunction with Marsh's testimony. In effect, after the surviving victim testified, Williams's confession, despite the redaction, clearly implicated the defendant in the plan to murder the victims.[118]

In addition, the majority opinion did not emphasize the fact that the introduction of Williams's confession into evidence placed the defendant in a precarious position.[119] The admission of the confession, combined with Williams's failure to testify, had the practical "real world"[120] effect of undermining Marsh's privilege against self-incrimination. Marsh was denied the right, guaranteed by the Sixth Amendment's confrontation clause, to confront Williams in order to rebut the presumption that she knew about and consented to the plan to kill the victims of the robbery.[121] She no doubt felt overwhelming pressure to testify so that she could deny any complicity in the plan.[122] Of course, Marsh testified at trial and denied any knowledge of or complicity in the plan to kill the victims.[123] This testimony further prejudiced Marsh by reminding the jury of Williams's plan to kill the victims and by affording the prosecutor another chance to highlight this evidence "on the close question of her specific intent."[124] This was the price Marsh had to pay for being denied the right to have a separate trial in which Williams's confession was not introduced into evidence.

Another faulty premise underlying Justice Scalia's opinion is the belief that a jury can be trusted to follow limiting instruction in a situation such as that presented in *Marsh*, where evidence other than the confession is necessary to link the defendant to the crime. The flaw behind this logic is exposed by the tentative manner in which the majority expresses its judgment. Indeed, Justice Scalia recognizes that "it may not always be simple for the members of a jury to obey the instruction that they disregard an incriminating inference."[125] He qualifies this by stating that, in such an instance of contextual implication, "there does not exist the overwhelming probability of [the jury's] inability to [disregard the limiting instruction] that is the foundation of *Bruton*'s exception to the general rule''[126] that juries may be presumed to follow limiting instructions.

Moreover, the likelihood that the jury in *Marsh* could easily follow the trial judge's instruction to disregard Williams's confession in determining Marsh's guilt is negligible, if not nonexistent, because the confession was the only direct evidence demonstrating Marsh's specific intent to kill the victims after the completion of the robbery.[127] The speciousness of the *Marsh* majority's blind leap of faith on this issue is clear when one realizes the powerfully incriminating nature of the confession.

Further, in more general terms, the assumption that in ''evidentiary linkage'' contexts the jury is more apt to follow limiting instruction is belied by the research of jury decision-making undertaken by cognitive psychologists. Relying on a ''hindsight bias model of decision-making'' in circumstances where information is to be disregarded, researchers have found that ''a juror's ability to disregard information is simply a function of the relevance of the information, not of the matter in which it is learned.''[128] Accordingly, jurors are unable to ignore information relevant to the crux of a case they must decide, despite an instruction to the contrary.[129]

The majority in *Marsh*, moreover, attempted to bolster its dubious holding by arguing that the application of *Bruton* in an evidentiary linkage context would be cumbersome and would lead to such undesirable results as mistrials and appeals.[130] This conclusion assumed that if *Bruton* were extended to evidentiary linkage situations, it would not be feasible to determine whether a confession was powerfully incriminating, thereby requiring a new trial, until the end of the first trial.[131] As Justice Stevens remarked in his dissent, however, a trial judge can evaluate the incriminating nature of a codefendant's confession at the end of the prosecution's case-in-chief, when the prejudicial effect of the confession can be judged in light of the government's entire case.[132] Furthermore, the dissent pointed to the unlikelihood of defense manipulation, because few defense attorneys would pursue the strategy of ''manipulating their evidence in order to enhance the prejudicial impact of a codefendant's confession.''[133]

Finally, the *Marsh* majority sought to justify its failure to apply *Bruton* in evidentiary linkage situations by noting that such an extension of *Bruton* would drastically reduce joint trials and therefore ''impair both the efficiency and the fairness of the criminal justice system.''[134] The majority in essence relied upon the arguments set forth by Justice White in his dissenting opinion in *Bruton*, in which he extolled the alleged advantages of joint trials.[135] As we have seen, however, the putative advantages of joint trials are greatly exaggerated.[136] In addition, as Justice Stevens noted in *Marsh*, the majority opinion in *Bruton* made clear that constitutional imperatives take precedence over administrative concerns.[137] The alleged ''efficiency'' of a joint trial must give way to a defendant's right to confrontation under the Sixth Amendment.

In sum, the Court in *Marsh* circumvented *Bruton*'s teachings by refusing to extend its application to cases in which, despite the redaction of all reference to the defendant, the admission of a confession provided the prosecution with a potent tool to convict the defendant. In fact, the Court also ignored the precedent established by *Douglas v. Alabama*,[138] where the Court held that when a confession is critical to the government's case, the defendant's inability to cross-examine the maker of the confession violates the accused's right to confrontation.[139]

The Court's failure to follow *Bruton*'s dictates in *Marsh* was combined paradoxically with its willingness to expand *Bruton* in the same term, when it decided *Cruz v. New York*.[140] This illustrates the Court's lack of consistency in adhering to the principles set out in *Bruton*. By eliminating the "interlocking confession" exception to *Bruton*, the Court in *Cruz* enlarged the boundaries established by *Bruton* and reversed the plurality opinion in *Parker v. Randolph*.[141] Before discussing both *Parker* and *Cruz* in depth, however, it is necessary to address in general the scope of the exceptions to *Bruton* that the Court has crafted.

EXCEPTIONS

Testimony by the Codefendant: *Nelson v. O'Neil*

Bruton was preeminently designed to avert a denial of confrontation when the confession of a nontestifying codefendant that inculpated another defendant was admitted into evidence at a joint trial. It would seem logical that this problem would be avoided when the confessing codefendant testified, thereby providing the defendant with the opportunity of testing the codefendant's credibility by confronting him at trial. The force of this logic is not, however, as compelling as it would first appear. Nevertheless, a majority of the Court accepted this simplistic reasoning in *Nelson v. O'Neil*.[142]

In *Nelson*, two codefendants were tried on the charges of kidnapping, robbery, and vehicle theft. At a joint trial, each defendant raised an alibi defense.[143] One defendant had confessed to the crimes and implicated the other defendant. This confession was admitted into evidence through the testimony of a police officer. Diverging from the situation presented in *Bruton*, however, the confessing defendant took the stand and staunchly denied having made the confession, despite a thorough cross-examination by the prosecutor.[144] The defense attorney of the codefendant who was implicated in the confession did not question the confessing defendant. The nonconfessing defendant also took the stand and corroborated the substance of his codefendant's testimony.[145]

The Supreme Court held that the defendant was not denied the right to confrontation under the Sixth Amendment[146] because, in effect, he was afforded a better substitute for what he could have accomplished through effective cross-examination of his codefendant. The Court viewed the denial of the confession by the codefendant as "more favorable to the respondent than any [evidence] that cross-examination by counsel could have produced, had Runnels 'affirmed the statement as his.' "[147]

As Justice Brennan asserted in dissent, however, the defendant in *Nelson* was harmed by the introduction of the confession, because a limiting instruction to the jury not to use the inadmissible hearsay in the codefendant's confession was not sufficient to protect the defendant.[148] In essence, the majority in *Nelson* embraced the position discarded in *Bruton* that a jury could be expected to follow limiting instructions and ignore the confession of a codefendant that inculpated the defendant. James Haddad points up the deficiency of *Nelson's* rationale by stressing that *Nelson* "leaves the co-defendant with fewer safeguards than before *Bruton*"[149] in cases where the codefendant testifies.

Furthermore, the testimony by the codefendant in *Nelson* served to link the interests of both defendants; that is, it tied the codefendant's credibility to the guilt or innocence of the defendant.[150] Given that premise, the defendant could not effectively cross-examine the codefendant.[151] In addition, to the degree that *Nelson* results in a linkage between the defendant's and the codefendant's interests, it also places an added burden on the defendant to waive the privilege against self-incrimination and take the stand in order to buttress the codefendant's version of the facts. Indeed, this actually occurred in *Nelson*, because the defendant testified and verified the substance of the codefendant's testimony. Alternatively, if the codefendant takes the stand and affirms the portion of the confession implicating the defendant, the defendant may feel compelled to testify in order to sever ties with the codefendant. Otherwise, the jury may in fact conclude that the codefendant's case is identical to that of the defendant and lump the two cases together when considering the relative guilt or innocence of both defendants.

The opportunity for full and effective cross-examination was conspicuous by its absence in *Nelson*. Even assuming a situation in which the codefendant affirmed the substance of the confession, the resulting conflict between the codefendants might have led a trial court to order severance or a mistrial.[152] In short, the Court in *Nelson* opted for an unsatisfactory approach to a problem that could have been effectively solved through the simple expedient of severance.

Harmless Error

The Court announced the first major exception to *Bruton* within a year of its issuance, in *Harrington v. California*.[153] Applying the constitutional standard of harmless error articulated by the Court in *Chapman v. California*,[154] the majority in *Harrington* held that a *Bruton* violation was not unconstitutional per se, but could rather be analyzed under the harmless error doctrine pronounced in *Chapman*.[155] A clear violation of *Bruton* occurred during Harrington's trial.[156] Despite this breach, the majority found the error harmless. The rationale underpinning the opinion rested on the majority's belief that "the case against Harrington was so overwhelming that we concluded that this violation of *Bruton* was harmless beyond a reasonable doubt.[157]

Justice Brennan's dissent, however, revealed the weakness of the majority's reasoning. He observed that the government could not establish beyond a reasonable doubt that the confessions by two codefendants admitted erroneously against Harrington did not contribute to his conviction.[158] In essence, the evidence against Harrington other than the confessions admitted in violation of *Bruton* consisted of testimony by witnesses who misidentified Harrington, an admission by Harrington that he was at the scene of the crime, and the ''self-serving'' testimony of the only codefendant who testified during the trial.[159]

By redefining the standard formulated in *Chapman*, which entailed a determination whether the constitutionally infirm evidence contributed to the conviction, the *Harrington* majority arrived at a result that deprived the defendant of effective confrontation pursuant to the Sixth Amendment. In addition, by focusing on the weight of evidence aside from the tainted confession introduced against the defendant, the Court denigrated the constitutional foundation of *Chapman*, which narrowly circumscribed the harmless error rule to circumstances in which an appellate court could establish beyond a reasonable doubt that the tainted evidence did not facilitate the conviction.[160]

Similarly, the Court in *Schneble v. Florida*[161] applied the harmless error doctrine to a factual pattern involving questionable proof against the defendant. In *Schneble*, the defendant was convicted largely on the basis of the confession of his codefendant, admitted in contravention of *Bruton*, and his own confession, obtained by the police under dubious, and perhaps coercive, circumstances.[162] In effect, the *Schneble* majority acknowledged that the only solid proof the government possessed to convict the defendant was his tainted confession,[163] but nonetheless made the unwarranted assumption that the codefendant's confession was not ''sufficiently prejudicial'' to the defendant and hence did not require a reversal of his conviction.[164]

Finally, in *Brown v. United States*[165] the Court reaffirmed the validity of the harmless error analysis with respect to *Bruton*, forswearing the notion that a ''*Bruton* error can never be harmless.''[166]

The harmless error rule applied in the *Bruton* context infringes significantly upon a defendant's privilege against self-incrimination under the Fifth Amendment. This argument might be countered by stressing that when overwhelming evidence of guilt exists against the accused, the introduction of the defendant's confession does not appreciably increase the defendant's need to rebut the government's case. A closer consideration of this premise, however, exposes the flaw in its foundation. The following examination demonstrates this flaw by focusing on two decisions which shed light on the issue.

As previously mentioned, in *Schneble v. Florida* the government's case was based principally on the codefendant's confession, introduced in contravention of *Bruton*, and on the defendant's own elaborate confession obtained by the police under allegedly coercive conditions. Given a proper application of *Bruton* in this case, however, the codefendant's confession would not have been admitted. In this circumstance, the government's case would have rested mainly on the defendant's confession. The defendant could have effectively challenged the accuracy and reliability of his own confession by cross-examining the police officers who secured the confession under such questionable circumstances.

Conversely, the defendant was faced with an insoluble dilemma when the codefendant's confession was admitted erroneously into evidence. The codefendant was not available for cross-examination, hence the defendant could not rebut effectively the incriminating nature of the codefendant's confession by testing the confession's validity and veracity. The only way the defendant could blunt the prejudicial impact of the codefendant's confession was to testify and thus challenge directly the basis of the codefendant's accusations.

This position, moreover, is powerfully illuminated in a case in which the defendant claimed that the government entrapped him into committing the crime. In *United States v. Vissars*,[167] the codefendant had given a statement to the government that implicated the defendant. The codefendant did not take the stand at trial. The confession, however, was introduced when the codefendant's attorney cross-examined the FBI agent to whom the codefendant had allegedly confessed.[168] The confession damaged considerably the defendant's entrapment defense because it called into question the defendant's contention that he was not predisposed to commit the crime. As Paul Marcus perceptively noted: "Once the trial court admitted this damaging statement [the codefendant's confession], Keenberg was forced to take the stand because the statement sharply challenged his credibility and raised the real possibility that he *did* have a preexisting intent to commit the crime."[169]

As these two cases demonstrate, a defendant is adversely affected when the patently unreliable confession of a nontestifying codefendant is admitted into evidence in transgression of the *Bruton* doctrine. This holds true regardless of the existence of other overwhelming evidence of the defendant's guilt. The harmless error doctrine, moreover, applied to a *Bruton* situation is not as innocuous as it seems on its face, given the harm suffered by the defendant with regard to his Fifth Amendment rights.

Interlocking Confessions

Another exception carved out by the Supreme Court pertains to the concept of "interlocking" confessions, according to which *Bruton* does not apply if a defendant has confessed and his confession dovetails considerably with that of his codefendant. However, this exception was relatively short-lived. The Court adopted the interlocking confession exception to *Bruton* in *Parker v. Randolph*,[170] but renounced the faulty logic undergirding the exception in *Cruz v. New York*.[171] The force of *Cruz* was diminished substantially, however, because the Court left open the possibility that the defendant's confession could be admitted as substantive evidence, despite the *Bruton* violation, if its reliability was beyond reproach.[172] The Court relied on *Lee v. Illinois*[173] to arrive at this dubious conclusion.

The Court's meandering course in this area clearly shows the inconsistency with which it has interpreted *Bruton*. In the search for a coherent rationale for the interlocking confession doctrine, the Court has ignored the principles embodied in *Bruton*, and has demonstrated a lack of fidelity to the values essential to a proper interpretation of the confrontation clause. Thus, the Court's decisions in this area merit further attention.

Parker v. Randolph

The precedential value of *Randolph* was diminished appreciably by the fact that only a plurality of the Court adhered to the flawed proposition that *Bruton* was not germane to a situation involving interlocking confessions.[174] Four justices firmly rejected this position as violative of *Bruton*.[175] The plurality opinion in *Randolph* held that the admission of interlocking confessions, coupled with proper limiting instruction warning the jury not to consider the codefendant's confession in determining the guilt of the defendant, "conforms to the requirements of the Sixth and Fourteenth Amendments to the United States Constitution."[176]

The plurality based its opinion on unsound reasoning. Justice Rehnquist summed up the opinion by stating that "the incriminating statements of a co-defendant will seldom, if ever, be of the 'devastating' character referred to in *Bruton* when the incriminated defendant has admitted his own guilt."[177] This expansive reading of the interlocking confession standard would "eliminate the need to determine whether the defendant and co-defendant's confessions would interlock and the issue would simply be whether the defendant confessed to the offense."[178]

Despite this patently fallacious definition of the interlocking confession rule by the plurality, Justice Blackmun's concurrence revealed the practical problems that would accompany the implementation of the interlocking confession exception to *Bruton*. As he pointed out, two confessions may only partially interlock or cover only a portion of the events in controversy at trial. Moreover, despite consistency between the confessions, one confession could implicate the confessor's codefendant to a greater degree than the other.[179] More importantly, Justice Blackmun properly assessed the adverse effect that the introduction of the codefendant's confession would have on the defendant's case. He stated that "admission of the confession of the co-defendant who does not take the stand could very well serve to prejudice the defendant who is incriminated by the confession, notwithstanding that the defendant's own confession is, to an extent, interlocking."[180]

Justice Stevens attacked the plurality opinion by pointing to the flaws behind some of its assumptions. The plurality assumed that a jury would find it easier to follow limiting instructions if the defendant also confessed and that "all unchallenged confessions by a defendant are equally reliable."[181] Neither proposition, as Stevens noted, has any foundation in fact.[182]

Paradoxically, the plurality opinion in *Randolph* conceded readily that a *Bruton* violation significantly undermines a criminal defendant's right against self-incrimination. The plurality observed correctly that when a codefendant's statement incriminating the defendant is admitted without providing the defendant the opportunity to cross-examine, such a statement stands unchallenged "unless the defendant waives his privilege and takes the stand."[183] Nevertheless, the plurality then sought to qualify this axiom by stating that it applied only to a situation in which the defendant's confession is introduced at trial because of its damaging character.[184]

Justice Stevens's dissent repudiated the fallacy on which this conclusion is based. Setting up a complex hypothetical case in which the government's case against the defendant is entirely circumstantial, absent the admission of the codefendant's incriminating confession,[185] Justice Stevens observed that nothing a defendant could do to blunt the impact of his confession would allay the "damning effect" of the codefendant's statement.[186] He expressed the fundamental maxim that a defendant should not suffer for exercising a constitutional right (the privilege not to testify) by having another (the right to confrontation under the Sixth Amendment) taken away.[187]

As this discussion indicates, the interlocking confession exception to *Bruton* is replete with inconsistency and lacks a coherent, principled rationale. Furthermore, the application of the exception, as noted above, erodes a criminal defendant's privilege against self-incrimination. The Supreme Court saw fit to reverse *Randolph* in *Cruz*, but not before taking a detour in *Lee v. Illinois*. It is instructive, therefore, to examine *Lee* before exploring the Court's reasons for reversing *Randolph* in *Cruz*.

Lee v. Illinois

Although *Lee v. Illinois*[188] did not, strictly speaking, encompass a *Bruton* issue,[189] it did pave the way for the Court's reversal of *Randolph* in *Cruz* by detailing the difficulties associated with the application of the interlocking confession exception to *Bruton*. In *Lee*, the defendant and her codefendant were tried jointly in a bench trial for committing a double murder. On the eve of trial, the attorneys for both defendants withdrew their motions for severance and for a jury trial on the express condition, agreed to by the trial judge, that the court consider the evidence separately as to each defendant.[190] Neither of the two defendants testified at the trial.[191] The trial judge, however, failed to abide by his promise to weigh the evidence separately with respect to each defendant and relied expressly on the codefendant's confession in finding the defendant guilty of the murder of one of the two victims.[192]

The issue resolved by the Court in *Lee* was whether the trial judge's improper use of the codefendant's confession as substantive evidence in assessing the defendant's guilt violated the defendant's right to confrontation. The Court rejected the government's argument. The government claimed that the defendant's confrontation rights were not contravened by the trial court's reliance on the hearsay contained within the codefendant's confession, because the codefendant was unavailable and his confession was sufficiently reliable to be admitted into evidence against the defendant.[193] Rather, the Court ruled that the codefendant's statement, "as the confession of an accomplice, was presumptively unreliable and that it did not bear sufficient 'indicia of reliability' to overcome that presumption."[194]

The codefendant's confession, in turn, was presumptively unreliable, according to the majority opinion, because it did not sufficiently interlock with the defendant's statement and because it was not given under circumstances justifying belief in its trustworthiness.[195] In effect, the *Lee* majority emphasized the shaky premise underlying the interlocking confession doctrine by noting that "a confession is not necessarily rendered reliable simply because some of the facts it contains 'interlock' with the facts in the defendant's statement."[196] Because the inherent unreliability of confessions by codefendants implicating other defendants was not rebutted in *Lee*, the Court concluded that Lee's conviction was obtained wrongfully through a violation of her right to confrontation under the Sixth Amendment.[197]

Though the *Lee* decision could be construed as facilitating the Court's reversal of the interlocking confession exception to *Bruton* in *Cruz*, the *Lee* Court also to a large extent nullified *Douglas v. Alabama*,[198] as evidenced in the Court's per curiam opinion in *New Mexico v. Earnest*.[199] In *Earnest*, the Court interpreted *Lee* as discarding the principle set forth in *Douglas* that the confrontation clause requires the defendant be afforded an opportunity for cross-examination as a prerequisite to the admission of a codefendant's confession.[200] Instead, reliability would determine the admissibility of a defendant's confession, despite the defendant's inability to cross-examine the codefendant.[201] Therefore, both *Lee* and *Earnest* portended an ominous trend: a defendant's constitutional right to confrontation and, concomitantly, his right to have a fair trial, are subordinated to the notion of "reliability," which governs the law of evidence.[202]

Cruz v. New York

In *Cruz v. New York*,[203] the Court rendered a decision that was replete with ambiguity in that it reversed *Randolph*'s weak adoption of the interlocking confession rule. At the same time, *Cruz* ties the admission of a nontestifying codefendant's confession incriminating the defendant at a joint trial to the concept of reliability, rather than to the concept of the constitutional right of confrontation. As such, the decision exemplifies the inconsistency with which the Court has applied the *Bruton* doctrine.

The defendant in *Cruz* was charged with felony murder along with his brother, a codefendant. The defendant was denied a separate trial,[204] which he had sought in order to avoid the damaging effect of the codefendant's videotaped confession incriminating him in the murder.[205] The codefendant's confession was admitted into evidence at trial, despite the defendant's objection.[206] The defendant, however, had allegedly made a statement to a witness in which he admitted playing a role in the murder.[207]

The majority in *Cruz* jettisoned the interlocking confession exception to *Bruton*, recognizing its illogical foundation. In fact, Justice Scalia, writing for the majority, observed correctly that "in the real world of criminal litigation" an interlocking confession by a codefendant can be "enormously damaging" if it corroborates the defendant's confession.[208] Contrary to the plurality's contention in *Randolph* that the introduction of a nontestifying codefendant's interlocking confession at a joint trial does not markedly harm a defendant, the majority in *Cruz* observed that the interlocking nature of the confessions adversely affects the defendant more than if the confessions diverge. The Court noted that in a criminal trial the defendant is "seeking to *avoid* his confession."[209] Therefore, to the degree that a codefendant's confession confirms the defendant's admission it places the defendant in the predicament of having to challenge not only one, but two damaging statements. Further, as noted in the previous analysis of *Parker v. Randolph*, the interlocking confession doctrine serves to undermine a criminal defendant's privilege against self-incrimination.[210]

The *Cruz* Court, however, hedged its rejection of the interlocking confession exception to *Bruton* by relying on *Lee v. Illinois*. The majority stated that the "interlocking" did not bear on the harmful nature of the codefendant's confession, but referred to its reliability—a criterion for admissibility established in *Lee*.[211] Consequently, if a codefendant's confession verified defendant's confession, its reliability could be assumed. In addition, the codefendant's confession could presumably be admitted as substantive evidence against the defendant, in spite of the defendant's lack of opportunity to cross-examine the codefendant.[212] Quoting *Lee* and *Bruton*, the *Cruz* Court stated that "the defendant's statements are supported by 'sufficient indicia of reliability' to be directly admissible against him . . . despite the lack of opportunity for cross-examination.[213] As an alternative to reversal of the defendant's conviction, if the codefendant's confession was reliable, the court of appeals could employ the harmless error doctrine in determining whether the confrontation clause violation in *Cruz* was harmless pursuant to *Harrington v. California*.[214]

In sum, the *Cruz* Court discarded the interlocking confession doctrine but simultaneously weakened a defendant's right to confrontation by allowing the admission of a nontestifying codefendant's confession incriminating the defendant as direct evidence against the defendant, provided the declarant's statement is sufficiently reliable. In effect, this second prong of the *Cruz* decision penalizes a defendant for confessing if the codefendant's confession is admissible against him as substantive evidence. Thus, it deprives him of his right to confrontation.[215]

Evidence Used for a "Nonhearsay" Purpose

Contrasting sharply with the amorphous nature of the Court's decision in *Cruz* is *Tennessee v. Street*,[216] the only decision applying the *Bruton* doctrine in which there were no dissenting opinions. In *Street*, the defendant was tried separately from his codefendants.[217] At the defendant's trial, the prosecution introduced the defendant's elaborate confession and the defendant elected to take the stand. The defendant attempted to rebut his own confession by claiming it was the product of police coercion and that it was derived from a written statement one of his codefendants had provided to the police.[218]

To challenge the defendant's testimony regarding the confession, the prosecution introduced into evidence the confession of the codefendant to highlight the differences between the two confessions and thereby rebut the defendant's claim that his confession was a "coerced imitation" of his codefendant's.[219] Before admitting the codefendant's confession, however, the judge cautioned the jury that it was going to be admitted "not for the purpose of proving the truthfulness of the [codefendant's] statement, but for the purpose of rebuttal only."[220] The defendant was convicted of murder and appealed his conviction, which was reversed by the Tennessee Court of Criminal Appeals[221] on the ground that the defendant's right to confrontation had been violated by the introduction of the codefendant's confession.

The Supreme Court granted certiorari and reversed the Tennessee appellate court's decision, holding that the admission of the codefendant's confession for the nonhearsay purpose of rebutting the defendant's testimony, coupled with the limiting instruction the trial judge issued to the jury that the confession was to be considered only for rebuttal purposes, did not contravene the Sixth Amendment's confrontation clause.[222]

The Court's reasoning in *Street* is sound. The defendant received the best possible remedy for a *Bruton* problem: his case was severed from those of his codefendants.[223] The defendant injected the codefendant's confession into his own trial through his testimony; the prosecution did not attempt to admit the codefendant's confession into evidence. In essence, the defendant opened the door to the prosecution's rebuttal of his testimony that his confession was a "coerced imitation" of his codefendant's statement. Street was asking for the best of two worlds; that is, he wanted to bring out the codefendant's confession as a means of challenging the veracity of his own confession, but he did not want the prosecution to use the codefendant's confession to rebut his testimony.

Moreover, the defendant could have cross-examined the sheriff who secured the codefendant's confession. Through cross-examination the defendant could have challenged the sheriff's testimony (that the sheriff did not read from the codefendant's statement and that the sheriff did not order the defendant to repeat its substance).[224] Therefore, the Court's assumption that the factual pattern of *Street* posed no confrontation clause violation stands on solid constitutional footing.

Hearsay Exceptions

As *Street* indicates, the *Bruton* doctrine does not apply to evidence used for a nonhearsay purpose. In a similar fashion, the Court suggested soon after handing down *Bruton* that it would not apply the *Bruton* rule to hearsay rule exceptions. The Court in *Dutton v. Evans*,[225] the seminal case in this area, focused on the question left open by the *Bruton* Court: whether the introduction of evidence that is admissible as an exception to the hearsay rule triggers confrontation clause issues.[226]

Dutton v. Evans

In *Evans*, Justice Stewart's plurality opinion indicated that exceptions to the hearsay rule do not present possible violations of the confrontation clause under all conceivable circumstances. Instead, quoting from *Pointer v. Texas*,[227] Justice Stewart noted that " '[i]t is not argued, nor could it be, that the constitutional right to confrontation requires that no hearsay evidence can ever be introduced.' "[228] The *Evans* plurality upheld the trial court's ruling that testimony by one coconspirator about statements by another coconspirator was admissible under a Georgia state hearsay exception that allowed post-arrest statements to be admitted as coconspirator declarations even though they were made after the conspiracy ended.[229]

As Justice Marshall's dissenting opinion indicated, the plurality's opinion should not be construed as meaning that a "a defendant's constitutional right of confrontation must give way to a state evidentiary rule."[230] More importantly, although *Evans* did not involve a *Bruton* issue, it affected the *Bruton* doctrine's vitality. Justice Marshall observed that, carried to its "logical end," the opinion could result in "wholesale avoidance" of *Bruton*.[231]

Ohio v. Roberts

The disturbing trend of equating the hearsay rule and the confrontation clause that began with *Evans* continued unabated in *Ohio v. Roberts*.[232] In *Roberts*, the Court held that a criminal defendant's right to confrontation is not violated when an incriminating hearsay statement not subject to cross-examination is introduced into evidence at trial if the declarant is unavailable and the hearsay bears sufficient "indicia of reliability" to warrant its admission.[233] In turn, a hearsay statement raises no confrontation clause concerns if it is particularly trustworthy or if it falls within a "firmly rooted" hearsay exception.[234] As Seidelson asserts, to a large degree *Roberts* demoted the confrontation clause "to nothing more than a 'constitutional hearsay rule' subject to many hearsay exceptions."[235]

United States v. Inadi

In *United States v. Inadi*,[236] the Court continued its frontal attack on the confrontation clause. In *Inadi*, the majority redefined *Roberts* to the extent that it held that unavailability was no longer indispensable to the admission of a hearsay statement not subject to confrontation. The Court relied on *Evans* to hold that unavailability was not a prerequisite to the admission of an absent coconspirator's statement at the trial of another coconspirator.[237] In *White v. Illinois*,[237a] the Court confirmed *Inadi* by holding that *Roberts*' unavailability analysis applies solely to out-of-court statements made in the course of judicial proceedings. In effect, the *Inadi* and *White* Courts took a giant step in the subordination of the constitutional value underlying the confrontation clause to evidentiary principles.

Bourjaily v. United States

The utter subservience of the confrontation clause to evidentiary law was completed in *Bourjaily v. United States*.[238] The *Bourjaily* Court held that an absent coconspirator's inculpatory statement may be introduced at the trial of another coconspirator regardless of a showing of both unavailability and particularized "indicia of reliability" with regard to the out-of-court declaration.[239] Rather, the Court held that coconspirator statements could be considered reliable because they fell within a "firmly rooted" hearsay exception, and therefore no independent inquiry into reliability of the statement was necessary to comply with the confrontation clause of the Sixth Amendment.[240] This analysis suggests a conclusive presumption that the confrontation clause is not violated as long as hearsay evidence falls within a "firmly rooted" exception. As Stanley Goldman points out, however, there is no assurance that a statement is reliable merely because it falls within a "firmly rooted" exception.[241]

LACK OF CONGRUENCE BETWEEN THE CONFRONTATION CLAUSE AND EVIDENTIARY LAW

As the preceding discussion demonstrates, and as several commentators have noted,[242] the Court has merged the confrontation clause and evidentiary principles. Randolph Jonakait goes so far as to suggest that the confrontation clause has become "a mere vestigial appendix of hearsay doctrine."[243] He indicates that the Court's approach stems from its misplaced emphasis on the confrontation clause's "mission" to achieve accuracy of fact-finding in a criminal trial rather than to advance the goals of the confrontation clause; these, read in conjunction with the other Sixth Amendment rights, the rights to notice and counsel, guarantee the accused an adversarial proceeding and a fair trial.[244] This novel interpretation of the confrontation clause by the Court is at odds with its recognition in *California v. Green*[245] that there exists a lack of congruence between evidentiary principles and the confrontation clause, though both are designed to protect similar values.[246]

Furthermore, the equation of the confrontation clause and evidentiary law could result in a potentially ominous curtailment of a criminal defendant's right to confrontation in a *Bruton* context. The Court's pronouncements in *Lee*, *Earnest*, and *Cruz* clearly show the negative consequences flowing from this flawed analysis. These three cases suggest strongly that the government may rely on hearsay evidence in the absence of confrontation provided the trial court finds the content of the hearsay is reliable. Reliability, in turn, may be inferred from the degree to which a defendant's confession interlocks with that of his codefendant.

As Roger Kirst observes, the Court's suggestion in both *Lee* and *Earnest* that reliability can be based on the content of hearsay could result in the "trial by affidavit" that the confrontation clause was designed to prevent.[247] What the Court declined to acknowledge in those cases, according to Kirst, is an important "procedural dimension" of the confrontation doctrine: that hearsay created by the government, as when the police questioned the accomplices in *Lee* and *Earnest*, can "revive the equivalent of trial by affidavit."[248] Another disturbing phenomenon is raised by the Court's emphasis on reliability in *Lee*: if the police can make the confessions of two codefendants coincide, then "the prosecutor will not have to use live witnesses for the trial of either defendant."[249] Again, the prosecution could conduct the quintessential trial by affidavit.

In *Cruz*, moreover, the Court's adherence to the reliability criterion adopted in *Lee* entails the possibility of a clear evisceration of *Bruton* where two confessions interlock sufficiently to ensure the "reliability" of the codefendant's confession. Of course, as Kirst notes, the mere fact that the confessions of codefendants coincide does not automatically translate into a finding of reliability.[250] Accordingly, the Court's analysis threatens to sacrifice the confrontation clause of a defendant in the *Bruton* context to the exigencies of principles grounded in evidentiary law.

In addition, if *Bruton* is construed not to apply to "firmly rooted" exceptions to the hearsay rule, this would create an anomalous result: It would effectively allow Congress to nullify a constitutional holding by merely rewriting the Federal Rules of Evidence, thus contravening the separation of powers doctrine.[251]

CONFLICT BETWEEN A CRIMINAL DEFENDANT'S FIFTH AMENDMENT PRIVILEGE AGAINST SELF-INCRIMINATION AND THE *BRUTON* PROBLEM

The recent decisions issued by the Supreme Court construing the *Bruton* doctrine not only threaten to revive the process of trial by affidavit through a denial of effective confrontation, but also encroach upon a criminal defendant's Fifth Amendment right against self-incrimination. Of course, this has been a major theme of this chapter. Nevertheless, we must revisit the issue by briefly reviewing the most egregious example of this trend in *Richardson v. Marsh*[252] and by setting forth a coherent rationale for the argument.

In *Marsh*, as the earlier discussion and analysis demonstrated,[253] the defendant was placed in the difficult position of having to rebut the confession of her nontestifying codefendant linking her to the crime. In essence Marsh faced the stark choice of allowing the codefendant's confession to stand unchallenged or surrendering her Fifth Amendment rights in order to rebut the incriminating nature of the confession. The devastating effect of introducing the codefendant's confession against Marsh was unmistakable given its great value to the prosecution—the confession "was the only evidence directly linking [the defendant] with the specific intent, expressed before the robbery, to kill the victims afterwards."[254] Thus, the government's case rested principally on the uncontested "affidavit" of the codefendant, leaving the defendant with no alternative other than to testify in order to rebut the negative inference the jury would surely draw from the out-of-court statement. The defendant was compelled to testify in order to challenge the confession's veracity and accuracy.

The practical, "real world" effect of the denial of the right to confrontation in a *Bruton* situation is akin to the dilemma faced by a defendant charged with a nonpossessory offense[255] who had to establish standing to contest the validity of a search before the Court decided *Simmons v. United States*.[256] Such a defendant had to admit some type of possessory interest in an incriminating item to establish standing to suppress the evidence, but risked the possibility that if she lost on the motion to suppress, her testimony at the suppression hearing could be used at trial. To relieve the defendant of the "Hobson's choice,"[257] the Court in *Simmons* held that a defendant's testimony supporting a motion to suppress on a Fourth Amendment issue may not be admitted to prove his guilt at trial unless he waives the objection.[258]

The *Simmons* Court, moreover, rejected the contention that the defendant's Fifth Amendment privilege against self-incrimination was waived voluntarily in such a context.[259] Such an argument was premised on the notion that the defendant had a choice in the sense that he would merely forgo a benefit if he did not testify.[260] However, the Court observed correctly that the "benefit" to be gained by the Fourth Amendment suppression motion was the protection provided by the Constitution: the right to be free from unreasonable searches and seizures. Consequently, the defendant in *Simmons* had the choice of waiving a colorable Fourth Amendment claim or surrendering his Fifth Amendment privilege against self-incrimination.[261] The Court remarked that it was "intolerable that a constitutional right should be surrendered in order to assert another."[262]

Applying this theory to the *Bruton* context, it is possible to see the "intolerable" import of the Court's denial of confrontation when a *Bruton* scenario arises. The defendant who is denied the right to confront the out-of-court statement of a nontestifying accomplice at trial must give up the benefit of her privilege against self-incrimination in order to compensate for the denial of another constitutional safeguard: the right to confront her accusers as stipulated in the Sixth Amendment. Such a result flies in the face of principled judicial decision making designed to protect a criminal defendant's constitutional rights when the potent resources of the government have been marshalled against him. In fact, the violation in this instance is more flagrant than that in *Simmons*, since in the *Bruton* context a constitutional right must be waived not only to assert another, but to compensate for the denial of another.

CONCLUSION

The *Bruton* doctrine has followed a winding path marked by doctrinal inconsistency and by the failure of the Supreme Court to adhere to the core values underlying the confrontation clause of the Sixth Amendment. In essence, the Court has wavered on the vital issue of the extent to which a criminal defendant should be entitled to a fair trial, with the opportunity to confront his accusers, and thereby not be convicted on the basis of the unverified and unchallenged assertions of an accomplice who does not testify at trial.

The inconsistency with which the Court has applied the *Bruton* doctrine is amply demonstrated by its approach to the remedies available to cure a *Bruton* problem. Rather than acknowledging that severance is the most effective means of affording a defendant a fair trial in which the unsubstantiated allegations of a nontestifying codefendant do not prejudice his defense, the Court has instead adopted Justice White's position in his dissenting opinion in *Bruton*.[263] In effect, such an approach serves to undermine the basis of the confrontation clause and substitutes the rationale of efficiency for the ideal of a fair trial firmly embedded in the Sixth Amendment.

Indeed, the incongruous method the Court has relied upon in interpreting *Bruton*'s mandate is illustrated in the last two decisions it handed down on the issue, *Richardson v. Marsh*[264] and *Cruz v. New York*.[265] In *Marsh*, the Court approved the logic behind the remedy of redaction when a *Bruton* issue arises as a viable alternative to severance. Even though all references to the defendant's existence were deleted from the confession,[266] the defendant still suffered prejudice when the nontestifying codefendant's confession implicated her in the crime charged. This holding ignores the principle which undergirds the *Bruton* decision: that a joint trial at which a nontestifying codefendant's confession implicating the defendant is introduced into evidence violates the defendant's right to confrontation pursuant to the Sixth Amendment.

If *Marsh* represents the Court's lack of fidelity to the *Bruton* doctrine, *Cruz v. New York* typifies the ambivalent and inconsistent manner in which the Court has attempted to apply *Bruton*'s lessons. Although the *Cruz* Court recognized the flaws associated with the interlocking confession exception to *Bruton*, as decreed by a plurality of the Court in *Parker v. Randolph*,[267] the Court nonetheless qualified its decision by remanding the case to the New York state court to determine "whether [Cruz's] co-defendant's statements are supported by 'sufficient indicia of reliability' to be directly admissible against [Cruz]."[268] Therefore, although the Court in *Cruz*, in contrast to its holding in *Marsh*, held true to the basic tenet of *Bruton*, it simultaneously paved the way for a possible dilution of the *Bruton* doctrine by linking evidentiary principles with the safeguards provided to a criminal defendant under the confrontation clause.

It is ironic in this regard that the Court in *Coy v. Iowa*[269] held that a defendant charged with lascivious acts with a child was denied the right to confrontation when the trial judge permitted a screen to be placed in front of the two complaining witnesses, blocking the defendant from their sight. To a large degree, the Court has succeeded in erecting a "screen" that prevents a criminal defendant from contesting the validity of a nontestifying codefendant's inculpatory confession at a joint trial through its inconsistent and restrictive interpretation of *Bruton*.

Furthermore, the Court's restrictive and inconsistent application of the *Bruton* doctrine has had the unfortunate ancillary consequence of diminishing appreciably a criminal defendant's right against self-incrimination under the Fifth Amendment. As this chapter has shown, the net effect of the Court's narrow interpretation in the "real world" of criminal law is that a criminal defendant is placed in the precarious situation of either testifying at trial in order to challenge the uncontested inculpatory affirmation of a nontestifying codefendant, or risking the very distinct probability that a jury will draw negative inferences from the accusations against the defendant contained in the codefendant's confession.

Such a result not only signifies a flagrant violation of the constitutional precepts embodied in the Fifth and Sixth amendments but also denies the defendant the benefit of a choice by compelling him to forsake the right against self-incrimination to redress the denial of the right to confront his accusers. As the *Simmons* Court aptly remarked in another context, the defendant is faced with what amounts to a Hobson's choice.[270] Moreover, such a waiver of the Fifth Amendment right against self-incrimination is not voluntary, since the defendant must testify, as in *Marsh*,[271] to blunt the damaging effect of the uncorroborated and unconfronted accusation leveled against her by the codefendant's confession.

The upshot of the Court's decisions interpreting *Bruton* is that, in a criminal trial, in which the defendant's liberty is at stake, the scales of justice are balanced in favor of the prosecution. As a consequence, one of the principal goals of our adversary system of adjudication, the right of the defendant to have a fair trial, has been significantly eroded.

NOTES

1. *California v. Green*, 399 U.S. 149, 176 (1970) (Harlan, J., concurring).

2. Westen, *Confrontation and Compulsory Process: A Unified Theory of Evidence for Criminal Cases*, 91 HARV. L. REV. 568 (1978).

3. Of course, our criminal justice system has adopted a "modified" rather than a "pure" adversary system of adjudication to the degree that parties do not have complete discretion to structure the case as they see fit; that is, restrictions exist on the partisan tactics each side may employ. Moreover, the judge does not play a strictly "passive" role in the process as would be the case in a "pure" adversary system. *See* Lafave & Israel, CRIMINAL PROCEDURE 23 (1985). In addition, the consensus underlying the adversary model in the criminal process focuses on the potential for a case to develop

into an "adversary struggle" rather than on the requirement that each case rigidly conform to the adversary standard. Packer, THE LIMITS OF THE CRIMINAL SANCTION 157 (1968).

4. The right to cross-examine witnesses is also available in other contexts outside of trial, as for example at the taking of depositions. McCormick, McCORMICK ON EVIDENCE 47 (3d ed. 1984).

5. The Sixth Amendment provides in pertinent part that "[i]n all criminal prosecutions the accused shall enjoy the right . . . to be confronted with the witnesses against him." U.S. CONST. Amend. VI.

6. As Westen observes, the Sixth Amendment's confrontation clause is applicable only at trial; that is, it does not apply to information provided by tipsters, nor to evidence furnished by witnesses who do not testify at trial. Rather, "the Sixth Amendment requires only that the defendant be allowed to confront those witnesses whose testimony is heard by the factfinder on the ultimate issue of guilt or innocence," Westen, *supra* note 2, at 57–72. However, this principle is qualified if the government attempts to use an out-of-court statement against the defendant. In that circumstance, the government must secure the declarant's attendance and call him as a witness if he is available, id. at 577. The Supreme Court has stressed that the confrontation clause is safeguarded primarily through the right of the defendant to cross-examine the witnesses against him at trial. *See*, e.g. *Douglas v. Alabama*, 380 U.S. 415, 418 (1965); *Pointer v. Texas*, 380 U.S. 400, 404 (1965); *Mattox v. United States*, 156 U.S. 237, 242 (1895).

7. The Supreme Court has emphasized that the "denial or significant diminution [of the right to confrontation] calls into question the ultimate 'integrity of the factfinding process,' " *Chambers v. Mississippi*, 410 U.S. 284, 295 (1973) (quoting from *Berger v. California*, 393 U.S. 314, 315 (1969)). The Court has also characterized the right to confrontation as "a fundamental right essential to a fair trial in a criminal prosecution," *Pointer v. Texas*, 380 U.S. at 404.

8. *Delli Paoli v. United States*, 352 U.S. 232, 241–42 (1957).

9. 391 U.S. 123 (1968).

10. Id. at 126. It should be pointed out that the applicability of the *Bruton* rule to bench trials is doubtful at best. The Supreme Court has not ruled on the matter, and federal appellate courts appear to be split on the issue. For example, compare *Cockrell v. Oberhauser*, 413 F.2d 256, 258 (9th Cir. 1969) (*Bruton* rule inapplicable to bench trials) with *Marsh v. Richardson*, 781 F.2d 1201, 1206 n.3 (6th Cir. 1986) (noting in dictum that *Bruton*'s applicability to nonjury trials is unclear), rev'd, 107 S. Ct. 1702 (1987). Haddad argues that the *Bruton* Court did not assume that a judge, rather than a jury, would be "unwilling or unable to decide the co-defendant's case without giving weight to the defendant's confession." Haddad, *Post-Bruton Developments: A Reconsideration of the Confrontation Rationale and a Proposal for a Due Process Evaluation of Limiting Instructions*, 18 AM. CRIM. L. REV. 1, 26 (1980).

11. E.g., Jonakait, *Restoring the Confrontation Clause to the Sixth Amendment*, 35 UCLA L. REV. 557, 570–74 (1988); Seidelson, *The Confrontation Clause, the Right Against Self-Incrimination and the Supreme Court: A Critique and Some Modest Proposals*, 20 DUQ. L. REV. 429, 433–36 (1982).

12. The Fifth Amendment provides, in part, that "[n]o person . . . shall be compelled in any criminal case to be a witness against himself." U.S. CONST. Amend. V.

13. 391 U.S. 123 (1968).

14. Graham observes that it is reasonable to ascribe more than one purpose to the

confrontation doctrine. He describes three purposes served by the doctrine that have been recognized by commentators: ensuring the reliability of convictions through the method of effective cross-examination; preventing unfair trials by controlling prosecutorial misconduct; and giving the defendant the "psychological" advantage of confronting the evidence ultimately used to convict him. *See*, e.g., Graham, *The Right to Confrontation and the Hearsay Rule: Sir Walter Raleigh Loses Another One*, 8 CRIM. L. BULL. 99, 105 (1972).

15. 399 U.S. 149, 173–74 (1970) (Harlan, J., concurring).

16. In the words of Justice Harlan, "[t]he Confrontation Clause comes to us on faded parchment. History seems to give us very little insight into the intended scope of the Sixth Amendment Confrontation Clause," id.

17. Heller, THE SIXTH AMENDMENT 104 (1961).

18. *See* Graham, *supra* note 14, at 100–101 (providing account of Sir Walter Raleigh's trial); Kirst, *The Procedural Dimension of the Confrontation Doctrine*, 66 NEB. L. REV. 485, 490–91 (1987) (same); Lily, *Notes on the Confrontation Clause and Ohio v. Roberts*, 36 U. FLA. L. REV. 207, 208–10 (1984) (same).

19. Graham, *supra* note 14, at 100 n.4 (citations omitted). Graham reaches the "tentative" conclusion that the Sixth Amendment emerged from the violations prevailing in trials conducted in vice-admiralty courts rather than from Raleigh's trial or the "supposed abuses of the Star Chamber," id. at 104 n.23.

20. 98 U.S. 145, 158 (1879).

21. Evidently, the defendant deliberately withheld information from the authorities regarding the location of the witness, his second wife (the defendant had been indicted for bigamy), id. at 159–60.

22. Id. at 161.

23. 178 U.S. 458 (1900).

24. Id. at 471, 474.

25. The witness had been incarcerated without bail until the eve of the defendant's trial. When the trial began, an official, without authority, released the witness into the custody of another government witness and instructed the custodian to allow the witness to stay in a hotel with his family. Predictably, the witness failed to appear when he was scheduled to testify, id. at 471.

26. Id. at 474.

27. 156 U.S. 237 (1895).

28. Id. at 242–43.

29. Id. at 243.

30. Id. at 243–44.

31. This is the portion adopted by Justice Harlan in his concurring opinion in *California v. Green*, 399 U.S. 149, 179–81 (1970) (Harlan, J., concurring).

32. 352 U.S. 231 (1957).

33. The confession was not admissible under the hearsay exception permitting the admission of statements by coconspirators made in the course of and in furtherance of a conspiracy because the defendant confessed after the conspiracy had ended, id. at 233.

34. Id. at 241–42.

35. Id. at 243.

36. As the majority opinion stated: "As a practical matter, the choice was between separate trials and a joint trial in which the confession would be admitted under appropriate instructions," id.

37. Id.

38. Id. at 241.

39. Id. at 247 (Frankfurter, J., dissenting). Justice Frankfurter quoted from Judge Learned Hand's opinion in *Nash v. United States*, 54 F.2d 1006, 1007 (2d Cir.), *cert. denied*, 285 U.S. 556 (1932), for the proposition that the limiting instruction to the jury to consider the confession only against the declarant and not against other defendants is "the recommendation to the jury of a mental gymnastic which is beyond, not only their powers, but anybody else's."

40. *Delli Paoli v. United States*, 352 U.S. at 248.

41. 380 U.S. 400 (1965).

42. Id. at 403.

43. Id. at 404.

44. Id.

45. Id. at 405.

46. 380 U.S. 415 (1965).

47. The trial judge initially threatened Douglas's codefendant with contempt for his refusal to testify, but did not carry out the threat. Instead, the judge interrupted Douglas's trial to impose a twenty-year sentence on the codefendant, whose sentencing had been deferred, id. at 416 n.1.

48. Id.

49. Id. at 416–17. The prosecutor accomplished this feat by reading a part of the document and then pausing to ask the codefendant whether he made the statement—which the codefendant replied to by asserting the privilege against self-incrimination—until the entire confession had been read. It should be noted that the confession was never formally introduced into evidence.

50. Id. at 419.

51. Id.

52. Id.

53. Id. at 419–20.

54. Id. at 420.

55. E.g., *Berger v. California*, 393 U.S. 314 (1969); *Barber v. Page*, 390 U.S. 719 (1968); *Brookhart v. Janis*, 384 U.S. 1 (1966); *Pointer v. Texas*, 380 U.S. 400 (1965); *Motes v. United States*, 178 U.S. 458 (1900); *Kirby v. United States*, 174 U.S. 47 (1899); see Westen, *supra* note 2, at 584 n.43 (suggesting this typology of confrontation cases).

56. 391 U.S. 123 (1968).

57. See *infra*, discussion of constraints and exceptions regarding *Bruton* doctrine.

58. *Bruton v. United States*, 391 U.S. at 124.

59. Id. at 125.

60. Id. at 126. It should be noted that the Court dealt with the Sixth Amendment issue in *Bruton* gratuitously, because Evans's confession was held inadmissible by the court of appeals on the ground that it violated *Miranda v. Arizona*, 384 U.S. 436 (1966). On retrial, Evans was acquitted. *Bruton v. United States*, 391 U.S. at 124.

61. *Bruton v. United States*, 391 U.S. at 127.

62. Id. at 128.

63. See *supra* text accompanying note 50 (discussing critical role of confession to prosecutor's case in *Douglas*).

64. 378 U.S. 368 (1964). In *Jackson*, the Court held that the trial judge must determine the admissibility of a defendant's confession before submitting it to the jury. The Court

concluded that a jury could not be expected to ignore a defendant's confession of guilt if it ultimately found the confession was given involuntarily, id. at 388–89.

65. *Bruton v. United States*, 391 U.S. at 128–31. The *Bruton* Court did not reach the issue whether the confrontation clause would have been violated if the hearsay statement by Evans implicating Bruton had fallen under an exception to the hearsay rule. Rather, the Court noted that Evans's statement was inadmissible hearsay as to Bruton under traditional rules of evidence, Id. at 128 n.3; see *infra*, discussion of uncertain relationship between confrontation clause and hearsay rule.

66. *Bruton v. United States*, 391 U.S. at 134.

67. 249 N.Y. 419, 432, 164 N.E. 336, 341 (1928) (Lehman, J., dissenting).

68. *Bruton v. United States*, 391 U.S. at 134.

69. Id. at 135–36 (citations omitted).

70. 380 U.S. 400 (1965); see *supra* text accompanying notes 41–45 (discussing decision in *Pointer*).

71. "A defendant is entitled to a fair trial but not a perfect one," *Bruton v. United States*, 391 U.S. at 135 (citing *Lutwak v. United States*, 344 U.S. 604, 619 (1953)).

72. Justice White also dismissed the "assumption of the majority that giving instructions to a jury to disregard a co-defendant's confession is an empty gesture," id. at 143 (White, J., dissenting).

73. The majority opinion referred to lower courts' use of deletion in a footnote, id. at 134 n.10.

74. Id. at 143 (White, J., dissenting).

75. Id.

76. Id. at 143–44.

77. Graham, *supra* note 14, at 115.

78. Id.

79. *See*, e.g., *Bruton v. United States*, 391 U.S. 123, 143 (1968) (White, J., dissenting) ("Unquestionably, joint trials are more economical and minimize the burden on witnesses, prosecutors and courts. They also avoid delays in bringing those accused of crime to trial."); *see also* Dawson, *Joint Trials of Defendants in Criminal Cases: An Analysis of Efficiencies and Prejudices*, 77 MICH. L. REV. 1379, 1381–89 (1979) (discussing "supposed efficiencies" generally invoked to justify joint trials).

80. Dawson lists two more alleged efficiencies of joint trials: the conservation of time for the prosecution and the reduction of the costs of appeal; Dawson, *supra* note 77, at 1383, 1387–88.

81. *See Bruton v. United States*, 391 U.S. at 143 (White, J., dissenting) ("[s]eparate trials are apt to have varying consequences for legally indistinguishable defendants"); Dawson, *supra* note 77, at 1391–97 (discussing various advantages and disadvantages of joint trials). Writing for a majority, Justice Scalia recently reiterated the putative advantages of joint trials; *Richardson v. Marsh*, 107 S.Ct. 1702, 1708 (1987) ("[j]oint trials generally serve the interests of justice by avoiding inconsistent verdicts and enabling accurate assessment of relative culpability").

82. *See* Dawson, *supra* note 77, at 1380–98 (rationales cited most frequently in defense of joint trials are based on dubious assumptions).

83. Id. at 1389.

84. Id. at 1389–90.

85. Not only does severance furnish the criminal defendant with the best protection from *Bruton*-related prejudice, but it also avoids the complexity of joint trials, in which

the jury may find it difficult to assess fairly the role and relative guilt of each individual defendant, id. at 1397–98.

86. Id. at 1413 (citing *United States v. Taylor*, 508 F.2d 761 (5th Cir. 1975) (prosecution violated its agreement not to introduce defendant's confession by contending defendant had "opened the door" on cross-examination of government witness)).

87. 107 S. Ct. 1702 (1987).

88. This term is a synonym for the deletion from a confession of a codefendant's references implicating another defendant in the crime charged. *See infra*, discussion of redaction remedy in detail.

89. This evidence included testimony by one of the victims to the crime and the testimony of the defendant, *Richardson v. Marsh*, 107 S. Ct. at 1704–06.

90. Id. at 1706.

91. Id. at 1706 n.2. The prosecutor in effect took contradictory positions in the closing argument. On the one hand, he stressed to the jury that it should not use the confession in evaluating the defendant's guilt. On the other, and at a later point in his closing argument, he invited the jury to do the exact opposite, id. Although the *Richardson* Court held that no *Bruton* violation occurred through the introduction of the nontestifying codefendant's confession, it nonetheless remanded the case for determination whether the prosecution's negation of the limiting instructions on closing argument constituted a sufficient ground for granting a writ of habeas corpus, id. at 1709.

92. *See* e.g., Note, *Richardson v. Marsh: Co-defendant Confessions and the Demise of Confrontation*, 101 HARV. L. REV. 1876, 1890–94 (1988); Note, *Sixth Amendment—Limiting the Scope of Bruton*, 78 J. CRIM. L. & CRIMINOLOGY 984, 1010–11 (1988); Calo, *Joint Trials, Spillover Prejudice, and the Ineffectiveness of a Bare Limiting Introduction*, 9 AM J.TRIAL ADVOC. 21, 37 (1985); Gaynes, *Two Juries/One Trial: Panacea of Judicial Economy or Personification of Murphy's Law*?, 5 AM. J. TRIAL ADVOC. 285, 285 (1981). But *see* Haddad, *supra* note 10, at 4–5, n.10–11; Dawson, *supra* note 79, at 1416–18.

93. *See* Dawson, *supra* note 79, at 1416–18 (discussing courts' recognition of flaws in various alternative remedies).

94. 470 F.2d 1158 (9th Cir. 1972).

95. Id. at 1170–71. But *see State v. Watson*, 397 So. 2d 1337, 1340–41 (La.) (where confessions of codefendants are substantially identical no prejudice results when the jury of one defendant learns of other's confession), *cert. denied*, 454 U.S. 903 (1981).

96. *United States v. Crane*, 499 F.2d 1385, 1388 (6th Cir.), *cert. denied* 419 U.S. 1002 (1974).

97. *See*, e.g., *People v. LaBelle*, 18 N.Y.2d 405 (1966) (separate trials ordered where redaction of codefendant's name from defendant's confession introduced at joint trial altered substance of confession and thereby prejudiced defendant). But *see People v. Boggs*, 63 Cal. Rpt. 430 (1967) (deletion of codefendant's name from defendant's confession held not prejudicial on issue of guilt where defendant had already confessed to offense "as a matter of law" by admitting participation in robbery).

98. Dawson, *supra* note 79, at 1414.

99. *See*, e.g., *West v. United States*, 499 A.2d 860, 868 (D.C. App. 1985) (substitution of "someone" or "somebody" in place of defendant's name adequately preserved defendant's confrontation right).

100. *See*, e.g., *United States v. De Parias*, 805 F.2d 1447, 1455 (11th Cir. 1968) (admission of codefendant confession does not violate *Bruton* if statements standing alone

do not "clearly inculpate" defendant); *Nelson v. Follette*, 430 F.2d 1055, 1059 (2d Cir. 1970) (where codefendant's confession did not mention defendant, that jury could have made "substantial inference" of defendant's culpability from confession and other evidence held not to violate *Bruton* if curative instructions given).

101. *See United States v. Belle*, 593 F.2d 487, 494 (3d Cir. 1979) (en banc) (codefendant statements held not "clearly inculpatory" to extent that jury must make inferences to inculpate defendant from other clearly admissible evidence).

102. 107 S.Ct 1702 (1987).

103. *See*, e.g., *United States v. Belle* 593 F.2d at 493–94 (evidentiary linkage or contextual implication does not render otherwide admissible statements inadmissible under *Bruton*). The Supreme Court overturned the Sixth Circuit's decision in *Marsh*. The appellate court in *Marsh* found a *Bruton* violation despite the redaction of all references to the defendant. The Supreme Court adopted the approach followed by six other circuit courts of appeals that *Bruton* does not extend to redacted confessions which make no references to the defendant, *Richardson v. Marsh*, 107 S. Ct. at 1709.

104. Her other codefendant, Kareem Martin, was a fugitive at the time of the trial, *Richardson v. Marsh*, 107 S. Ct. at 1704.

105. Id.

106. Id. at 1704, 1706.

107. Id. at 1705.

108. The surviving victim, Cynthia Knighton, testified that Marsh arrived at the home where the crimes occurred—the residence of victim Ollie Scott—in the company of codefendant Martin and that, shortly thereafter, she let codefendant Martin into the house. Williams's confession related a conversation that allegedly occurred in the car on the way to the victim's residence in which Martin suggested he would have to kill the victims after the robbery, id. at 1704–05. Thus, the jury could easily infer from Williams's confession that Marsh was aware of and acquiesced in the plan to kill the victims at the conclusion of the robbery.

109. Id. at 1710–11 (Stevens, J., dissenting).

110. This was the term used by the Supreme Court in *Simmons v. United States*, 390 U.S. 377, 391 (1968).

111. *Richardson v. Marsh*, 107 S. Ct. at 1705–06.

112. Id. at 1706.

113. Id. at 1707–09.

114. Id. at 1709.

115. In a footnote, Justice Scalia took issue with the dissent's argument that the majority assumed that Williams's confession did not incriminate Marsh. Rather, he contended that "the very premise of our discussion is that respondent would have been harmed by Williams's confession if the jury had disobeyed its instructions," id. at 1707 n.3 (emphasis in original).

116. Id. at 1707.

117. *See supra* note 115 and accompanying text (discussing majority's recognition of prejudice).

118. *See supra* note 108 (describing content of confession).

119. The dissent also glossed over this point.

120. In *Lee v. Illinois*, 476 U.S. 530 (1986), Justice Blackmun castigated his colleagues for stressing the theoretical underpinnings of criminal procedure and slighting "the sig-

nificant realities that so often characterize a criminal case.'' As he observed, ''[t]here is a real world as well as a theoretical one,'' Id. at 547–48 (Blackmun, J., dissenting).

121. As Justice Stevens pointed out, since Williams did not testify, Marsh's lawyer did not have an opportunity to challenge his credibility nor to establish that the car radio was playing so loudly that Marsh could not hear the conversation between Martin and Williams from the back seat and she could not have been privy to Martin's plan to kill the victims. *Richardson v. Marsh*, 107 S. Ct. at 1711–12 (Stevens, J., dissenting).

122. *See infra*, developing this argument in detail.

123. *Richardson v. Marsh*, 107 S. Ct. at 1705–06.

124. Id. at 1712 (Stevens, J., dissenting).

125. Id. at 1708.

126. Id.

127. The point that the confession was the only direct evidence of Marsh's specific intent was made by the dissent, id. at 1711.

128. *See* Note, *Richardson v. Marsh: Co-defendant Confessions and the Demise of Confrontation*, 101 HARV. L. REV. 1876, 1880–81 (1988) (citing Casper, Benedict, & Perry, JUROR DECISION-MAKING, ATTITUDES, AND THE HINDSIGHT BIAS 3–5 (American Bar Foundation Working Paper No. 8702, 1987).

129. Id. at 1881.

130. *Richardson v. Marsh*, 107 S. Ct. at 1708.

131. Id.

132. Id. at 1713 (Stevens, J., dissenting).

133. Id. at 1714.

134. Id. at 1708.

135. *See supra* text accompanying notes 73–74 (discussing dissenting arguments in *Bruton*).

136. *See supra* notes 80–84 and accompanying text (discussing commentators' criticisms of joint trial remedy's effectiveness).

137. *Richardson v. Marsh*, 107 S. Ct. at 1712–13 (Stevens, J., dissenting) (footnotes omitted).

138. 380 U.S. 415 (1965).

139. Id. at 419–20.

140. 481 U.S. 186 (1987).

141. 442 U.S. 62 (1979) (plurality opinion).

142. 402 U.S. 622, 626–27 (1971).

143. Id. at 623–24.

144. Id. at 624.

145. Id. at 624–25.

146. Id. at 629–30.

147. Id. at 629.

148. Id. at 633–34 (Brennan J., dissenting).

149. Haddad, *supra* note 10, at 15.

150. *See* Seidelson, *supra* note 11, at 446.

151. Id.

152. *See* Dawson, *supra* note 79, at 1416 (noting that increasing number of courts grant severance or mistrial where antagonism between codefendants likely exists).

153. 395 U.S. 250 (1969).

154. 386 U.S. 18 (1972). The Court in *Chapman* held that certain constitutional

violations were subject to harmless error analysis provided an appellate court was convinced beyond a reasonable doubt that the error complained of was harmless, id. at 24. Since *Chapman*, the Court has found that most constitutional violations fall within the harmless error analysis. *See, e.g., Michigan v. Tucker*, 417 U.S. 433 (1974) (Fifth Amendment privilege against self-incrimination and *Miranda* rule); *Chambers v. Maroney*, 399 U.S. 42 (1970) (Fourth Amendment violation); *United States v. Wade*, 388 U.S. 218 (1967) (right to counsel at proceedings other than trial).

155. *Harrington v. California*, 395 U.S. at 254.

156. Id. at 252–53.

157. Id. at 254.

158. Id. at 257 (Brennan, J., dissenting).

159. Id. at 256–57.

160. Id. at 255–56 (Brennan, J., dissenting). Justice Brennan pointed out that the majority in *Harrington* misconstrued *Chapman* by "shifting the focus of inquiry from whether the constitutional error contributed to the conviction to whether the untainted evidence provided 'overwhelming' support for the conviction," id. at 255. He remarked that the proper application of *Chapman* should oblige appellate courts to examine "the character and quality of the tainted evidence as it relates to the untainted evidence and not just on the amount of untainted evidence," id. at 256.

161. 405 U.S. 427 (1972).

162. As Justice Marshall noted in dissent, the confession of the defendant was secured "[o]nly after he was subjected to a series of bizarre acts by the police intended to frighten him into making incriminating statements," id. at 434 (Marshall, J., dissenting).

163. Id. at 430–31.

164. Id. at 432.

165. 411 U.S. 223 (1973).

166. Id. at 231.

167. 596 F.2d 400 (9th Cir. 1979).

168. Id. at 403.

169. Marcus, *The Confrontation Clause and Co-defendant Confession: The Drift from Bruton to Parker v. Randolph*, 1979 U. ILL. L.F. 559, 574 (emphasis in original).

170. 442 U.S. 62 (1969) (plurality opinion).

171. 107 S. Ct. 1714 (1987).

172. Id. at 1719.

173. 476 U.S. 530 (1986).

174. Justice Rehnquist, who wrote the plurality opinion joined by Chief Justice Burger and Justices Stewart and White, adopted this approach, *Parker v. Randolph*, 442 U.S. at 64.

175. Justices Stevens, Marshall and Brennan dissented, id. at 81. Justice Blackmun concurred in the result reached by the majority, but renounced the notion that the interlocking confession rule should constitute an exception to *Bruton*. He believed that the majority abandoned the harmless-error rule applied in previous cases. In applying this rule, he stated that the error committed in *Randolph* was harmless beyond a reasonable doubt under *Harrington*'s rationale, id. at 77 (Blackmun, J., concurring). Justice Powell did not take part in the decision.

176. Id. at 75.

177. Id. at 73.

178. Dawson, *supra* note 79, at 1421.

179. *Parker v. Randolph*, 442 U.S. at 79 (Blackmun, J., concurring).

180. Id.

181. Id. at 84 (Stevens, J., dissenting).

182. Id. at 84–86.

183. Id. at 72.

184. Id. at 72–73.

185. Id. at 84–85 (Stevens, J., dissenting).

186. Id. at 86.

187. Id. (citing *United States v. Jackson*, 390 U.S. 570 (1968) (holding Federal Kidnapping Act not unconstitutional where impermissible death penalty provision can be severed from remainder of act).

188. 476 U.S. 530 (1986).

189. The majority noted that *Lee* was distinguishable from *Bruton* because it did not involve the question of the "effectiveness of limiting instructions in preventing spill-over prejudice to a defendant when his co-defendant's confession is admitted against the co-defendant at a joint trial." Instead, the Court likened *Lee* to *Douglas v. Alabama*, id. at 542; *see supra* text accompanying notes 47–56 (discussing *Douglas* in detail).

190. *Lee v. Illinois*, 476 U.S. at 536.

191. Id.

192. Id. at 538. The defendant was found guilty of the murder of both victims, but the trial judge relied particularly on the codefendant's confession in finding the defendant guilty of the murder of one victim, id.

193. Id. at 539. The state based its argument on the holding of *Ohio v. Roberts*, 448 U.S. 56, 66 (1980), that a hearsay statement is admissible into evidence even though a defendant is denied the right to confront the maker of the statement provided the declarant is unavailable and that the statement bears sufficient indicia of reliability as to assure its trustworthiness. *See infra*, analyzing *Roberts* decision.

194. *Lee v. Illinois*, 476 U.S. at 539.

195. Id. at 544–46.

196. Id. at 545 (quoting *Parker v. Randolph*, 442 U.S. 62, 79 (1979) (Blackmun, J., concurring)). Ironically, Justice Blackmun wrote the dissenting opinion in *Lee*, in which he maintained that the codefendant's confession was sufficiently reliable to warrant its admission against the defendant, id. at 547 (Blackmun, J., dissenting). His opinion in *Lee* contrasts sharply with his cogent concurring opinion in *Randolph*. *See supra* notes 179–180 and accompanying text (discussing Justice Blackmun's concurrence in *Randolph*).

197. *Lee v. Illinois*, 476 U.S. at 546.

198. 380 U.S. 415 (1965); *see supra*, discussing *Douglas* decision in detail.

199. 477 U.S. 648 (1986) (per curiam).

200. Id. at 649.

201. The Court quoted from *Lee* to justify its conclusion that "[i]n the instant case, therefore, the State is entitled to overcome the weighty presumption of unreliability attaching to co-defendant statements by demonstrating that the particular statement at issue bears 'sufficient indicia of reliability' to satisfy Confrontation Clause concerns," id. at 649–50 (quoting *Ohio v. Roberts*, 448 U.S. 56, 66 (1980)).

202. *See infra*, developing this argument in greater detail.

203. 107 S. Ct. 1714 (1987).

204. Id. at 1716.

205. The trial judge issued a limiting instruction to the jury not to use the codefendant's confession against the defendant, id. at 1717.

206. Id. at 1716–17.

207. Id. at 1716.

208. Id. at 1718.

209. Id. (emphasis in original). In fact, the defendant in *Cruz* attempted to challenge the veracity of his confession by alleging that the witness to whom he supposedly confessed had a motive to fabricate the confession because the witness suspected the defendant was responsible for his brother's murder.

210. *See supra* discussing *Randolph* decision in detail.

211. *Cruz v. New York*, 107 S. Ct. at 1718.

212. Id. at 1718–19.

213. Id. at 1719.

214. 395 U.S. 250 (1969); *see supra* discussing *Harrington* decision.

215. As one commentator observes: "By confessing, the defendant should not lose his constitutional right, including the right to confront his accuser, namely, the co-defendant," Note, *Sixth Amendment-Confrontation and the Use of Interlocking Confessions at Joint Trial*, 78 J. CRIM. L. & CRIMINOLOGY 937, 949 (1988).

216. 471 U.S. 409 (1985). Justices Brennan and Marshall filed concurring opinions, accepting the rationale that a codefendant's confession may be admitted for nonhearsay purposes but rejecting the notion that the trial court's limiting instruction by itself justifies the admission of the confession.

217. Id. at 411.

218. Id.

219. Id. at 411–12. The sheriff who obtained Street's confession testified that he did not coerce the defendant; he denied both reading the codefendant's confession to the defendant and compelling the defendant to repeat the codefendant's confession, id. at 411.

220. Id. at 412. The codefendant's statement was admitted through the sheriff's testimony and was also formally introduced into evidence as an exhibit, id. at 411.

221. *State v. Street*, 674 S.W. 2d 741 (Tenn. Crim. App. 1984).

222. *Tennessee v. Street*, 471 U.S. at 417.

223. As the Court remarked, there were no possible alternatives to both eliminate jury prejudice and maintain the trial's "truth-seeking function" as the defendant's case had already been severed from that of his codefendants, id. at 415 n.7.

224. Id. at 414.

225. 400 U.S. 74 (1970) (plurality opinion).

226. The *Bruton* majority acknowledged in a footnote that the codefendant's confession did not constitute a hearsay exception, and left open the question of *Bruton*'s relevance to hearsay exceptions by stating that "we intimate no view whatever that such exceptions necessarily raise questions under the Confrontation Clause," *Bruton v. United States*, 391 U.S. at 128 n.3.

227. *See supra* discussing *Pointer* decision in detail.

228. *Dutton v. Evans*, 400 U.S. at 80 (quoting *Pointer v. Texas*, 380 U.S. 400, 407 (1965) (plurality opinion)).

229. Id. at 81. The Georgia statute's rationale was that such statements were made during the concealment phase of the conspiracy, id.

230. Id. at 105 (Marshall, J., dissenting).

231. Id. at 107.
232. 448 U.S. 56 (1980).
233. Id. at 66.
234. Id.
235. Seidelson, *supra* note 9, at 433.
236. 475 U.S. 387 (1987).
237. Id. at 400.
237a. 112 S. Ct. 736 (1992).
238. 107 S. Ct. 2775 (1987).
239. Id. at 2782.
240. Id. at 2782–83.
241. Goldman, *Not so "Firmly Rooted": Exceptions to the Confrontation Clause*, 66 N.C.L. REV. 1, 9 (1987).
242. *See*, e.g., Seidelson, *supra* note 11, at 431, 433: Jonakait, *supra* note 11, at 558, 570–71 (confrontation clause equated with postulates governing hearsay rule and its exceptions).
243. Jonakait, *supra* note 11, at 575.
244. Id. at 576–84.
245. 399 U.S. 149 (1970).
246. Id., at 155–56.
247. *See* Kirst, *supra* note 18, at 486–88 (Sir Walter Raleigh's conviction was based on alleged coconspirator affidavit of questionable reliability).
248. Id. at 488.
249. Id. at 492.
250. Id.
251. Note, *Inculpatory Statements Against Penal Interest and the Confrontation Clause*, 83 COLUM. L. REV. 159, 168 (1983).
252. 107 S. Ct. 1702 (1987).
253. *See supra* notes 95–139 and accompanying text (no confrontation clause violation was held to have occurred because limiting instructions to the jury not to consider confession in determining guilt protected Marsh's Sixth Amendment rights).
254. *Richardson v. Marsh*, 107 S. Ct. at 1711 (Stevens, J., dissenting).
255. The Supreme Court established "automatic standing" for defendants charged with possessory offenses in *Jones v. United States*, 362 U.S. 257 (1960). The Court, however, eradicated automatic standing for possessory offenses in *United States v. Salvucci*, 448 U.S. 83 (1980).
256. 390 U.S. 377 (1968).
257. This is the term employed by the Court in *Simmons*, id. at 391. It originated in a seventeenth-century work entitled *England's Reformation*, written in 1630 by Thomas Ward (1577–1639): "Where to elect there is but one,/ 'Tis Hobson's choice—take that or none."
258. Id. at 394.
259. Id. at 393.
260. Id. at 394.
261. Id.
262. Id.
263. *Bruton v. United States*, 391 U.S. at 143 (White, J., dissenting).
264. 107 S. Ct. 1702 (1987).

265. 107 S. Ct. 1714 (1987).

266. *Richardson v. Marsh*, 107 S. Ct. at 1707 n.3.

267. 442 U.S. 62 (1979) (plurality opinion).

268. *Cruz v. New York*, 107 S. Ct. at 1719 (citing *Lee v. Illinois*, 476 U.S. 530, 546 (1986)).

269. 108 S. Ct. 2798, 2803 (1988).

270. *Simmons v. United States*, 390 U.S. 377, 391 (1968).

271. *Richardson v. Marsh*, 107 S. Ct. at 1705–06.

3

The Compulsory Process Clause and the "Sporting Theory of Justice"

More than eight decades have elapsed since Roscoe Pound delivered an iconoclastic address entitled "The Causes of Popular Dissatisfaction with the Administration of Justice"[1] to the twenty-ninth annual meeting of the American Bar Association. A conspicuous deficiency of our adversary system of adjudication, according to Pound, derives from its inordinate emphasis on procedure to the detriment of substantive justice.[2] This stress on procedure results in an adjudicatory process that resembles a game in which the primary objective is to ensure scrupulous adherence to procedural rules rather than to achieve substantive justice. The outcome of such a process, Pound maintained, is that our system of adversary adjudication transforms the law into a "mere game"; as Pound put it, "[Our] sporting theory of justice awards new trials, or reverses judgments, or sustains demurrers in the interest of regular play."[3]

The theme Pound elaborated in that momentous address has been echoed by legal scholars, particularly in the context of our criminal justice system.[4] Indeed, the resiliency of Pound's message, which centered on the deleterious effects of our adversary system of adjudication,[5] is evidenced by the spate of legal commentary on the relative merits or disadvantages of the adversary process.[6]

The debate over the effectiveness of the adversary system as a mechanism for arriving at the truth has gained considerable attention in the context of our criminal justice process.[7] A salient feature of that controversy focuses on whether procedural protections accorded to criminal defendants impede the "search for truth" by excluding probative, relevant evidence.[8] The centerpiece of this controversy, of course, is the exclusionary rule, which affords criminal defendants the benefit of the suppression of otherwise relevant, material evidence as a remedy for the violation of protections delineated in the Fourth, Fifth, and Sixth amendments to the U.S. Constitution.[9]

The rationale supporting the exclusionary remedy is grounded upon three fundamental tenets: the interest in individual dignity, the requirement of judicial integrity, and the need to curb official power.[10] Although the primary function of the exclusionary remedy is to deter police misconduct, the ancillary purposes of the preservation of judicial integrity and of individual dignity are equally compelling bases for the rule. The Supreme Court, however, has completely discarded these rationales, maintaining that the sole object of the rule is the deterrence of official misconduct.[11] Furthermore, the Court has held that the rule is not mandated by the Constitution, arguing that it is merely a "judicially created remedy" designed to achieve a deterrent effect instead of being a personal constitutional right of the party whose rights are violated.[12]

Within the past decade and a half, the Court has significantly narrowed the scope of the rule by employing a balancing approach that weighs the costs of excluding material evidence against the benefits derived from the application of the exclusionary remedy.[13] Given the Court's restrictive interpretation of the purposes served by the exclusionary rule, such a balancing test tips the scale in a manner that clearly favors the admission of evidence gathered in violation of a criminal defendant's constitutional rights. A corollary of this perspective is that it supposedly furthers "the public interest in prosecuting those accused of crime and having them acquitted or convicted on the basis of all the evidence which exposes the truth."[14] Of course, such a view rests on the cornerstone of Pound's critique of the "sporting theory" of justice; that is, that the adjudicatory process should determine the outcome of a controversy on the substantive merits rather than on the slavish enforcement of procedural rules.

It is evident, therefore, that the exclusionary rule has come under increasing negative scrutiny by the Court in recent years in large part due to its "costs"; that is, the rule excludes probative, relevant, evidence. In *Taylor v. Illinois*,[15] however, the Court excluded probative, material evidence offered by a defendant in a criminal trial.[16] Paradoxically, the *Taylor* decision relies heavily on the integrity rationale, previously jettisoned by the Court as a basis for the exclusionary rule, to support the exclusion of relevant, probative evidence.[17] The decision, moreover, portends an ominous abridgment of a defendant's right to present a defense by administering the exclusionary remedy, previously applied only to vindicate an aggrieved defendant's constitutional rights, to prevent a criminal defendant from offering exculpatory evidence.

In effect, the *Taylor* Court elevated procedure over substance, thereby succumbing to the "sporting theory" of justice. This chapter argues that the *Taylor* decision reflects a result-oriented jurisprudence that decisively alters the balance of power in a criminal trial by denying a defendant the right to present critical evidence. The decision, moreover, is inconsistent with our adversary system of adjudication and runs counter to precedent. Further, *Taylor* flies in the face of the Court's previous derogation of reliability and integrity as attributes worthy of constitutional concern.[18]

The *Taylor* decision is grounded upon a strained construction of the Sixth

Amendment's compulsory process clause.[19] Therefore, this chapter delves first into the historical background and modern doctrinal basis of the clause. Next, it will undertake a detailed critique and analysis of *Taylor*, emphasizing its departure from precedent and its logically flawed analysis. In turn, it will juxtapose *Taylor*'s premises with the Court's recent devaluation of the twin goals of integrity and reliability as values meriting constitutional protection.

THE EMERGENCE OF COMPULSORY PROCESS

As the architect of the Sixth Amendment to the U.S. Constitution, James Madison included within its parameters the right of the criminal defendant to obtain compulsory process of witnesses in his favor.[20] In comparison with other provisions of the Bill of Rights, the Sixth Amendment was passed without major modifications and with little controversy.[21] It is also apparent that the provision of the Sixth Amendment relating to compulsory process had gained wide acceptance at an early date in our history. As the foremost authority on the compulsory process clause persuasively demonstrates, by 1791 the right of compulsory process was firmly entrenched within the American criminal process and "represented the culmination of the long-evolving principle that the defendant should have a meaningful opportunity, at least on a par with the prosecution, to present a case in his favor through witnesses."[22]

The vitality of the clause, moreover, was made clear in its forceful application less than two decades after the passage of the Bill of Rights in the misdemeanor and treason trials of former Vice President Aaron Burr.[23] A harbinger of the Burr decisions had been provided by Justice Chase in *United States v. Cooper*.[24] In that case, the defendant was on trial for libeling the President and he requested that the court issue a letter to members of Congress imploring their attendance as witnesses on his behalf. Chase summarily denied the defendant's request, explaining that the defendant could rely on the compulsory process clause. The clause, he believed, applied to members of Congress, thus rendering superfluous the issuance of the letter, since members of Congress could be ordered to appear at trial.

Similarly, Justice Marshall concluded in the *Burr* cases that the clause must be implemented even when the President of the United States is the subject of its reach.[25] Marshall enshrined the clause by asserting that "[T]he right given by this article must be deemed sacred by courts, and the article should be so construed as to be something more than a dead letter."[26] In placing such a high value on the protections afforded by the right to compulsory process, Marshall rejected President Jefferson's interest in secrecy. Although recognizing the President's need for secrecy, Marshall remarked that such an interest must give way to the defendant's need for information "absolutely necessary in [his] defense."[27] Of course, the claim of executive privilege would be pitted against the demands of compulsory process more than a century and a half later in *United States v. Nixon*.[28]

The Modern Doctrinal Basis of Compulsory Process

Despite the forceful manner in which Marshall construed the compulsory process clause in the *Burr* case, the clause lay dormant for a considerable period of time,[29] until the Supreme Court resurrected it in the landmark case of *Washington v. Texas*.[30] In light of the significance of the decision, and the *Taylor* Court's flawed and incomplete application of *Washington*'s doctrinal imperatives, it is worthwhile to examine in detail that seminal decision.

The *Washington* Court gave new impetus to the right to compulsory process by equating it with the right to present a defense and by characterizing compulsory process as a "fundamental element of due process of law."[31] The Court thereby invalidated two Texas statutes that prohibited persons charged or convicted as coparticipants in the same crime from testifying for one another, although the same restriction was not applicable to the prosecution.[32] The factual predicate of *Washington*, therefore, must be examined in order to derive the doctrinal essence of the decision.

Jackie Washington was charged and then convicted by a jury of murder. His defense rested on the contention that he did not shoot the victim, but that he unsuccessfully attempted to dissuade the codefendant, Fuller, from shooting the victim.[33] The record clearly indicated that the codefendant would have been willing to testify at Washington's trial and would have corroborated Washington's testimony. However, since Fuller had been previously convicted of the murder, the Texas statutes precluded him from testifying on Washington's behalf.[34]

The Court first determined that the compulsory process clause was applicable to the states through the operation of the Fourteenth Amendment's due process clause.[35] In arriving at this conclusion, the Court revitalized the right to compulsory process by placing it on an equal footing with such other Sixth Amendment guarantees as the right to confrontation, the assistance of counsel, and the right to a speedy and public trial.[36] In strong terms, the Court defined the clause as implicating "[t]he right to offer the testimony of witnesses, and to compel their attendance . . . [and] the right to present the defendant's version of the facts as well as the prosecution's to the jury so that it may decide where the truth lies."[37]

The rationale undergirding the *Washington* decision is based on the principle that our adversary system of adjudication values the introduction of relevant, probative evidence over a court's "interest in preventing perjury."[38] In rejecting the reasoning behind the Texas rule, namely that if alleged accomplices to a crime were permitted to testify for one another, "each would try to swear each other out of the charge,"[39] the Court instead opted for a rationale that placed trust on jurors to weigh the credibility of relevant testimony. Indeed, the *Washington* Court believed that if truth were one of the fundamental goals of the adversary system, it was "[m]ore likely to be arrived at by hearing the testimony of all persons of competent understanding who may seem to have knowledge of the facts involved in such a case, leaving the credit and weight of such testimony to be determined by the jury or by the court.''[40]

Given the *Washington*'s Court emphasis on the need to present relevant, crucial evidence to a jury, despite the risk that such testimony might be tainted, it was natural that the Court would find the violation of Jackie Washington's right to compulsory process. As the Court cogently put it:

> We hold that the petitioner in this case was denied his right to have compulsory process for obtaining witnesses in his favor because the State arbitrarily denied him the right to put on the stand a witness who was physically and mentally capable of testifying to events that he had personally observed, and whose testimony would have been relevant and material to his defense. The Framers of the Constitution did not intend to commit the futile act of giving to a defendant the right to secure the attendance of witnesses whose testimony he had no right to use.[41]

Implicit in the majority opinion is the notion that the defendant ought to have an equal opportunity to present her version of events, given the prosecution's inherent power to present its case. To the degree that arbitrary rules designed to prevent perjury forestall crucial witnesses from testifying for the defendant, the ends of justice are not served. In essence, the *Washington* Court nullified the Texas rules that prevented Fuller from testifying on Washington's behalf by classifying them as arbitrary because they ''[p]revent whole categories of defense witnesses from testifying on the basis of *a priori* categories that presume them worthy of unbelief.''[42] Indeed, Justice Harlan's concurring opinion was premised not on the compulsory process clause but rather on the notion that fairness dictated that the defense ought to have the same opportunity as the prosecution for presenting a coparticipant's crucial testimony.[43]

The principal teaching of *Washington* is that testimony on a critical issue must be presented to the trier of fact even if the possibility exists that such testimony might be perjured.[44] A byproduct of this precept is that the finder of fact ought to be trusted with the task of ferreting out the relative weight and credibility of testimony that is relevant and probative rather than being shielded from such testimony because it might be tainted. The *Washington* Court, in fact, quoted approvingly from *Benson v. United States*[45] the proposition that the common law notion that only disinterested parties should be allowed to testify ought to be rejected. The reason for this rigid common law rule was that, ''[t]he courts were afraid to trust the intelligence of jurors.''[46] In effect, the *Washington* Court made the clear choice that the presentation of crucial evidence in a criminal trial superseded a court's interest in precluding a jury from hearing testimony that might be perjured.

The main teaching of *Washington* was foreshadowed in *Hoffa v. United States*.[47] In *Hoffa*, however, the principle was applied to the prosecution rather than to the defendant. Hoffa's conviction hinged on the testimony of a government informer whose credibility was subject to question. The defendant thus contended that the prosecution's use of such an informer, who had a great motive to lie, violated the Fifth Amendment's due process clause.[48] The Court agreed with Hoffa's argument that the informer had a great incentive to lie.[49] Nevertheless, it rejected Hoffa's due process argument because the testimony of the informant was not *ipso facto* untrue and because the built-in safeguards of the adversary system, namely cross-examination and the ability of the jury to assess the weight and credibility of the testimony, counterbalanced the probability that the informer's testimony was perjured.[50]

The results of both *Washington* and *Hoffa* are in accord with our adversary system of adjudication, which places responsibility on the fact-finder to determine the truthfulness and credibility of witnesses.[51] This burden is shouldered by the fact-finder, in most criminal cases the jury, because the parties in an adversary system are primarily entrusted with the task of weakening their opponent's case through the impeachment of presumptively false or inconsistent evidence. In fact, the Supreme Court has asserted that cross-examination is the most effective means of exposing false testimony.[52] The risk of admitting testimony that might be false, therefore, is outweighed by the benefit of permitting the fact-finder to assess its weight and credibility, assisted by the inherent protections afforded by the adversary system.

Application of *Washington*

The vigorous implementation of the right to compulsory process in *Washington* continued unabated as the Court on several occasions in the 1970s applied, either directly or tangentially, the principal teachings of *Washington*. It is instructive, therefore, to analyze the decisions construing *Washington*. This examination is necessary to counterpoise these decisions with the Court's misapplication of *Washington* in *Taylor*.

Cool v. United States

In a *per curiam* opinion, the Court in *Cool v. United States*[53] held that a defendant was deprived of his right to compulsory process when the trial court instructed the jury that the exculpatory testimony of an accomplice should be disregarded unless the jury deemed that such testimony was true beyond a reasonable doubt.[54] In applying *Washington* to the facts in *Cool*, the Court concluded that such an instruction impermissibly infringed upon a criminal defendant's right to compulsory process and violated *Washington*'s mandate because it excluded relevant evidence absent the jury's determination that the accomplice's testimony was "extremely reliable."[55]

The *Cool* Court correctly construed *Washington* by emphasizing the defendant's right to present exculpatory evidence over the trial court's interest in preventing a jury to reach a verdict based on testimony that might be "tainted."[56]

The Court thereby stressed the primary teaching of *Washington* that in a criminal trial the defendant's right to present relevant exculpatory evidence takes precedence over the trial court's interest in preventing the jury from hearing testimony that might be perjured. Implicitly, the *Cool* Court also implemented the precept enunciated in *Washington* that the fact-finder should determine the weight and credibility of possibly false testimony rather than being preempted from considering such testimony by the trial judge or, alternatively, by instructions issued by the court.

It is also natural to draw the inference from the *Cool* decision that the Court viewed the impermissible jury instruction as conflicting with *Washington*'s prohibition against assuming that some witnesses' testimony is not worthy of belief. To the extent that the trial court's instructions in *Cool* clearly suggested to the jury that the accomplice's testimony was not credible, the message conveyed to the jury was unmistakable; that is, accomplices fit the category of witnesses who are *a priori* "suspect" and thus not credible.

The second prong of the *Cool* decision relied on the fundamental principle established by *In re Winship*[57] that the prosecution must prove the defendant's guilt beyond a reasonable doubt. Through its instruction on how to weigh the accomplice's testimony, the trial court in essence "[created] an artificial barrier to the consideration of relevant evidence putatively credible by a preponderance of the evidence . . . [reducing] the level of proof necessary for the Government to carry its burden."[58] The upshot of the trial judge's instruction was to require the defendant to prove his innocence beyond a reasonable doubt, since the defendant's case relied almost exclusively on the accomplice's testimony.[59]

Webb v. Texas

In a similar vein, the Court in *Webb v. Texas*[60] affirmed *Washington*'s dictates, although it decided the case on due process grounds rather than on the compulsory process clause.[61] In *Webb* the defendant was prevented from presenting a witness when the trial judge in effect intimidated the witness into not testifying. The sole defense witness in *Webb* had a previous criminal record and was serving a prison term when he was called by the defense.[62] The trial judge proceeded to issue a stern warning to the witness, suggesting that the witness could face perjury charges if he testified for the defense.[63] The witness did not testify, and the defendant could not present a defense given the trial judge's success in dissuading the witness from testifying.[64]

The *Webb* Court quoted approvingly from *Washington*[65] in holding that the defendant's due process rights under the Fourteenth Amendment were violated by the judge's coercion of the defense witness.[66] Specifically, the Court affirmed the proposition established by *Washington* that the defendant has a right to present a defense coextensive with the prosecution's right to present its case and that the jury serves the function of determining "where the truth lies."[67]

Chambers v. Mississippi

In *Chambers v. Mississippi*,[68] the Court again relied on the underlying premises of *Washington* while deciding that the defendant was denied due process of law under the Fourteenth Amendment. The defendant in that case was denied the right to present the testimony of three witnesses who would have testified that someone else committed the crime with which Chambers was charged.[69] The trial court excluded this testimony on the basis that it violated the hearsay rule.[70] Noting that a defendant's right to compulsory process is "essential to due process,"[71] the *Chambers* Court reasoned that the right of the defendant to present witnesses on his behalf, as set forth in *Washington*, *Webb*, and *Oliver*,[72] overrides the "mechanistic" application of the hearsay rule.[73]

Although the *Chambers* majority acknowledged the need for evidentiary rules that ensure fairness and reliability in the ascertainment of guilt, the Court nonetheless rejected the procrustean application of such rules to "defeat the ends of justice."[74] *Chambers*, therefore, rejected the "sporting theory" of justice and instead favored a result grounded in substantive justice. In effect, the right to present a defense triumphed over strict fealty to procedure.

United States v. Nixon

The high point for the compulsory process clause in the 1970s occurred when the Court issued its decision in *United States v. Nixon*.[75] The Court harked back to the basic postulate announced by Chief Justice Marshall in the *Burr* cases[76] that the compulsory process clause takes precedence over claims of executive privilege. Underscoring the importance of compulsory process to the attainment of a correct result in a criminal trial, the majority noted that, "[t]o ensure that justice is done, it is imperative to the function of the courts that compulsory process be available for the production of evidence needed either by the prosecution or by the defense."[77]

More important, the Court stressed the constitutional aspect of compulsory process,[78] noting that implicit in the notion of a fair trial was the "constitutional need" that the outcome be based upon the weighing of all relevant evidence.[79] The claim of executive privilege, therefore, had to give way to the "specific need for evidence in a criminal trial."[80]

If *Nixon* represents the culmination of the Court's expansive interpretation of the compulsory process clause, a series of cases dealing with the tension between the demands imposed by discovery rules and the right to compulsory process in the 1970s reflected a certain ambivalence on the part of the Court. Those cases did not resolve the issue whether discovery rules could, in certain instances, take precedence over a criminal defendant's constitutional right to compulsory process. A discussion and analysis of those cases will be reserved and will constitute a backdrop to the discussion of *Taylor*, since in that case the Court grappled with the question posed by the conflict between discovery rules and the compulsory process clause.[81]

The Countertrend of the 1980s

The fidelity to *Washington*'s dictates manifested in the robust application of its fundamental premises waned with the advent of the 1980s and concluded with the Court's apathy and, indeed, antipathy toward *Washington* in *Taylor*. The Court's decision in *United States v. Valenzuela-Bernal*[82] heralded the attenuation of the expansive application of the compulsory process clause that had prevailed during the previous decade.

In signaling its retreat from *Washington*, the *Valenzuela-Bernal* Court held that when the government deports witnesses who may possess evidence relevant to the defense, such a procedure does not necessarily violate the compulsory process clause absent a showing that "[t]he evidence lost would be both material and favorable to the defense."[83] Moreover, the Court also evinced its willingness to undertake a balancing approach in which governmental administrative considerations would be weighed against the defendant's right to compulsory process.[84]

In *Valenzuela-Bernal*, the defendant was charged with knowing transportation of an illegal alien into the United States.[85] He was arrested at a Border Patrol checkpoint with three other passengers of the car he drove.[86] Two of those passengers were deported to Mexico on the determination by an assistant United States attorney that the passengers were not material witnesses either for the prosecution or for the defense.[87] The defendant, who did not have an opportunity to interview the two passengers before they were deported, maintained that the deportation violated his right to compulsory process pursuant to the Sixth Amendment and his right to due process of law under the Fifth Amendment.[88]

The reasoning adopted by the *Valenzuela-Bernal* Court was in part based upon the administrative burdens shouldered by the government as a result of not deporting aliens who "possess no material evidence relevant to a criminal trial."[89] Giving free rein to prosecutorial discretion,[90] the majority deemed that the prosecution could be trusted to decide whether a witness was material and relevant to the defense.[91] The Court thus diminished the value of the right to compulsory process by counterbalancing the defendant's need for evidence with governmental, bureaucratic considerations.

The primary rationale of *Valenzuela-Bernal* rests on the dubious proposition that the defendant can depend on the prosecution to determine the materiality of the evidence; and that the defendant bears the burden of proving, without any means of interviewing the witness, that the witness's testimony would have been material and favorable to the defense.[92]

Furthermore, the majority in *Valenzuela-Bernal* misconstrued the core meaning of *Washington* by relying on a crabbed reading of the case. The *Valenzuela-Bernal* Court quoted *Washington* to support its holding that the defendant had not established that the testimony of the deported witnesses would have been material, relevant, and vital to the defense.[93] The majority noted that, "[i]n, *Washington*, this Court found a violation of the [compulsory process] Clause of the Sixth Amendment when the defendant was arbitrarily deprived of 'testimony [that] would have been *relevant* and *material*, and . . . *vital* to the defense.' "[94] In essence, the *Valenzuela-Bernal* Court not only quoted *Washington* out of context, but it also clearly missed the holding and the underlying message conveyed by *Washington*.

The clear holding of *Washington* is that the prosecution may not arbitrarily deny a criminal defendant the right to "put on the stand a witness who [is] physically and mentally capable of testifying to events that he [has] personally observed, and whose testimony [is] relevant and material to the defense."[95] It is discernible that the word "vital" is conspicuously missing from the Court's holding. Although the testimony excluded from Washington's trial was vital, the Court's holding was not circumscribed to the facts of Washington's case but rather stands for the broad principle that the compulsory process clause protects a criminal defendant's right to present *any* relevant and material evidence.

In fact, the majority in *Valenzuela-Bernal* was acutely aware that *Washington* did not provide a firm basis for its holding. Consequently, the Court resorted to *Roviaro v. United States*[96] to bolster its rationale. In *Roviaro*, the Court held that the government's interest in shielding an informant's identity must yield to a criminal defendant's right to the informant's testimony.[97] Although the *Roviaro* Court's holding was not constitutionally based, the *Valenzuela-Bernal* Court cited *Roviaro* for the precept that "[w]hile a defendant who has not had an opportunity to interview a witness may face a difficult task in making a showing of materiality, the task is not an impossible one."[98]

As Justice Brennan pointed out in dissent, the *Valenzuela-Bernal* Court's reliance on *Roviaro* is also misplaced.[99] *Roviaro* emphasized, according to Justice Brennan, the accused's right to decide whether a witness might be helpful to the defense.[100] Accordingly, the Court in *Valenzuela-Bernal* should have allowed the defendant, not the prosecution, to determine whether the illegal-alien eyewitnesses could have furnished testimony material and favorable to his defense.[101]

The *Valenzuela-Bernal* decision underscored the Court's deviation from the principles sustaining *Washington*. The ruling also marked a disturbing trend toward giving governmental administrative concerns equal, if not greater, weight than a criminal defendant's constitutional rights.[102] In effect, the *Valenzuela-Bernal* Court bowed to the "sporting theory" of justice by allowing administrative reasons to play a role in determining a criminal defendant's right to present a defense. The ultimate glorification of the "sporting theory" of justice and of procedure over substantive justice, however, occurred in *Taylor v. Illinois*.[103]

TAYLOR V. ILLINOIS

In *Taylor* the Court decided the question it had left unanswered in both *Williams v. Florida*[104] and *Wardius v. Oregon*[105] and on which it had refused to grant certiorari on several occasions[106]: that is, whether the compulsory process clause prohibits the exclusion of admissible evidence as a sanction to enforce discovery rules against criminal defendants. The *Taylor* Court answered the question negatively, thereby championing the ''sporting theory'' of justice and detracting from the ideal of a criminal trial: to seek justice and truth based on all of the relevant, material evidence available to the fact-finder. Moreover, the Court in *Taylor* completely ignored the teachings of *Washington* and related cases.[107] Before analyzing *Taylor*, however, it is necessary, as a point of departure, to discuss its background.

Discovery and the Compulsory Process Clause

In *Williams v. Florida*[108] the Court came to grips with the issue of whether Florida's pretrial discovery rule requiring the defendant, in response to the prosecution's demand, to give notice of an alibi defense prior to trial was constitutional.[109] The Court held that the rule was constitutional and hence not violative of the defendant's Fifth Amendment right against self-incrimination because it did not compel him to reveal any information but merely accelerated the timing of his disclosure.[110] More important for our purposes, however, is the Court's discussion of the relationship between discovery rules and the defendant's right to compulsory process under the Sixth Amendment.

Noting that ''the adversary system of trial is hardly an end in itself,''[111] the Court legitimized notice-of-alibi rules as consistent with the search for truth and as congruent with the rational concern of the prosecution to prevent ''eleventh hour'' defenses based on false testimony.[112] The Court, however, qualified its holding by stressing that Florida's notice-of-alibi rule was ''carefully hedged with reciprocal duties requiring state disclosure to the defendant.''[113]

The *Williams* Court did not rule on the constitutionality of the sanction imposed by the Florida notice-of-alibi rule because the defendant complied with the rule. The sanction stipulated in the rule involved the exclusion at trial of the defendant's alibi evidence, with the exception of his testimony.[114] In a footnote, the Court unequivocally stated that it was not deciding whether the prosecution could enforce discovery rules against the defendant who failed to comply with such rules by excluding ''probative, relevant evidence.''[115]

It is significant, moreover, that the *Williams* decision set forth the appropriate solution to the problem notice-of-alibi rules are intended to protect against: unfair surprise to the prosecution. In the event that a jurisdiction lacked a notice-of-alibi provision similar to Florida's statute, the adequate resolution to the prejudice suffered by the prosecution is for the trial court to grant a continuance as soon as the alibi witness is called.[116] The continuance would negate the strategic advantage sought by the defense because the prosecution would then have an opportunity to take the deposition of or interview the alibi witness and thus discover rebuttal evidence.[117] In fact, the *Williams* Court averred that such a procedure would comport with the U.S. Constitution.[118] The *Taylor* Court, however, rejected this solution as a means of remedying a discovery violation by the defense.[119]

In contrast to the Court's approval of Florida's notice-of-alibi rule, Oregon's alibi statute was found constitutionally deficient in *Wardius v. Oregon.*[120] The Court in *Wardius* held that nonreciprocal alibi rules violate the due process clause of the Fourteenth Amendment.[121] The defendant in *Wardius* was not permitted to present an alibi defense at his trial either through a witness he called or through his own testimony.[122]

Once again, like the *Williams* Court, the *Wardius* Court declined to rule on the constitutionality of the preclusion sanction as applied to the defendant in a criminal trial. The defendant in *Wardius* contended that the exclusion of his testimony or that of other defense witnesses at trial would be unconstitutional, even conceding the validity of Oregon's notice-of-alibi rule. The Court, however, did not decide the issue, arguing that the matter was rendered moot in light of the unconstitutionality of the Oregon statute.[123]

In an enlightening analysis of the purposes served by discovery rules, the *Wardius* Court viewed such rules as helpful devices that "by increasing the evidence available to both parties, [enhance] the fairness of the adversary system."[124] More important, the Court grounded its decision on the essential premise that the due process clause of the Fourteenth Amendment requires a "balance of forces" between the prosecution and the defense.[125] The majority emphasized the importance of discovery for the defense as well as for the prosecution.[126] Indeed, the majority in *Wardius* clearly intimated that discovery rules should favor the defense, given the superior advantages in resources the prosecution enjoys over the defendant.[127]

In a trenchant concurring opinion, Justice Douglas elaborated on the suggestion by the *Wardius* majority that discovery rules should favor the defense. He assailed the development of discovery rules, such as notice-of-alibi statutes, that compelled the defendant to reveal information to the prosecution. The trial-related rights afforded criminal defendants in the Bill of Rights,[128] according to Douglas, "[do] not envision an adversary proceeding between two equal parties."[129] Instead, those rights acknowledge the "awesome power of indictment and the virtually limitless resources of government investigators."[130] In essence, the rights enjoyed by the defendant under the United States Constitution are "designed to redress the advantage that inheres in a government prosecution."[131]

Although both the *Williams* and the *Wardius* decisions deferred resolution of the constitutionality of the preclusion sanction as a remedy for a defendant's violation of a discovery rule, they suggest that the Court would have been loath to uphold such a drastic measure. The *Williams* Court outlined the pragmatic solution to the problem by approving a continuance for the prosecution to nullify any strategic advantage the defendant sought to gain by "ambushing" the prosecution. Similarly, it is possible to infer from the *Wardius* decision that the Court would have been reluctant to augment the prosecution's decisive advantage over the defendant by excluding relevant, material defense witnesses from testifying.

The Court's affirmation of the defendant's right to present a defense in *Wardius* was contrasted with the obligation of the defendant to make available all of her evidence to the prosecution in *United States v. Nobles.*[132] *Nobles* presented the issue whether the defense had the right to offer a selective portion of certain facts, thus thwarting the prosecution's right to cross-examination. The defendant in that case attempted to question the credibility of prosecution witnesses through the use of the testimony of his investigator, who had interviewed the witnesses.[133] The trial court did not allow the investigator to testify, however, because the defense refused to disclose the written report of the investigator, which summarized the interviews.

Upholding the trial court's exclusion of the investigator's testimony, the Court determined that the defendant's right to compulsory process was not implicated in the case because "[t]he District Court did not bar the investigator's testimony . . . [i]t merely prevented [defendant] from presenting to the jury a partial view of the credibility issue."[134] The Court referred to the restriction on the prosecution's opportunity to cross-examine the investigator by remarking that "[t]he Sixth Amendment does not confer the right to present testimony free from the legitimate demands of the adversarial system."[135]

The *Nobles* decision is crucial to our analysis because the majority in *Taylor* patently misconstrued its import.[136] The *Nobles* Court did not impose the exclusionary sanction, as the previous discussion demonstrates; rather, it merely prevented the defendant from presenting a partial view of the testimony free from the constraints imposed by cross-examination. The majority in *Taylor*, however, would employ *Nobles* for the proposition that the exclusion of relevant, probative defense evidence is constitutionally permissible.[137] Such an application of *Nobles* is fundamentally flawed.[138]

Prelude to *Taylor*: *Crane*, *Ritchie*, and *Rock*

Although the Court in *Nobles* did not undermine the key elements of *Washington* and its progeny, it did intimate in *Valenzuela-Bernal* that it was willing to dilute the protections embodied in *Washington* to accommodate governmental interests.[139] Nevertheless, the Court gave no hint immediately before the *Taylor* decision that it was willing to decimate the doctrinal underpinnings of *Washington* to the degree it did in *Taylor*. In fact, the three rulings bearing on the compulsory process clause rendered by the Court prior to *Taylor* strongly reasserted the basic rationale underlying the defendant's right to compulsory process. It is instructive, therefore, to examine these three decisions as a basis of comparison with the *Taylor* Court's distorted perspective of the compulsory process clause.

Crane v. Kentucky

In *Crane v. Kentucky*,[140] the Court held that a sixteen-year-old defendant was deprived of a fair trial when the trial court prohibited the admission of testimony relating to the circumstances under which his confession was given to the police.[141] The Court cited the Sixth Amendment guarantees of compulsory process and confrontation, as well as the due process clause of the Fourteenth Amendment, for the proposition that the Constitution entitles the defendant to "a meaningful opportunity to present a complete defense."[142] Since the government's case relied almost exclusively on the defendant's confession,[143] a unanimous Court concluded that the opportunity to present a defense would be hollow indeed if the "[s]tate were permitted to exclude competent, reliable evidence bearing on the credibility of a confession when such evidence is central to a defendant's claim of innocence."[144]

Not only did the *Crane* Court vigorously uphold the right of a criminal defendant to present a "complete" defense, but it also did so when that right clashed with a state evidentiary rule. Though the Court acknowledged the right of states to craft their evidentiary and trial procedural rules, it also recognized that, given the factual predicate of *Crane*, the exclusion of testimony regarding the circumstances of the defendant's confession did not afford him a fair trial.[145]

Pennsylvania v. Ritchie

In the second case in which the Court had the opportunity to address the scope of the compulsory process clause, *Pennsylvania v. Ritchie*,[146] a majority expounded a restricted view of the compulsory process clause; in effect, the *Ritchie* Court equated the compulsory process clause with the due process clause of the Fourteenth Amendment, thus diminishing the status of the clause established by *Washington*.[147] The Court expressed this narrow conception of the right to compulsory process by declining to "decide . . . whether and how the guarantees of the Compulsory Process Clause differ from those of the Fourteenth Amendment."[148] It seems that the *Ritchie* Court conveniently ignored the fact that in *Washington* the specific protections of the compulsory process clause were made applicable to the states through the operation of the Fourteenth Amendment's due process clause.[149]

Nevertheless, the *Ritchie* Court in dicta reasserted the basic postulates of the compulsory process clause. Referring to the precedent set forth in *Washington*, *Chambers*, *Cool*, and *Webb*, the Court observed that criminal defendants have "the right to the Government's assistance in compelling the attendance of favorable witnesses at trial and the right to put before a jury evidence that might influence the determination of guilt."[150]

Furthermore, the Court in *Ritchie* affirmed a criminal defendant's right to discover material exculpatory evidence even though such evidence is shielded by a state evidentiary privilege. In *Ritchie*, the defendant was charged with the rape of his thirteen-year-old daughter[151] and attempted to discover records about his daughter kept by a state agency that investigated child-abuse cases.[152] Invoking a state statute,[153] the prosecutor convinced the trial judge that the records the defendant sought were privileged.[154] The Court held that the due process clause of the Fourteenth Amendment entitled defendant to a review of the file by the trial court to determine whether it contained "information that probably would have changed the outcome of the trial."[155]

Rock v. Arkansas

The ambiguity concerning the appropriate boundaries of the compulsory process clause evident in *Ritchie* was dispelled by the Court's decision in *Rock v. Arkansas*.[156] In *Rock*, the Court held that an Arkansas evidentiary rule that *per se* excluded any testimony that was hypnotically refreshed contravened a criminal defendant's right to testify on her behalf.[157] The *Rock* Court analyzed the issue it confronted as involving a dichotomy between a state evidentiary rule designed to ensure reliability in fact-finding and the right of the defendant to present a defense by offering material testimony.[158]

More important, the majority in *Rock* correctly interpreted the major doctrinal underpinning of *Washington*: that evidentiary rules based on the need for reliability in the fact-finding process are subservient to a criminal defendant's right to present a defense.[159] In fact, the Court likened the statute at issue in *Rock* with the rule of competence it declared unconstitutional in *Washington*.[160] Moreover, the Court quoted *Chambers v. Mississippi* for the principle that a rule of evidence that prevents a criminal defendant from presenting a complete defense by excluding material parts of his testimony is constitutionally impermissible.[161]

The *Rock* Court recognized that the "right [of a criminal defendant] to present relevant evidence is not without limitation."[162] Nonetheless, the Court was careful to stress that restrictions on the defendant's right to testify must not "be arbitrary or disproportionate to the purposes they are designed to serve."[163] Rather, the Court proposed a delicate balancing approach in which the burden rests with the state to justify an evidentiary rule that limits a defendant's "constitutional right to testify."[164]

Moreover, the Court in *Rock* allayed concerns about the reliability of hypnotically refreshed testimony by pointing to the potent weapon of cross-examination, which constitutes an "effective tool for revealing inconsistencies."[165] Therefore, the Court enunciated the fundamental tenet expressed in *Hoffa* that cross-examination in our adversary system of adjudication serves to bring to light the truthfulness, or lack thereof, of a witness's testimony.[166]

Standing in stark contrast to the *Rock* Court's sound interpretation of the compulsory process clause is the Court's egregious misinterpretation of the clause as well as its disdainful indifference to *Washington*'s mandate in *Taylor*. The irony of the decision is that the author of *Rock*, Justice Stevens, produced the diametrically opposed opinion in *Taylor*.

Taylor v. Illinois

In *Taylor*, the Supreme Court allowed the preclusion of testimony by a defense witness as a sanction for a discovery violation by the defense.[167] Unlike the situation in *Washington*, a rule of competence did not disqualify the witness from testifying.[168] Neither, for that matter, did a rule creating a privilege, such as the rule in *Roviaro* protecting the identity of government informers,[169] nor the statute creating a privilege for certain juvenile records in *Ritchie*,[170] pose an obstacle to the testimony the defendant sought to present in *Taylor*. Rather, the testimony was excluded by the trial court on the basis of a violation of a reciprocal discovery rule which required the defendant before trial to reveal the names and addresses of witnesses he intended to call.[171]

Furthermore, unlike the notice-of-alibi statutes in *Williams* and *Wardius*,[172] whose primary goal was to prevent the likelihood of fabricated testimony engendered by an alibi defense, the discovery rule the defense violated in *Taylor* was not chiefly designed to prevent perjury through the means of an "eleventh hour" defense. Therefore, the *Taylor* Court applied the exclusionary sanction to otherwise relevant, admissible evidence merely for the violation of a discovery rule.

Given the foregoing analysis, it is imperative to scrutinize the reasoning of *Taylor* and to critique its faulty logic. A starting point for such an exercise is the factual predicate of the decision. After an exposition of the facts, the *Taylor* decision will be analyzed against the backdrop of the three fundamental premises of *Washington v. Texas*: that a defendant's right to present relevant, probative evidence outweighs a trial court's interest in preventing perjury; that, as a corollary to this principle, a jury ought to be allowed to assess relevant testimony rather than being "protected" from weighing the credibility of such testimony by exclusion of the testimony; and that to the extent that evidentiary rules prevent defense witnesses from testifying based on "*a priori* categories that presume them worthy of unbelief" such rules violate the defendant's right to compulsory process.[173]

After examining *Taylor* from this vantage point, the analysis will critique the part of the decision that penalizes the defendant for the violations of discovery rules committed by his defense counsel.[174] Finally, the last section will deal with the impact of *Taylor* on the criminal adversary process; that is, the extent to which *Taylor* affects the balance of power in a criminal trial and contradicts the fundamental premises of the criminal justice system.

Facts

The defendant, Ray Taylor, was charged with and convicted (by a jury) of the attempted murder of Jack Bridges.[175] The conviction rested on the testimony of Bridges, his brother, and three other witnesses.[176] These witnesses described an altercation that began when Bridges slapped one Derrick Travis for sitting on Bridges's car. Taylor came to the aid of Travis.[177] After a twenty-minute argument, Bridges left the scene "to cool off."[178] Bridges apparently had not "cooled off" when he returned to the scene about an hour later.[179]

Bridges testified at trial that when he returned to the scene with his brother, Maurice Bethany, they were confronted by Taylor, Travis, and several other individuals. Bridges testified that he fled, but that Taylor pursued him and ultimately fired four shots, the last of which struck Bridges in the back. After he was struck by the bullet, Bridges testified that Taylor pointed the gun at his head and pulled the trigger, but that the gun misfired.[180]

The altercation was supposedly witnessed by twenty or thirty bystanders.[181] Two of those eyewitnesses, Hattie and Regina Algood, sisters and friends of Taylor, testified for the defense.[182] Their version of the event in question differed from the prosecution's account in one significant respect: They testified that Bridges's brother, not Taylor, had a gun and fired into the group, hitting Bridges by mistake.[183]

Before trial, the prosecutor filed a discovery motion pursuant to Illinois rules that requires the defense to disclose the names and addresses of witnesses it intends to call at trial.[184] This was in accordance with Illinois Practice Rules, which provide for reciprocal discovery in all felony criminal cases.[185] Part of that reciprocal discovery includes a provision that requires the disclosure by both sides, upon written motion by either the prosecution or defense, of the names and addresses of all witnesses they intend to call at trial.[186]

In the response to the prosecution's request, defense counsel in *Taylor* provided the names of the two sisters who testified as well as the names of two men who did not testify.[187] He was permitted to amend his answer on the first day of trial by adding the name of two witnesses who did not testify. In fact, the only two witnesses who testified for the defense at trial were the two sisters.[188]

The source of controversy arose on the second day of trial. After the prosecution's two main witnesses completed their testimony, defense counsel sought to add the names of two witnesses to his answer to discovery. One of those two witnesses was Alfred Wormley,[189] whose testimony the trial judge would ultimately exclude.[190] To justify his addition of the two witnesses, defense counsel explained that "he had just been informed about them and that they had probably seen the 'entire incident.' "[191]

The trial judge questioned the late revelation of these two witnesses. Defense counsel explained that the defendant had informed him of these witnesses in advance of the trial but maintained that he had been unable to locate Wormley.[192] The judge was not satisfied with defense counsel's explanation, stating that the witnesses' names could have been furnished to the prosecution, even though their addresses were unknown. At that point in the trial, the trial court told defense counsel to produce the two new witnesses the next day, when he would decide whether they would testify. Further, the trial judge made the statement that "witnesses are being found that really weren't there."[193]

The next day Wormley appeared in court, whereupon the trial judge allowed defense counsel to make an offer of proof with Wormley's testimony outside the jury's presence.[194] Wormley testified that he had not witnessed the incident but that before the altercation he saw Jack Bridges and his brother with two guns in a blanket. Wormley also asserted that he heard Bridges and his brother say "they were after Ray [Taylor] and the other people," and that prior to the incident he had run into Taylor and his group and warned them "to watch out because they got weapons."[195]

The prosecutor, on cross-examination, elicited from Wormley that he first met the defendant (formally) two years after the incident occurred. He also admitted that defense counsel had visited him at his home the week before the trial began.[196] At the end of Wormley's testimony, the trial judge excluded Wormley's testimony as a sanction for the discovery violation.[197]

The trial judge's justification for excluding Wormley's testimony is instructive because it strikes at the core of the compulsory process clause and, specifically, at the precedent established by *Washington*. The trial judge's reasons for excluding the testimony were threefold: as a sanction for a "blatant" and "willful" violation of discovery rules; to deter further violations of discovery rules because of previous discovery violations by other defense attorneys in his courtroom; and because he seriously questioned the credibility of Alfred Wormley.[198]

It is also worthwhile to note that the trial judge chose to impose the most drastic remedy for noncompliance provided by the Illinois discovery rules.[199] Illinois Practice Rule 415 stipulates the penalties a trial judge may impose for violation of reciprocal discovery: The judge may order the noncomplying party to disclose the withheld information; she may grant a continuance; she may exclude the undisclosed evidence; and finally, she may enter whatever order she deems "just under the circumstances."[200] The conclusion one may draw from a full reading of the remedies provided by the rule is that exclusion is reserved for cases in which the evidence remains "undisclosed." In the *Taylor* case, however, the evidence was disclosed: Wormley was produced and testified subject to cross-examination, though admittedly he was produced late in the trial.

The Illinois Appellate Court affirmed Taylor's conviction,[201] holding that exclusion of evidence was a permissible sanction for the violation of discovery rules and leaving to the unfettered discretion of the trial judge the severity of the sanction imposed. The court thus reasoned that the trial court in Taylor "was within its discretion in refusing to allow the additional witnesses to testify."[202] After the Illinois Supreme Court rejected Taylor's appeal, the United States Supreme Court granted certiorari.[203]

Reliability and Integrity vs. Compulsory Process

The majority in *Taylor*[204] refers to *Washington v. Texas* only once in the main body of the opinion.[205] The answer to the *Taylor* Court's lack of reliance on *Washington*, however, is evident. The Court did not emphasize *Washington* because it ignored the basic postulates of the decision. In fact, the *Taylor* Court missed the primary lesson of *Washington*: that the defendant's right to present exculpatory evidence outweighs the court's interest in preventing perjured or otherwise potentially unreliable testimony.

The rationale of the *Taylor* decision is predicated upon a balancing perspective that weighs the "fundamental" right of the defendant "to offer the testimony of witnesses in his favor" against "countervailing public interests."[206] Those competing "interests" are the integrity of the adversary system, which depends on the admissibility of reliable evidence and the rejection of unreliable evidence; the need for the "fair" and "efficient" administration of justice; and the axiom that ascertaining truth is the ultimate objective of a trial.[207]

The linchpin of the *Taylor* decision is the Court's concern with the values of reliability and integrity as indispensable to the operation of the criminal justice system. The Court rejected Taylor's contention that the exclusion sanction should never override a criminal defendant's right to compulsory process by claiming that the public "has an interest in a full and truthful disclosure of critical facts"[208] and that the central feature of the discovery rule at issue in *Taylor* was "to minimize the risk that fabricated testimony will be believed."[209] At one juncture in *Taylor* the majority opinion stresses that the trial court has a "vital interest in protecting the trial process from the pollution of perjured testimony."[210]

Of course, this reasoning is at variance with the principal teaching of *Washington*. When the *Washington* Court invalidated the Texas competence statute disqualifying accomplices from testifying for one another, it unmistakably rejected the logic behind the rule. The underlying basis of the statute was to shield the jury from hearing potentially perjured testimony. The *Washington* Court repudiated such a rationale; in essence, it deemed the court's interest in preventing perjury subordinate to defendant's right to compulsory process.[211] Moreover, this fundamental axiom was applied to the prosecution in *Hoffa v. United States*.[212]

Admittedly, one may raise the objection that the testimony barred in *Washington* bore certain indicia of reliability because it was consistent with the defendant's testimony that the codefendant had fired the fatal shot that killed the victim.[213] On the other hand, Wormley's testimony in *Taylor* was regarded as "suspect" because he was identified by the defense at the "eleventh hour."[214] However, if one examines the testimony of Wormley, it does not seem as tainted as the *Taylor* Court implies.

Wormley testified that he saw the victim and his brother with guns wrapped in a blanket prior to the altercation.[215] In response to cross-examination by the prosecutor, Wormley admitted that he had met Taylor four months before the trial, or more than two years after the shooting occurred. Wormley also acknowledged during cross-examination that defense counsel had visited him the week before the trial began.[216]

Given this testimony, the likelihood that Wormley's testimony was not reliable or was "polluted" by perjury is negligible. If Wormley wanted to help Taylor by lying, he would not have admitted during cross-examination that he had not witnessed the shooting. Nor, for that matter, is it likely that Wormley would have acknowledged that he had formally known Taylor for four months and that defense counsel had visited him before the trial. Further, if Wormley had been properly coached by defense counsel, perhaps he would have verified the account of the sisters who testified on Taylor's behalf at trial. Finally, Wormley appears to have had little incentive to lie for Taylor, since they had known each other for a relatively short period of time. The bonds of friendship did not seem to have solidified to the point of giving Wormley a strong inducement to lie in Taylor's behalf.

Indeed, it is anomalous that the *Taylor* majority adopted the trial court's reasoning that "witnesses are being found that weren't there" to uphold the court's exclusion of Wormley's testimony.[217] In fact, Wormley admitted that "he wasn't there." Nevertheless, his testimony was critical to the defense.

In fact, the crucial issue the *Taylor* majority chose to ignore was the critical nature of Wormley's testimony for Taylor's defense. As Justice Brennan pointed out in dissent, the jury that convicted Taylor was "not permitted to hear evidence that would have both placed a gun in Bridges' brother's hands and contradicted the testimony of Bridges and his brother that they possessed no weapons that evening."[218] This testimony did not threaten the "integrity" of the criminal justice system, as the majority maintains.

Furthermore, Wormley's testimony was not cumulative or duplicative of the testimony of the other two defense witnesses. In effect, Wormley's testimony added a crucial ingredient to Taylor's defense: it established that the victim might have been armed. Moreover, the testimony was bolstered by the fact that Wormley was, by all indications, a relatively disinterested party. As the *Taylor* Court observed, the sisters who testified on Taylor's behalf were the defendant's "friends."[219] On the other hand, Wormley could hardly be classified as Taylor's "friend" because they had met a mere four months before the trial. Thus, Wormley's testimony would have corroborated the sisters' version of the incident and served to exculpate Taylor.

Even if the stringent criterion applied in *Valenzuela-Bernal* was employed by the *Taylor* Court, Wormley's testimony would not have been excluded. Of course, in *Valenzuela-Bernal* the Court stated that for the defendant to make a *prima facie* showing of a violation of compulsory process, she must establish the evidence was material and favorable to the defense.[220] As the preceding discussion and analysis clearly indicates, the testimony excluded in *Taylor* was material and favorable to the defense.

Wormley's testimony, moreover, suffered from no infirmity that would have warranted its exclusion under evidentiary rules. It is baffling that the *Taylor* Court, in rejecting the defendant's argument that the Sixth Amendment absolutely bars the exclusion of a defense witness's testimony, raised the objection that a criminal defendant "does not have the unfettered right to offer testimony that is incompetent, privileged, or otherwise inadmissible under standard rules of evidence."[221] As indicated, however, the testimony excluded in *Taylor* did not suffer from any of those deficiencies.[222] Rather, Wormley's testimony was excluded because it violated the Illinois reciprocal discovery rule.

As a result of the trial court's exclusion of Wormley's testimony, Taylor was prevented from presenting a "complete" defense. One may contrast the *Taylor* ruling, therefore, with the Court's holding in *Crane v. Kentucky* that the right to present a defense is superior to state evidentiary and procedural rules when such rules exclude competent, reliable evidence that supports a criminal defendant's claim of innocence.[223]

The *Taylor* majority upheld the trial court's exclusion of Wormley's vital testimony by rejecting Taylor's contentions that the compulsory process clause absolutely precludes the exclusion of defense evidence as a sanction for the violation of a discovery rule; and that even conceding the lack of an absolute preclusion of defense evidence, the exclusion of Wormley's testimony was inconsistent with the right to compulsory process.[224]

It is possible to argue, as Peter Westen has done, that a criminal defendant has a constitutional right to introduce any material evidence, regardless whether it is protected by an evidentiary privilege.[225] As Welsh White reminds us, however, such an approach might not be "pragmatic" in light of the current makeup of the Supreme Court.[226] Nonetheless, the defendant's second argument, that is, that given the specific facts of *Taylor* the preclusion of Wormley's testimony was constitutionally impermissible, is well-founded. It is worthwhile, therefore, to explore further the justifications for such an argument.

The underlying rationale of Taylor's argument that the preclusion sanction was unnecessary in his case rests on the commonsense notion that less drastic alternatives than exclusion were available to the trial court. Indeed, the majority readily acknowledged that Taylor was correct in making such an assumption.[227] The Court recognized that such alternative sanctions as a continuance, declaration of a mistrial, or disciplinary sanctions against the defendant or defense counsel could have minimized any harm to the prosecution.[228] In effect, the prosecution suffered little harm in *Taylor* because it was given the opportunity of cross-examining Wormley. In fact, the prosecution was able to discover more evidence than it would have under the discovery rule Taylor's counsel violated.[229] Under that rule, all the prosecution was entitled to discover before trial was the name of defense witnesses and any "relevant written or recorded statements." Admittedly, the prosecution may have been "surprised" by the defense's "eleventh-hour" witness, but any disadvantage the state may have endured was redressed when it was given the chance of cross-examining Wormley outside of the jury's presence.

Although the *Taylor* majority could not seriously rely on the argument that the prosecution suffered prejudice when Wormley was produced the second day of trial, it resorted again to its primary rationale: that the integrity of the adversary process required the drastic sanction of exclusion to prevent potentially perjured or unreliable evidence from tainting the outcome of the trial.[230] Of course, as the preceding discussion has demonstrated, such a rationale is entirely without foundation.

The proper solution to the trial court's problem in *Taylor* is suggested by the Court's discussion of the remedies available to cure unfair surprise to the prosecution in *Williams v. Florida*.[231] In that case the Court suggested the remedy of a continuance to negate the strategic advantage sought by the defense when it failed to reveal an alibi witness prior to trial.[232] In this connection, moreover, the supreme court of Mississippi has devised a solution that the trial court in *Taylor* could have profitably employed.

In *Houston v. State*,[233] the Mississippi supreme court discussed a procedure it has developed that reconciles the conflicting goals of the utilization of relevant, admissible evidence and the imperative of fairness to the party surprised by the late production of evidence or witnesses.[234] The standard summarized and applied in *Houston* directs the trial court to use a three-step procedure when confronted with any discovery violation. The procedure entails the following process: (1) upon objection by a party, the aggrieved party should be afforded a reasonable opportunity to become familiar with the undisclosed evidence; (2) if after this opportunity is offered, the objecting party still believes that it might suffer prejudice, it must request a continuance (failure to do so constitutes a waiver of the party's objection to the evidence); and (3) if the objecting party requests a continuance, the discovery violator may choose to proceed with the trial and forgo the use of the undisclosed evidence (if, however, the discovery violator is not willing to proceed without the evidence, the court must grant the requested continuance).[235]

Before the *Taylor* decision was rendered by the Court, in fact, most state courts had followed the ''less drastic'' means approach in dealing with discovery violations.[236] Furthermore, as Justice Blackmun's dissent in *Taylor* makes clear, the discovery rule at issue in *Taylor* was merely a general reciprocal discovery rule and did not involve the dangers normally associated with alibi defenses that notice-of-alibi rules are designed to prevent.[227] As Justice Brennan put it in dissent, the harsh sanction of preclusion imposed by the trial court and ratified by the majority of the Court in *Taylor*, ''distorts the truthseeking process by excluding material evidence of innocence in a criminal case.''[238] Furthermore, alternative sanctions ''are not only adequate to correct and deter discovery violations but are far superior to the arbitrary and disproportionate penalty imposed by the preclusion sanction.''[239]

Finally, the majority opinion seems to find support for its holding in the ''efficiency'' rationale by noting that the state's interest in an ''orderly conduct of a criminal trial'' warrants the invocation of ''firm'' rules regarding the presentation of evidence.[240] It is indeed perplexing that the Court values administrative efficiency to the extent of sacrificing a criminal defendant's right to present relevant, probative exculpatory evidence. This emphasis on ''efficiency'' and administrative concerns marks a disturbing trend for the Court in which it resorts to this reasoning to deny criminal defendants vital Sixth Amendment rights.[241]

In sum, the *Taylor* Court's misguided emphasis on reliability and integrity to sustain the exclusion of material, relevant evidence resulted in a "distortion" of the truth and the concomitant misapplication and denigration of the principal dictate of *Washington v. Texas*. The majority opinion, moreover, slighted the key corollaries of *Washington*'s mandate.

Is a Jury "Intelligent" Enough to Weigh Credibility?

One of the maxims the *Washington* opinion embodied is the right of a criminal defendant to present exculpatory, relevant evidence to a jury despite the possibility that such evidence might be perjured or otherwise unreliable.[242] The Court thereby renounced the assumptions of the common law rule that only disinterested parties should be permitted to testify because the "intelligence of jurors" could not be trusted.[243] As Justice Brennan's dissent asserts, by allowing the exclusion of Wormley's testimony because it was "presumably" unworthy of belief, the *Taylor* Court "usurped" the jury's chief function in our adversary system: to weigh the credibility of witnesses.[244] Of course, such an arrogation of the jury's function also contradicts the teachings of *Rock v. Arkansas*, as well as *Washington v. Texas*, that rules precluding a jury from hearing testimony because of its "presumptive unreliability" are constitutionally suspect.[245]

In our adversary system of adjudication, of course, cross-examination serves to ferret out false or unreliable testimony. Therefore, in *Taylor*, had the trial court permitted Wormley's testimony, the prosecutor could have effectively brought out any inconsistencies and discovered the "real" story during cross-examination. In fact, the prosecutor accomplished this task when he cross-examined Wormley outside of the jury's presence.[246] Instead, the jury's "intelligence" was called into question when the trial judge deprived it of the right to hear and assess the weight and credibility of Wormley's testimony.[247]

A Priori Categories and Compulsory Process

Closely connected with the principle that the jury ought to determine the credibility of relevant, probative, and otherwise admissible evidence is *Washington*'s holding that evidentiary rules designed to curtail perjury by precluding defense witnesses from testifying violate the compulsory process clause.[248] Of course, those rules are based on the notion that certain categories of defense witnesses are presumptively not worthy of belief.[249] In effect, as Justice Brennan argues, the majority in *Taylor* ratified the concept repudiated in *Washington* by implying that a defense witness who is not identified until the trial has begun is presumptively unworthy of belief and thus should be barred from testifying.[250]

Furthermore, the majority's exclusion of Wormley's testimony in *Taylor* contravenes the dictates of *Chambers* and *Rock*, which sanctioned the introduction of reliable hearsay statements as well as a defendant's post-hypnosis testimony despite evidentiary rules to the contrary.[251] The proper course for the trial court to follow in *Taylor* would have been to admit Wormley's testimony and to permit the prosecutor to comment on the defense's late disclosure of Wormley.[252] Rather than pursuing this sensible approach to the problem, however, the trial court indulged in the presumption of unbelief that *Washington* and its progeny repudiated. Unfortunately, the Supreme Court endorsed the trial court's arbitrary preclusion of Wormley's testimony.

Visit the Sins of the Lawyer on the Client?

An intriguing part of the *Taylor* decision is the majority's rejection of Taylor's contention that his constitutional right to compulsory process should not be curtailed because of an ethical violation by his counsel.[253] The majority's response to this argument is disingenuous and utterly lacking in logic. In essence, the majority's argument is that a criminal defendant is bound by the tactical decisions of his attorney because the lawyer must have "full authority to manage the conduct of the trial."[254] The efficiency rationale again rears its ugly head, as the Court maintains that "the adversary process could not function effectively if every tactical decision required client approval."[255]

As Justice Brennan argued in dissent, this argument presupposes that one may categorize defense counsel's conduct in failing to identify Wormley as "tactical" in nature. An attorney does not have the freedom to engage in conduct that "includes misconduct as an option."[256] Moreover, the Court's perspective leads to a conflict of interest between defendant and counsel. Justice Brennan observed that defense counsel in *Taylor* became less than zealous when the trial judge threatened to expose his actions to the bar disciplinary commission.[257] In a case where a willful discovery violation by defense counsel occurs, therefore, it is unrealistic to expect that defense counsel will protect his client's interests when those interests clash with counsel's professional reputation.[258]

More importantly, the majority's position in this respect significantly abridges a criminal defendant's *personal* constitutional right to compulsory process and to a complete and effective defense as a sanction for her counsel's violation of a procedural rule and possible violation of the professional code of ethics. If we accept Justice Brennan's conclusion that the trial court excluded Wormley's crucial testimony to punish defense counsel for "purposely lying" about when he had located Wormley,[259] then the sins of the defense attorney were visited upon the defendant. The upshot of this decision was that Taylor's personal constitutional rights were sacrificed as punishment for his attorney's alleged "ethical" violation.

Given the notion advanced by the Court that constitutional rights are personal and cannot be vicariously asserted,[260] it is ironic indeed that the *Taylor* Court is willing to circumscribe a vital constitutional trial right of a criminal defendant in part to sanction defense counsel for a procedural or ethical violation. Indeed, as Justice Brennan remarks, such alternatives as the imposition of fines, or the threat of incarceration or disciplinary proceedings, are far more effective in deterring attorney misconduct than the exclusionary remedy.[261]

In fact, the dissent in *Taylor* could have marshalled another effective argument to counter the majority's approval of the exclusionary sanction for defense counsel's discovery violation. The Court in *United States v. Leon*[262] gave its approval to the "good-faith" exception to the exclusionary rule.[263] The majority's rationale centered on the assumption that a police officer who secured a search warrant in "good faith" reliance of its validity would not be deterred by the exclusionary sanction. The same argument could be applied to *Taylor*. That is, why should the defendant be penalized by the exclusionary sanction from presenting critical, probative exculpatory evidence when he acts in good-faith reliance on his counsel's representation? Further, if one accepts *Leon*'s rationale, why impose the exclusionary remedy when the likelihood of deterrence is minimal, if not illusory?

Furthermore, the Court recently held in *Arizona v. Youngblood*[264] that the good-faith rationale should apply when the government loses or destroys potentially useful evidence in good faith. In fact, the interesting aspect of *Youngblood* is that the Court employs *Valenzuela-Bernal* to bolster its holding that "unless a criminal defendant can show bad faith on the part of the police, failure to preserve potentially useful evidence does not constitute a denial of due process of law."[265] The Court clearly proposes a double standard in which good faith may be asserted by the prosecution to rebut a due process claim by the defendant but the defendant may not reciprocate by resorting to a good-faith argument in attempting to preserve a vital trial-related constitutional right.

Justice Brennan's dissenting opinion, therefore, is not only more consistent with precedent but also is grounded on a strong logical foundation. His position, briefly stated, is that if the defendant does not participate in the discovery violation, the exclusionary sanction is "arbitrary and disproportionate to the purposes of discovery and criminal justice and should be *per se* unconstitutional."[266]

Taylor and the Criminal Justice System: An Assessment

The majority opinion in *Taylor* has distressing implications for criminal defendants as well as for the criminal process in general. It seems that the Court is willing to apply severe sanctions to the defense but not to the prosecution. The Court's "misgivings" about applying the exclusionary rule to prevent the prosecution from introducing otherwise admissible, probative evidence did not worry the majority in *Taylor*.[267] More important, the Court's application of the exclusionary rule in *Taylor* alters the balance of power in a criminal trial by making it easier for the prosecution to obtain a conviction.

The prosecution's advantage in *Taylor* may be readily discerned by examining the dynamics of the case and, in particular, the effect of the discovery rule at issue in the case. One may readily conclude that the discovery rule Taylor's counsel contravened clearly favors the prosecution. This proposition is supported by Justice Douglas's prescient concurring opinion in *Wardius v. Oregon*.[268] In that opinion, Justice Douglas maintained that the guarantees accorded criminal defendants in the Bill of Rights do not contemplate an "adversary proceeding between two equal parties."[269] Rather, these rights are designed to rectify the prosecution's enormous advantage in investigative and other resources *vis-à-vis* the criminal defendant.[270]

Viewed from this perspective, the reciprocal discovery rule at issue in *Taylor*[271] does not seem as neutral as it appears at first glance. By allowing the prosecution to discover the names and addresses of witnesses the defendant intends to call at trial and any statements made by the witnesses, the rule gives the government an insight into the defense's case. Therefore, the prosecution not only enjoys its inherent investigative advantage over the defendant but also gets a glimpse of the defendant's possible strategy at trial. Further, the reciprocal discovery rule in *Taylor* was not intended to prevent the last-minute fabricated testimony that notice-of-alibi rules supposedly guard against.

The exclusion in *Taylor* of Wormley's testimony, moreover, diminished the prosecution's burden to establish *Taylor*'s guilt beyond a reasonable doubt. *In re Winship*[272] establishes the prosecution's burden of proof and delineates the fundamental tenet that our criminal adversary process prefers a wrongful acquittal over a mistaken conviction.[273] Furthermore, in *Cool v. United States*[274] the Court invalidated an instruction to the effect that an accomplice's testimony should be disregarded unless the jury believed that it was true beyond a reasonable doubt because the instruction reduced the government's burden of proof.[275] The Court in *Cool* reached this conclusion on the ground that the instruction created "an artificial barrier" to the jury's weighing of relevant, material exculpatory evidence.[276]

In *Taylor*, of course, the jury did not have the opportunity to hear Wormley's material, exculpatory evidence linking the victim's brother to the gun that injured the victim. This evidence could have created reasonable doubt in the juror's minds and therefore led to an acquittal or, possibly, to a hung jury. The trial court's exclusion of Wormley's testimony, however, precluded the defendant from planting the seed of doubt in the jury's mind and thereby eased the prosecution's burden of proving guilt beyond a reasonable doubt.

The *Taylor* decision represents the crowning triumph of the "sporting theory" of justice. The ruling exalts procedure over substance to unparalleled heights. The Court engages in "doublespeak" when it quotes *United States v. Nixon* for the proposition that ends of justice are ill-served if "judgments were to be founded on a partial or speculative presentation of the facts."[277] By denying the defendant the right to present a complete defense, the *Taylor* Court permitted his conviction to rest on an incomplete presentation of the facts. In an effort to rigidly preserve the "sanctity of discovery,"[278] the Court upheld Taylor's conviction "in the interest of fair play."[279] The Court's attempt to achieve "fairness" in the criminal justice process produced an eminently "unjust" result for Ray Taylor and for the criminal justice system.

Postscript to *Taylor*: *Michigan v. Lucas*

In keeping with its philosophy in *Taylor*, the Court has ratified the preclusion remedy in circumstances where a defendant charged with rape does not notify the prosecution before trial of his intention to introduce evidence of his previous sexual conduct with the victim. In *Michigan v. Lucas*,[280] the defendant was prevented from offering testimony at trial of his previous sexual relationship with the victim because of his failure to comply with a "notice-and-hearing" requirement of the applicable "rape-shield" statute. Naturally, the defendant's defense at trial was consent.[281]

Though the *Lucas* Court remanded the case to the state courts to determine whether preclusion was warranted under the circumstances of the case, it held that failure to comply with a notice requirement of a "rape-shield" statute "may in some cases justify even the severe sanction of preclusion."[282] Therefore, where the defendant raises a defense of consent, and the alleged victim and the accused have had a previous sexual relationship, evidence of that relationship is relevant. The *Lucas* majority intimates that, given a flagrant violation of the notice rule, preclusion might be appropriate. This would be a perverse result in a case such as *Lucas*, where the prosecution could not claim surprise because the victim had admitted to prior sexual relations with Lucas at the preliminary hearing.[283] Again, the ruling comports with the Court's restrictive view of the purposes served by the compulsory process clause.

INTEGRITY, RELIABILITY, AND THE EXCLUSIONARY RULE: ARE THEY REALLY THAT IMPORTANT TO THE SUPREME COURT?

Paradoxically, the *Taylor* Court's ratification of the exclusionary remedy in *Taylor* is at odds with the Court's recent antipathy toward the exclusionary rule. In fact, Justice Brennan expresses this contradiction in his dissenting opinion in *Taylor*.[284] Justice Brennan's analysis of this dichotomy, however, is conclusory. This section, therefore, will elaborate upon the dissent's exposition of this contradiction in light of the Court's devaluation of the exclusionary remedy as applied to the prosecution and will examine the enigmatic stress on integrity and reliability by the *Taylor* Court in light of the Court's recent depreciation of those values.

The Exclusionary Rule and *Taylor*

The Supreme Court's hostility toward the effects of the exclusionary remedy reached its apogee in *United States v. Leon*.[285] *Leon* was previously analyzed in relation to the *Taylor* Court's imposition of the exclusionary remedy as a sanction for defense counsel's discovery violation.[286] It is necessary to revisit *Leon*, however, in order to apply it in a broader context. Of course, in *Leon* the Court fashioned the "good-faith" exception to the exclusionary rule. In broad terms, *Leon* stands for the proposition that in circumstances wherein police officers obtain a search warrant in "good faith" and the warrant is subsequently invalidated because it was issued without probable cause, the exclusionary rule will not be applied.[287] The policy rationale of the majority centered on the argument that the cost of suppressing such evidence far outweighed the benefits, since the deterrence objective underlying the exclusionary remedy would not be served when police officers obtain a warrant in the objectively reasonable "good faith" belief that is valid.

If the *Taylor* Court had adhered to the reasoning upon which *Leon* is grounded, it would not have suppressed Wormley's testimony. Weighing the "costs" and "benefits" of exclusion in *Taylor* yields the unequivocal conclusion that the costs of excluding Wormley's testimony superseded the benefits of suppression. The costs of suppression were substantial: the exclusion of material, relevant evidence that exculpated the defendant and that might have swayed the jury by creating reasonable doubt. By contrast, the benefits of excluding Wormley's testimony are negligible. If the Court was seeking general deterrence of future discovery violations by defense counsel, it is unlikely that the suppression of Wormley's testimony had its desired effect. Defense counsel did not suffer any punitive sanctions for the violation; rather, Taylor paid the "costs" of his counsel's transgression through the exclusion of Wormley's testimony.

If the *Taylor* Court's concern with the integrity of the criminal process and the reliability of testimony is the focus of its decision, as this chapter maintains, the benefits again fall short of the costs exacted by exclusion. Quite simply, the primary cost of suppression was significant: the jury that convicted Taylor was barred from hearing testimony that would have had an effect on the determination of guilt. The worst-case scenario of this suppression is that, because of the delay in discovery, "an innocent man may be serving ten years in prison."[288] The benefits, on the other hand, are minimal at best, nonexistent at worst. Apart from the Court's deviation from precedent, even if it believed that the trial court was correct in keeping perjured or presumptively perjured testimony from the jury, the net effect of its ruling was to insult the intelligence of the jurors, who had the option of rejecting Wormley's testimony.

Integrity, the Exclusionary Rule, and *Taylor*

Not only is the *Taylor* Court's deprecation of its own doctrine regarding the exclusionary rule contradictory, but it also is rather baffling that the key reasoning of *Taylor* rests on the integrity rationale. Indeed, the Court weighs the right of the defendant to compulsory process against the "integrity of the adversary process" and finds that integrity is more important than compulsory process.[289]

By contrast, the Court has abandoned integrity as a rationale for the exclusionary rule.

As previously mentioned,[290] the principal objective of the exclusionary rule is deterrence of police misconduct. However, another compelling rationale of the exclusionary rule is "the imperative of judicial integrity."[291] Of course, the "imperative of judicial integrity" is predicated on the notion that courts condone the violation of the Constitution by admitting evidence that is tainted because it was illegally obtained. The erosion of the integrity rationale as support for the exclusionary rule, however, is unmistakable. It began with *United States v. Calandra*[292] and has continued unabated, to the point that the Court has completely dispensed with integrity as a basis for the rule.[293]

In light of this eradication of the integrity rationale as a basis for the exclusionary rule, it is ironic that the *Taylor* decision relies so heavily on integrity to exclude the testimony of a witness who was willing to offer material, relevant evidence helpful to the defendant. One can only explain this manifest inconsistency by assuming that integrity is important to the Court when it adversely affects the defendant but is irrelevant when integrity might detract from the government's ability to secure a conviction.

Reliability, *Connelly*, and *Taylor*

The integrity of the adversary system, the majority in *Taylor* insists, "depends . . . on the presentation of reliable evidence and the rejection of unreliable evidence."[294] What is truly remarkable about this statement is that the Court in *Colorado v. Connelly*[295] rejected out of hand the notion that reliability was worthy of constitutional concern or protection under the due process clause of the Fourteenth Amendment.[296] The *Connelly* Court held that, absent coercion by the police, the confession of an insane defendant is "voluntary" and hence admissible into evidence and does not violate the due process clause of the Fourteenth Amendment.[297]

More important, the *Connelly* Court emphasized the considerable costs exacted by the exclusionary rule and cited the deterrence rationale as the sole basis for the rule.[298] It is instructive, moreover, to juxtapose the *Connelly* Court's statement that it had "previously cautioned against expanding 'currently applicable exclusionary rules by erecting additional barriers to placing truthful and probative evidence before state juries,"[299] with the *Taylor* decision.

The "truthful and probative" evidence the Court in *Connelly* declared constitutionally admissible into evidence was the confession of a defendant who suffered from chronic schizophrenia at the time he confessed.[300] The *Connelly* Court readily acknowledged that such a confession might be less than "reliable." Nonetheless, although the Court recognized that Connelly's confession might "be proved to be quite unreliable," it deemed such an issue not worthy of constitutional concern and best left to "the evidentiary laws of the forum."[301] Indeed, the Court went as far as to declare that, "[t]he aim of the requirement of due process is not to exclude presumptively false evidence, but to prevent fundamental unfairness in the use of evidence, whether true or false."[302]

A comparison of the evidence suppressed because of its putative "unreliability" in *Taylor* and the confession the Court in *Connelly* did not view as constitutionally suspect yields only one conclusion: Reliability is important for the Court as far as the defendant is concerned but is of no consequence with regard to the prosecution. Wormley's testimony was that of a sane, competent individual who was subject to cross-examination by the government. Although one might argue that Wormley's testimony was tainted by its "eleventh-hour" nature, it surely bore as many, if not more, indicia of reliability as Connelly's confession. In effect, the Court seems to be comfortable with a double standard that favors the government and curtails a criminal defendant's critical trial-related constitutional rights.

CONCLUSION

Is our adversary process of adjudication excessively procedural and therefore "blind" to justice, as Pound argued in his landmark address to the American Bar Association more than eight decades ago? The Supreme Court seems to agree with Pound's assessment of our adjudicatory system, at least insofar as it affects the criminal process and, particularly, to the degree it suppresses material, relevant evidence sought to be introduced by the prosecution at trial.

In *Taylor v. Illinois*, however, the Court subscribed to the "sporting theory" of justice with a vengeance. In the name of "procedural" consistency, the *Taylor* Court excluded relevant, probative, otherwise admissible exculpatory evidence that could have altered the course of the trial. In the process of doing so, the Court deprived the defendant of a vital constitutional right deeply embedded in our jurisprudence: the right of the defendant to compulsory process for obtaining and presenting witnesses in her favor.

It is a sad commentary on the jurisprudence of the Supreme Court that a state supreme court has shed more wisdom on the issue of the extent to which discovery rules should interfere with a defendant's right to compulsory process than the *Taylor* Court's flawed analysis of the matter. In *Houston v. State*,[303] the Mississippi supreme court described the function of a criminal trial as a "trial for life and liberty [and] not a game."[304] The court put discovery rules in perspective by classifying them as "not an end in themselves but a means to the end that we dare call justice."[305] More important, the court adhered to principle first enunciated in *Washington v. Texas*[306] that procedural and, specifically, discovery rules ought to be applied with a view toward the fact-finder, whether judge or jury, receiving all "relevant and otherwise admissible" evidence.[307]

The decision of the Court in *Taylor* represents the ultimate glorification of the "sporting theory" a majority of the Court has decried on many occasions. Procedural rigidity, however, seemed to suit the purposes of the *Taylor* Court because the aggrieved party was the defendant, not the government. In essence, the *Taylor* Court ''evened'' the score by reversing the trend begun in *Washington* that stressed substantive justice and eschewed strict procedural conformity.

NOTES

1. Pound, *The Causes of Popular Dissatisfaction with the Administration of Justice*, 29 A.B.A. REP. 395 (1906).

2. Id. at 404–06.

3. Id. at 406.

4. Pound limited his comments to the civil area, specifically excluding the criminal realm, because he thought the civil arena more worthy of concern, id. at 396. For three examples of the application of Pound's theory to the criminal process, *see* Caplan, *Questioning* Miranda, 38 VAND. L. REV. 1417, 1440–43 (1985) (arguing that the sporting theory gives the defendant an undue advantage); Grano, Miranda v. Arizona *and the Legal Mind: Formalism's Triumph over Substance and Reason*, 24 AM. CRIM. L. REV. 243, 267 (1986) (sporting theory as applied in *Miranda* leads to unwarranted formalism to the detriment of justice); Grano, *Implementing the Objectives of Procedural Reform: The Proposed Michigan Rules of Criminal Procedure—Part I*, 32 WAYNE L. REV. 1007, 1019–22 (1986) (attacking the sporting theory of justice in the criminal context).

5. Pound explained that the adversary process undermined public confidence in the legal system by fostering the skewed notion that procedure was a means toward evasion of substantive justice. He noted that, ''The effect of our contentious procedure is not only to irritate parties, witnesses and jurors in particular cases, but to give the whole community a false notion of the purpose and end of law. Hence comes, in large measure, the modern American race to beat the law. If the law is a mere game, neither the players who take part in it nor the public who witness it can be expected to yield to its spirit when their interests are served by evading it,'' Pound, *supra* note 1, at 406.

6. *See*, e.g., Simon, *The Ideology of Advocacy: Procedural Justice and Professional Ethics*, 1978 WIS. L. REV. 29; Miller, *The Adversary System: Dinosaur or Phoenix*, 69 MINN. L. REV. 1 (1984); Saltzburg, *Lawyers, Clients, and the Adversary System*, 37 MERCER L. REV. 647 (1986); Steffen, *Truth as Second Fiddle: Reevaluating the Place of Truth in the Adversarial Trial Ensemble*, 1988 UTAH L. REV. 799.; Sward, *Values, Ideology, and the Evolution of the Adversary System*, 64 IND. L. J. 301 (1986); Weinreb, DENIAL OF JUSTICE (1977); Frankel, PARTISAN JUSTICE (1980) and *The Search for Truth: An Umpireal View*, 123 U. PA. L. REV. 1031 (1975); Landsman, THE ADVERSARY SYSTEM: A DESCRIPTION AND DEFENSE (1984).

7. *Compare*, e.g., Saltzburg, *supra* note 6 at 651 (arguing that ''The American adversary system is misdescribed as a search for truth''); *with* Steffen, *supra* note 6 at 803 (contending that ''truth should be the reigning objective of every trial''). The specific application of the adversary system to the criminal sphere has multiple facets; that is, a criminal trial allegedly serves the varied objectives of finding the truth, producing a fair decision, protecting the defendant from possible governmental abuse, and generating norms accepted by the public. These goals are not mutually exclusive; rather, they shade into one another. *See* Goodpaster, *On the Theory of American Adversary Criminal Trial*, 78 J. CRIM. L. & CRIMINOLOGY 118, 121–44 (1987).

8. *See*, e.g., Grano, Miranda v. Arizona *and the Legal Mind*, *supra* note 4, at 276.

("Under the dictates of *Miranda*'s black-letter formalism, we have thus reached a point in our jurisprudence that judges feel constrained to suppress reliable statements even though they acknowledge that the *Miranda* warnings in the particular context would be counterproductive in terms of everyone's interest and even though the statements obtained have not been compelled.") *But see*, Maclin, *Constructing Fourth Amendment Principles from the Government Perspective: Whose Amendment Is It, Anyway?*, 25 AM. CRIM. L. REV. 669 (the U.S. Supreme Court's interpretation of the Fourth Amendment has resulted in the diminution of rights afforded defendants pursuant to that amendment).

9. The rule was initially applied by the United States Supreme Court in the seminal case of *Weeks v. United States*, 232 U.S. 383 (1913). In *Mapp v. Ohio*, 367 U.S. 643, 655 (1961), the Court made the application of the rule a constitutional requirement. The rule was invoked for a Fourth Amendment violation in *Mapp*. It was also applied with respect to the Fifth Amendment initially in *Bram v. United States*, 168 U.S. 532, 542–43 (1897) (Fifth Amendment privilege against self-incrimination bars the use of involuntary confessions in federal court) and also in *Miranda v. Arizona*, 384 U.S. 436 (1966), in which the Court held that any inculpatory or exculpatory statements in response to police questioning made by a defendant in custody without the appropriate *Miranda* warnings and a proper waiver of the *Miranda* rights is inadmissible, id. at 444–45. The Court has also applied the rule with regard to the Sixth Amendment. *See*, e.g., *United States v. Wade*, 388 U.S. 218, 237–39 (1967) (excluding identification by witness because of post-indictment lineup conducted without counsel in violation of the Sixth Amendment); and *Massiah v. United States*, 377 U.S. 201, 206–07 (1964) (excluding statements deliberately elicited by government agent after the defendant had been indicted and secured counsel).

10. *Mapp v. Ohio*, 367 U.S. 643, 656, 659 (1961).

11. *See*, e.g., *United States v. Leon*, 468 U.S. 897, 921 (1984).

12. *United States v. Calandra*, 414 U.S. 338, 348 (1974).

13. *See*, e.g., *United States v. Leon*, 468 U.S. at 920–21, crafting a "good-faith" exception to the rule for evidence obtained by police officers relying on a search warrant later determined to be lacking probable cause. The Court's reasoning was that the exclusionary rule would not deter police misconduct under such circumstances.

14. In holding that constitutional rights are personal and that the exclusionary rule is not applicable to a party whose rights are not violated by public officials, the Court noted in *Alderman v. United States*, 394 U.S. 165, 174–75 (1969), that: "[W]e are not convinced that the additional benefits of extending the exclusionary rule to other defendants would justify further encroachment upon the public interest in prosecuting those accused of crime and having them convicted on the basis of all the evidence which exposes the truth."

15. 484 U.S. 400 (1988).

16. Id. at 415–16.

17. Id. at 416.

18. In *Colorado v. Connelly*, 479 U.S. 157, 166 (1986), the Court did not object to the admission of a presumptively unreliable confession. *See infra*. For a critique and analysis of *Connelly*, *see* Garcia, *Mental Sanity and Confessions: The Supreme Court's New Version of the Old "Voluntariness" Standard*, 21 AKRON L. REV. 275 (1988).

19. The Sixth Amendment provides in pertinent part that "[i]n all criminal prosecutions, the accused shall enjoy the right to . . . have compulsory process for obtaining witnesses in his favor," U.S. CONST. Amend. VI.

20. Madison drafted all of the provisions incorporated in the Sixth Amendment with the exception of the part dealing with trial in the state and district where the crime was committed. *See*, e.g., Westen, *The Compulsory Process Clause*, 73 MICH. L. REV. 76, n. 7 (1974) (citing Goebel, 1 HISTORY OF THE SUPREME COURT OF THE UNITED STATES 430–31, 437–38, 442–43, 449, 455 (1971)); Heller, THE SIXTH AMENDMENT TO THE CONSTITUTION OF THE UNITED STATES 29–30 (1951).

21. *See* Westen, *supra* note 20, at 77; Heller, *supra* note 20, at 30–34.

22. Westen, *supra* note 20, at 78, 79–101.

23. *United States v. Burr*, 25 F. Cas. 30 (No. 14,692d) (C.C.D. Va. 1807); *United States v. Burr*, 25 F. Cas. 27 (No. 14,694) (C.C.D. Va. 1807).

24. 4 Dall. (4 U.S.) 341 (Cir. Ct., D. Pa., 1800). Justice Chase, of course, was "riding circuit" when he decided this case.

25. The compulsory process Burr sought revolved around two crucial letters that formed the heart of the case against him. The letters allegedly exposed Burr's plot to create a separate country under his control by invading Mexico and dissolving the states west of the Alleghenies. These letters were allegedly in President Jefferson's possession, since he had used them to inform Congress of Burr's plot and to establish Burr's supposed guilt in the matter. As a result of Jefferson's message, Burr was arrested and bound over to a grand jury in Richmond, Virginia. *See* Westen, *supra* note 20, at 102–03.

26. *United States v. Burr*, 25 F. Cas. at 33.

27. Marshall noted that: "Perhaps the court ought to consider the reasons which would induce the president to refuse to exhibit such a letter as conclusive on [the privilege], unless such letter could be shown to be absolutely necessary in the defense. . . . But on objections being made by the president to the production of a paper, the court would not proceed further in the case without such an affidavit as would clearly show the paper to be essential to the case," *United States v. Burr*, 25 F. Cas. at 192.

28. 418 U.S. 683, 709–13 (1974). *See infra* for a discussion of *Nixon*.

29. As Westen notes, until 1967, the Supreme Court dealt with the clause on five occasions, twice in dictum and three times in refusing to construe it, Westen, *supra* note 20, at 108. Those five cases were: *Pate v. Robinson*, 383 U.S. 375, 378, n.1 (1966); *Blackmer v. United States*, 284 U.S. 421, 442 (1932); *United States v. Van Duzee*, 140 U.S. 169, 173 (1891); *Ex parte Harding*, 120 U.S. 782 (1887); *United States v. Reid*, 53 U.S. (12 How.) 361, 363–65, *overruled* in *Rosen v. United States*, 245 U.S. 467 (1918); id. n.164.

30. 388 U.S. 14 (1967).

31. Id. at 19.

32. Id. at 22–23.

33. Id. at 15–16.

34. Id. at 16–17.

35. Id. at 17–19.

36. Id. at 18.

37. Id. at 19.

38. Id. at 21–22.

39. Id. at 21 (quoting *Benson v. United States*, 146 U.S. 325, 335 (1892)).

40. Id. at 22. The Court quoted from *Rosen v. United States*, 245 U.S. 467, 471 (1918). The Court also noted that even though *Rosen* was not constitutionally based, its logic was required by the Sixth Amendment, id.

41. Id. at 23. The Court qualified its holding by asserting in a footnote that "Nothing

in this opinion should be construed as disapproving testimonial privileges . . . which are based on entirely different considerations from those underlying the common law disqualifications for interest. Nor do we deal in this case with nonarbitrary state rules that disqualify as witnesses persons who, because of mental infirmity or infancy, are incapable of observing events or testifying about them,'' id. n. 21.

42. Id. at 22. The Court correctly observed that the testimony of an accomplice who testified for the prosecution had a greater likelihood of being perjured, since such an accomplice obviously had a tremendous inducement to lie, id. Moreover, the majority exposed the faulty logic of the statutes by stating that: ''To think that criminals will lie to save their fellows but not to obtain favors from the prosecution for themselves is indeed to clothe the criminal class with more nobility than one might expect to find in the public at large,'' id. at 22–23.

43. Id. at 24–25 (Harlan, J., concurring).

44. Id. at 21. In rejecting the justification for the Texas statutes disqualifying co-participants in a crime from testifying for each other, the Court remarked that such rules ''[r]ested on the unstated premises that the right to present witnesses was subordinate to the court's interest in preventing perjury, and that erroneous decisions were best avoided by preventing the jury from hearing any testimony that might be perjured, even if it were the only testimony available on a crucial issue,'' id.

45. 146 U.S. 325 (1892).

46. *Washington v. Texas*, 388 U.S. at 21 (quoting from *Benson v. United States*, 146 U.S. at 336).

47. 385 U.S. 293 (1966).

48. Id. at 310–11.

49. Id. at 311.

50. Id. at 311–12. It should be pointed out that the trial judge in *Hoffa* instructed the jury on weighing the informer's testimony as follows: ''You should carefully scrutinize the testimony given and the circumstances under which each witness has testified, and every matter in evidence which tends to indicate whether the witness is worthy of belief. Consider each witness' intelligence, his motives, state of mind, his demeanor and manner while on the witness stand. Consider also any relation each witness may bear to either side of the case. . . . All evidence of a witness whose self-interest is shown from either benefits received, detriments suffered, threats or promises made, or any attitude of the witness which might tend to prompt testimony either favorable or unfavorable to the accused should be considered with caution and weighed with care,'' id. at 312 n.14.

51. *See*, e.g., *Imbler v. Pachtman*, 424 U.S. 404, 440 (1976) (White, J., concurring); *Jackson v. Virginia*, 443 U.S. 307, 319 (1979); *Bronston v. United States*, 409 U.S. 352, 359–60 (1973); *Brooks v. Tennessee*, 406 U.S. 605, 611 (1972); *Hoffa v. United States*, 385 U.S. at 311.

52. *See*, e.g., *Pointer v. Texas*, 380 U.S. 400, 404 (1965); *Bronston v. United States*, 409 U.S. at 358–60.

53. 409 U.S. 100 (1972).

54. Id. at 104.

55. Id. The trial judge issued the following instruction to the jury: ''[I] charge you that the testimony of an accomplice is competent evidence and it is for you to pass upon the credibility thereof. If the testimony carries conviction and you are convinced it is true *beyond a reasonable doubt*, the jury should give it the same effect as you would to a witness not in any respect implicated in the alleged crime and you are not only justified,

but it is your duty, not to throw this testimony out because it comes from a tainted source,'' id. at 102 (emphasis added by the Court).

56. In effect, the trial court suggested to the jury that the accomplice's testimony was not worthy of belief by stating in its instruction that the jury should not disregard the testimony because it derived from a ''tainted'' source, id. at 102.

57. 397 U.S. 358 (1970).

58. *Cool v. United States*, 409 U.S. at 104.

59. Id.

60. 409 U.S. 95 (1972) (per curiam).

61. Id. at 98.

62. Id. at 95.

63. Id. at 96. The judge told the witness: ''If you take the witness stand and lie under oath, the Court will personally see that your case goes to the grand jury and you will be indicted for perjury and the liklihood [*sic*] is that you would get convicted of perjury and that it would be stacked onto what you have already got, so that is the matter you have got to make up your mind on. If you get on the witness stand and lie, it is probably going to mean several years and at least more time that you are going to have to serve. It will also be held against you in the penitentiary when you're up for parole and the Court wants you to thoroughly understand the chances you're taking by getting on that witness stand under oath. You may tell the truth and if you do, that is all right, but if you lie you can get into real trouble. The court wants you to know that. You don't owe anybody anything to testify and it must be done freely and voluntarily and with the thorough understanding that you know the hazards you are taking,'' id.

64. Id.

65. Id. at 98.

66. Id.

67. Id. (quoting *Washington v. Texas*, 388 U.S. at 19).

68. 410 U.S. 284 (1972).

69. Id. at 292–93.

70. Id.

71. Id. at 294.

72. *In re Oliver*, 333 U.S. 257 (1948).

73. *Chambers v. Mississippi*, 410 U.S. at 302.

74. Id. The hearsay evidence in this case bore assurances of trustworthiness since it was corroborated by other evidence in the case: to wit, the confession of Gabe McDonald, who Chambers claimed committed the crime, the testimony of eyewitnesses to the shooting (Chambers was charged with murdering a policeman), testimony establishing that McDonald owned a revolver of the same caliber as the murder weapon, and testimony that McDonald was seen with a gun at the scene or the crime, id. at 300.

75. 418 U.S. 683 (1974).

76. *See supra* notes 23–27 and accompanying text.

77. *United States v. Nixon*, 418 U.S. at 709.

78. Id. at 711. The Court affirmed that: ''The right to the production of all evidence in a criminal trial has constitutional dimensions.''

79. Id. at 713.

80. Id. at 713.

81. *See infra*.

82. 485 U.S. 858 (1982).

83. Id. at 872–73.

84. Id. at 864–65.

85. Id. at 860. Specifically, the defendant was indicted for violating 8 U.S.C. Sec. 1324 (a)(2), which prohibits the transportation of ''any alien,'' ''knowing that [the alien] is in the United States in violation of law, and knowing or having any reasonable grounds to believe that his last entry into the United States occurred less than three years prior'' to the transportation or attempted transportation with which the person is charged, id., n.1.

86. Id. at 861.

87. Id. A third passenger was detained to establish the defendant's violation of the statute, id.

88. Id. at 860–61.

89. Id. at 865.

90. The majority was concerned with restricting prosecutorial discretion to deport aliens, noting that the ''conceivable benefits'' rule ''significantly constrains the Government's prosecutorial discretion,'' id. at 865.

91. The Court rejected as overly broad the ''conceivable benefits'' rule embodied in *United States v. Mendez-Rodriguez*, 450 F.2d 1 (9th Cir. 1971), which found a constitutional violation when ''the alien's testimony could conceivably benefit the defendant.'' *United States v. Valenzuela-Bernal*, 458 U.S. at 862. The majority in *Valenzuela-Bernal* added that the adoption of the ''conceivable benefits'' test unduly restricted prosecutorial discretion, id. at 865.

92. Id. at 867.

93. Id.

94. Id. (emphasis added by the Court) (quoting from *Washington v. Texas*, 388 U.S. at 16).

95. *Washington v. Texas*, 388 U.S. at 23.

96. 353 U.S. 53 (1957).

97. Id. at 64–65. In *Roviaro*, the informer was the only witness, other than the defendant, to the crime (a drug sale), id.

98. *United States v. Valenzuela-Bernal*, 458 U.S. at 871.

99. Id. at 883–84 (Brennan, J., dissenting).

100. Id. at 884.

101. Id. at 884–85.

102. *See*, e.g., *Richardson v. Marsh*, 481 U.S. 200 (1987). In that case, the Court emphasized administrative considerations (i.e., the efficiency of a joint trial for the smooth operation of the criminal justice system) in denying a criminal defendant the right to confront her accuser (that is, her codefendant). *See* Garcia, *The Winding Path of* Bruton v. United States: *A Case of Doctrinal Inconsistency*, 26 AM. CRIM. L. REV. 401, 420 (1988) for a critique of *Marsh*.

103. 484 U.S. 400 (1988).

104. 399 U.S. 78 (1970).

105. 412 U.S. 479 (1973).

106. *See*, e.g., *Taliafero v. Maryland*, 461 U.S. 948 (1983); *United States* ex rel. *Robinson v. McGinnis*, 593 F. Supp. 175 (C.D. Ill. 1984), *aff'd*, 753 F.2d 1078, *cert. denied* 471 U.S. 1116 (1985); *Lane v. Enoch*, 475 U.S. 1053 (1986); *Smith v. Jago*, 470 U.S. 1060 (1985) (White, J., dissenting from denial of certiorari).

107. *See infra*.

108. 399 U.S. 78 (1970).

109. Id. at 79. Rule 1.200 of the Florida Rules of Criminal Procedure provided that the defendant, before trial, must furnish, upon a written request by the prosecution, notice of her intent to rely on an alibi and to provide the prosecution with information of the place where she claimed to have been and with the names and addresses of witnesses she intends to use at trial. The rule also required the prosecution to disclose to the defense the names of witnesses it intended to use to rebut the alibi, id. at 100. The full text of the rule is published in *Williams*, id. at 104.

110. Id. at 85. The *Williams* Court also rejected the defendant's contention that the Sixth Amendment's guarantee of a jury trial mandates a twelve-person jury, id. at 103.

111. Id. at 82.

112. Id. at 81–82.

113. Id. at 81.

114. Id. at 80.

115. Id. at 83, n.14. The footnote, in its entirety, reads as follows: "We emphasize that this case does not involve the question of the validity of the threatened sanction, had petitioner chosen not to comply with the notice-of-alibi rule. Whether and to what extent a State can enforce discovery rules against a defendant who fails to comply, by excluding relevant, probative evidence is a question raising Sixth Amendment issues which we have no occasion to explore. Cf. Brief for *Amicus Curiae* 17–26. It is enough that no such penalty was exacted here."

116. Id. at 85.

117. Id. at 86.

118. Id. at 85.

119. *See infra.*

120. 412 U.S. 470 (1972).

121. Id. at 472.

122. Id. at 472–73. The defendant called one witness to establish an alibi. When the witness testified, the prosecution moved to strike the testimony on the grounds that the defendant had not filed a notice of alibi. The trial judge granted the prosecution's request. The defendant then attempted to bring forth the alibi through his testimony, but the prosecution objected and the trial judge excluded the evidence.

123. Id. at 472, n.4. The full text of the footnote is as follows: "Petitioner also argues that even if Oregon's notice-of-alibi statute were valid, it could not be enforced by excluding either his own testimony or the testimony of supporting witnesses at trial. But in light of our holding that Oregon's rule is facially invalid, we express no view as to whether a valid rule could be so enforced" (citation omitted).

124. Id. at 474.

125. Id.

126. Id. at 475. The Court observed that discovery is a "two-way street" and that "[t]he state may not insist that trials be run as a 'search for truth' so far as defense witnesses are concerned, while maintaining 'poker game' secrecy for its own witnesses," id.

127. Id. at 475, n.9.

128. The rights encompass the Fifth Amendment privilege against self-incrimination, Sixth Amendment rights to a trial by jury, to confront adverse witnesses, to compulsory process for obtaining favorable evidence, to the assistance of counsel, and, of course,

Fifth and Fourteenth amendment due process rights. *See* U.S. CONST. amends. V, VI and XIV, Sec. I.

129. *Wardius v. Oregon*, 412 U.S. at 480 (Douglas, J., concurring).

130. Id.

131. Id.

132. 422 U.S. 225 (1975).

133. Id. at 227–29.

134. Id. at 241.

135. Id.

136. For the majority's misapplication of *Nobles*, *see Taylor v. Illinois*, 484 U.S. at 412.

137. Id.

138. *See* Justice Brennan's dissent in *Taylor*, id. at 426–27 (Brennan, J., dissenting).

139. *See supra* notes 82–103 and accompanying text.

140. 476 U.S. 683 (1986).

141. Id. at 690.

142. Id. (citations omitted) (citing *Strickland v. Washington*, 466 U.S. 668, 684–85 (1984)).

143. Id. at 685. The defendant unsuccessfully attempted before trial to suppress the confession. After the opening statement, during which defense counsel questioned the credibility and reliability of the confession, the prosecution convinced the trial court to prevent any testimony about the circumstances surrounding the confession, id. at 684–86.

144. Id. at 690.

145. Id. at 689–90. The Court noted that, "[W]ithout signaling any diminution in the respect traditionally accorded to the States in the establishment and implementation of their own criminal trial rules and procedures, we have little trouble concluding on the facts of this case that the blanket exclusion of the proferred testimony about the circumstances of petitioner's confession deprived him of a fair trial," id. at 690 (citing *Chambers v. Mississippi*, 404 U.S. 284, 302–03 (1973)).

146. 480 U.S. 39 (1986).

147. Id. at 56.

148. Id.

149. *See supra* note 35 and accompanying text.

150. *Pennsylvania v. Ritchie*, 480 U.S. at 56.

151. Id. at 43.

152. Id.

153. A Pennsylvania statute provided that records of the Pennsylvania Children and Youth Services were confidential subject to certain exceptions. One exception authorized disclosure to a "court of competent jurisdiction pursuant to a court order," id. at 44 n.2 (quoting PA. STAT. ANN. tit. 11, section 2215 (a)(5) (Purdon Supp. 1986)).

154. Id.

155. Id. at 58.

156. 483 U.S. 44 (1987).

157. Id. at 62.

158. Id. at 53. Citing *Washington v. Texas*, the majority noted that "[t]his is not the first time this Court has faced a constitutional challenge to a state rule, designed to ensure

trustworthy evidence, that interfered with the ability of the defendant to offer testimony,'' id.

159. Id. at 53–55. It is significant that the Court quoted at length from *Washington* to reaffirm this proposition.

160. Id.

161. Id. at 55.

162. Id.

163. Id. at 55–56.

164. Id. at 56.

165. Id. at 61.

166. *See infra* notes 49–50 and accompanying text.

167. *Taylor v. Illinois*, 484 U.S. at 402.

168. *See supra* notes 32–34 and accompanying text.

169. *See supra* notes 96–100 and accompanying text.

170. *See supra* notes 152–55 and accompanying text.

171. *Taylor v. Illinois*, 484 U.S. at 403. The rule the defense violated is Illinois Sup. Ct. Rule 413(d), which provides in pertinent part that:

> Subject to constitutional limitations and within a reasonable time after the filing of a written motion by the State, defense counsel shall inform the State of any defenses which he intends to make at a hearing or trial and shall furnish the State with the following material and information within his possession or control:
>
> (i) *the names and last known addresses of persons he intends to call as witnesses* together with their relevant written or recorded statements, including memoranda reporting or summarizing their oral statements, any record of prior criminal convictions known to him.'' Id. n.2 (emphasis added by the Court)

172. *See supra* notes 108–23 and accompanying text.

173. *See supra* notes 32–46 and accompanying text.

174. *Taylor v. Illinois*, 484 U.S. at 417–18.

175. Id. at 402.

176. Id.

177. *People v. Taylor*, 141 Ill. App. 3d 839, 842, 491 N.E. 2d 3, 5 (1986).

178. Id.

179. Id.

180. Id.

181. *Taylor v. Illinois*, 484 U.S. at 402.

182. *People v. Taylor*, 141 Ill. App. 3d 839, 842, 491 N.E. 2d 3, 5 (1986).

183. *Taylor v. Illinois*, 484 U.S. at 402–03.

184. Id. at 403. See *supra* note 171 to see a partial text of the rule.

185. ILL. ANN. STAT. ch. 110A, para. 411 (Smith-Hurd 1985).

186. Rule 412 obligates the State to disclose the names and addresses of its witnesses upon written motion by the defense, id. at para. 412 (a)(i). Rule 413 requires the defense to reciprocate, id. para. 413 (d)(i).

187. *Taylor v. Illinois*, 484 U.S. at 402.

188. Id. at 403.

189. Id.

190. Id. at 405.

191. Id. at 403.

192. Id. at 404.

193. Id. at 404. The judge told defense counsel:

There's all sorts of people on the scene, and all of these people should have been disclosed before.

When you bring up these witnesses at the very last moment, there's always the allegation and the thought process that witnesses are being found that really weren't there. And it's a problem in these types of cases, and it should be—should have been put on that sheet a long time ago.

At any rate, I'll worry about it tomorrow. Id. n.6 (quoting appellate record at 13–14)

194. Id. The appellate record does not account for the fact that the second witness, Pam Berkhalter, did not appear, id. n.7.

195. Id. at 404–05.

196. Id. at 405.

197. Id.

198. Id. The judge's comments are reproduced in the Supreme Court's opinion. They read as follows:

THE COURT: All right, I am going to deny Wormley an opportunity to testify here. He is not going to testify. I find this is a blatant violation of the discovery rules, (*sic*) willful violation of the rules. I also feel that the defense attorneys have been violating discovery in this courtroom in the last three or four cases blatantly and I am going to put a stop to it and this is one way to do so.

Further, for whatever value it is, because this is a jury trial, I have a great deal of doubt in my mind as to the veracity of this young man that testified as to whether he was an eyewitness on the scene, sees guns that are wrapped up. He doesn't know Ray but stops Ray.

At any rate, Mr. Wormley is not going to testify, (*sic*) be a witness in this courtroom. (Id.)

199. *See supra* notes 184–86 and accompanying text.

200. ILL. ANN. STAT. ch. 110A, para. 415 (g)(i).

201. 141 Ill. App. 3d 839, 491 N.E.2d 3 (1986).

202. Id. at 844–45, 491 N.E.2d at 7.

203. 479 U.S. 1063 (1987).

204. Justice Stevens wrote the majority opinion and was joined by Chief Justice Rehnquist and Justices White, O'Connor, and Scalia. Justice Brennan wrote the dissenting opinion and was joined by Justices Marshall and Blackmun. At the time *Taylor* was decided, Justice Powell's replacement on the Court had not been confirmed.

205. *Taylor v. Illinois*, 484 U.S. at 409. The Court employs *Washington* to establish the proposition that the compulsory process clause embraces the right to offer testimony and not merely the empty right to subpoena witnesses. The Court therefore rejected the State of Illinois's contention that the compulsory process clause merely guarantees the right of the defendant to subpoena witnesses, id. at 406. The other references to *Washington* in the majority opinion are contained in note 1, in which *Washington* is cited for the proposition that the compulsory process clause is applicable to the states, *Taylor v. Illinois*, 484 U.S. at 402 n.1; and in note 9 to resolve the issue of whether Taylor had preserved a constitutional issue at the trial level because he invoked only a due process violation, though he relied on *Washington* and *Chambers* to support his position. The Court concluded that such reliance on the Sixth Amendment was "clear," id. at 406 n.9.

206. *Taylor v. Illinois*, 484 U.S. at 414.

207. Id. at 414–15.

208. Id. at 412.

209. Id. at 413.

210. Id. at 417.

211. *See supra* notes 38–44 and accompanying text.
212. *See supra* notes 47–50 and accompanying text.
213. *See supra* notes 32–34 and accompanying text.
214. *Taylor v. Illinois*, 484 U.S. at 414.
215. Id. at 404.
216. Id. at 405.
217. Id. at 404.
218. Id. at 438 (Brennan, J., dissenting).
219. Id. at 402.
220. *See supra* notes 92–101 and accompanying text.
221. *Taylor v. Illinois*, 484 U.S. at 410.
222. *See supra* notes 168–72 and accompanying text.
223. *See supra* notes 140–45 and accompanying text.
224. *Taylor v. Illinois*, 484 U.S. at 406.
225. *See* Westen, *supra* note 20, at 161–77. *See* also *United States v. Davis*, 639 F.2d 239, 243 (1981). The court in *Davis* held that "the compulsory process clause of the Sixth Amendment forbids the exclusion of otherwise admissible evidence solely as a sanction to enforce discovery rules or orders against defendants," id. at 243.
226. White, *Evidentiary Privileges and the Defendant's Constitutional Right to Introduce Evidence*, 80 J. CRIM. L. & CRIMINOLOGY 377, 385–86 (1989).
227. *Taylor v. Illinois*, 484 U.S. at 413.
228. Id.
229. *See* note 171 for the text of the rule.
230. *Taylor v. Illinois*, 484 U.S. at 413.
231. *See supra* notes 116–19 and accompanying text.
232. Id.
233. 531 So.2d 598 (Miss. 1988).
234. Id. at 611.
235. Id. at 611–12. It is ironic that while the *Houston* case, decided after *Taylor*, reserves the exclusion sanction for extreme cases, it cites *Taylor* for the incorrect proposition that the sanction ought to be applied only in cases in which the *defendant* (emphasis added) participates in some "cynical scheme to gain a substantial tactical advantage," id. at 612. In *Taylor*, no evidence existed that the defendant participated in the decision to conceal Wormley's identity, *see infra*.
236. *See* Lafave and Israel, CRIMINAL PROCEDURE Section 19.5 (1985).
237. *Taylor v. Illinois*, 484 U.S. at 438 (Blackmun, J., dissenting). Justice Blackmun joined the dissent on the condition that it was confined to general reciprocal discovery rules and did not take a position with regard to sanctions for noncompliance with notice-of-alibi rules, id. *See* also in this respect, *Fendler v. Goldsmith*, 728 F.2d 1181, 1190 n.19 (9th Cir. 1983) (distinguishing in its analysis general discovery rules from the federal notice-of-alibi rule, "a rule designed to deal with particular types of evidence").
238. Id. at 419 (Brennan, J., dissenting).
239. Id. In reaching this conclusion, Justice Brennan relied on *Rock v. Arkansas* 483 U.S. 44, 55–56, for the proposition that the right to offer defense evidence can be limited only to the degree such limitations serve "legitimate interests in the criminal trial process" and are not "arbitrary or disproportionate to the purposes they are designed to serve," id. at 660–61 (citations omitted). *See supra* notes 163–64 and accompanying text for a discussion of this standard enunciated in *Rock*.

240. Id. at 411.

241. The Court employed this rationale in *Richardson v. Marsh*, 481 U.S. 200 (1987). *See* Garcia, *supra* note 102, at 420 for a discussion of *Marsh*'s implications. Furthermore, the *Valenzuela-Bernal* Court also employed this reasoning to bolster its holding, *see supra* notes 89–91 and accompanying text.

242. *See supra* notes 33–44 and accompanying text.

243. *Washington v. Texas*, 388 U.S. at 21 (quoting from *Benson v. United States*, 146 U.S. 325, 336 (1892)). *See supra* notes 45–46 and accompanying text.

244. *Taylor v. Illinois*, 484 U.S. at 430, n.5 (Brennan, J., dissenting).

245. Id. For a discussion of *Rock* regarding this issue, *see supra* notes 156–66 and accompanying text.

246. *See supra* notes 215–16 and accompanying text.

247. According to Justice Brennan's dissent, the trial judge in *Taylor* did not exclude Wormley's testimony solely on its apparent lack of credibility because Illinois law forbade exclusion of testimony based on lack of credibility, *Taylor v. Illinois*, 484 U.S. at 427 (Brennan, J., dissenting) (citations omitted). On a reading of the appellate record, Justice Brennan concluded that the trial court excluded the testimony because defense counsel misrepresented to the court when he had located Wormley, id. at 432.

248. *Washington v. Texas*, 388 U.S. at 22.

249. Id.

250. *Taylor v. Illinois*, 484 U.S. at 428 (Brennan, J., dissenting).

251. Id. at 429.

252. Id. at 430. The defendant conceded this point on appeal, id.

253. Id. at 417–18.

254. Id. at 418.

255. Id.

256. Id. at 435 (Brennan, J., dissenting).

257. Id. at 436–37.

258. Id. at 437. As Justice Brennan put it, ''I cannot see how we can expect defense counsel in this or any other case to act as vigorous advocates for the interests of their clients when those interests are adverse to their own,'' id.

259. Id. at 432.

260. This, of course, is the concept of ''standing'' to assert a constitutional violation. *See*, e.g., *Rakas v. Illinois*, 439 U.S. 128 (1978) (standing explained as it relates to the Fourth Amendment); *United States v. Wade*, 388 U.S. 218 (1967) (standing concept employed as to Fourth Amendment applied by analogy to the Sixth Amendment).

261. *Taylor v. Illinois*, 484 U.S. at 433 (Brennan, J., dissenting).

262. 468 U.S. 897 (1984).

263. Id. at 921.

264. 109 S.Ct. 333 (1988), *reh'g denied*, 109 S.Ct. 885 (1988).

265. Id. at 337.

266. *Taylor v. Illinois*, 484 U.S. at 419, 436.

267. Justice Brennan did notice this irony by stating in his dissenting opinion that ''It seems particularly ironic that the Court should approve the exclusion of evidence in this case when several of its members have expressed serious misgivings about the evidentiary costs of exclusionary rules in other contexts,'' id. at 437. *See infra* for an elaboration of this argument.

268. 412 U.S. 470, 480 (Douglas, J., concurring). *See supra* notes 129–31 and accompanying text for a discussion of Douglas's opinion.

269. *Wardius v. Oregon*, 412 U.S. at 480 (Douglas, J., concurring).

270. Id.

271. *See supra* note 171 for the text of the rule.

272. 397 U.S. 358 (1970).

273. Id. at 372 (Harlan, J., concurring). Justice Harlan stated that: "[T]he requirement of proof beyond a reasonable doubt in a criminal case . . . [is] bottomed on a fundamental value determination in our society that it is far worse to convict an innocent man than to let a guilty man go free," id.

274. 409 U.S. 100 (1972).

275. *See* notes 53–59 and accompanying text for an extended analysis of *Cool.*

276. *Cool v. United States*, 409 U.S. at 104.

277. *Taylor v. Illinois*, 484 U.S. at 408–09 (quoting from *United States v. Nixon*, 418 U.S. 683, 709 (1974)).

278. This is the apt phrase used by Justice Brennan in his dissent. *Taylor v. Illinois*, 484 U.S. at 437 (Brennan, J., dissenting).

279. This language is taken from Pound's address to the A.B.A. *See supra.*

280. 111 S.Ct. 1743 (1991).

281. Id. at 1745.

282. Id. at 1748.

283. Id.

284. *Taylor v. Illinois*, 484 U.S. at 437 (Brennan, J., dissenting).

285. 468 U.S. 897 (1984). The companion case to *Leon* is *Massachusetts v. Sheppard*, 468 U.S. 981 (1984).

286. *See supra* notes 262–63 and accompanying text.

287. *United States v. Leon*, 468 U.S. at 920–21.

288. *Taylor v. Illinois*, 484 U.S. at 438 (Brennan, J., dissenting).

289. Id. at 414.

290. *See supra.*

291. This rationale was first expressed by the Court in *Elkins v. United States*, 364 U.S. 206 (1960).

292. 414 U.S. 338 (1974) (the majority focused solely on the deterrence rationale in holding that a grand jury witness may not refuse to answer questions because they are based on illegally seized evidence).

293. *See*, e.g., *United States v. Leon*, 468 U.S. 897 (1984). For an argument that the principal goal of the exclusionary rule is to maintain judicial integrity rather than to deter police illegality, *see*, e.g., Baldwin, *Due Process and the Exclusionary Rule: Integrity and Justification*, 39 U. FLA. L. REV. 505.

294. *Taylor v. Illinois*, 484 U.S. at 414–15.

295. 479 U.S. 157 (1986).

296. Id. at 167. For a critique of this position, *see* Garcia, *supra* note 18, at 280–81.

297. *Colorado v. Connelly*, 479 U.S. at 167.

298. Id. at 166 (citations omitted).

299. Id. (quoting *Lego v. Twomey*, 404 U.S. 477, 488–89 (1972)).

300. Id. at 161–62.

301. Id. at 167 (citations omitted).

302. Id. (quoting *Lisenba v. California*, 314 U.S. 219 (1941)).

303. 531 So.2d 598 (Miss. 1988).
304. Id. at 611.
305. Id.
306. 388 U.S. 14 (1967).
307. *Houston v. State*, 531 So.2d at 611.

4

Speedy Trial, Swift Justice: Full-Fledged Right or "Second-Class Citizen"?

The constitutional right of a criminal defendant to a speedy trial, ingrained within the Sixth Amendment to the U.S. Constitution,[1] has been variously characterized by the U.S. Supreme Court as "relative,"[2] "amorphous,"[3] and "slippery."[4] At the same time, the Court has emphasized that the right to a speedy trial is "fundamental"[5] and that it constitutes "one of the most basic rights preserved by our Constitution."[6] The dichotomy posed by these apparently contradictory views of such an important facet of the Sixth Amendment requires an explanation. Unfortunately, neither the Supreme Court nor legal scholars have managed to provide a satisfactory answer to this glaring paradox.

In critiquing the ambivalent fashion in which the Court has dealt with the right to a speedy trial, Richard Uviller points to the faulty premise embraced by the Court in *Barker v. Wingo* that society has a countervailing interest in swift justice which sometimes clashes with a defendant's stake in a speedy trial.[7] As he cogently remarks, the Bill of Rights is not meant to protect governmental or societal concerns or interests; rather, its sole purpose is to furnish basic procedural safeguards to criminal defendants in order to assure fairness in the criminal process.[8]

Although this explication may furnish a partial response to the seeming inconsistency with which the Court has dealt with the right to a speedy trial, it fails to account fully for the Court's incongruous position. Rather, the Court's contradictory approach may be a function of the strategic interplay between the right to a speedy trial and a criminal defendant's calculus of the extent to which the passage of time may erode the prosecution's case. Indeed, Justice Powell stressed the link between delay and the deterioration of the government's case by noting that "delay is not an uncommon defense tactic."[9] In fact, the right to be afforded a speedy trial is a double-edged sword for most criminal defendants: It is a potent weapon if the prosecution is not prepared to effectively establish the accused's guilt; on the other hand, a speedy trial may seal the defendant's fate to the extent that the prosecution's case is fresh and hence does not suffer from the staleness that necessarily flows from the lapse of a lengthy period of time.[10]

Notwithstanding the advantage that a defendant may potentially derive from the passage of time, delay may severely prejudice the defense.[11] Moreover, the delay may prejudice the defendant not only in limiting her ability to put forth a viable defense, but also because it may interfere with her liberty and her right to remove the stigma associated with a criminal accusation. As the Court has noted, the defendant's right to a speedy trial involves three distinct interests: freedom from oppressive pretrial incarceration, mitigation of the "anxiety and concern accompanying public accusation," and avoidance of delay that "impairs the ability of the accused to defend himself."[12]

Part of the doctrinal confusion engendered by the Court's conflicting perspective on the defendant's right to a speedy trial also stems from its failure to identify which of these discrete, yet somewhat related, interests that the clause is designed to protect takes precedence in determining whether a speedy-trial violation has occurred. The Court's seminal case interpreting the right to a speedy trial, *Barker v. Wingo*,[13] affirms that the most important interest protected by the right is the possibility that delay may impair the defense.[14] In singling out this concern, the *Barker* Court reasoned that if a defendant is prevented from preparing her defense, the fairness of the criminal justice system would be called into question.[15] On the other hand, the Court has asserted that the safeguards built into the speedy trial clause "exist quite apart from actual or possible prejudice to an accused's defense."[16]

The doctrinal morass in which the right to a speedy trial has been mired is compounded by the remedy the Court has fashioned for its infringement. Because in *Strunk v. United States*,[17] the Court decreed that the only remedy for a violation of a defendant's right to a speedy trial is dismissal,[18] the right has been transformed into "the right of a few defendants, most egregiously denied a speedy trial, to have the criminal charges against them dismissed on that account."[19]

In order to remedy the deficiencies inherent in the Court's balancing, *ad hoc*, inadequate approach to the speedy trial right,[20] Congress enacted the Speedy Trial Act of 1974.[21] The Speedy Trial Act, however, has failed to fulfill the legislature's expectations. As a consequence, criminal defendants have scant remedies, from either a constitutional or a statutory standpoint, available to secure a speedy trial.

The thesis of this chapter is that, even though the reach of the speedy trial clause's protection has significant practical ramifications, the right of a defendant to a speedy trial has been relegated to second-class status. Furthermore, the statutory counterpart to the constitutional right, that is, the Speedy Trial Act of 1974, has not accomplished its primary objectives: It has not afforded criminal defendants a more concrete remedial device than its constitutional analogue. This phenomenon, moreover, is largely attributable to the equivocal fashion in which the Court has interpreted the right and to its reticence in acknowledging the pragmatic importance of a speedy trial to the fair adjudication of a criminal case.

HISTORICAL ORIGINS

The constitutional right to a speedy trial has a rich historical lineage. Beginning with the Magna Carta (1215), and even as far back as the Assize of Clarendon (1166), the defendant's right to speedy justice was deemed central to notions of fairness.[22] Accordingly, the right to a speedy trial was enshrined in the Virginia Declaration of Rights of 1776 as well as in the constitutions of other states.[23] Given its importance, therefore, the framers of the United States Constitution incorporated the right to a speedy trial into the Sixth Amendment.[24] Although its historical basis and inclusion within the Sixth Amendment seemed to foreshadow its significance, the speedy trial clause receded into relative obscurity, overshadowed by other provisions of the Bill of Rights.[25]

The United States Supreme Court first explored the contours of the speedy trial clause in *Beavers v. Haubert*.[26] In that case, the defendant faced formal charges in both New York and the District of Columbia. New York voluntarily relinquished its jurisdiction over the defendant in favor of the District of Columbia. The defendant contended that such a waiver violated jurisdictional principles as well as the defendant's right to a speedy trial with respect to the New York case.[27]

Rejecting Beaver's speedy-trial challenge, the Court circumscribed the boundaries of the right, describing a defendant's right to a speedy trial as qualified and "relative."[28] In fact, the *Beavers* Court juxtaposed the defendant's right to a speedy disposition with the interests of "public justice." The Court even deemed the speedy-trial right to be dependent upon circumstances and hence to be "consistent with delays."[29] Thus, the defendant's contention that his removal to the District of Columbia interfered with his right to a speedy resolution of the New York charges was summarily rebuffed by the Supreme Court.[30]

Although the *Beavers* Court properly assessed the flawed nature of the defendant's contention, it strayed beyond what was necessary to decide the case. By classifying the right to a speedy trial as relative and qualified, it created the impression that speedy justice was not as important as other procedural rights accorded criminal defendants through the Bill of Rights. Further, the Court in *Beavers* weighed a vital constitutional right against the "ends of public justice"; therefore, it intimated that a constitutional right created for the benefit of criminal defendants might have to yield to societal or governmental interests.

As a consequence of the Court's narrow construction of the speedy trial clause, lower courts classified this provision of the Sixth Amendment as "a privilege rather than a right," and deemed the right to be "subordinate to the broader aims of public justice."[31] *Frankel v. Woodrough*[32] furnishes an apt illustration of the lower courts' concurrence with and adoption of the *Beavers* rationale.

Following the precept enunciated in *Beavers* that the right to speedy justice was reciprocal, the *Frankel* court subsumed the right of a defendant to a speedy trial to ends of justice. Therefore, speed was intricately bound up with and subservient to "justice both to the accused and the public."[33]

The sparse treatment accorded the speedy trial clause through the early and mid-twentieth century did not augur well for its centrality to the criminal process. Moreover, to the extent that speedy justice was subordinated to other goals of the criminal justice system and hence viewed as "relative," its resuscitation seemed unlikely. Nevertheless, the Supreme Court revived the clause, and stressed its relevance to criminal defendants and the criminal justice system in the 1960s, when *Klopfer v. North Carolina*[34] became a part of the constitutional landscape.

MODERN CONSTITUTIONAL BASIS OF SPEEDY TRIAL

Klopfer v. North Carolina

In *Klopfer*, the Supreme Court placed the right to a speedy trial on equal footing with other constitutional rights enumerated in the Sixth Amendment.[35] Tracing the English, colonial, and modern historical roots of the right to a speedy trial, the Court concluded that speedy justice was "one of the most basic rights preserved by our Constitution"[36]; therefore, the right to a speedy trial was made applicable to the states through the operation of the due process clause of the Fourteenth Amendment.[37] The factual predicate of *Klopfer*, moreover, evinces the Court's commitment to an energetic construction of the speedy trial clause.

Klopfer was an atypical defendant: He was a zoology professor at Duke University.[38] The defendant was indicted for the misdemeanor offense of criminal trespass. After a trial in which the jury failed to reach a verdict, the trial court declared a mistrial. The prosecutor requested a continuance and, ultimately, over the defendant's objection, entered a *nolle prosequi* with leave (i.e., with the option of reinstituting charges anytime in the future).[39] Klopfer maintained that such untrammeled prosecutorial discretion violated his right to a speedy trial.[40]

Agreeing with Klopfer's argument, the Court found an infringement of the defendant's right to a speedy trial.[41] The opinion gave vitality to the speedy trial clause in light of its factual background. In effect, Klopfer was not being prosecuted for the misdemeanor offense; nor was he subject to restraint. Rather, the defendant was awaiting the prosecutor's exercise of discretion in determining whether to proceed with the case. The *Klopfer* Court, however, called the limbo in which the defendant remained intolerable and in contravention of his right to a speedy disposition of the charges. Thus, the defendant could not remove the cloud of suspicion and anxiety surrounding the charges; as the Court put it, Klopfer had no means of resolving the pending charges either through dismissal or adjudication of the merits.[42]

Klopfer's significance derives not only from its infusion of life into a relatively moribund right, but also from the forceful manner in which the Court realized such a transformation. In the larger scheme, an indifferent prosecution of a misdemeanor charge hardly inspires the implication of constitutional imperatives. Despite this inauspicious factual basis, the *Klopfer* Court perceived the need to remind trial courts that the right to speedy justice was as integral to the proper functioning of the criminal process as other procedural safeguards afforded criminal defendants in the Sixth Amendment.

Smith v. Hooey

Ratifying the underlying premise behind *Klopfer*, the Court in *Smith v. Hooey*[43] held that a prison inmate was entitled to the protections embodied in the speedy trial clause.[44] The *Smith* Court refused to countenance bureaucratic lassitude on the part of the state of Texas as an excuse for denying an inmate imprisoned on federal charges the right to a speedy resolution of his state case. In doing so, the Court recognized the "corrosive effect" of the passage of time on the ability of a defendant to defend herself.[45] This danger was especially acute for an imprisoned defendant, who faces difficult obstacles in gathering evidence and locating witnesses. Consequently, Texas had a duty to comply with Smith's persistent, yet futile, demands for a speedy disposition of his case.[46]

In a thoughtful concurring opinion, Justice Harlan raised a critical question left unanswered by the *Smith* majority: What is the proper remedy for a speedy trial violation?[47] Smith contended that he had been prejudiced by a nine-year delay in his state case. Justice Harlan suggested that if Smith came forward with proof of prejudice, the burden would shift to the prosecution to rebut the defendant's claim.[48]

Dickey v. Florida

Although the Court would ultimately resolve Justice Harlan's query,[49] it moved towards that step in *Dickey v. Florida*.[50] In that case, the defendant, while serving a federal sentence, repeatedly attempted to secure a trial on pending state charges. A period of seven years elapsed before he was tried and convicted, however. During those seven years two defense witnesses died and a third became unavailable.[51]

In strong terms the Court characterized the speedy trial clause as not merely "theoretical and abstract," but as a vital constitutional protection in the context of the criminal process. More important, the *Dickey* majority mandated the dismissal of charges against the accused, thus portending the remedy it would definitely establish in *Strunk*.[52]

Dickey, moreover, is noteworthy largely for the concurring opinion of Justice Brennan. Criticizing the inchoate doctrinal underpinnings of the right to a speedy trial, Justice Brennan sought to provide a more coherent framework.[53] In essence, he erected a three-pronged inquiry into determining whether delay impinges on the accused's right to speedy justice: the source of the delay, the reasons for it, and the impact of the delay on interests preserved by the speedy trial clause.[54] Ultimately, this test would be adopted by the Court in *Barker v. Wingo*.[55]

Perhaps the most cogent part of Brennan's opinion dealt with the question whether prejudice is a necessary condition for providing a speedy trial violation. Pointing to the difficulty in showing prejudice in the speedy trial context, Brennan drew an analogy to other Sixth Amendment rights. Since the defendant does not have to establish prejudice with regard to other Sixth Amendment safeguards, it is proper to "assume prejudice once the accused shows he was denied a rapid prosecution."[56] The dilemma remained, however, of setting a threshold period of time when such prejudice to the accused would be presumed. Nevertheless, though Justice Brennan did not specify such a threshold, he maintained that, once it was reached, the government's only recourse would be to invoke the harmless error doctrine.[57]

DEFINITION OF THE RIGHT TO A SPEEDY TRIAL

Though the Court made halting progress in defining the constitutional boundaries of speedy justice in *Dickey*, Justice Brennan's concurring opinion highlighted the gaps in the Court's jurisprudential delineation of the scope of the right to a speedy trial.[58] Accordingly, the Court sought to provide a more adequate framework in the 1970s. Specifically, the Court endeavored to establish the necessary conditions in determining a violation of the right; and it had to determine the precise point at which the defendant's right to a speedy trial attached. In framing a conceptual solution to these questions, the Court faltered in its mission to fashion a comprehensive vision of the right to speedy justice according to the ideals represented by the Sixth Amendment. Therefore, it is imperative to survey the Court's failed attempt at furnishing such a vision and to explain why it was unsuccessful in doing so.

WHEN DOES THE RIGHT ATTACH?

A critical issue attending the application of a constitutional protection afforded a criminal defendant is ascertaining when the right attaches. In assessing this demarcation with respect to speedy trials, the Court adopted a facile conceptual appraisal: The right comes into play only when a formal accusation has been lodged against the suspect.[59] At first blush, this approach seems proper and sensible; upon closer scrutiny, however, the flawed analysis underlying such a conclusion becomes apparent.

United States v. Marion

In *Marion*, the government appealed the dismissal of an indictment because three years elapsed between the criminal act and the filing of an indictment.[60] The majority held that such a delay did not implicate the right to a speedy trial because "[o]n its face, the protection of the [Sixth] Amendment is activated only when a criminal prosecution has begun and extends only to those persons who have been 'accused' in the course of that prosecution."[61] Interpreting the Sixth Amendment in a literal fashion, the *Marion* majority sought to justify and rationalize its holding by resorting to history, legislative provisions, and judicial interpretation.[62]

Ultimately, the *Marion* Court's holding rested on the rationale that the evils the speedy trial clause guards against do not arise until a formal arrest occurs. Dispensing with the view that the right of a defendant to a speedy trial is principally designed to avoid prejudice to the accused's defense, the majority in *Marion* instead focused upon the way an arrest infringed on the accused's liberty interests.[63] Consequently, since the accused suffers none of the infirmities, anxiety, and possible incarceration accompanying an arrest, the safeguards embedded in the speedy trial clause are not triggered until a formal arrest occurs.[64] Further, the possibility of prejudice to the defendant caused by pre-arrest delay is not a "sufficient reason to wrench the Sixth Amendment from its proper context."[65]

Nevertheless, the *Marion* Court did not foreclose the possibility of a remedy pursuant to the due process clause if the defendant showed that she suffered substantial prejudice to her right to a fair trial from the pre-indictment delay. In addition, the defendant had to prove that such delay was prompted by the government's intent to gain a tactical advantage over the accused.[66] Given such demanding criteria, it is doubtful whether a defendant can successfully establish a due process violation based on pre-indictment delay. The obstacle posed by such stringent requirements is transparent when the majority concludes that the mere possibility of prejudice stemming from the delay is necessarily "speculative" or "premature" and does not warrant reversal on due process grounds. Indeed, the majority intimates that only after the trial is concluded will a defendant be able to demonstrate prejudice.[67]

The conceptual basis upon which *Marion* is grounded suffers from serious flaws. The anxiety and concern associated with a formal arrest are equally compelling when a citizen is publicly accused of a crime. Moreover, the prejudice flowing from the passage of time is not ameliorated because the delay occurs at the pre-indictment versus the post-indictment stage of the prosecution.[68] The speedy trial clause loses its force when the government is given virtually unfettered discretion in deciding when to begin a prosecution.[69]

More important, the majority's analysis is replete with inconsistencies. At one level, the Court strains to evade the truism that the speedy trial clause safeguards the defendant's right to a fair trial by averting prejudicial delay. On the other hand, when it excludes pre-indictment delay from the purview of the clause, the majority in *Marion* uses prejudice, combined with prosecutorial bad faith, as the guiding standard for proving a due-process violation. One can explain the incongruous reasoning by inferring that the Court sought to achieve a particular result, and resorted to *post hoc* rationalizations to attain it.

United States v. Lovasco

Consistent with the cumbersome *Marion* due-process standard, the Court elaborated upon its tightly circumscribed parameters in *Lovasco*. Qualifying the due-process test the *Marion* Court enunciated, the *Lovasco* Court asserted that proof of prejudice is "a necessary but not sufficient" element of a due process claim.[70] It correctly noted that the *Marion* test required not only proof of prejudice but also prosecutorial bad faith as a reason for the delay.[71]

The primary reason for the *Lovasco* holding was the Court's reluctance to impinge upon prosecutorial discretion in the filing of charges. Citing systemic, practical, and institutional considerations, the majority sanctioned investigative delay in the filing of formal charges because such deferral is supposedly not motivated by the government's desire to obtain a tactical advantage over the accused.[72] The *Lovasco* Court rejected the notion that the government ought to be compelled to prosecute once it amasses sufficient evidence to establish guilt. The majority offered three explanations for its reluctance to impose this requirement: it would impede prosecutions of multiple-defendant cases; it would pressure the government to file charges in marginal cases; and, it would unnecessarily interfere with prosecutorial discretion.[73]

As Phyllis Goldfarb has demonstrated in a thoughtful evaluation of the Court's jurisprudence in *Marion* and *Lovasco*, the Court's doctrinal underpinning is deficient.[74] Speedy trial interests are the same whether the delay occurs before formal accusation or after the commencement of formal proceedings.[75] Moreover, the Court could have employed analogical reasoning and found that pre-accusation delay infringes the defendant's right to compulsory process or to traditional due process.[76] The problem with the due process analysis the Court relies upon is that it overlooks a fundamental component of due process: the value of fair process norms in conjunction with reliable determination of guilt in legitimating the criminal process.[77]

Finally, the almost insuperable barrier set by both *Marion* and *Lovasco* distorts the meaning of due process by viewing it from a prosecutorial rather than a defendant-oriented perspective. Fairness is measured by the absence of prosecutorial misconduct rather than "on the defendant's injury."[78] Due-process norms are designed to protect the defendant's right to a fair process rather than to safeguard governmental interests.

The circumscribed constitutional shield for pre-accusation delay delineated by the Court leaves the defendant with a sole practical remedy: the applicable statute of limitations. Therefore, as one commentator has aptly noted, "these statutes are [the accused's] only legal protection in the precourt phase, except the distant . . . protection afforded by the due process guarantee of a fair trial."[79]

CRITERIA FOR DETERMINING VIOLATION OF THE RIGHT

Having set an artificial boundary by which to judge pre-accusation delay, the Court then strove to fashion a coherent foundation for determining the parameters of the right to a speedy trial. Unfortunately, the *Barker* opinion failed to advance the doctrinal development of the speedy trial clause; to a large extent, the Court's jurisprudence was a throwback to the nebulous, flawed treatment accorded the defendant's interest in speedy justice. Furthermore, the aftermath of *Barker* did not furnish any more hope that the right to a speedy trial would be placed on an equal footing with its Sixth Amendment counterparts. An explanation for this failure lies in the Court's ambivalent attitude toward speedy justice and in its reluctance to embrace a realistic outlook on the interests preserved by the right.

Barker v. Wingo

The factual predicate underlying *Barker* proves the degree to which the passage of time may be a double-edged sword for either the prosecution or the defense. The government requested sixteen continuances in *Barker*, which led to a five-year delay between Barker's indictment and his trial. The reason for the prosecution's successful delaying maneuvers was tactical; the government did not believe it could secure Barker's conviction without the testimony of his codefendant, Manning. In turn, Manning's testimony against Barker became possible only after the prosecution tried Manning six times for the murders he committed in concert with Barker.[80] Having been released on bail after ten months of confinement, Barker gambled on the government's inability to obtain Manning's conviction. He failed to object to the state's first eleven continuances, but demurred unsuccessfully twice thereafter to the delay on speedy trial grounds. He was convicted at trial, principally on Manning's testimony against him.[81]

In a footnote, the *Barker* Court pointed to the irony behind Barker's hapless tactical choice. Had Barker sought and been granted a speedy trial at the outset, he would have been acquitted because Manning's testimony was indispensable to the state. Nevertheless, the majority pointed out that the defense could not have foreseen that the government would have to try Manning six times over a four-year period before securing the necessary convictions.[82] In effect, Barker gambled on time's being his ally and lost; by contrast, the prosecution successfully relied on delay to obtain an otherwise inconceivable conviction.

It is precisely this fortuity which explains the *Barker* Court's approach toward developing a comprehensive framework for the right to a speedy trial. In differentiating the speedy trial clause from other defendant-oriented rights, the *Barker* majority identified the public's countervailing interest in speedy justice[83]; as a corollary, the Court reaffirmed the previous characterization of the right as amorphous, relative, and slippery.[84] It is possible to discern the rationale undergirding this perspective by emphasizing a key passage in *Barker*. In endeavoring to distinguish the speedy trial right from other protections granted to criminal defendants, the Court asserted that "deprivation of the right may work to the accused's advantage"; and that "delay is not an uncommon defense tactic."[85]

Taking such a position to its logical limit, the majority maintained that denial of the right to a speedy trial does not necessarily entail prejudice to the defendant.[86] It is this logic that led to the basis for the Court's decision in *Barker*. If the defendant is not able to prove prejudice or if he has not shown his desire for a prompt disposition of the case, his speedy trial argument will not succeed.

To a large extent, the *Barker* Court's equivocal viewpoint on the speedy trial clause is attributable to its conclusion that delay usually favors the defense. In ratifying the staid, shopworn classification of the right to a speedy trial as relative, amorphous, and slippery, the majority in *Barker* evinced its reluctance to give this ''fundamental'' right its due recognition. Moreover, the rationale that Justice Powell, the author of *Barker*, adduced to bolster his characterization of the right to speedy justice as relative is without foundation.

Justice Powell argued that the right to a speedy trial ''is a more vague concept than other procedural rights'' because it is difficult to pinpoint when the right has been denied. In addition, he maintained that no ''fixed point'' exists when the defendant may be compelled to either invoke or surrender the right.[87] One can effectively counter this faulty logic by stressing the amorphous, vague, and slippery nature of such procedural remedies as ''reasonableness'' in the search and seizure context, ''double jeopardy,'' or the right to confrontation. In fact, the government is more aware of the passage of time after formal proceedings commence than it is of ''illegalities which occur beyond its sight.''[88]

In light of the *Barker* Court's predilections regarding the supposedly nebulous aspect of speedy justice, it came to the conclusion that a flexible, rather than a rigid, delineation of the scope of the right was warranted. Accordingly, the majority rejected two options that would have drawn a clear line in determining when a violation of the right occurs: the demand-waiver rule and a specified time limit within which a defendant would have to be brought to trial.[89] Paradoxically, Justice Powell spurned the demand-waiver rule (i.e., a defendant who fails to demand a speedy trial waives the right) because he acknowledged that delay can be detrimental to the defendant.[90] Yet, the gist of *Barker* rests on the unstated proposition that if the defendant wishes to invoke the benefits associated with a speedy disposition, she must either suffer prejudice or demand a rapid trial. In addition, the *Barker* majority repudiated a specific time frame within which a defendant would have to be tried because it deemed such a rule to encroach upon the legislative function.

Given the Court's aversion to a bright-line approach, it essentially adopted the balancing test set forth by Justice Brennan in his concurring opinion in *Dickey*.[91] Thus, in assessing whether a defendant has been deprived of the right to a speedy trial, the *Barker* majority took four factors into account: the length of the delay, the reason for the delay, the defendant's assertion of his right, and the prejudice to the defendant. The length of the delay serves as a triggering mechanism. The reason for the delay is weighed in terms of governmental motives: that is, whether the delay was due to negligence or overcrowded dockets, bad-faith efforts by the prosecution to delay trials to secure tactical advantages, or valid reasons, such as missing witnesses.[92]

Identifying none of the four factors as indispensable to the finding of a speedy trial violation,[93] the *Barker* Court nevertheless stressed two as quintessential: prejudice and the accused's invocation of the right. One may cast doubt on the fairness of the system if the accused is inhibited in her ability to mount an effective defense. Logically connected to prejudice, according to the Court's analysis, is the defendant's assertion of the right. The majority sets a high threshold by stating that "failure to assert the right will make it difficult for a defendant to prove that he was denied a speedy trial."[94]

In assessing *Barker*'s factual predicate, Justice Powell stressed the apparent lack of prejudice Barker suffered as a result of the delay. The critical determinant, however, was Barker's failure to demand a speedy trial because he was gambling on Manning's acquittal.[95] Therefore, Justice Powell ignored the five-year delay between Barker's indictment and his trial because Barker neither requested a rapid disposition nor did he suffer appreciable prejudice from the lapse of time. Indeed, the Court emphatically affirms that, absent "extraordinary circumstances," a defendant would be hard pressed to prove a speedy trial violation without invoking the right.[96]

The faulty premises underlying *Barker* are manifold. Although the Court purports to renounce the demand-waiver rule, in effect it endorses the precept in muted form by seemingly adopting a "balancing" test rather than a rigid one. Nonetheless, *Barker* ignored a five-year delay because the defendant allegedly suffered no prejudice and waited a long time to invoke his right to a speedy disposition.

In making such a determination, the *Barker* majority ignored *Marion*'s injunction that the evils safeguarded against by the speedy trial guarantee are divorced from actual or possible prejudice to the accused.[97] *Barker* overtly focused on the alleged lack of actual prejudice the defendant suffered as a consequence of the delay. However, Barker was prejudiced by the delay, as the majority acknowledged. He spent ten months in jail before trial, and lived under the stigma and anxiety associated with a public prosecution for a period of four years.[98] The majority took the procrustean position that Barker was not prejudiced merely because none of his witnesses vanished as a result of the delay.

More important, Barker suffered prejudice because, had he been tried before Manning was convicted, he would have been acquitted. In essence, the *Barker* Court sanctioned the prosecution's dilatory tactics in trying the defendant. Interestingly, the *Barker* opinion conveniently overlooks the fact that the reason for the delay in Barker's case stemmed from the prosecution's tactical decision to forestall the trial until it obtained Manning's conviction. Further, that decision was a deliberate attempt by the state to secure a tactical advantage over the defendant. Combined with the length of the delay, this transparent abuse by the government in using time as a weapon against the defendant is presumably what the speedy trial clause is designed to prevent.

As Justice Brennan has pointed out, equating silence or inaction with waiver of a fundamental constitutional right is at odds with precedent.[99] The Supreme Court has unequivocally held that a criminal defendant's waiver of a constitutionally protected right must be intentional and that courts should presume against such waivers.[100] Indeed, a criminal defendant should not bear the burden of making sure he is brought to trial. The presumption ought to be that the accused desires a speedy trial "unless he affirmatively accepts delay."[101]

By adhering to a sanitized version of the demand-waiver standard, the *Barker* Court depreciated the fundamental nature of the accused's right to speedy justice. Rather than advancing the rudimentary doctrinal basis upon which the right rested, the Court ratified the status quo. In essence, the defendant's right to a speedy trial was pitted against societal aims; consequently, the speedy trial clause remained a privilege which had to be invoked rather than a fundamental right whose benefits the defendant must intentionally relinquish.[102] Justice Powell's opinion in *Barker* provided an answer to Justice Brennan's rhetorical question in *Dickey*: Is affirmative action by the defendant required to preserve rather than waive the right?[103] It is clear that *Barker* goes far toward compelling a defendant to invoke her right to a speedy trial or, alternatively, risk waiving its safeguards.

As Uviller notes, the *Barker* Court erred in linking inferred desire and implied waiver. A fundamental constitutional right should not be afforded solely to those defendants "judicially determined to want its benefit." Justice Powell's analysis is faulty to the extent he likened Barker's tactical error in betting on Manning's acquittal to his subjective intent.[104] The right to a speedy trial, as Justice Brennan observed in *Dickey*, is not waived tacitly or subjectively. To put it simply, "waiver not wish governs; law not psychology."[105] In short, Barker's tactical error should not have been construed as the equivalent of his wish not to have a speedy trial.

In order to dissect the basis for the *Barker* Court's reasoning, one must go beyond criticizing its faulty logic and lack of adherence to precedent. Rather, one must focus on the underlying policy rationale animating the Court. To the degree that the majority of the Court believed that "delay in criminal cases is welcomed by defendants as it usually operates in their favor,"[106] it felt constrained to underscore the two factors which would militate against a successful speedy trial claim: prejudice and, most importantly, demand. If Barker's gambit did not pay off, then he should not be afforded the constitutional benefit conferred by the speedy trial clause. Deterrence would hardly be served if a defendant can unsuccessfully gamble on the failure of the government's dilatory tactics and still secure the benefits conferred by the speedy trial clause.

Intertwined with this rationale is the *Barker* Court's reluctance to grant the defendant's claim and thereby abort his prosecution. In *Barker*, the Court made clear that the unduly harsh remedy of dismissal is the "only possible remedy" for a speedy trial violation.[107] Furthermore, the majority exhibited its distaste for such a "severe" remedy by stressing its negative consequences; that is, a defendant guilty of a serious crime will go free, without an adjudication on the merits.[108] Therefore, Justice Powell sent a powerful message that Barker would not prevail despite a five-year delay in bringing him to trial. Barker committed a serious crime: the murder of an elderly couple.[109]

Remedies: *Strunk v. United States*

One year after rendering its opinion in *Barker*, the Court reaffirmed its position that dismissal was the sole cure for a speedy trial violation. *Strunk v. United States*[110] was an inauspicious vehicle to portray dismissal as the sole relief available to cure a speedy trial transgression. In that case, a ten-month delay between indictment and trial led the trial court to conclude that the defendant's right to a speedy disposition had been violated. Ironically, the defendant was partially responsible for the delay, endured no prejudice to his defense from the postponement, and the prosecution did not act in bad faith in failing to bring Strunk to trial earlier.[111]

Given these mitigating circumstances, the ten-month delay in *Strunk* stands in sharp contrast to the five-year postponement in *Barker*. Moreover, the appellate court in *Strunk* afforded the defendant a sensible and practical remedy: it gave him credit for the part of his sentence which was attributable to the unreasonable delay.[112] More important, the lower court pointed to the primary inadequacy of dismissal as a remedy: it made courts extremely hesitant to find a speedy trial violation due to the severity of the remedy.[113]

Despite the lower court's practical solution, Chief Justice Burger, the author of *Strunk*, reiterated the interests the speedy trial clause safeguards and, in light of these concerns, quoted from *Barker* for the proposition that dismissal was the "only possible remedy."[114] Juxtaposing the speedy trial clause with other rights guaranteed by the Sixth Amendment, Chief Justice Burger distinguished it on the basis that the right to a speedy trial is an all-or-nothing proposition, whereas other rights denied the accused can be afforded at a new trial.[115] It is interesting to compare the *Strunk* opinion's rigid approach toward the remedies available to cure a speedy trial violation with the *Barker* Court's flexible, *ad hoc* perspective in fashioning viable criteria to determine a speedy trial violation.

As Anthony Amsterdam has aptly noted, the accused's right to a speedy trial is multifaceted rather than monolithic.[116] It is not an "indivisible" right that calls for a severe remedy. Rather, an elastic approach that takes into account the interests protected by the right is more prudent. Therefore, if the concern is oppressive incarceration, then the remedy ought to be release from pretrial confinement; if anxiety associated with a public accusation is the malady, then dismissal without prejudice is the appropriate relief; finally, only if the delay significantly infringes the defendant's ability to defend herself should the drastic remedy of dismissal be invoked.[117]

Related to the Court's constricted vista regarding the remedies trial courts may conjure for a speedy trial violation is its confusion of a breach of the right with the proper relief. The *Strunk* Court, as well as lower courts, failed to distinguish between the question whether a speedy trial violation has occurred and the question whether the violation warrants dismissal.[118] As a consequence, the right to speedy justice has been perverted into "a windfall benefit of criminal immunity for a very few accuseds'' who benefit from the deplorable failure of courts to provide speedy trials.[119]

Perplexing though Chief Justice Burger's draconian remedy for a speedy trial violation may seem,[120] it is possible to offer a pragmatic basis for the Court's holding in *Strunk*. When analyzed in conjunction with *Barker, Strunk* may be seen as its logical extension. Since the *Barker* Court was loath to recognize a vibrant, defendant-oriented right to speedy justice, it necessarily adopted fluid criteria which made the showing of a violation extremely difficult. If the Court had subscribed to a flexible perspective with respect to the appropriate relief for a violation, the right to a speedy trial would not have squared with the Court's characterization: that is, that speedy justice is a vague, amorphous, or slippery concept. Moreover, had the *Strunk* Court espoused less drastic sanctions, lower courts would have found it easier to find violations. Instead, most lower courts have assessed speedy trial deprivations chiefly on impairment of the defendant's ability to defend, thus denigrating other speedy trial interests.[121]

THE COURT'S MISSPENT OPPORTUNITY

The development of the Court's speedy trial jurisprudence in both *Barker* and *Strunk* failed to advance the inchoate doctrinal underpinnings of a fundamental constitutional right. Rather than using *Klopfer* as a point of departure for expanding the parameters of the right, the Court resurrected old shibboleths, resorted to flawed logic, and endorsed the discredited notion that speedy justice merits secondary status in comparison with other procedural guarantees embodied in the Sixth Amendment. In sum, the Court's prescription reduced the speedy trial clause to a ''feeble farce.''[122]

Furthermore, the Court's failure to promote a more definite procedural mechanism by which the accused could establish a speedy trial violation left defendants with a hollow remedy. As Justice Brennan remarked in *Dickey*, it is difficult for a defendant to adduce evidence of prejudice. The mere passage of time potentially wreaks havoc upon the accused's ability to present a viable defense: Memories dim, evidence may be lost, and the anxiety surrounding pending charges weighs heavily on the defendant.[123] In addition, other Sixth Amendment rights are not conditioned upon the defendant's proving prejudice stemming from their violation. Rather, prejudice is presumed to flow from the infringement of these rights because evidence of prejudice is so elusive.[124]

In fact, the *Barker* Court could have followed Justice Brennan's suggestion that, once delay raises the probability of substantial prejudice, the burden should shift to the government to justify why the delay was necessary or to rely on the harmless error doctrine.[125] It is possible to object to this solution on the ground that it is difficult to measure when the delay becomes presumptively prejudicial. Additionally, one could cavil with this approach because, unless the defendant produces evidence of how he was prejudiced, it would be onerous for the government to rebut such a claim.

These objections may be countered with a standard that builds upon Justice Brennan's analysis. First, if the defendant demands an early trial, and the government unjustifiably disregards such a request, prejudice should be presumed without placing the burden of production upon the accused. On the other hand, the defendant should come forward with some evidence of prejudice if he has not requested a speedy trial. Once the defendant comes forward with some evidence of potential prejudice, however, then the burden of persuasion should shift to the government; the prosecution must justify the delay or establish harmless error.[126]

Instead of fashioning a realistic standard, the *Barker* Court erected a supposedly flexible balancing test that made it difficult for a defendant to obtain relief. Combined with the unusually harsh sanction of dismissal as the sole remedy for a speedy trial violation, the Court fostered the notion that speedy justice was different from other fundamental rights and thereby less worthy of protection.

THE ILLUSORY REMEDY: *MACDONALD* AND *LOUD HAWK*

The confused nature of speedy trial jurisprudence continued unabated with the Court's decisions in *United States v. MacDonald*[127] and *United States v. Loud Hawk.*[128] In those two cases, the Court identified different interests safeguarded by the clause and rejected the prejudice prong of the *Barker* balancing test in order to arrive at results inimical to the defendants' speedy justice claims. Viewed in tandem, both opinions illustrate the hostility with which the Court has treated defendants' speedy trial interests and the extent to which it has refused to adhere to the principle of fair play assimilated in the Sixth Amendment.

MacDonald

A cause célèbre, the *MacDonald* case exemplifies the Court's disdain for *Klopfer*'s mandate; it shows that *Klopfer* has become an anomaly, a convenient abstraction whose invocation serves to mask how unfundamental the defendant's speedy trial rights have become.

Captain MacDonald, a physician, was formally charged with and absolved by the army of the murders of his wife and two daughters in 1970. Subsequent to that dismissal, MacDonald sought and was granted an honorable discharge from the army.[129] At the Justice Department's behest, however, the Army Criminal Investigation Division (CID) continued its investigation of the case after MacDonald's discharge. In 1972, the CID forwarded a voluminous report to the Justice Department, followed by reports in late 1972 and August 1973. Ultimately, the Justice Department presented the case to a grand jury in August of 1974 and the grand jury returned an indictment on January 25, 1975.[130]

MacDonald was aware of the continuing investigation, urged the government to complete its inquiry as soon as possible, and even volunteered to submit to further questioning. The Justice Department, however, failed to respond to

MacDonald's requests. MacDonald's sincerity was corroborated by the fact that he waived his Fifth Amendment right to remain silent by testifying before the grand jury that ultimately indicted him.[131] Further, the government did not adduce any legitimate reason for waiting more than two years between the time it acquired the army's comprehensive report and it presented MacDonald's case to the grand jury in August 1974.[132]

The majority in *MacDonald* did not find a speedy trial violation because it deemed that during the period between the army's dismissal of the charges and MacDonald's indictment by the grand jury, MacDonald "was not under arrest, not in custody, and not subject to any 'criminal protection.' "[133] Though the *MacDonald* Court acknowledged that the defendant suffered from the anxiety and opprobrium cast by a continuing criminal investigation, it dismissed such interests as not within the contours of the speedy trial clause. Rather, the majority indulged in the disingenuous legal fiction that while the government continued its investigation, "MacDonald was legally and constitutionally in the same posture as though no charges had been made."[134]

To support this position, the *MacDonald* majority had to grapple with *Klopfer*'s dictates. Therefore, it sought to distinguish *Klopfer* on the basis that, technically speaking, the charges against Klopfer had not been dismissed, and those against MacDonald had.[135] The flimsy basis of this distinction is betrayed by the majority's relegating the differentiation to a footnote. Moreover, the distinction is without foundation because Klopfer did not face pending charges to the degree that the government was required to take an affirmative step in order to reinstitute a formal prosecution.[136]

The interest *Klopfer* furthers—and that the majority ignores in *MacDonald*—is the defendant's right to be free from the anxiety accompanying a public accusation.[137] Interestingly, the *MacDonald* majority relied upon *United States v. Marion*, as well as on Justice White's concurring opinion in *Barker*, for the proposition that the right to speedy justice is not principally designed to limit prejudice to the defense deriving from the passage of time.[138] As we have seen, however, the *Barker* majority focused on prejudice as a critical factor in determining whether a speedy trial violation has occurred.[139] In *MacDonald*, however, it suited the majority's purposes to revive *Marion*'s dictum: in order to deny speedy trial relief to the defendant.

A critical look at the rationalizations employed by the *MacDonald* majority reveals the poverty of the Court's speedy trial jurisprudence. MacDonald faced a cloud of suspicion for more than two years. He sought relief and asserted his right to resolve the public accusation against him by repeatedly asking the Justice Department to interview him and by requesting that it move expeditiously in deciding whether to reprosecute the case. MacDonald, like Klopfer, was also an atypical defendant; he was a doctor whose reputation was under suspicion while the government made up its mind to prosecute. He suffered from doubt and anxiety over serious charges, which haunted him for a long time.

Comparing *McDonald* with *Barker* also yields an important parallel: Both defendants were charged with gruesome murders of victims who evoked particular sympathy. In *Barker*, an elderly couple suffered a slow death; in *MacDonald*, a mother and two young children met a bizarre and untimely death. One may assume that the Court was loath to grant the defendants relief in both cases. In fact, the *MacDonald* Court refused to hear the case on an interlocutory basis until MacDonald's trial was completed.[140]

The Expansion of *MacDonald*: *United States v. Loud Hawk*

Broadening the principles set forth in *MacDonald*, the Court validated its reluctance to categorize lengthy delays as speedy trial transgressions in *United States v. Loud Hawk*.[141] *Loud Hawk* involved a ninety-month delay from arrest and indictment until dismissal of charges against the defendant. Finding no speedy trial violation, the Court held that speedy disposition is not constitutionally required when the government appeals a district court's dismissal of an indictment as long as the defendant is not incarcerated during the pendency of the appeal.[142]

The *Loud Hawk* majority managed to expand *MacDonald*'s reach through a clever artifice: that is, by categorizing the dismissal of an indictment by a district court as analogous to the dropping of charges by the government. In *MacDonald*, the army voluntarily dropped charges against the defendant. Therefore, the government's commitment to prosecute MacDonald had not solidified—and triggered the liberty interests advanced by the speedy trial clause. By contrast, the defendants in *Loud Hawk* could have had their liberty revoked by a stroke of a pen during the government's appeal.[143] The government's desire to prosecute had not only been formalized but also had been reaffirmed through its appeal of the court's dismissal of the indictment. The specious character of the distinction the *Loud Hawk* Court sought to create is evident when the majority concedes that *MacDonald* would not have applied if the defendants had either been incarcerated or compelled to post bail.[144]

What is revealing about the Court's discourse in *Loud Hawk* is its candid admission that the seriousness of the crime ought to be weighed in determining the existence of a speedy trial violation. Among the factors the majority believes should be considered when a court assesses the reasonableness of an interlocutory appeal by the government is the gravity of the crime.[145] In effect, the *Loud Hawk* majority makes explicit what is implicit in the Court's speedy trial jurisprudence; that is, courts should seldom invoke the drastic dismissal remedy for a speedy trial violation when the defendant is charged with a serious crime. It is logical, therefore, that the *Loud Hawk* Court denied relief to a defendant who was a fugitive from the siege and occupation of Wounded Knee and who faced charges of possession of firearms and explosives.[146]

Furthermore, *Loud Hawk* is instructive because it explains the Court's reluctance to focus on prejudice to the defendant as an interest worthy of protection. Dismissing the possibility of prejudice to the defendant as a sufficient basis for a speedy trial violation, the *Loud Hawk* majority emphasizes that delay is a ''two-edged sword'' equally deleterious to the prosecution and to the defense.[147] Although the Court is correct from a practical standpoint, the right to speedy justice is partly designed to safeguard the defendant's constitutionally derived right to a fair trial and does not protect the prosecution from prejudice stemming from the passage of time.[148]

The *Loud Hawk* opinion, like *Barker*, reflects the Court's deeply rooted belief that delay benefits the defense. Through its circuitous logic, *Loud Hawk* minimizes the potential prejudice the defendant is exposed to when prolonged delay occurs. Instead, the *Loud Hawk* majority turns the constitutional right afforded defendants on its head; it seems more concerned with the adverse impact of delay upon the government's ability to successfully prosecute the defendant than it is with securing speedy justice for persons formally accused of a crime. As the latest pronouncement by the Court on the constitutional right to a speedy trial, *Loud Hawk* represents the obvious culmination of the Court's antipathy toward a significant component of the Sixth Amendment.

THE SPEEDY TRIAL ACT: AN INEFFECTIVE ANTIDOTE

In response to the nebulous and ill-defined constitutional criteria set forth in *Barker*, Congress sought to delineate a more concrete speedy trial remedy by passing the Speedy Trial Act of 1974.[149] The impulse behind the act, however, was not to provide the defendant with an effective antidote to the feeble relief fashioned by the Supreme Court's constitutional standard; rather, the preamble to the Act identifies its main thrust as ''reducing crime and the danger of recidivism by requiring speedy trials and by strengthening the supervision over persons released pending trial.''[150]

Despite the Act's societal impetus, it does provide definite limits within which a defendant must be formally charged and brought to trial. Specifically, the act mandates that an indictment of information be presented within thirty days from arrest or issuance of a summons, with a thirty-day extension if no grand jury is in session.[151] Furthermore, a defendant must be afforded a trial within seventy days, but not less than thirty days, from the filing date of the information or indictment, or from the date he appeared before a judicial officer of the court in which the charge is pending, whichever date occurs last.[152]

These time limits are substantially negated by the excludable delays exempted from the length of time within which a trial must begin. For example, the following exemptions are delineated in the act: delays owing to proceedings involving the mental competency or physical capacity of the accused,[153] pretrial motions,[154] the absence or unavailability of an ''essential witness,''[155] and ''any reasonable period of delay when the accused is joined for trial with a codefendant whose time for trial has not expired and a motion for severance has not been granted.''[156]

The provision that gives virtually untrammeled discretion to the trial judge and threatens the validity of the specific time limits specified in the act permits the exclusion of:

> Any period of delay resulting from a continuance granted by any judge on his own motion or at the request of the [accused] or his counsel or at the request of the attorney for the Government, if the judge granted such continuance on the basis of his findings that the ends of justice served by taking such an action outweigh the best interest of the public and the [accused] in a speedy trial.[157]

As Malcolm Feely has demonstrated, the exceptions set forth in the Speedy Trial Act have been artfully employed by trial judges to violate the intent and spirit of the act. Thus, trial courts have successfully evaded the time-limit provisions of the act by invoking the loopholes and thereby creating the image of compliance.[158] Candidly admitting that the act had not changed matters in his court, a judge asserted that, "We don't care if [the act is] repealed or not; our court has figured out ways to deal with the act that don't cause us to change our practices at all. The act has caused us to be a little creative; that's all."[159]

Even if the defendant finds a judge not bent upon circumventing the act, he must convince the trial court to dismiss the case with prejudice. Under the act, failure to comply with section 3161 requires dismissal of the charge (if no information or indictment is filed) or of the indictment or information (if the defendant is not tried within the applicable time limit). Under section 1962, the trial court is given discretion to dismiss the charges with or without prejudice. The criteria the act sets forth to guide the trial judge in her decision are: "the seriousness of the offense; the facts and circumstances of the case which led to the dismissal; and the impact of a reprosecution on the administration of this chapter and on the administration of justice."[160]

It is clear that the accused must persuade the trial court to dismiss the charge with prejudice in order to attain a satisfactory remedy; otherwise, the government is free to re-institute the charges against the defendant. Further, in cases where the government may re-initiate the prosecution, it would have little incentive to comply with the time strictures outlined in the act.

As a prelude to the passage of the Speedy Trial Act, the appropriate remedy for a violation of its provisions generated intense debate in Congress. Those who favored barring reprosecution upon a violation contended that, to have any teeth, the act required a stringent penalty. The opposing viewpoint was that criminals would not receive their just deserts if reprosecution was precluded.[161] Ultimately, a compromise emerged in which the decision to dismiss with or without prejudice was left to the "guided" discretion of the district court based on specified criteria.[162] Given the Supreme Court's interpretation of the circumstances in which dismissal with prejudice is warranted, however, most trial judges are unlikely to exercise their discretion in favor of barring reprosecution.

In *United States v. Taylor*,[163] the United States Supreme Court implicitly constrained the discretion accorded district judges in determining the proper sanction for a Speedy Trial Act violation. A clear breach of the act occurred in *Taylor*. The circumstances under which the transgression developed were unusual, however. Taylor's trial was set to begin one day before the expiration of the seventy-day period between indictment and trial required by the act. Taylor failed to appear for trial and became a fugitive. He was subsequently arrested on another charge; ultimately he was brought back to federal court to face the pending charges as well as a new charge based on his failure to appear at the scheduled trial. Taylor requested a dismissal of the original charges on the basis of a Speedy Trial Act violation.[164]

After excluding the time the defendant was a fugitive as well as a reasonable period for transporting Taylor to Seattle, the district court judge found that a violation of the act had occurred because the clock had expired fourteen days before the government obtained a superseding indictment.[165] Therefore, the trial judge exercised her discretion to dismiss the charges with prejudice, finding that the government's "lackadaisical behavior" in failing to ensure the defendant's prompt return to Seattle warranted a severe sanction.[166] Significantly, in her dismissal order, the judge explained that if the government's behavior was "tacitly condoned" by the toothless sanction of dismissal without prejudice, the "Speedy Trial Act would become a hollow guarantee."[167]

Reversing the trial judge's decision to dismiss the charges with prejudice, the *Taylor* Court imported constitutional speedy trial notions into the interpretation of the Speedy Trial Act. Although the majority rejected the argument that the defendant's flight restarted the speedy trial clock, it nevertheless maintained that such behavior should be considered in assessing the remedy for a breach of the Speedy Trial Act. Borrowing from *Barker* and *Marion*, moreover, the *Taylor* majority focused on the brevity of the delay caused by the government's conduct and the corresponding lack of prejudice suffered by the defendant.[168]

In effect, the *Taylor* Court resorted to the seldom-invoked, drastic measure of disturbing a district judge's exercise of discretion allegedly because of the inadequacy of the judge's explanation for her ruling.[169] In fact, as Justice Stevens pointed out in dissent, the judge's written order carefully dissected the basis for her ruling. She applied the three factors outlined in Section 1962(2) of the act, which guide the district judge by asking her to consider the seriousness of the offense, the circumstances provoking the dismissal, and the impact of a reprosecution upon the administration of the act and of justice in determining the proper remedy for a violation.[170]

The clear message conveyed to district judges by the *Taylor* decision is unmistakable: The best way to avoid reversal is to dismiss without prejudice.[171] Although the *Taylor* majority disingenuously sought to portray dismissal without prejudice as an effective sanction,[172] the only hurdle the government faces when this remedy is invoked is the relatively simple one of obtaining another indictment. The statute of limitations does not present a meaningful impediment; if the statute does run, a district court judge has no option to choose between dismissal with or without prejudice.[173]

If one views the Speedy Trial Act as a concrete remedial alternative to the ambiguous constitutional standard fashioned by the Supreme Court, the import of *Taylor* emerges in bold relief: In the phrase employed by the district judge in *Taylor*, the Speedy Trial Act is transformed into a "hollow guarantee."[174]

Indeed, to the extent the *Taylor* majority adopts the factors of length of delay and prejudice underlying the constitutional speedy trial right, it melds the constitutional and statutory rights. Since the Court has expressed its distaste for the only sanction that could give real meaning to the act, it necessarily has adopted constitutional criteria not meant to play a role in the construction of the Speedy Trial Act. Thus, *Taylor* implies that the accused must establish a lengthy delay prejudicing the defense to convince the district judge that dismissal with prejudice is warranted. Given that scenario, the time limits prescribed in the act lose their force.

CONCLUSION

The right to a speedy trial has been the subject of considerable confusion, inconsistency, and divergent viewpoints. From a constitutional perspective, the Court has viewed the right as a "second-class" citizen and thus not worthy of equal treatment with other comparable safeguards afforded criminal defendants. The Court's ambiguous jurisprudence results from the assumption that delay most often favors the defendant and prejudices the prosecution. Therefore, the Court has failed to develop a consistent, principled approach protective of defendants' speedy trial interests. Although time may be "the greatest cocounsel in the world,"[175] it also wreaks devastating harm to the defendant's right to speedy justice. Moreover, the fundamental rights embodied in the Sixth Amendment serve to protect the defendant, not the government or society's interest in deterring crime. Furthermore, it is the government's burden to provide the accused with speedy justice. Failure to invoke a fundamental right is not synonymous with its waiver.

As an alternative to the inadequate remedies evident in the constitutional right to a speedy trial, the Speedy Trial Act has proved to be a disappointment. Not only is the act subject to manipulation and evasion, but the Court's construction of the sanctions available under the statute has resulted in an amalgamation of constitutional and statutory "remedies." In effect, a defendant wishing to invoke his right to a speedy trial in the federal system, either constitutionally or statutorily, will encounter "hollow guarantees."

NOTES

1. The Sixth Amendment stipulates in pertinent part that "In all criminal prosecutions, the accused shall enjoy the right to a speedy and public trial," U.S. CONST. Amend. VI.
2. *Beavers v. Haubert*, 198 U.S. 77, 87 (1905).
3. *Barker v. Wingo* 407 U.S. 515, 522 (1972).

4. Id.
5. *Klopfer v. North Carolina*, 386 U.S. 213, 223 (1967).
6. Id. at 226.
7. Uviller, *Barker v. Wingo: Speedy Trial Gets a Fast Shuffle*, 72 COLUM. L. REV. 1376, 1378 (1972). Uviller's criticism was aimed at Justice Powell's opinion in *Barker*, which attempted to distinguish the right to a speedy trial from other defendant-protective rights in the Constitution because of a "societal interest in providing a speedy trial which exists separate from, and at times in opposition to, the interests of the accused," *Barker v. Wingo*, 407 U.S. at 519.
8. Uviller, *supra* at 1378.
9. *Barker v. Wingo*, 407 U.S. at 521.
10. *See* Godbold, *Speedy Trial-Major Surgery for a National Ill*, 24 ALA. L. REV. 265 (1972).
11. *Barker v. Wingo*, 407 U.S. at 526. The *Barker* Court recognized that in certain instances, "delay appreciably harms the defendant's ability to defend himself," id.
12. *United States v. Ewell*, 383 U.S. 116, 120 (1966); *Smith v. Hooey*, 393 U.S. 374, 377–78 (1969); *Barker v. Wingo*, 407 U.S. at 532.
13. 407 U.S. 514 (1972).
14. Id. at 532.
15. Id.
16. *See*, e.g., *United States v. Marion*, 404 U.S. 307, 320 (1971); *Barker*, 407 U.S. at 538 (White, J., concurring); *United States v. MacDonald*, 456 U.S. 1, 7–8 (1982).
17. 412 U.S. 434 (1973).
18. Id. at 435.
19. Amsterdam, *Speedy Criminal Trial: Rights and Remedies*, 27 STAN. L. REV. 525 (1975).
20. The *Barker* Court set forth a four-part balancing test to determine a violation of a defendant's speedy trial right based upon the length of the delay, the reason for it, the defendant's invocation of the right, and prejudice to the defendant, *Barker v. Wingo*, 407 U.S. at 530–32. Nevertheless, the majority insisted that none of the four factors "was a necessary or sufficient condition" to the finding of a violation, id. at 533.
21. 18 U.S.C. Sec. 3161 (1982).
22. *See Klopfer v. North Carolina*, 386 U.S. at 223–24.
23. Id. at 225. The Virginia constitution asserted that, "in all capital or criminal prosecutions a man hath a right . . . to a speedy trial," Va. Bill of Rights Sec. 8 (1776). Other states that inserted the right in their constitutions included Delaware (Del. Const. art. I, Sec. 7; Maryland (Md. Const.—Declarations of Rights art. XXI); Massachusetts (Mass. Const. art. XI); Pennsylvania (Pa. Const. art. I, Sec. 9). *See* 2 THE FEDERAL AND STATE CONSTITUTIONS, COLONIAL CHARTERS, AND OTHER ORGANIC LAWS OF THE UNITED STATES, 1909, 1920 (B. Poore, comp. 2d ed. 1878).
24. U.S. Const. Amend. VI. *See* Heller, THE SIXTH AMENDMENT TO THE CONSTITUTION OF THE UNITED STATES, 30 (1951).
25. Id. at 60–63. The right to a speedy trial was principally eclipsed by the defendant's right to a jury trial.
26. 198 U.S. 77 (1905).
27. Id. at 84–85.
28. Id. at 86–87.
29. Id. at 87.

30. Id.
31. Heller, *supra* note 23 at 61.
32. 7 F.2d 796 (8th Cir. 1925).
33. Id. at 798.
34. 386 U.S. 213 (1967).
35. Id. at 223.
36. Id. at 226.
37. Id.
38. Id. at 218.
39. Id. at 217–18.
40. Id. at 218.
41. Id. at 216.
42. Id.
43. 393 U.S. 374 (1969).
44. Id. at 383.
45. Id. at 379–80.
46. Id. at 383.
47. Id. at 384 (Harlan, J., concurring).
48. Id.
49. *See* notes 17–19 *infra* and accompanying text.
50. 398 U.S. 30 (1970).
51. Id. at 32–36.
52. *Strunk v. United States*, 412 U.S. 434 (1973).
53. *Dickey V. Florida*, 398 U.S. at 40–56 (Brennan, J., concurring).
54. Id. at 48.
55. 407 U.S. 514 (1972). The *Barker* Court adopted the same test based on a four-part inquiry: length of delay, reason for it, prejudice to the defendant, and waiver by the accused. However, Justice Brennan subsumed length under reason and prejudice; he deemed waiver by the defendant to be a function of the source of the delay, *Dickey v. Florida*, 398 U.S. at 48 n.12 (Brennan, J., concurring).
56. *Dickey v. Florida*, 398 U.S. at 53–55.
57. Id. at 55. (In *Chapman v. California*, 386 U.S. 18 (1967), the Court held that appellate reversals are not warranted for errors which do not affect the substantive rights of criminal defendants).
58. Brennan identified two ''group of issues to be met in interpreting the rights: first, those concerned with when during the criminal process the speedy-trial guarantee attaches; and second, those concerned with the criteria by which to judge the constitutionality of the delays to which the right does attach,'' id. at 41.
59. *United States v. Marion*, 404 U.S. 307, 313 (1971); *United States v. Lovasco*, 431 U.S. 783, 796 (1977).
60. *United States v. Marion*, 404 U.S. at 308.
61. Id. at 313.
62. Id. at 313–20.
63. Id. at 320.
64. Id. at 321.
65. Id. at 322.
66. Id. at 324.
67. Id. at 326.

68. Id. at 331–32 (Douglas J., concurring).
69. Id.
70. *United States v. Lovasco*, 431 U.S. at 790.
71. Id.
72. Id. at 790–95.
73. Id. at 792–95.
74. Goldfarb, *When Judges Abandon Analogy: The Problem of Delay in Commencing Criminal Prosecutions*, 31 W. & MARY L. REV. 607 (1990).
75. Id. at 632.
76. Id. at 638–59.
77. Id. at 651–59.
78. Id. at 657–58.
79. Amsterdam, *supra* note 19 at 528.
80. *Barker v. Wingo*, 407 U.S. at 516–17.
81. Id.
82. Id. at 535, n.39.
83. Id. at 519–20.
84. Id. at 521–22.
85. Id. at 521.
86. Id.
87. Id.
88. Uviller, *supra* note 7 at 1380–81.
89. *Barker v. Wingo*, 407 U.S. at 523–30.
90. Id. at 526–27.
91. Id. at 530. Brennan suggested the standard in *Dickey*, 398 U.S. at 48.
92. Id. at 530–31.
93. Id. at 533.
94. Id. at 532.
95. Id. at 534–35.
96. Id. at 536.
97. Id. at 537–38 (White, J., concurring). Justice White cited *United States v. Marion*, 404 U.S. at 320.
98. *Barker*, 407 U.S. at 534.
99. *Dickey v. Florida*, 398 U.S. at 49 (Brennan, J., concurring).
100. Id. at 49–50 (Citing *Johnson v. Zerbst*, 304 U.S. 458, 464 (1938); *Aetna Insurance Co. v. Kennedy*, 301 U.S. 389, 393 (1937); *Ohio Bell v. Public Utilities Comm'n*, 301 U.S. 292, 307 (1937)).
101. *Dickey v. Florida*, 398 U.S. at 50 (Brennan, J., concurring).
102. Heller, *supra* note 24 at 61.
103. *Dickey v. Florida*, 398 U.S. at 50 (Brennan, J., concurring).
104. Uviller, *supra* note 7 at 1391.
105. Id.
106. *United States ex. rel. Von Cseh v. Fay*, 313 F.2d 620, 623 (2d. Cir. 1963).
107. *Barker v. Wingo*, 407 U.S. at 522.
108. Id.
109. Id. at 516.
110. 412 U.S. 434 (1973).
111. Id. at 435–36.

112. Id. at 438.
113. Id.
114. Id. at 438–39.
115. Id. at 439.
116. Amsterdam, *supra* note 19 at 537.
117. Id. at 535.
118. Id. at 538–39.
119. Id. at 539.
120. Id. at 536 (Amsterdam describes the *Strunk* Court's holding as ''extremely puzzling'').
121. Id. at 539.
122. Id. at 538.
123. *Dickey v. Florida*, 398 U.S. at 53–54 (Brennan, J., concurring).
124. Id. at 54–55.
125. Id. at 55–57.
126. This solution was adopted by the Supreme Court of New Mexico in *Zurla v. State*, 109 N.M. 640, 789 P.2d 588 (N.M. 1990).
127. 456 U.S. 1 (1982).
128. 474 U.S. 302 (1986).
129. *United States v. MacDonald*, 456 U.S. at 4–5.
130. Id. at 5.
131. Id. at 13–14 (Marshall, J., dissenting).
132. Id. at 14–15.
133. Id. at 10.
134. Id. Of course, the majority relied on *Marion* for the principle that the speedy trial clause is not triggered until a defendant is formally charged with a crime via arrest, indictment, or other formal accusation, id. at 6–7.
135. Id. at 8–9, n.8.
136. Id. at 16 (Marshall, J., dissenting).
137. Id. at 16–17.
138. Id. at 7–8.
139. *See supra*.
140. The Court held that a criminal defendant cannot appeal a denial of a motion to dismiss on speedy trial grounds until the merits of the case are adjudicated, *United States v. MacDonald*, 435 U.S. 850 (1978); *United States v. MacDonald*, 456 U.S. at 5.
141. 474 U.S. 302 (1986).
142. Id. at 304–05, 312–14.
143. Id. at 319–21 (Marshall, J., dissenting).
144. Id. at 311, n.13. This critique was aptly made by Justice Marshall in his dissent, id. at 321 (Marshall, J., dissenting).
145. Id. at 315.
146. Id. at 305–06.
147. Id. at 315.
148. *See* notes 7–8 and accompanying text.
149. The Speedy Trial Act of 1974, Pub. L. No. 93–619, 88 Stat. 2076 (codified as amended at 18 U.S.C. Sec. 3161–3174 (1982 & Supp. III 1985)). The view that congressional disenchantment with *Barker* led to the passage of the act is reflected in *United States v. Mehrmanesh*, 652 F.2d 766, 769 (9th Cir. 1980). The Congressional Committee

Reports also indicate the legislature's dissatisfaction with the Court's speedy trial jurisprudence.

150. 18 U.S.C. Sec. 3161 (1982 & Supp. III 1985). *See* also, Doyel, *The Federal Speedy Trial Act: Stampede into Ambush*, 16 J. MARSHALL L. REV. 27–28 (1982). Nonetheless, the House Report indicates that the motivation behind the act was to provide a more concrete remedy than that furnished by the Supreme Court's jurisprudence. The report states: "The Committee finds that the adoption of speedy trial legislation is necessary in order to give real meaning to that Sixth Amendment right. Thus far, neither the decisions of the Supreme Court nor the implementation of Rule 50(b) of the Federal Rules of Criminal Procedure, concerning plans for achieving the prompt disposition of criminal cases, provides the courts with adequate guidance on this question," H.R.Rep. No. 93–1508, p. 11 (1974), U.S. Code Cong. & Admin.News 1974, pp. 7401–04. For a thorough description and analysis of the Speedy Trial Act of 1974, *see* Misner, SPEEDY TRIAL—FEDERAL AND STATE PRACTICE (1983).

151. Id. at Sec. 3161 (b).

152. Id. at Sec. 3161 (c).

153. 18 U.S.C. Sec. 3161 (h)(1)(A) (1982).

154. Id. Sec. 3161 (h)(1)(F).

155. Id. Sec. 3161 (h)(8)(3)(A).

156. Id. Sec. 3161 (h)(7).

157. Id. at Sec. 3161 (h)(8)(A).

158. Feely, COURT REFORM ON TRIAL 173 (1983).

159. Id.

160. 18 U.S.C. Sec. 3162 (a)(1)–(2).

161. Partridge, LEGISLATIVE HISTORY OF TITLE I OF THE SPEEDY TRIAL ACT OF 1974, 31–33, 1980, cited in *United States v. Taylor*, 487 U.S. 326, 334 (1988).

162. *United States v. Taylor*, 487 U.S. at 334–35. For the criteria enumerated in the act, *see* note 160 and accompanying text.

163. 487 U.S. 326 (1988).

164. Id. at 328–29. Taylor was originally indicted by a federal grand jury for conspiracy to distribute cocaine and possession of 400 grams of cocaine with intent to distribute.

165. Id. at 329–30.

166. Id. at 330–31.

167. Id. at 331.

168. Id. at 340–41.

169. Id. at 350 (Stevens, J., dissenting).

170. The explicit and adequate basis of the district judge's order is evident in Justice Stevens's dissent, *United States v. Taylor*, 487 U.S. at 350–52.

171. Id. at 350.

172. Id. at 342. Justice Blackmun, speaking for the majority, stated that "Dismissal without prejudice is not a toothless sanction: it forces the Government to obtain a new indictment if it decides to reprosecute, and it exposes the prosecution to dismissal on statute of limitations grounds."

173. Id. at 350 (Stevens, J., dissenting).

174. Id. at 352–53.

175. McNamara, CONSTITUTIONAL LIMITATIONS ON CRIMINAL PROCEDURE (1972).

5

The Jury Trial in Criminal Context: Link Between the Defendant and the Community

A jury trial represents America's ratification of participatory democracy. From our colonial roots to the present day, the right to be judged by one's peers is a safeguard which Americans hold in high esteem. Correlatively, the jury provides a vital link between the law and the community.[1] In the criminal realm, these two functions coincide to the extent that full-fledged societal participation furnishes a check against unbridled abuse by either the prosecution or the court. Thus, a jury in a criminal trial has been characterized as a fundamental right that assures the accused a fair trial by interposing between the prosecution and the defendant "the commonsense judgment of a group of laymen."[2] These complementary roles illuminate the distinctive feature of a jury trial within the adversary system of adjudication.

An inextricable nexus to the community and a democratic form of government, therefore, informs the development of the jury trial in America. As a prominent constitutional scholar has written, "The jury mediate[s] between 'the law' in the abstract and the human needs of those affected by it."[3] Within the criminal process, community participation enhances the fairness of a criminal trial by protecting against prosecutorial or judicial excesses. However, a jury trial is fundamentally designed to preserve the defendant's liberty interests. An ancillary component of a criminal trial is to advance societal privileges through heightened citizen participation in governmental functions.

The distinction between the structural and individual values fostered by a criminal jury trial was starkly elucidated by the Supreme Court in the early twentieth century. In *Patton v. United States*,[4] the majority stressed the defendant-oriented character of a jury trial in the criminal context. Searching in vain for a historical or contemporary societal anchoring of the criminal jury trial, the Court emphasized the individual focus of the right:

The record of English and colonial jurisprudence outdating the Constitution will be searched in vain for evidence that trial by jury in criminal cases was regarded as part of the structure of government, as distinguished from a right or privilege of the accused. On the contrary, it uniformly was regarded a valuable privilege bestowed upon the person accused of crime for the purpose of safeguarding him against the oppressive power of the King and the arbitrary or partial judgment of the court.[5]

From the historical record, the Court presumed that the framers' intent was to preserve the jury trial for the benefit of the accused and not necessarily to promote communitarian, democratic values.[6] In labeling the jury trial a "fundamental right," and making it applicable to the states through the Fourteenth Amendment, the Court underscored the principal feature of a jury trial as a safeguard against "miscarriages of justice," and as indispensable to secure a fair trial for all defendants.[7] At the same time, however, the Court has espoused the premise that the right to a jury trial is not exclusively the defendant's, but encompasses prosecutorial and societal objectives.[8] The Court's ambivalence with regard to the foundations, functions, and values served by a criminal jury trial has resulted in a conflicting array of holdings.

Flowing from this contradictory drift is an evident dichotomy: a constrained view of what communitarian and defendant-oriented goals demand with respect to jury size and unanimity; and a broader perspective on what a defendant and society at large deserve in terms of jury pool and grand jury composition. The Court's constricted vision about jury size and unanimity stems from its limited sense of the accused's right to a fair trial by an impartial jury and from its equally narrow view of how broad and diverse citizen participation in a jury supports a defendant's fair trial rights. Conversely, the Court's attitude toward the jury pool and the grand jury's composition relies on representative democracy as the core attribute of a criminal jury trial. Unfortunately, the Court's expansive view of the second prong of the dichotomy is the right result for the wrong reasons.

In order to analyze the ambivalent jurisprudence generated by this revered freedom, it is imperative to examine its historical sources and to explore its functional and pragmatic objectives. After undertaking this analysis, one must inquire about and offer an explanation for the Court's ambidextrous interpretation. To a great degree, this conflicting jurisprudence may be untangled by reference to the interplay between the jury's role in a democracy and the defendant's right to select an impartial jury of peers who will judge her guilt or innocence in a fair manner.

A jury trial formed an inestimable part of our heritage from colonial days and from the early days of the new nation. The American colonial jury system differed from its British counterpart in that colonial juries exercised the power to judge the legitimacy of the law.[9] Indeed, American independence coincided with the ascendancy of the jury system as a hallmark of individual liberty. Further, the roots of the revolt against English rule may be partially traced to fierce resistance to British attempts to restrict or evade the right to a jury trial.[10]

The Founding Fathers valued the right to a jury trial as an instrument of the democratic process. John Adams, the primary colonial exponent of the power of juries, described jury trials as one of the two key elements, together with popular elections, of the British system.[11] In the *Federalist 83*, Alexander Hamilton asserted that both proponents and foes of the new constitution agreed upon the centrality of the jury trial. The only differences, if any, between them lay in the fact that opponents regarded the jury trial as a "valuable safeguard to liberty," while proponents viewed it as the "very palladium of free government."[12] Similarly, Thomas Jefferson saw the jury trial as a means of assuring government fidelity to the principles underlying the constitution.[13]

Although the jury trial played a key role in our historical development as a nation, its history is shrouded in ambiguity and confusion. Other than agreement on the importance of the jury trial to the democratic form of government, little else is settled from a historical standpoint. As Toni Massaro tells us, "The recorded history of the jury is ambiguous, sometimes incomplete, and often conflicting. The role and form of the jury have changed significantly over time."[14] Consequently, history may buttress contradictory perspectives on the role of the jury due to its uncertain origins.

The open-ended texture of the constitutional provisions guaranteeing a jury trial for those accused of crimes, moreover, do not furnish much guidance. Both Article III, section 2 of the Constitution and the Sixth Amendment speak generally of the right to a jury trial but do not define its parameters.[15] Evidently, the generic language of those provisions embodied a desire to permit flexibility, thereby preserving local customs.[16] Unfortunately, such fluidity in the constitutional text has led to "confusion about what procedures are included in the Sixth Amendment mandate."[17] Therefore, recourse to either history or the text of the Constitution will not assist courts in construing the scope, letter, and spirit of the right to a jury trial in the criminal context.

If history does not furnish a definitive guide to the scope and breadth of a jury trial, it nonetheless facilitates analysis of the functions and values fostered by the right. The primary aim of a criminal jury trial is to prevent governmental abuse by using laypersons as a shield between the prosecution and the defendant. The second goal of a jury is to promote community participation in the determination of guilt or innocence.[18] These two objectives are complementary; that is, the defendant receives a fair trial if she is able to select a jury of her peers from a representative cross-section of the relevant community. Thus, the overarching function of a jury in a criminal trial is to provide an impartial body of defendant's peers who are drawn from a representative cross-section of the populace.[19] An impartial jury ideally affords the defendant a fair trial as well as cementing the appearance of fairness through full-fledged community participation in the verdict.[20]

Agreement upon these values and functions leaves open the question of how they are best implemented. In this respect, the historical, common law foundation of the jury trial has loomed large. The historical antecedents have produced an aberration in Supreme Court jurisprudence with respect to jury size and unanimity. From a jurisdictional perspective, a criminal defendant in the federal system is entitled to a twelve-person jury in unanimous agreement on his guilt[21]; on the contrary, an accused at the state level may be convicted by a jury not unanimous about his guilt and he may be tried by a six-person jury.[22] To explain this anomaly, we must trace the path taken by the Court in construing the principal requisites for a fair, representative jury.

Deciphering the appropriate boundaries of a criminal jury trial, the Supreme Court in *Patton v. United States*[23] delineated three critical elements underlying a jury trial at common law. Those three features entail a twelve-person jury, supervised by a judge, that arrives at a unanimous verdict. Furthermore, the common law attributes of the jury are indispensable components inherent in both the Article III and Sixth Amendment provisions guaranteeing a jury trial for criminal defendants.[24] *Patton*, in turn, relied on the clear precedent established more than three decades earlier in *Thompson v. Utah*.[25] Succinctly setting forth the intent behind the constitutional right to a jury trial, the *Thompson* Court declared that, "[t]he wise men who framed the Constitution . . . and the people who approved it [believed] that life and liberty . . . in criminal prosecutions, would not be adequately secured except through the unanimous verdict of twelve jurors."[26]

Indeed, the impulse behind both *Thompson* and *Patton* was a deep-seated notion that a unanimous verdict by a jury of twelve was a "substantial and essential" condition of the right to a trial by jury.[27] A product of this proposition was the holding by the *Thompson* Court that the liberty interests of the accused, as well as the accuracy of the fact-finding process, required a verdict by twelve, not eight, jurors.[28] Moreover, any statutory efforts to circumscribe the elements of size and unanimity would abridge the right to a jury trial.[29]

In viewing the right to a jury trial as a defendant-oriented safeguard, the Court in *Patton* gave the accused the prerogative to waive the right, subject to the approval of the court and the government.[30] Therefore, the unmistakable trend evinced by the Court's early twentieth-century jurisprudence pointed to a solicitous regard for the defendant's right to a fair trial. The Sixth Amendment guarantees a criminal defendant a jury trial in the common law sense: that is, a unanimous verdict by a jury composed of twelve "men."[31] In the 1970s, however, a majority of the Court decided to reverse the message conveyed by *Patton* and *Thompson*; it curtailed the requirements of jury size and unanimity so vigorously defended decades earlier.

The retreat from the principles enunciated in *Thompson* and *Patton* began with *Williams v. Florida*.[32] Explaining away the imperative common law requirement it had previously ratified, the *Williams* Court dismissed the twelve-person jury as a "historical accident."[33] The crux of the majority rationale rested on the severance of twelve-person jury from the key objectives of the jury trial. Given the interposition of the common-sense judgment of six laypersons and the participation of a broad segment of the community, a six-person jury served the same functions as that performed by one composed of twelve.[34] Thus, as long as the number permits group deliberation and provides "a fair possibility for obtaining a representative cross-section of the community," the jury comported with the Sixth Amendment.

Ironically, the edifice upon which *Williams* is built collapsed a few years later in *Ballew v. Georgia*.[35] The rhetorical question posed by Justice Harlan's concurring opinion in *Williams* came back to haunt the Court: if twelve jurors are not essential, why are six?[36] Ultimately, the *Ballew* decision recognized the obvious, supported by an impressive collection of empirical data: reducing jury size prejudices the defendant by increasing the risks of erroneous conviction and diminishing the consistency and reliability of verdicts.[37] As one study concluded: "Larger juries (size twelve) are preferable to smaller juries (six). They produce longer deliberations, more communication, far better community representation, and, possibly, greater verdict reliability (consistency)."[38]

Justifying *Williams*'s rationale became a difficult feat in light of *Ballew*. Therefore, the Court had to concede that the distinction between five- and six-person juries was necessarily arbitrary. Rather than overruling *Williams*, however, Justice Blackmun reaffirmed its chief premise while acknowledging that "the purpose and functioning of the jury in a criminal trial is seriously impaired . . . to a constitutional degree, by a reduction in size to below six members."[39] The flawed basis of such an aberrational result confirms the wisdom and judgment shown by the decisions which adopted the common law jury form. As Justice Harlan noted, history provides the best foundation for requiring a jury of twelve.[40]

The second part of the common law jury, unanimity, seemed unassailable if one read *Williams* carefully. In a footnote Justice White assumed that unanimity, unlike the twelve-person requirement, was vitally linked to the jury's function because it buttressed the government's burden of proving guilt beyond a reasonable doubt.[41] However impregnable unanimity appeared, it was rapidly punctured in companion cases scarcely two years after *Williams* was decided.[42] Furthermore, a majority of the Court rejected Justice White's proposition that reasonable doubt was tied to the jury's purpose.

A unanimous jury verdict, the Court concluded, is not required by the Sixth Amendment. Although the Court had held that the reasonable doubt standard was a component of the Fourteenth Amendment's due process clause, the jury clause of the Sixth does not mandate proof beyond a reasonable doubt. The fact that one, two, or three persons are not convinced of the defendant's guilt does not translate to reasonable doubt because those who vote to convict are presumably firm in their belief.[43] As long as a "substantial majority" of the jury votes to convict, the integrity of the verdict remains intact. In his concurring opinion, Justice Blackmun expressed doubts that a guilty verdict by less than 75 percent of the jury would be satisfactory.[44]

The flaw in the Court's internal logic is evident when one examines the rationale and purpose supporting the Sixth Amendment. As the linchpin of the adversary process, the rights guaranteed by the Sixth Amendment are meant to "shield the defendant against state power." It is axiomatic, therefore, that these guarantees assure that the burden of proof is borne by the government, not the defendant.[45] The reasonable doubt standard, endorsed by the Court in *In re Winship*,[46] complements Sixth Amendment rights by making the government earn convictions. The right to a jury trial is not designed to ease the state's burden in obtaining a guilty verdict; on the contrary, its principal thrust is to protect the accused from governmental or judicial abuse by placing his fate in the hands of "peers" selected from a representative sample of the community. Thus, to the degree that the government's burden of proof is diluted, the safeguards inhering in a jury trial dwindle.

How does a less than unanimous verdict adversely affect a defendant's right to compel the government to shoulder the burden of proof? It obliterates the possibility that a minority could persuade the majority to acquit or, alternatively, to convict of a less serious offense. Further, it allows the prosecution to attain a greater number of convictions than it would if unanimous verdicts are required.[47] In sum, the argument that neither the Sixth Amendment nor the reasonable doubt standard is compromised by a majority verdict runs counter to logic, experience, and empirical analysis.

If the structural and doctrinal bases upon which *Johnson v. Louisiana* and *Apodaca v. Oregon* rest are flawed, it is necessary to marshal a more convincing rationale. Justice Powell made an attempt to fill the gaps in the majority's faulty reasoning by resorting to a state sovereignty argument.[48] While recognizing the convincing historical and precedential bases for unanimity, Powell determined that the Fourteenth Amendment's due process clause was sufficiently flexible to permit the states to tinker with the unanimity requirement. Thus, he rejected the assumption that the Fourteenth Amendment incorporates "jot-for-jot and case-for-case" every element of the Sixth Amendment.[49]

Justice Powell's "federalism" justification produces anomalous results. While a defendant charged with a federal crime must be convicted through a unanimous jury decision, her counterpart at the state level can be stripped of her liberty and stigmatized as a criminal by a substantial majority of the jury. As Justice Douglas asked rhetorically, "How can that be possible when both decisions stem from the Sixth Amendment?"[50] Why should a defendant's liberty interests be jeopardized on the fortuity of the type of violation he is alleged to have committed? In essence, the Court's opinions dispensing with unanimity define a jury trial differently for defendants in state and federal trials.

By reshaping the boundaries of the criminal jury trial, the Court has departed from the perspective it subscribed to in the early part of the twentieth century. Although *Patton* viewed a twelve-person, unanimous jury as indispensable components of the Sixth Amendment, *Williams, Johnson*, and *Apodaca* saw the jury trial through a different lens. This novel view stripped the jury requirement to its bare essentials: jurors must be "laymen, drawn from the community without systematic exclusion of any group, who exercise commonsense judgment."[51]

As a consequence of the limited requisites of the jury trial, the Sixth Amendment has undergone a profound alteration from what the Founding Fathers envisioned. Although one may agree that the jury trial provisions of both the Sixth Amendment and Article III of the Constitution are fluid, it is evident that the framers intended "to preserve the jury safeguard as it was known to them at common law."[52] Moreover, precedent established the Court's sensitivity to preserving the vital common law elements of a jury trial. Circumscribing the parameters of the common law right to a jury trial for the sake of "federalism" detracts from the overriding goal of the Sixth Amendment. That goal is to subject the prosecution's case to the crucible of the adversary process, thereby ensuring that the defendant's liberty interests are adequately protected.

From a practical standpoint, one may dismiss the Court's restricted view of the jury by arguing that only a few states have chosen to discard either unanimity or the twelve-person jury. Nevertheless, allowing such a dilution of the jury trial concept lessens the appearance of fairness which underlies the values advanced by the Sixth Amendment. Symbolically, these two features of the jury trial impress upon society the system's concern with according the defendant maximum protection from an erroneous conviction or an unreliable verdict. Permitting majority verdicts and allowing six-person juries create the impression that the prosecution may obtain a conviction with greater ease than the Constitution anticipates.

In contrast to its narrow vision of the common law jury, the Court has striven to maintain inviolate the precept of both grand and petit jury representativeness. Participatory democracy is at odds with exclusion of identifiable groups from an essential governmental function: serving on a grand or petit jury. Ideally, a jury should be selected from a "cross-section of the community." It is impossible, however, for a petit jury ever to mirror the community. Thus, it is sufficient to ensure the legitimacy of the criminal justice system if the parties are enabled to choose a jury from a representative sample of the affected community. This requirement validates the criminal justice system by "injecting representative community voices into the decision process."[53]

Though in some circumstances the cross-section standard may interfere with the accused's right to a fair trial,[54] in most instances representativeness bolsters the defendant's opportunity to obtain a fair trial. In fact, the cross-section requirement is tied to the concept of peers that inheres in the right to a jury trial. A "peer" collectively represents the accused's "neighbors, fellows, associates, persons having the same legal status in society as that which he holds."[55] In effect, our heritage reflects a deep-rooted desire to be judged by people like ourselves. We desire a jury of our peers because they can supposedly empathize with our "feelings, volitions, or ideas."[56] Therefore, to the extent that a defendant may choose a jury from a representative part of the community, she has the opportunity of choosing jurors whose experiential background is similar to hers.[57]

As every trial lawyer knows, however, what attorneys want in a jury differs from the ideal of a fair and impartial jury. The ideal embodies "an impartial representative group of people who will listen to and consider all the evidence fairly and bring in a verdict." Pragmatically, "they [attorneys] want people who have some disposition, some tilt, toward their client, or who can be tilted. Jury selection is, in the end, the manipulation of bias."[58] Ultimately, enabling the defendant to choose a jury from a representative cross-section of the community fosters fairness by not allowing the prosecution to exclude members of the community who will empathize with the accused's position. On the opposite side of the spectrum, the jury drawn from a cross-section of the community "achieves symbolically what cannot be achieved practically—the presence of the entire populace at every trial."[59]

Historically, the Supreme Court has endeavored to adhere to the ideal of a jury selected from a representative sample of the community. It has striven to prevent exclusionary practices which preclude segments of the populace from performing jury service. Traditionally, the Court relied on the equal protection clause of the Fourteenth Amendment to prohibit states from excluding blacks from grand or petit jury service.[60] Once the right to a jury trial was extended to the states,[61] the Court characterized the cross-representation requirement as an "essential component of the Sixth Amendment right to a jury trial."[62] However, the Court has refused to apply the Sixth Amendment requirement to preclude the prosecutor from using the peremptory challenge process to exclude blacks from criminal juries.[63]

Beginning with a series of cases decided in the 1880s, the Court has declined to countenance racial exclusion in jury selection.[64] *Strauder v. West Virginia*[65] evoked the ideal that a jury necessarily entails "a body of men composed of the peers or equals of the person whose rights it is selected or summoned to determine."[66] As a corollary to this proposition, exclusion of blacks from a jury pool denied the accused equal protection because he could not select a jury from a body that included his peers; while a white man could enjoy the privilege of choosing a jury of his counterparts, or at least from a jury pool that included persons of his race.[67] Such discrimination contravened the equal protection clause of the Fourteenth Amendment, enacted chiefly to remove the incidents of exclusion that denied blacks the entitlements of full citizenship.[68]

Strauder was predicated upon the equal protection clause because the Supreme Court did not extend the right to a jury trial to the states until it decided *Duncan v. Louisiana* in 1968. Thus, the West Virginia statute making blacks ineligible to serve on grand or petit juries had to be invalidated on equal protection grounds. Nevertheless, the reasoning of *Strauder* relies in large part upon the right to a jury trial. The Court explicitly referred to the fact that West Virginia, through its constitution, guaranteed the right to trial by jury and that this right involved a trial by one's peers.[69] Implicitly, the *Strauder* Court ruled that exclusion of blacks from either a grand jury or a petit jury pool denied the defendant the right to be tried by a jury of his peers. A jury of the defendant's peers, in turn, meant a jury drawn from a representative sample of the community: that is, a jury from which no identifiable groups are omitted.

Given the historical straitjacket under which the *Strauder* Court operated, it had to justify its holding by resorting to equal protection, rather than jury trial, analysis. While it is true that West Virginia denied blacks equal protection by preventing them from jury service, it was the accused who complained that his right to a fair trial was abridged. How could the defendant obtain a fair and impartial jury when members of his own race were precluded from judging his guilt? To the extent that the deck was stacked against him, the possibility of the accused's receiving a fair trial was illusory.

As a consequence of the constraints imposed by the failure of the Supreme Court to extend the Sixth Amendment right to a jury trial to the states until the late 1960s, state laws excluding blacks from jury service had to be nullified on equal protection grounds. Therefore, since *Strauder* the Court "[has] repeatedly invalidated criminal convictions on equal protection grounds where state laws or practices excluded potential jurors from service on the basis of race."[70] This practice continued, moreover, after the Court had the defendant's right to a jury trial applicable to the states.

In *Taylor v. Louisiana*,[71] however, the Court held that the Sixth Amendment jury trial provision requires that panels from which a petit jury is drawn must represent a "fair cross-section of the community."[72] An impartial jury, therefore, can be secured only through a broad-based, representative pool which does not exclude distinctive groups of the community.[73] Excluding women from jury service contradicted the ideal of an impartial jury because a distinctive group was omitted from the jury pool.[74] Thus, impartiality and cross-representation are linked: to the degree that the defendant is deprived of the prospect of selecting a jury from a representative cross-section of the community, she is denied the Sixth Amendment right to an impartial jury.

Broad representation is satisfied through a representative jury pool and does not mandate a representative petit jury. The *Taylor* decision made clear that the cross-section requirement does not mean that "juries actually chosen must mirror the community and reflect the various distinctive groups in the population."[75] Rather, what the Sixth Amendment compels is that panels from which juries are selected must not systematically exclude identifiable groups in the community. A defendant who complains of a violation of the *Taylor* requirement has to meet a three-pronged test: that the group excluded is distinctive within the community; that the group is underrepresented in the pools from which juries are selected in relation to the group's size in the community; and that the underrepresentation stems from systematic exclusion of the group in the jury selection process.[76]

Taylor is grounded upon a three-fold rationale: The fair cross-section standard protects the defendant from the arbitrary power of either the prosecutor or the court; it furthers the legitimacy of the criminal justice system by conveying the appearance of fairness to the public; and it sustains the democratic ideal that "sharing in the administration of justice is a phase of civic responsibility."[77]

Of course, what *Taylor* failed to elucidate is what constitutes a "distinctive" group for "representative cross-section" purposes. Although the Court has not explicitly defined the concept of "distinctiveness," it has included groups distinguished by such "immutable characteristic[s] as race, gender, or ethnic background" within its boundaries.[78] By contrast, groups sharing attitudes that prevent them from fulfilling their duties as jurors fall outside *Taylor*'s ambit.[79]

Comparing the cross-section requirement with the dictates set forth in *Strauder* yields a simple conclusion: Excluding identifiable groups from jury service deprives the defendant of an impartial jury. Of course, *Strauder* reached the conclusion based on equal protection principles because constitutional constraints prevented a Sixth Amendment analysis. *Taylor*, on the other hand, linked representativeness, and hence nonexclusion, with the right to an impartial jury. In essence, both decisions achieve the same result through different constitutional provisions. Perhaps one can construe *Strauder* to mean that granting some defendants the right to an impartial jury trial and denying it to others violates the equal protection clause.[80] Nonetheless, the text of the Sixth Amendment is the better avenue to follow in determining lack of representation in a jury panel. Equal protection precepts filled the void in the late nineteenth and early twentieth centuries. In light of *Duncan*, however, the need to rely on equal protection is obviated. It is reliance on equal protection that has led the Court into a treacherous road of inconsistency and doctrinal confusion.

The difficult road traversed by the Court involves a futile attempt to reconcile the right to an impartial jury trial with the "most undemocratic feature of our democratic trial system,"[81] the peremptory challenge. A peremptory challenge is undemocratic because it permits either side to strike potential jurors from service on grounds unrelated to their ability to impartially decide the accused's guilt or innocence. As described by the Court, the peremptory challenge is "frequently exercised on ground normally thought irrelevant to legal proceedings or official action, namely the race, religion, nationality, occupation or affiliations of people summoned for jury duty."[82] Racial neutrality in jury selection is therefore at odds with the fundamental nature of the peremptory challenge. Moreover, exercise of peremptories conflicts with the fair cross-section standard as well as with the defendant's right to a jury of her peers.[83]

In *Swain v. Alabama*,[84] the defendant challenged the prosecutor's use of peremptory challenges in a discriminatory fashion. The defendant was a black man convicted and sentenced to death by an all-white jury in Talladega County, Alabama, for raping a seventeen-year-old white girl. Since 1950, no black had served on a jury in Talladega County; furthermore, the prosecution in *Swain* used peremptories to remove from the jury panel all six blacks who were eligible to serve.[85]

Finding no constitutional violation, Justice White held that striking blacks in a particular case is not a denial of equal protection. He recognized that the nature of the peremptory challenge would be subverted if the prosecution would have to explain why it exercised challenges in a particular case. Application of equal protection principles to the peremptory challenge would undermine its purpose. As he put it, the prosecution's judgment would be scrutinized for reasonableness and sincerity. Thus, "a great many uses of the challenge would be banned."[86] A presumption of prosecutorial good faith would attend the use of peremptory challenges to exclude blacks from jury service; such a presumption, moreover, would not be overcome with evidence that the prosecutor employed peremptories to remove all blacks from the jury.[87]

The Court acknowledged that removal of blacks from juries for nontrial-related reasons was impermissible. In order to establish discriminatory intent, however, the defendant had to establish the prosecutor's systematic use of peremptories to exclude blacks over a prolonged period of time.[88] Given the near-insurmountable hurdle *Swain* presented, criminal defendants had no practical remedies with which to combat discriminatory use of peremptories based on a potential juror's race.

It is instructive to explore the reasoning of *Swain*, in order to clarify the Court's deferential treatment of an inherently undemocratic procedure. The peremptory challenge, Justice White recognized, is not constitutionally compelled.[89] Nonetheless, the vitality and persistence of the challenge in American trial procedure pointed to its fundamental nature. Indeed, the *Swain* Court characterized the peremptory challenge as "a necessary part of trial by jury."[90] Supposedly, peremptories ensure an impartial jury by "eliminating extremes of partiality"and by removing biased jurors.[91] These explanations are without foundation. In essence, peremptories are used by skillful attorneys to obtain a jury which favors their side or, at a minimum, which is not tilted toward the opposition. Bias, moreover, is eliminated through the challenge for cause, which removes jurors who cannot impartially weigh the defendant's guilt or innocence.

Despite the illogical grounding of *Swain*, its rationale is consistent with the foundation underlying the peremptory challenge. The nature of peremptories clashes with the notion that the prosecution must justify exclusion of particular jurors. Justice White was correct in postulating the dichotomy between the challenge and race neutrality in jury selection. Irrational, instinctive, and stereotypical reasons for removing potential jurors are precisely what the peremptory challenge preserves. If one agrees with this fundamental premise, making the prosecutor explain the exercise of a particular challenge, for whatever benevolent reason, defeats the nature of the privilege.

Swain represented a misguided effort to "reconcile the command of racial neutrality in jury selection with the utility, and tradition, of peremptory challenges."[92] Furthermore, the discriminatory exercise of peremptories precludes the selection of a jury from a broad cross-section of the community. While it is true that a defendant is not entitled to a jury that mirrors the relevant community, she nevertheless should have the "fair possibility" of choosing a jury from a broad spectrum of the community. This means that identifiable groups are not excluded, whether at the stage of selecting the jury pool or at the level of attempting to choose the jury. A prosecutor who uses peremptory challenges to exclude all blacks from a jury deprives a defendant of the opportunity of selecting a jury from a cross-section of the community as surely as a state that excludes all blacks from jury service.[93]

Ultimately, the Court revisited *Swain*, casting aside its onerous requirements, yet missing the opportunity to discard the peremptory challenge as an undemocratic concept at variance with the Sixth Amendment. Instead, the Court opened a Pandora's Box that is not likely to be closed in the near future. *Batson v. Kentucky*[94] is a well-meaning reform gone astray. Doctrinally and practically, *Batson* is flawed because it relies on equal protection, rather than Sixth Amendment, grounds; and because it fails to abolish that quintessentially undemocratic device, the peremptory challenge. A look at *Batson* and its progeny amply demonstrates its defective character.

Batson challenged his conviction because he was tried by an all-white jury after the prosecutor used his peremptories to remove the only four blacks on the jury panel. Cognizant of the imposing obstacles presented by *Swain*, the defendant sought to reverse his conviction on the basis that the state's use of peremptories to remove all blacks from the jury violated his Sixth Amendment right to a jury drawn from a cross-section of the community.[95] Inexplicably, the Court ignored Batson's fair cross-section contention, and instead relied upon equal protection grounds to overturn part of *Swain*'s holding.

Discarding the "crippling burden of proof" established by *Swain*,[96] the *Batson* Court held that "a defendant may establish a prima facie case of purposeful discrimination in selection of the petit jury solely on evidence concerning the prosecutor's exercise of peremptory challenges at the defendant's trial."[97] Once the defendant sets forth her prima facie case, the burden shifts to the prosecution to establish a "neutral" explanation for challenging black jurors. Though Justice Powell did not elaborate on what constitutes a "neutral explanation," he did eliminate as a neutral reason the prosecutor's assumption that blacks "would be partial to the defendant because of their shared race." The trial court then will have to determine whether the defendant has established purposeful discrimination.[98]

Batson represents a well-intentioned effort to eliminate the pernicious effects of discrimination in the petit jury system. The solution proffered by the Court, however, has resulted in a quagmire. What *Batson* wrought was an "enforcement nightmare."[99] By narrowly limiting the peremptory challenge, the majority created more problems than it solved. Moreover, *Batson*'s misguided reliance on the equal protection clause raised thorny issues which would not have surfaced had the Court resorted to the Sixth Amendment's fair cross-section requirement.

One of the most troublesome issues posed by *Batson* is how a court determines purposeful discrimination by the prosecution. As Justice Marshall pointed out in his concurring opinion, discriminatory use of peremptories is subject to attack only in the most flagrant instances.[100] Albert Alschuler notes that discrimination "means taking more than one or two 'shots' at prospective black jurors."[101]

Hence, if the prosecutor's use of peremptories doesn't rise to the level of a "pattern" of strikes against black jurors, an inference of purposeful discrimination is unwarranted.

Similarly, weighing the prosecutor's motives to determine neutrality versus discriminatory purpose creates numerous difficulties. Discerning neutral motive involves tricky resolution of social, psychological, and racial issues.[102] Lower courts, moreover, have been more than generous in categorizing trivial explanations as "neutral." For example, exclusions based on demeanor, attitude, and lack or excess of eye contact, have been approved by appellate courts.[103] A savvy prosecutor will be able to offer a "neutral" explanation for striking a black juror. In effect, the message for such a prosecutor is: "When your quota of free shots is exhausted, you must make up some plausible reasons."[104]

The circumscribed basis of the "neutral" reason was confirmed by the Court in *Hernandez v. New York*.[105] In that case, the prosecutor used peremptory challenges to remove Hispanic jurors from the jury. The purported explanation was that "the specific responses and the demeanor of the two individuals during voir dire caused him to doubt their ability to defer to the official translation of Spanish-language testimony."[106] Writing for the majority, Justice Kennedy asserted that unless a discriminatory intent is evident in a prosecutor's explanation, the "reason offered will be deemed race-neutral."[107]

Though language is closely tied to ethnicity, the *Hernandez* majority dismissed the disproportionate impact of using language as a ground upon which to remove potential jurors. Absent discriminatory intent on the prosecutor's part, disproportionate impact of such a criterion does not violate the principle of race-neutrality.[108] Justice O'Connor's concurring opinion best expresses the majority's constricted view of what constitutes an unacceptable reason for striking a juror on *Batson* grounds: "No matter how closely tied or significantly correlated to race the explanation for a peremptory strike may be, the strike does not implicate the Equal Protection Clause unless it is based on race."[109]

Of course, the majority did not go quite as far as Justice O'Connor; it balked at approving a reason based solely on the fact that the prosecutor did not want Spanish-speaking jurors.[110] The cue prosecutors receive from *Hernandez*, however, is crystal clear: Make sure you don't offer Spanish-speaking ability as the sole reason for striking a juror; rather, offer some trivial "race-neutral" explanation such as demeanor, attitude, or unwillingness to abide by the official translation.

Hernandez converts the *Batson* mandate into a hollow prescription. If the guiding standard is a facially neutral explanation, despite its disparate impact, *Batson* is transformed into a symbolic requirement. It will be difficult for a defendant to establish discriminatory intent by the prosecutor when any trivial reason which is not facially discriminatory will rebut a prima facie case. The "heightened quantum of proof" created by *Hernandez* creates a difficult hurdle for a defendant, who will have to present evidence of the prosecutor's subjective intent to discriminate.[111]

In fact, *Hernandez* has borne out Justice Marshall's dire prediction in his *Batson* concurring opinion. He discerned the imaginary safeguard created by the majority opinion because of the nettlesome issue of detecting prosecutors' motives. Indeed, Marshall observed that "any prosecutor can easily assert facially neutral reasons for striking a juror, and trial courts are ill-equipped to second-guess those reasons."[112] Trial courts now will be virtually powerless to question a prosecutor's motives in light of *Hernandez*. A petty explanation will be deemed sufficient to rebut a prima facie case of discrimination, even though its disproportionate impact thwarts the possibility of selecting a jury from a fair cross-section of the community.

Given the ease with which the prosecution can rebut a claim of purposeful discrimination in the exercise of peremptories, the need to abolish the peremptory challenge becomes compelling. Some scholars contend that the prosecution, but not the defense, should be banned from using peremptory challenges.[113] This disparity is grounded on the notion that peremptory challenges assure the accused's right to a fair trial by countering the natural adversarial advantage enjoyed by the prosecution. On the other hand, the opposite view is that balance constitutes the cornerstone of the adversarial system and that it is antithetical to equal protection precepts to allow any discrimination to infect the trial process.[114]

Discriminatory practices serve no function in a jury trial. Should we be comfortable with a white defendant, accused of an interracial crime, who employs peremptory challenges to exclude all black jurors from the venire? Such discrimination would test the legitimacy of the criminal justice system. It would undermine confidence in the trial process and engender the same feelings of displacement among black potential jurors as would the discriminatory use of peremptories by the prosecution. Further, since the peremptory challenge is not constitutionally required, its proscription cannot be deemed to violate a defendant's Sixth Amendment right to a fair trial by an impartial jury.[115] Limiting the peremptory for the defense pursuant to *Batson*-like standards generates the same problems the Court has encountered in delineating *Batson*'s scope.

To a large extent, this debate has been rendered moot by the Supreme Court's extension of Batson to the civil arena. In *Edmonson v. Leesville Concrete Co. Inc.*,[116] the Court held that race-based peremptory challenges implicate state action in a purely civil proceeding between two private parties.[117] Therefore, in a civil trial, removal of jurors on racial grounds violates a prospective juror's right to equal protection. Furthermore, a litigant may vicariously raise the prospective juror's right on her behalf.[118] The logical effect of *Edmonson*'s dictate is that criminal defendants will be precluded from using peremptory challenges to exclude black jurors.[119]

At bottom, as *Edmonson* illustrates, the worst doctrinal implications of *Batson* were provoked by the Court's reliance upon equal protection analysis. Batson's counsel never invoked the equal protection clause as a basis for reversal of his client's conviction. Rather, he took the position that exclusion of blacks from the venire violated Batson's right to a jury drawn from a fair cross-section of the community. In view of *Swain*'s dictates, this was a strategically wise decision. Nevertheless, the Supreme Court chose to ignore that issue and instead opted to decide the case on equal protection grounds.[120] This decision was misguided because historical reasons no longer bound the Court to rely on the equal protection clause.[121] In addition, *Taylor v. Louisiana* stands for the proposition that "the American concept of the jury trial contemplates a jury drawn from a fair cross section of the community."[122]

Why did the Court reject Batson's Sixth Amendment theory? It is difficult to hazard an educated guess. However, what the Court accomplished in doing so was to create a dilemma it would ultimately have to resolve. In effect, what *Batson* represents is the Court's position that discrimination in the use of peremptories by the prosecution contravenes a juror's equal protection right to be free from discrimination. The majority, however, could have rested upon the defendant's right to a jury selected from a broad cross-section of the community. The cross-section requirement ensures a neutral jury selection procedure "that is not arbitrarily skewed for or against any particular group or characteristic."[123] Therefore, *Batson* arguably protects the integrity of the factfinding process in a criminal jury trial by protecting a defendant's "interests in neutral jury selection procedures."[124]

The faulty constitutional predicate of *Batson* is evident in the Court's later pronouncements. Thus, the Court has stated that the decision is founded on both equal protection grounds and a defendant's right to a "fair and impartial factfinder."[125] Ultimately, however, the Court contradicted its earlier pronouncements; it made the equal protection right of jurors to be free from discrimination the sole constitutional rationale on which *Batson* rests. Such reasoning created doctrinal problems which would have been obviated had the Court relied upon the Sixth Amendment fair cross-section requirement in invalidating the prosecutor's discriminatory use of peremptories.

Batson's house of cards began to fall apart with the Court's fundamentally flawed opinion in *Holland v. Illinois*.[126] Explicit within *Batson*'s parameters is the requirement that a defendant must show she is a member of a "cognizable racial group" who is a victim of the prosecutor's use of peremptories to remove from the venire members of the defendant's race.[127] Therefore, the opinion indicated that shared racial identity was a prerequisite to an equal protection challenge under its mandate. But the question left unanswered was: could a white defendant object to a prosecutor's discriminatory use of peremptories to exclude all blacks from the venire? The *Batson* Court's equal protection analysis indicated that such a challenge was not within its range.

When a white defendant did raise such an objection, he logically did so according to Sixth Amendment fair cross-section criteria. Under those principles shared identity between the defendant and the prospective juror is irrelevant, as the Court had made clear on numerous occasions.[128] The majority in *Holland*, however, rejected the defendant's claim that when the prosecution employs peremptory challenges to remove all black prospective jurors because of their race, it deprives the accused of the right to choose a jury from a representative cross-section of the community. The majority's rationale was ingenious: that the Sixth Amendment cross-section standard assures the defendant not a representative jury but an impartial one.[129] Of course, the Sixth Amendment fair cross-section requirement had never been construed to dictate that juries should perfectly reflect the composition of the community; instead, representativeness merely entails the fair possibility that the jury be drawn from a broad section of the community.[130]

Another false premise the majority trumpeted in *Holland* was the belief that applying *Batson* in a Sixth Amendment context would destroy the peremptory challenge. This reasoning is disingenuous; the damage to the traditional peremptory challenge system had already been done in *Batson* under the aegis of the Fourteenth Amendment.[131]

Examining *Holland* from an objective legal standpoint reveals its manifold deficiencies. The prosecution can defeat a defendant's Sixth Amendment right to a neutral jury selection procedure by exercising peremptories to exclude all prospective blacks from the venire. The Sixth Amendment protects a defendant's right to an impartial jury, which means a jury that is "skewed" toward a particular group because it is not selected through a neutral procedure. As Justice Stevens points out, "The Sixth Amendment's [fair cross-section] protection is not so frail that it can be defeated by the State's creation of an additional level of selection."[132]

In a concurring opinion, however, Justice Kennedy revisited *Batson*, interpreting it to mean that racial exclusion of a juror violates a juror's constitutional rights. Along with Justice Marshall, Justice Kennedy suggested that Holland would have prevailed on the merits had he relied upon the Fourteenth Amendment equal protection clause.[133] Justice Kennedy got the opportunity to reach that conclusion on behalf of a majority of the Court in *Powers v. Ohio.*[134]

With *Powers*, the Court's equal protection analysis in *Batson* produced skewed logic and strained results. The Court confronted the doctrinal and practical foundation of *Batson*'s holding. What did *Batson* mean? That a juror could not be excluded from a jury on race-based grounds, or that a defendant's fair trial rights were infringed when members of his own race were excluded from the jury? A close reading of *Batson* indicated that the latter explanation was its fundamental underpinning.[135] Such an interpretation, however, would permit race-based peremptory challenges by the prosecution when the defendant and the potential juror did not share racial identity.

If *Batson* had been decided on fair cross-section grounds, then the Court's strained analysis in *Powers* would have been unnecessary. Whatever the defendant's race or background, he would have been entitled to complain when deprived of the right to select a jury from a representative sample of the community. Shared racial, ethnic, or gender identity is irrelevant under Sixth Amendment, fair cross-section requirements. The accused's right to a jury trial means she cannot be denied the fair possibility of selecting a jury from a broad segment of the community. To the degree that a prosecutor attempts to stack the deck by exercising race-based peremptory challenges, he compromises the defendant's ability to select a jury that is "not arbitrarily skewed for or against any particular group or characteristic."[136]

A look at *Powers* is instructive because it reveals the flaw behind *Batson*'s equal protection approach and because it exposes the majority's ultimate reliance upon the fair cross-section standard. *Powers* has two prongs: a prospective juror's right to equal protection is abridged when a prosecutor uses race-based peremptories[137]; and a defendant may vicariously raise the excluded juror's equal protection rights.[138] The first part of the holding is defensible; that is, a juror should have the right to protest her exclusion from jury service because of her race. However, the likelihood of such an occurrence is negligible. Practical considerations militate against such claims; the most imposing is the cost of undertaking formal litigation.[139]

The second prong of *Powers* collapses under searching scrutiny. Why should a defendant have standing to raise the equal protection rights of an excluded juror? In essence, the majority employs a three-part test: the defendant has suffered a concrete injury; the defendant has a close relation to the juror; and the juror is hindered in pursuing his own interests.[140] The Court's analysis fails to justify the first prong of its "third-party standing" test.

In effect, the majority boldly asserts that "The discriminatory use of peremptory challenges by the prosecution causes a defendant a cognizable injury, and the defendant has a concrete interest in challenging the practice."[141] How does a third party's lost right affect the defendant? On equal protection grounds, the defendant has not been deprived of the right to equal protection when a juror is struck from the panel on the basis of race. Rather, the defendant, as the *Powers* majority ultimately recognizes, is denied the right to a neutral jury selection procedure. In its turn, a neutral, race-blind selection procedure, the Court acknowledges, ensures the *fairness* of the trial.[142]

Underscoring the Court's insistence that the defendant suffers from the same injury as the excluded juror is a fair cross-section, Sixth Amendment rationale. The fair cross-section requirement of the right to a jury trial is designed to assure a fair criminal trial in which neither side gains an advantage by arbitrarily removing an identifiable group from the jury. Indeed, the majority betrays this reasoning when it declares that "The purpose of the jury system is to [ensure] . . . that a verdict of conviction or acquittal is given in accordance with the law by persons who are fair."[143] Thus, a fairness, Sixth Amendment, not equal protection, argument underlies the *Powers* decision.

The upshot of the Court's misguided jurisprudence in this critical area is an appropriate remedy under a logically and doctrinally faulty analysis. Neither constitutional precedent nor legal reasoning dictated an equal protection basis for *Batson*. Nonetheless, the Court was bent upon employing the equal protection clause rather than the Sixth Amendment in reaching the conclusion that the criminal process would be perverted by the prosecutor's discriminatory use of peremptory challenges. Somehow, the Court failed to recognize that communitarian values could be equally advanced by protecting the accused's right to select a jury drawn from a broad cross-section of the community. As a consequence, a strained logic pervades the subsequent cases which elaborate upon and fill in the gaps left by Batson.

Viewing two specific facets of the jury trial system evokes the ambiguous, confused jurisprudence the Supreme Court has produced in this vital sphere of the criminal justice system. In determining the proper scope of the jury trial guarantee, the Court adopted a narrow, tightly circumscribed perspective. Thus, the size and unanimity requirements set forth by the Court demonstrate a myopic view of the history and function of the jury in the criminal process. This jurisprudence reflects an antidefendant as well as an anticommunitarian perspective. On the other hand, the Court's well-meaning attempt to eradicate invidious discrimination in all parts of jury selection has yielded correct results but a confused, illogical doctrinal interpretation. This jurisprudence derives in large part from the Court's inability to amalgamate mutually complementary values: the important role the jury plays in fostering democratic interests and the defendant's right to fair jury selection procedures.

Fortunately, the jury trial remains a vital part of the adversary criminal process. Although the Court's jurisprudence has not been a model of consistency and rationality, the jury trial is alive and well. Moreover, the Court's commitment to eliminate discriminatory practices from jury selection, though not altogether successfully, attests to the important symbolic meaning of the jury system in our democratic form of government. The jury has served us well and will continue to represent the criminal justice system's devotion to the accused's right to a trial free from potential governmental abuse on the part of either judges or prosecutors.

NOTES

1. *Johnson v. Louisiana*, 406 U.S. 356, 399 (1972) (Stewart, J., dissenting).
2. *Williams v. Florida*, 399 U.S. 78, 100 (1970).
3. Tribe, *Trial by Mathematics: Precision and Ritual in the Legal Process*, 84 HARV. L. REV. 1329, 1376 (1971). Tribe focuses upon the ritualistic nature of a criminal trial.
4. 281 U.S. 276 (1930).
5. Id. at 296–97.
6. Id. at 297.
7. *Duncan v. Louisiana*, 391 U.S. at 157–58.
8. *See*, e.g., *Singer v. United States*, 380 U.S. 34 (1965). The Court held that a defendant has no right to a nonjury trial; hence, the prosecution has a right to preclude the defendant from waiving her right to a jury trial by objecting to the waiver.
9. *See* Stimson, THE AMERICAN REVOLUTION IN THE LAW: ANGLO-AMERICAN JURISPRUDENCE BEFORE JOHN MARSHALL, 12–14 (1990).

10. Id. at 34.

11. Id. at 71. As he put it, "These two popular powers are the heart and lungs, the mainspring and centre wheel, and without them the body must die, the watch must run, the government become arbitrary," Id. (quoting from *Works of John Adams* III, 481).

12. THE FEDERALIST No. 83, at 521–22 (B. Wright ed. 1961).

13. Id. at 87.

14. Massaro, *Peremptories or Peers?—Rethinking Sixth Amendment Doctrine, Images, and Procedures*, 64 N. CAR. L. REV. 501, 504–510 (1986).

15. Article III, Sec. 2 stipulates that: "The trial of all crimes, except in cases of impeachment, shall be by jury; and such trial shall be held in the State where the said crimes shall have been committed." The Sixth Amendment provides that: "In all criminal prosecutions, the accused shall enjoy the right to a . . . trial, by an impartial jury of the State and district wherein the crime shall have been committed."

16. Massaro, *supra* note 14, at 508–09.

17. Id. at 508.

18. *Duncan v. Louisiana*, 391 U.S. at 156; *Williams v. Florida*, 399 U.S. at 100; *Apodaca v. Oregon*, 406 U.S. 404, 410–13 (1972).

19. *See* Massaro *supra* note 14, at 541–55.

20. *See*, e.g., *Batson v. Kentucky*, 476 U.S. 79, 87 (1986) (discriminatory jury selection "undermine[s] public confidence in the fairness of our system of justice").

21. *Patton v. United States*, 281 U.S. 276 (1930).

22. *Apodaca v. Oregon*, 406 U.S. 404 (1972); *Johnson v. Louisiana*, 406 U.S. 356 (1972) (unanimity not required at state level); *Williams v. Florida*, 399 U.S. 78 (1970) (six-person jury constitutionally permissible); *Ballew v. Georgia*, 435 U.S. 223 (1978) (five-person jury violates Sixth Amendment); *Burch v. Louisiana*, 441 U.S. 130 (1979) (six-person jury must return unanimous verdict).

23. 281 U.S. 276 (1930).

24. Id. at 288–92.

25. 170 U.S. 343 (1898).

26. Id. at 353.

27. *Patton v. United States*, 281 U.S. at 290; *Thompson v. Utah*, 170 U.S. at 352–53.

28. *Thompson v. Utah*, 170 U.S. at 353.

29. *Patton v. United States*, 281 U.S. at 290.

30. Id. at 312.

31. The Court invalidated exclusion of women from jury service in *Taylor v. Louisiana*, 419 U.S. 522 (1975); and *Duren v. Missouri*, 439 U.S. 357 (1979).

32. 399 U.S. 78 (1970).

33. Id. at 89.

34. Id. at 100.

35. 435 U.S. 223 (1978).

36. *Williams v. Florida*, 399 U.S. at 127 (Harlan, J., concurring in part and dissenting in part).

37. Id. at 232–42.

38. Saks, JURY VERDICTS, 207 (1977), cited in *Ballew*, 435 U.S. at 242.

39. *Ballew v. Georgia*, 435 U.S. at 239.

40. *Williams v. Florida*, 399 U.S. at 125–26 (Harlan, J., concurring in part and dissenting in part).

41. Id. at 100, n.46.

42. *Apodaca v. Oregon*, 406 U.S. 404 (1972); *Johnson v. Louisiana*, 406 U.S. 356 (1972).

43. *Johnson v. Louisiana*, 406 U.S. at 360–63; *Apodaca v. Oregon*, 406 U.S. at 411–12.

44. *Johnson v. Louisiana*, 406 U.S. at 366 (Blackmun, J., concurring). Justice Whiite's plurality opinion indicated that the verdict was sufficiently reliable when nine out of twelve jurors voted to convict, id. at 362. Similarly 10–2 and 11–1 verdicts were approved in *Apodaca v. Oregon*, 406 U.S. at 411.

45. *Williams v. Florida*, 399 U.S. at 112 (Black, J., concurring in part and dissenting in part).

46. 397 U.S. 358, 363–64 (1970) (holding that the due process clause of the Fourteenth Amendment requires that the state prove guilt beyond a reasonable doubt).

47. *Johnson v. Louisiana*, 406 U.S. at 388–92 (Douglas, J., dissenting). Justice Douglas relied upon the acclaimed jury study undertaken by Kalven and Zeisel. *See* Kalven and Zeisel, THE AMERICAN JURY (1966).

48. Id. at 375–77 (Powell, J., concurring).

49. Id. Justice Powell endorsed Justice Harlan's position, which repudiated the selective incorporation view that once a right enumerated in the Bill of Rights is applicable to the states through the operation of the Fourteenth Amendment's due process clause, all aspects of the right prevailing in the federal system must be guaranteed by the states. *See*, id. at 375, n.14.

50. Id. at 383 (Douglas, J., dissenting).

51. Id. at 400 (Marshall, J., dissenting).

52. Id. at 371 (Powell, J., concurring).

53. Massaro, *supra* note 14, at 545–47.

54. Id. at 547. Thus, if the community in which the defendant is tried is homogeneous and reflects antipathy to the accused's race or background, his right to a fair jury may be illusory.

55. *Strauder v. West Virginia*, 100 U.S. 303, 309 (1880).

56. Massaro, *supra* note 14, at 547–56.

57. Id. at 552.

58. Hanley, *The Last Thirty Days*, 10 LITIGATION, Winter 1984, at 10.

59. Di Perna, JURIES ON TRIAL 21 (1984).

60. *See*, e.g., *Strauder v. West Virginia*, 100 U.S. 303 (1880); *Neil v. Delaware*, 103 U.S. 370 (1881); *Martin v. Texas*, 200 U.S. 316 (1906).

61. *Duncan v. Louisiana*, 391 U.S. at 149 (1968).

62. *Taylor v. Louisiana*, 419 U.S. 522, 528 (1975); *Duren v. Missouri*, 439 U.S. 357 (1979).

63. *Holland v. Illinois*, 110 S.Ct. 803 (1990).

64. *Strauder v. West Virginia*, 100 U.S. 303 (1880); *Virginia v. Rives*, 100 U.S. 313 (1880); *Ex parte Virginia*, 100 U.S. 339 (1880).

65. 100 U.S. 303 (1880).

66. Id. at 308.

67. Id. at 309.

68. Id. at 309–10.

69. Id. at 308.

70. *Powers v. Ohio*, 111 S.Ct. 1364, 1374–75 (1991) (Scalia, J., dissenting) (citations

omitted). The term "race" is used by Justice Scalia to include ethnic groups. *See*, e.g., *Cataneda v. Partida*, 430 U.S. 482 (1977) (intentional discrimination against Mexican-Americans in grand jury selection violates equal protection clause of Fourteenth Amendment).

71. 419 U.S. 522 (1975).
72. Id. at 527.
73. Id. at 527–31.
74. Id. at 531–35.
75. Id. at 538.
76. *Duren v. Missouri*, 439 U.S. 357, 364 (1979).
77. *Taylor v. Louisiana*, 419 U.S. at 530–31 (quoting from *Thiel v. Southern Pacific Co.*, 328 U.S. 217, 227 (1946) (Frankfurter, J., dissenting); *Lockhart v. McCree*, 476 U.S. 162, 174–75 (1986).
78. *Lockhart v. McCree*, 476 U.S. at 175.
79. Id. at 174 (i.e., jurors excluded from the guilt phase of capital murder trials because their scruples against the death penalty would preclude them from imposing death in the penalty phase of the trial).
80. Alschuler, *The Supreme Court and the Jury: Voir Dire, Peremptory Challenges, and the Review of Jury Verdicts*, 56 U. CHICAGO L. REV. 153, 190–91 (1989).
81. Id. at 156.
82. *Swain v. Alabama*, 380 U.S. 202, 220 (1965).
83. *See*, e.g., Alschuler, *supra* note 80, at 167.
84. 380 U.S. 202 (1965).
85. Id. at 205.
86. Id. at 221–22.
87. Id. at 222.
88. Id. at 223–27.
89. Id. at 219 (citing *Stilson v. United States*, 250 U.S. 583, 586 (1919).
90. Id.
91. Id. at 219–20.
92. *Powers v. Ohio*, 111 S.Ct. 1364, 1367 (1991).
93. As Justice Stevens noted in dissent, "The Sixth Amendment's protection is not so frail that it can be defeated by the State's creation of an additional level of selection," *Holland v. Illinois*, 110 S.Ct. 825–26 (1990).
94. 476 U.S. 79 (1986).
95. Id. at 82–83.
96. Id. at 92 (citing *McCray v. Abrams*, 750 F.2d 1113 (2d Cir. 1984)).
97. Id. at 96.
98. Id. at 97–98.
99. Pizzi, Batson v. Kentucky: *Curing the Disease but Killing the Patient*, 1987 S CT REV 97, 134.
100. Id. at 105 (Marshall, J., concurring).
101. Alschuler, *supra* note 80, at 200.
102. Id. at 174.
103. Id. at 176 (citations omitted).
104. Id.
105. 111 S.Ct. 1859 (1991).
106. Id. at 1867.

107. Id. at 1866.
108. Id. at 1867.
109. Id. at 1874 (O'Connor, J., concurring).
110. Id. at 1872–73.
111. Id. at 1876 (Stevens, J., dissenting).
112. *Batson v. Kentucky*, 476 U.S. at 106.
113. *See*, e.g., Massaro *supra* note 14; Goldwasser, *Limiting a Defendant's Use of Peremptory Challenges: On Symmetry and the Jury in a Criminal Trial*, 102 HARV. L. REV. 808 (1989).
114. *Batson v. Kentucky*, 476 U.S. at 107–08 (Marshall, J., concurring).
115. Id. at 108 (citing *Frazier v. United States*, 335 U.S. 497, 505, n.11 (1948); *United States v. Wood*, 299 U.S. 123, 145 (1936); *Stilson v. United States*, 250 U.S. 583, 586 (1919); *Swain v. Alabama*, 380 U.S. at 219.
116. 111 S.Ct. 2077 (1991).
117. Id. at 2083.
118. Id. at 2087–88.
119. Id. at 2095 (Scalia, J., dissenting).
120. *Batson v. Kentucky*, 476 U.S. at 112–16 (Burger, C. J., dissenting).
121. *Duncan v. Louisiana*, 391 U.S. 145 (1968).
122. 419 U.S. at 527.
123. *Holland v. Illinois*, 110 S.Ct. at 826 (Stevens, J., dissenting).
124. *Allen v. Hardy*, 478 U.S. 255, 259 (1986).
125. Id. Justice Stevens' dissent in *Holland* makes this point clear. He states that, "Batson has underpinnings both in the juror's equal protection right to be free of discrimination and in the defendant's right to a fair and impartial factfinder," *Holland v. Illinois*, 110 S.Ct. at 827 (Stevens, J., dissenting) (citing and quoting from *Allen v. Hardy*, 478 U.S. 255 (1986)).
126. 110 S.Ct. 803 (1990).
127. *Batson v. Kentucky*, 476 U.S. at 96.
128. *Holland v. Illinois*, 110 S.Ct. at 805 (citing *Duren v. Louisiana*, 439 U.S. 357 (1979); and *Taylor v. Louisiana*, 419 U.S. 522 (1975)).
129. Id. at 807.
130. Id. at 824 (Stevens, J., dissenting) (citing *Williams v. Florida*, 399 U.S. at 100; *Ballew v. Georgia*, 435 U.S. at 236–37).
131. Id. at 819 (Marshall, J., dissenting).
132. Id. at 825–26 (Stevens, J., dissenting).
133. Id. at 811–12 (Kennedy, J., concurring).
134. 111 S.Ct. 1364 (1991).
135. Id. at 1379 (Scalia, J., dissenting).
136. *Holland v. Illinois*, 110 S.Ct. at 826 (Stevens, J., dissenting).
137. Id. at 1370.
138. Id. at 1371–73.
139. Id. at 1373.
140. Id. at 1370–73 (citations omitted).
141. Id. at 1371.
142. Id. (citing *Allen v. Hardy*, 478 U.S. 255, 259 (1986) (per curiam); *Rose v. Mitchell*, 443 U.S. 545, 556 (1979)).
143. Id. at 1372.

6

Clash of the Titans: The Difficult Reconciliation of a Fair Trial and a Free Press in Modern American Society

In an epoch marked by the pervasive influence of the mass media in daily life, a fundamental clash sometimes evolves between a criminal defendant's right to a fair trial by an impartial jury and the media's liberty to report on matters it deems worthy of public interest. This conflict is unique because it involves two of our most hallowed rights, shielded by the First and Sixth amendments to the United States Constitution.[1] The dichotomy is compounded by the fact that neither the Constitution nor the wisdom of the Founding Fathers sheds light on the problem.[2] Although the drafters of the Bill of Rights could not have been oblivious to the potential conflict,[3] they can hardly be faulted for not envisaging the widespread role the media would play in twentieth-century America.

Under normal circumstances, the rights to a fair trial and to a free press dovetail; that is, a free press satisfies the public's legitimate concern with the workings of the criminal justice system and thereby enhances the fairness of a criminal proceeding. As the Court has noted, "[t]he knowledge that every criminal trial is subject to contemporaneous review in the forum of public opinion is an effective restraint on possible abuse of judicial power. . . . Without publicity, all other checks are insufficient; in comparison of publicity, all other checks are of small account."[4] When criminal activity becomes the object of intense media scrutiny, however, the right of the accused to a fair trial may be imperiled. As a consequence, the judicial system confronts the nettlesome dilemma posed by Justice Black of accommodating "two of the most cherished policies of our civilization," free speech and fair trials.[5]

The source of this predicament lies with the contradictory purposes served by the Sixth and the First amendments. Historically and functionally, the right to free speech and press does not promote fairness. As a prominent scholar tells us, the First Amendment does not demand press "responsibility," and the Framers "knew a partisan and scurrilous press, not a fair one."[6] In fact, fairness might interfere with the media's role in serving as a check on government. In contrast, the rights conferred on the accused by the Sixth Amendment are designed to ensure fairness in the criminal process.[7] The difficult task the judiciary faces when these two titans clash is to reconcile them without sacrificing the critical values fostered by each right.

When these two fundamental guarantees are pitted against each other, achieving a harmonious balance between them is a formidable exercise. Given two competing constitutional interests, must a court necessarily choose which one takes precedence? If a defendant's right to a fair trial is "the most fundamental of all freedoms,"[8] must the right to a free press yield to such an overriding interest? The Supreme Court has emphatically asserted that no hierarchy of values inheres in the safeguards enumerated in the Bill of Rights.[9] On other occasions, however, former Chief Justice Burger has suggested that the accused's right to a fair trial transcends the freedom of the press to keep the public informed about the criminal process.[10] Nevertheless, when free speech and press and fair trial have collided, the Court has striven to resolve the conflict "without essentially abrogating one right or the other."[11]

Although the Court's struggle to harmonize these sometimes conflicting rights has been a valiant one, its solution to the problem has not been successful. Understandably, the Court has been loath to encroach upon the right of the media to report on the criminal justice system because public access to the process advances fairness as well as the appearance of fairness.[12] Despite this justifiable reluctance, the Court has failed to produce a workable method for protecting a criminal defendant's right to a fair trial by an impartial jury when freedom of speech and press potentially infringes on that precious right. To a large extent, this flaw derives from the failure to recognize that the media's role is not to promote fairness; on the other hand, fairness is the preeminent value advanced by the Sixth Amendment's safeguard of a fair trial by an impartial jury.[13]

Conceptually, the attempt to resolve the conflict between free press and fair trial may be divided into two categories: (1) the degree to which the press may be restrained from divulging information that threatens the right to a fair trial; and (2) what viable remedies exist to blunt the damaging effects of prejudicial pretrial publicity. These two classifications are analytically linked because the resolution of the first category dictates the strength of the remedies required by the second. Accordingly, we will view these categories in sequence in order to determine whether the Court's approach represents an equitable solution to a delicate quandary.

In the late nineteenth century, the Supreme Court presciently appreciated the widespread repercussions of mass communication and universal education for criminal cases. Those cases that generate extensive public interest garner the "attention of all the intelligent people in the vicinity, and scarcely any one can be found among those best fitted for jurors who has not heard or read of it."[14]

Indeed, nearly a century before, Chief Justice Marshall encountered the problem of selecting an unbiased, impartial jury in the celebrated treason trial of Aaron Burr. Media coverage of the controversy between Burr and President Jefferson led Burr's attorneys to question the ability of jurors who had followed the feud to act impartially.[15]

Technological advances in the twentieth century, combined with the media's increasing coverage of government and politics, have made the task of selecting an impartial jury in a highly publicized criminal case a difficult proposition.[16] Consequently, a trial court in such a situation must attempt to keep prejudicial publicity from reaching the public in the hope that a jury untainted by the information may be selected. If that arrangement is not possible, then the judge must ensure that a jury exposed to such information is willing and able to set aside its preconceived notions and decide the case solely on the evidence presented.[17] Though the first alternative is preferable since it enhances the probability of finding an impartial jury, it runs head-on into the freedom of the media to report on matters of public interest.

In *Nebraska Press Assn. v. Stuart*,[18] the trial judge sought to prevent confessions, admissions, and facts "strongly implicative of the accused" from being disseminated by the media. His concern was justified by the fact that the defendant was charged with six murders of the members of one family in a small community. In addition, the crime had attracted considerable local, regional, and national media coverage. Therefore, he imposed a "gag order" on the release of such information by the media, which encompassed details relating to the crime revealed in the defendant's "open" preliminary hearing. The rationale backing the judge's order was the "clear and present danger that pre-trial publicity could impinge on the defendant's right to a fair trial."[19]

Finding the trial court's order "speculative," the majority believed the court's remedy was deficient; in the process, the Court fashioned a three-part test to determine whether a pretrial restraint complies with constitutional strictures. The criteria the *Stuart* Court adopted were the nature and scope of pretrial coverage; whether other measures would effectively counter the adverse pretrial publicity; and whether a gag order would achieve its intended effect.[20] Applying these standards to the facts at hand, the *Stuart* Court concluded that other remedies would have sufficed and that the restraining order would have been futile given the small size of the community and the gravity of the crime.[21]

More important, the majority acknowledged the obstacles to "managing and enforcing pretrial restraining orders." Specifically, such problems center on the difficulty of overinclusiveness or underinclusiveness: that is, the extent to which the trial court can predict accurately what information will poison potential jurors and the limited jurisdiction of a state court in enjoining the national press from publishing details about the crime.[22] Though the trial judge in *Stuart* attempted not to craft an overly sweeping order, the Supreme Court was reluctant to sanction his proposed solution. The decision conveys the distaste with which the Court regards a pretrial restraining order as a resolution to the problem of prejudicial pretrial publicity. Thus, the court bears a "heavy burden" in establishing before trial that prior restraint is the only means of securing a fair trial.[23]

A major blunder committed by the trial judge in *Stuart* was his attempt to preclude the media from reporting the results of a proceeding open to the public. As a result, he could not rely on precedent to prevent the press from reporting a public event. What the Court left open, however, was the possibility that closing the hearing to the press and public was an option a trial judge could exercise.

Taking the cue from *Stuart*, the trial judge in *Gannett v. DePasquale*[24] closed a pretrial hearing on a motion to suppress a confession and a gun in a publicized murder prosecution. The publicity surrounding the murder was neither sensational nor unusual; indeed, it may be characterized as largely factual in nature and not particularly prejudicial toward the defendants' right to a fair trial. Nevertheless, the defense sought closure of the suppression hearing because "the unabated buildup" of pretrial publicity endangered their clients' right to a fair trial. The prosecution did not oppose the motion and the press representative did not object when the defense made the request.[25]

In sharp contrast to its solicitude for freedom of the press in *Stuart*, the *Gannett* Court focused on the accused's stake in a fair trial. Heralding a novel approach to the free press–fair trial controversy, the *Gannett* majority found no common law or constitutional right for public attendance at pretrial or trial proceedings. Rather, the fact that the accused's right to a public trial is grouped with other defendant-related rights meant that it inured to the accused and not to the public (or press) at large.[26] Nonetheless, the Court left open the question not squarely before it; that is, whether the First and Fourteenth amendments provided a right for the public to attend criminal trials.[27] The tone and rationale underlying *Gannett*, however, strongly suggested that perhaps the Court was willing to subordinate the public's and, derivatively, the press's right to attend pretrial or trial proceedings if such access jeopardized a criminal defendant's right to a fair trial by an impartial jury.

Precisely one year later, however, the Court granted the press and the general public a constitutional right of access to criminal trials in *Richmond Newspapers, Inc. v. Virginia*.[28] Relying on common law tradition, and the implicit notion that the First Amendment protects the right of access, the Court reasoned that a presumption of openness inheres in the nature of a criminal trial.[29] The structural dimension to the First Amendment is integral to our democratic system and compels a public trial to safeguard the judicial process and the "republican system of self-government."[30]

Richmond Newspapers provided inauspicious circumstances under which to persuade the Court to close a trial to the public. Nonetheless, the trial judge certainly had sufficient basis to believe that his order would be upheld, given the message conveyed in *Gannett*. Given a shaky set of facts justifying closure, however, the Court would have been hard-pressed to ratify the trial court's order.

The flimsy excuse to close the trial to the press and public was that the defendant's murder trial had ended in mistrials on four previous occasions, one mistrial occurring because a prospective juror had read about the defendant's previous trials in a newspaper and had told other jurors before the retrial began. Therefore, the accused's counsel was concerned about prejudicial information being exchanged by the jurors, especially since the crime had taken place in a small community.[31]

The factual predicate underlying *Richmond* buttresses the *Stuart* Court's contention that closure of any part of a criminal proceeding on the basis of speculative prejudice to the defendant's right to a fair trial is risky business. What made the trial judge's decision in *Richmond* indefensible was that his order was overly broad in comparison with the danger presented. The publicity was apparently less pervasive in *Richmond* than in *Stuart*. After all, the crime in *Richmond* did not attract national publicity, as did the crime in *Stuart*. Moreover, the community in *Stuart* was exceedingly small (850), casting doubt on the apprehension expressed by defense counsel in *Richmond*. Finally, the trial court in *Richmond* closed the entire trial to the public; the trial judge in *Stuart* drafted a narrow order designed to prevent disclosure of the defendant's damaging admissions.

Consistent with the nexus between openness and fair process, and the "structural" role played by the First Amendment, the teaching of *Richmond* meshes with a defendant's right to a fair trial. Further, it is unlikely in an "age of mass media" that closing a trial to the press and public will be an effective antidote to adverse prejudicial publicity. Publicity in a notorious case will begin when the crime is discovered.[32] The impact of such publicity will continue unabated during the course of pretrial hearings. Thus, closing a trial to the public and precluding the media from reporting it is akin to attempting to turn back the clock. Sequestering the jury or admonishing jurors to avoid media exposure about the case, although not foolproof remedies, furnish better alternatives to closure.[33]

Evidently, *Richmond* laid to rest the question whether a trial could be closed to the public, though four justices intimated that the right to attend a trial was not absolute, and might yield to an "overriding" interest.[34] The overriding interest would presumably be a defendant's right to a fair trial, though the plurality in *Richmond* failed to articulate that interest because the trial court's justification for closure was deficient. At any rate, *Richmond* makes clear that closing a trial is an extreme measure warranted, if at all, only under exceptional circumstances.

Clarifying its stance on the matter, the Court held in *Globe Newspaper Co. v. Superior Court*[35] that a state must justify its attempt to close a criminal trial by showing a compelling interest. Additionally, the government must establish that the denial of access is "narrowly tailored" to serve the compelling interest.[36] As a result, the Court invalidated a Massachusetts statute that sought to protect minor victims of sex crime by excluding the press and the public from the courtroom.[37] The *Globe* majority rejected the two interests advanced by the state:

sparing the alleged victims from further trauma and embarrassment, and prodding victims to report sexual crimes and to testify truthfully. Although the majority agreed that avoiding "psychological trauma" of young victims was a compelling interest, such a concern did not justify a *per se* closure rule. Instead, a case-by-case approach was proper, with the trial judge taking into account such factors as the minor victim's age and psychological maturity, the nature of the crime, and the wishes of the victim and her parents.[38]

An interesting facet of *Globe Newspapers* is the defendant's objection to the closure of the trial proceedings to the press and public.[39] Since the defendant has a constitutional right to insist on a public trial according to the Sixth Amendment, to what extent may the government's interest in closing a trial override a defendant's constitutional right? If the government satisfies the "compelling" interest standard delineated in *Globe Newspapers*, and the defendant objects, is the trial judge justified in denying access to the media and the public? This question was not explored by the Court in *Globe Newspapers*.

The crucial issue in *Globe* inexorably leads to the conclusion that, in such circumstances, closure comports neither with the Constitution nor with the purposes served by the First and Sixth amendments. To the degree that openness enhances the structural role of the First Amendment by keeping the public informed and ensuring the integrity and fairness of the judicial process, closure ill serves that function. Juxtaposed against the fair play values fostered by the Sixth Amendment, a governmental interest, no matter how "compelling," hardly supports a denial of the defendant's Sixth Amendment right to a public trial.

Despite the elaboration of *Richmond*'s dictates in *Globe Newspapers*, a majority of the Justices saw fit to return to the issue raised by *Gannett*: Under what conditions, if any, may a court exclude the media and public from a pretrial hearing to safeguard a defendant's right to a fair trial? Before reaching that inquiry, however, it had to determine whether the presumption of open criminal trials extended to the jury selection process.

Answering that question affirmatively, the Court viewed the jury selection process as a central component of the criminal justice system. *Press Enterprise Co. v. Superior Court*[40] (*Press Enterprise I*) involved the interracial sexual attack and murder of a fifteen-year-old.[41] In order to encourage honest responses by potential jurors, the prosecutor requested the closure of the jury selection process to the press and public; the trial court complied with the state's wishes, closing all but three days of the six-week selection process to the public.[42] Holding that an alternative method (i.e., questioning the juror in chamber upon an affirmative request) would have sufficiently protected the jurors' privacy concerns, the Court found that the stringent test set forth in *Globe* was not satisfied.[43] Therefore, absent a compelling interest for a juror's privacy, closing voir dire proceedings to the public violates the First Amendment.[44]

Buoyed by its victory, Press Enterprise Company subsequently challenged the exclusion of the media and the public in a mass-murder case. The facts of *Press Enterprise II*[45] constitute the stuff the media thrives on: the murder of twelve patients by a male nurse who allegedly administered massive doses of the heart drug lidocaine. Invoking a state statute,[46] the defendant, unopposed by the state, successfully moved to close his preliminary hearing from media and public scrutiny. The hearing lasted forty-one days, consisting largely of scientific and medical evidence. Subsequently, the court acceded to the accused's desire to keep transcripts of the hearing from the press and public for the same reason he sought to exclude the public from the preliminary hearing: the potential infringement of his right to a fair and impartial trial.[47]

Reaching a conclusion opposite to the one embodied in *Gannett, Press Enterprise II* saw a tradition of accessibility to pretrial hearings. Moreover, the unique adversarial features of the preliminary hearing in California approximate a trial in many respects. These two premises led the majority to conclude that a preliminary hearing may be closed only if a "substantial probability" exists that the defendant's fair-trial rights will be compromised. A second prong of the formulation requires the court to determine that other "reasonable" alternatives to closure will not preserve the accused's right to an unbiased jury.[48]

Press Enterprise II represents the logical culmination of the Court's efforts to jealously safeguard the tradition of openness with respect to criminal proceedings. The defendant faces a nearly insurmountable barrier: She must show a substantial probability that pretrial publicity will so taint the community as to preclude the selection of an unbiased jury. In light of the speculative nature of such an endeavor, closure of a pretrial proceeding is highly unlikely in the wake of *Press Enterprise II*. If the Court is not content with the accused's demonstrating a "reasonable likelihood of prejudice," then its value judgment is predicated upon the notion that the community "therapeutic" value of openness[49] predominates over the defendant's right to a fair trial.

The bottom line to the Court's doctrinal approach inescapably leads to one conclusion: Absent compelling, and highly unusual, circumstances, a criminal defendant will not be able to prevent the media and the public from attending either pretrial proceedings or a trial on the basis that prejudicial pretrial publicity might impinge upon his right to a fair trial by an impartial jury. Nor, for that matter, will the accused successfully prohibit "the publication by the press of any information pertaining to pending judicial proceedings or the operation of the criminal justice system, no matter how shabby the means by which the information is obtained."[50]

Usually, fair process norms advanced by both the tradition of openness and the defendant's interest in a jury untarnished by preconceived notions of the accused's guilt coincide. When they conflict, however, the Court has not embraced the remedy of excluding the media as a means of avoiding prejudicial publicity from poisoning jurors' attitudes toward the defendant. One can certainly understand the Court's reluctance to do so, for it contravenes the essence of a democratic form of government. Secrecy is not a cherished value in a "republican" society. Accessibility has its price, however; when it conflicts with a defendant's equally important right to a fair trial, an accommodation is called for. If we are unwilling to tolerate closed criminal proceedings, then we must avert "the sacrifice of Sixth Amendment rights on the altar of the First Amendment."[51]

Given the Court's aversion to closure as a remedy to protect a defendant's right to an impartial jury, only one alternative exists to ensure a fair trial: removing from jury service potential jurors with strong biases against the defendant who are unwilling or unable to set aside their partiality. Since the treason trial of Aaron Burr,[52] courts have grappled with the problem of identifying and accurately assessing the extent and intensity of the venire's predispositions toward the defendant. In addition, courts have sought to determine the applicable criteria for disqualifying a potential juror on grounds of bias. Finally, courts have constructed remedies designed to attenuate the effects of partiality and thereby enhance the prospect of a fair trial. Unfortunately, these palliatives have not proved effective, thus hampering the search for an equitable balance between a free press and fair trial. The reasons for this failure merit a historical and pragmatic approach to the issue.

Historical Underpinnings

Building upon the edifice created by John Marshall in the treason trial of Aaron Burr,[53] Chief Justice Waite developed a visionary perspective on the issue of juror partiality in *Reynolds v. United States*.[54] Waite followed Marshall's lead in *Burr*. Marshall rejected the suggestion by Burr's defense counsel that the constitutional guarantee to an "impartial jury" meant that jurors should be "perfectly indifferent and free from prejudice."[55] Waite aptly concluded that such a threshold would be insuperable in light of modern advances in communications.[56] Opinions as to the guilt of the defendant would not preclude a juror from serving; rather, the defendant ought to bear the burden of demonstrating that the juror's opinion was strong enough to raise a "presumption of partiality."[57]

Moreover, Waite believed that a trial court's finding on the issue of partiality should be accorded deference. A trial court's determination should "not be set aside by a reviewing court, unless the error is manifest."[58] Although Waite's calibration placed the onus on the defendant to establish juror bias, he did not put forth a coherent test for determining when the presumption of partiality arises. Indeed, he admitted that courts had not reached accord on when an opinion disqualified a juror, other than agreeing upon the notion that the opinion must be unyielding and not a "mere impression," subject to dissipation through evidence presented in court.[59]

Perhaps we ought not to chastise Chief Justice Waite for failing to develop a comprehensive standard of jury impartiality. What is troubling about *Reynolds* is the tremendous burden the defendant must shoulder in order to exclude a presumptively biased juror. Assuming the juror has formed an opinion of the defendant's guilt, it is up to the accused to identify the bias, demonstrate its intensity, and convince the trial judge that the jurors' "impressions" are not light but are firmly etched in the mind. More important, if the defendant seeks to reverse her conviction on the basis of juror bias, the trial court's findings are to be given wide latitude by the appellate tribunal.

Recent Trends

Nearly a century later, the Court lessened the defendant's burden in proving bias. In *Irvin v. Dowd*[60] Justice Clark recognized that a crime may engender such a "pattern of deep and bitter prejudice" in a community that bias against the defendant may be presumed.[61] *Irvin* represents a perfect example of a small community poisoned by pervasive publicity against a defendant charged with six murders. Under those circumstances, the jurors' assertions of impartiality could not be given credence, because "the psychological impact requiring such a declaration before one's fellows is often its father."[62] The unbelievability of such statements was betrayed by the fact that the voir dire revealed most prospective jurors had some opinion about the defendant's guilt and that eight of the twelve jurors in the case thought the defendant was guilty.[63]

Irvin is enlightening in four other respects. First, Justice Clark emphasized the elusive nature of impartiality. Quoting Chief Justice Hughes, Justice Clark observed that impartiality is not a "technical conception"; rather, it is "a state of mind." Therefore, no talismanic formula is available to flesh out this "mental attitude."[64] Second, *Irvin* establishes the proposition that a trial by jurors "having a preconceived, fixed opinion" of the accused's guilt violates due process.[65] As a corollary, such a fixed belief exists, despite protestations to the contrary, when deep prejudice against the defendant permeates the community. Third, *Irvin* acknowledges that juror impartiality is not synonymous with the lack of a preconceived notion of guilt. Instead, a juror is deemed to be impartial if he can "lay aside his impression or opinion and render a verdict based on the evidence presented in court."[66] Fourth, when a community in which the crime occurred is so prejudiced against the defendant, presumably a change of venue, the relief requested in *Irvin*, is warranted.

Irvin has subsequently been construed as fashioning a two-part test for detecting juror bias derived from their knowledge or opinions about the case. The first part permits the defendant to show actual prejudice through responses elicited in voir dire and other evidence. The second part provides relief by presuming prejudice from the circumstances surrounding the trial.[67]

Faithfully applying the *Irvin* formula, the Court in *Rideau v. Louisiana*[68] presumed prejudice when the defendant's confession was televised three times to a viewing audience comprising the bulk of the community.[69] Consequently, the accused was denied a fair trial, and due process of law, when his request for a change of venue was denied. The "spectacle" of the defendant's televised confession was tantamount to Rideau's trial.[70] Under these circumstances, review of the voir dire to determine partiality was not necessary.[71]

The presumed prejudice standard was substantially diluted by two cases in which extensive pretrial publicity exposed potential jurors to the defendants' prior convictions as well as other inadmissible evidence. *Murphy v. Florida*[72] dealt with the burglary, robbery, and assault charges against the notorious convicted murderer and jewel thief Jack ("Murph the Surf") Murphy. The venire in Murphy's case was aware of his prior convictions for murder and his famous theft of the Star of India sapphire from a museum in New York. Further, potential jurors were also exposed to news accounts of the crimes he was charged with. These circumstances augured ill for Murphy's ability to obtain a fair trial; however, the Supreme Court thought the defendant's right to a fair trial was not abridged.[73]

The majority's puzzling conclusion derived from its narrow and somewhat skewed reading of the record as well as its restrictive interpretation of the presumed prejudice test. Presumed prejudice, according to the *Murphy* majority, occurs only when criminal proceedings take on a circus atmosphere and thus lack the "solemnity and sobriety to which a defendant is entitled."[74] In contrast, mere juror exposure to the defendant's prior convictions or to news accounts surrounding the crime he is charged with do not automatically lead to prejudice.[75] In the absence of a "circus atmosphere," therefore, the accused bears the burden of proving actual juror bias through voir dire questioning.

Pointing to jurors' professions of impartiality, and distinguishing familiarity with the defendant's past and a predisposition against him, the Court found no evidence of juror partiality against Murphy.[76] Moreover, the majority stressed that most of the publicity about the defendant had appeared seven months before the jury was chosen.[77] Finally, the Court took comfort in the fact that only twenty out of seventy-eight potential jurors were excused because they indicated a predisposition against Murphy. This led to the assumption that the jurors' assertions of impartiality could be taken at face value, for the jury pool was not as poisoned as in *Irvin*.[78]

A distorted view of the record colored the majority's facile perceptions in *Murphy*. Contrary to its factual premises, at least one juror obtained her knowledge from a newspaper article the week of the trial that described Murphy as a "beach boy hoodlum serving a life sentence for murder."[79] Another juror stated that other comments by venire members had made him "sick to [his] stomach." In fact, venirepersons had characterized Murphy as "thoroughly rotten," and called for Murphy's conviction.[80] These comments do not convey the sense of impartiality and fairness which the majority readily subscribed to.

If *Murphy* made difficult a showing of presumed or actual prejudice, *Patton v. Yount*[81] converted the process into a herculean exploit. In *Patton*, the defendant had been previously convicted of the rape and murder of an eighteen-year-old student in a small Pennsylvania community. His conviction was reversed because an illegally secured confession was used against him at trial. He was subsequently tried and convicted of murder four years after the first trial.[82] Before Yount's second trial, publicity disclosed his previous conviction for murder, his confession, and his previous plea of temporary insanity, all of which were inadmissible, and not admitted, at trial. The voir dire also revealed that nearly all members of the jury pool (161 out of 163) had heard about the case and that 77 percent admitted they would carry an opinion into the jury box.[83] Additionally, eight of the fourteen jurors who found Yount guilty admitted that they had formed an opinion on his guilt.[84]

Though these factual circumstances paralleled those present in *Irvin*,[85] the *Patton* majority found no prejudice to the defendant's right to a fair trial by an impartial jury. Rather, it seized upon *Murphy*'s rationale that the passage of time mitigates the damaging effects of pretrial publicity. Noting that four years passed between Yount's two trials, the majority stressed the lapse of time as having "a profound effect on the community and, more important, on the jury, in softening or effacing opinion."[86] To bolster its weak rationale, the Court emphasized the factual nature of articles which appeared daily during jury selection.[87]

It is disingenuous to suggest that jurors exposed to negative publicity about the accused can maintain their impartiality. Specifically, in both *Murphy* and *Patton*, jurors learned about otherwise inadmissible evidence. In Murphy's case, they knew about his previous escapades with the Star of India theft and his prior murder conviction. In Yount's case, jurors were aware of his confession, his previous conviction of the crime he was on trial for, and his use of the insanity defense at his first trial, a defense he abandoned in the second trial. The evidence the jurors were exposed to in both *Murphy* and *Yount* was inadmissible. Of course, such evidence is inadmissible not only because it is deemed irrelevant or because it was unconstitutionally obtained; it is inadmissible because of its devastating and negative impact upon the jury. Common sense dictates that a juror will consciously or unconsciously hold a conviction against the accused. As one juror in the *Murphy* case readily admitted, he would be hard pressed to ignore Murphy's criminal record during deliberations.[88]

The adverse influence of such inadmissible evidence is confirmed by the attitude it generates among potential jurors. In *Patton*, for example, nine veniremen who were unsuccessfully challenged for cause asserted that their opinions concerning Yount's guilt would be changed only if the defendant could convince them otherwise. A juror who ultimately decided Yount's fate shared the same attitude.[89] Similarly, a juror who was seated for Murphy's trial testified during voir dire that, in light of what he knew about Murphy's past through pretrial publicity, he would find him guilty if Murphy did not testify or offer other exculpatory evidence.[90]

Despite these negative effects created by pretrial publicity, a criminal defendant faces incredible odds in showing either actual or presumed prejudice. The teaching of *Murphy* and *Patton* is that a case must be of a "rare breed" in order to "exceed the extremely high threshold test of presumed prejudice requiring a change of venue."[91] Absent a carnival atmosphere in which the defendant is tried and convicted before the trial process begins, it is unlikely a defendant will successfully meet the presumed prejudice criterion. The upshot of this is unmistakable; the recourse for a defendant who is the subject of prejudicial pretrial publicity is to establish actual prejudice by eliciting juror bias through the jury selection process.

Extracting an admission of bias by a potential juror is exceedingly difficult. This problem may stem from the juror's desire to conceal her bias or from the juror's failure to recognize the prejudice.[92] Indeed, this phenomenon emerges graphically in *Smith v. Phillips*.[93] In that case, a juror sought employment with the prosecution as an investigator during the defendant's trial. Unaware of this during the trial, the defendant attempted to reverse his conviction on due process grounds based on the juror's conduct as well as on the prosecution's failure to divulge the fact to the defense. Finding no "implied bias" in the juror's conduct, the Court held that his action did not impair his ability to render an impartial verdict.[94]

What option did the accused have in *Phillips*? According to the Court, he could prove actual bias, thereby maintaining his right to an impartial jury.[95] This conclusion is predicated upon the Court's overly sanguine view that voir dire adequately identifies juror bias. In fact, the Court's assumption is that questioning potential jurors is sufficient to identify juror bias, "even in a community saturated with publicity adverse to the defendant."[96] Even though the Court has not formally embraced this proposition, for practical purposes its doctrine has faithfully adopted it.

The Efficacy of Remedies Designed to Elicit Actual Bias

As the preceding discussion indicates, the judicial system has placed confidence in the ability of trial courts to elicit actual juror bias through the voir dire process. This reliance lacks an empirical or commonsense foundation. One recent study shows that no direct empirical evidence points to the effectiveness of judges' and attorneys' voir dire challenges as an antidote to prejudicial pretrial publicity.[97] From a practical standpoint, one can discern the failure of voir dire to draw accurate or honest responses from potential jurors. The available evidence, moreover, shows that jurors do not admit their biases and preconceptions during voir dire. A variety of reasons accounts for this: jurors' inability or unwillingness to recognize bias; a defensive attitude generated by suggestions of prejudice; lack of candor fostered by the inhibiting nature of judicial questioning; haste and the nature and detail of voir dire questions.[98]

Other remedies designed to cure prejudicial pretrial publicity also fall short of the mark. For example, continuances granted to ameliorate public passion conflict with a defendant's right to a speedy trial. Judicial instructions admonishing jurors to disregard information gleaned outside the courtroom are unavailing from a practical as well as an empirical perspective. Jury deliberation serves to magnify, rather than diminish, existing biases. Finally, a change of venue is at variance with the defendant's right to be tried in the community in which the crime occurred and may clash with the community's desire to mete out justice in the case.[99]

Despite the deficiencies inherent in these remedies, the American judicial system has put faith in the jury selection process as the most effective means of identifying actual juror bias. In *Nebraska Press Assn. v. Stuart*, for example, the Supreme Court advised trial courts to engage in "searching questioning" of potential jurors to detect those with "fixed opinions as to guilt or innocence."[100] Given courts' aversion to a change of venue as a way of remedying pretrial publicity, the defendant's primary weapon is a thorough voir dire process, conducted by the judge or by the attorneys, which is designed to flesh out potential jurors' real attitudes and feelings about the case.

The ability of the defendant to employ the jury selection process to extract admissions of prejudice by potential jurors has been severely curtailed by the Court's opinion in *Mu'Min v. Virginia*.[101] In that case, the majority held that questioning about the content of pretrial publicity a potential juror has been exposed to is not constitutionally mandated.[102] Therefore, a trial judge may, at her discretion, ask general questions of a jury panel *en masse*, and assure herself of a juror's supposed impartiality without even evoking a response from the juror. In essence, the trial court may presume impartiality from a juror's silence in response to generic questions posed by the judge about the effect of pretrial publicity on the juror's ability to render a fair verdict.[103]

In *Mu'Min*, the defendant was charged with the murder of a store owner in Prince William County, Virginia. Mu'Min committed the crime after escaping from his work detail assignment during a lunch break. The defendant was a convicted murderer serving a forty-eight-year prison sentence. Considerable publicity attended the circumstances of the crime. Specifically, forty-seven newspaper articles detailed the nature of the crime, Mu'Min's criminal record, and the fact that the defendant had been rejected for parole six times and had committed numerous prison infractions. In addition, the pretrial accounts described the circumstances of the murder of which Mu'Min had been convicted, the fact that he escaped the death penalty for the murder because it was not available when he was convicted, and indicated that the defendant had confessed to the murder of the store owner. Finally, newspaper articles described the flaws associated with and suggested reform of the prison work-crew system.[104]

Rejecting the accused's motion for a change of venue, the trial judge instead relied upon the voir dire process to elicit juror bias. Further, the court refused the defendant's request to ask potential jurors questions about the content of news accounts they may have seen or read. In fact, sixteen out of twenty-six potential jurors admitted to having read or heard information about the offense or the accused through the news media or other sources. In an attempt to discern the jurors' impartiality, the trial judge asked four generic, open-ended, questions which essentially asked jurors whether the information they were exposed to had destroyed their impartiality; and whether they could render an impartial verdict based on the evidence presented in court.[105] Interestingly, eight of the twelve jurors who decided Mu'Min's fate had either heard or read something about the case.[106]

The rationale of the *Mu'Min* decision centers on the nexus between content questioning and the defendant's right to a fair trial. The majority opinion recognizes the common-sense notion that content-based questions "would materially assist in obtaining a jury less likely to be tainted by pretrial publicity than one selected without such questions."[107] As a corollary, content questioning would be helpful in fleshing out juror partiality. Nevertheless, the majority, while conceding these arguments, draws the line by stating that failure to ask content-based questions does not necessarily infringe upon the accused's right to a fair trial. Accordingly, content questioning in a criminal trial affected by pretrial publicity is not constitutionally compelled.[108]

Several reasons may be adduced to rebut the *Mu'Min* majority's narrowly crafted rationale. Content questioning sorts out the extent and intensity of publicity a prospective juror has been exposed to, thereby determining whether such exposure would lead to disqualification as a matter of law. Additionally, such questioning is necessary to buttress the trial court's finding of impartiality. A third reason for exploring the content of publicity is to assist the trial judge in assessing the credibility of the juror's responses.[109]

Perhaps the most compelling justification for requiring content questioning is the balance fostered by the procedure. The defendant is at a disadvantage when he has no opportunity to discover what prospective jurors have read or seen. Not only are trial judge and counsel in a weak position to weigh challenges for cause, but the defendant's intelligent use of peremptory challenges is seriously impaired.

As Judge Celebrezze has argued, "[w]here veniremen have been exposed to prejudicial publicity, the nature and degree of that exposure is certainly a matter of legitimate concern to a defense attorney . . . deciding on peremptory challenges."[110] Hampering the defense's intelligent use of peremptory challenges calls into question the delicate adversarial symmetry essential to a fair trial.

To the extent peremptory challenges help counsel eliminate from the jury venirepersons who are otherwise qualified on the basis of gut reaction or psychological theories, content questioning enhances the intelligent use of those challenges. It is difficult to assess a juror's claim of impartiality when one is not allowed to probe the basis for the affirmation. Furthermore, a defendant may be stripped of the ability to exclude jurors for cause when content questioning is not permitted. A telling example of this phenomenon occurred in the murder and robbery trial of Susan Saxe. One juror, who had read about the case but professed impartiality, was questioned at length. The questioning prompted the juror to reveal that, "[w]e all know the girl went in and held up the bank and the policeman was shot there."[111]

A fair trial in the criminal context entails an impartial jury; in turn, the Supreme Court has equated impartiality not with lack of opinion or preconceptions, but with the willingness to put aside impressions or opinions and "to render a verdict based on the evidence presented in court."[112] It is exceedingly difficult, however, to determine true impartiality without exploring in depth the nature and degree of bias that may have been prompted by exposure to prejudicial pretrial publicity. Content questioning facilitates the task through a searching inquiry into the sources of pretrial publicity a prospective juror has encountered. In the absence of content questioning, intelligent decisions on peremptory challenges or challenges for cause become highly unlikely. Therefore, a defendant is disadvantaged in eliciting juror bias and in assessing the validity of prospective jurors' assertions of impartiality.

Contrary to the *Mu'Min* majority's deceptive reasoning, preclusion of content questioning thwarts the defendant's right to a fair trial by an impartial jury. Although voir dire is not an effective mechanism to ensure an impartial jury, it is the predominant method employed by trial courts, and endorsed by the Supreme Court, to detect juror bias. Thus, the defendant who is the subject of prejudicial pretrial publicity suffers a tremendous disadvantage: She is prevented from using any method, however flawed, that measures the extent and intensity of a prospective juror's predispositions toward her.

The effect of *Mu'Min* is to leave a criminal defendant virtually powerless in her quest for an impartial jury. Not only does she face formidable odds in establishing presumptive prejudice but she is prevented from proving actual prejudice by probing the extent and nature of juror exposure to adverse pretrial publicity. Short of candid responses from potential jurors or extraordinary circumstances leading to presumed prejudice, a defendant will find it difficult to ensure she will be tried by an impartial jury. Within this context, the search for an impartial jury has degenerated into a game of chance.

Examining the contours of the free press–fair trial controversy leaves one with the feeling of hopelessness. When these titans collide, it seems that a proper balance is an unattainable goal. Such an accommodation, however, is not an impossible task. Unfortunately, the Supreme Court has failed to achieve a proper equilibrium principally for two reasons. First, it has not acknowledged the crucial link between the extent of media freedom and the ability of the accused to receive a fair trial. Second, the Court has ignored the contradictory purposes served by a free press and a fair trial. As noted at the outset, freedom of the press does not promote fairness; rather, freedom of expression often causes harm.[113] On the other hand, the Sixth Amendment is the hallmark of fairness within the criminal justice system.

The Court's failure to achieve an accommodation of these important rights stems from its failure to analytically discern the connection between freedom of expression and the ideal of a fair trial. Although the Court has been reluctant to close criminal proceedings to the media and the public, or to place restraints on media reporting about criminal activity, it has not compensated for this freedom by according more leeway to a defendant who has been the subject of pretrial publicity. At first, the Court seemingly accounted for this disparity by creating what appeared to be a fairly broad standard for establishing presumed prejudice. With its decision in *Murphy*, however, the Court began hampering the ability of the accused to establish presumed prejudice except in egregious circumstances.[114]

Furthermore, the Court has placed an imposing obstacle in the defendant's path with regard to proof of actual prejudice. *Mu'Min* represents the culmination of the Court's blind faith in the process of voir dire as a means of discovering juror bias. The new doctrine fashioned in *Mu'Min* obtusely relies on the efficacy of a process discredited from a pragmatic as well as an empirical standpoint.[115] This misplaced reliance has reached ridiculous proportions with the Court's assumption that open-textured, generic questions asked of panels of prospective jurors are adequate to detect juror bias.

Rather than fashioning such unrealistic standards, the Court ought to have recognized its aversion to closure or pretrial restraints and given defendants in highly publicized cases the remedy most often sought: a change of venue. While it is true that with mass communication, a notorious defendant such as Manuel Noriega will find it difficult to find a jury oblivious to his case, it is nonetheless true that in most circumstances a change of venue will assist the defendant in selecting an impartial jury. Even in such extraordinary circumstances, a change of venue could increase the likelihood of a fair trial. In General Noreiga's case, jury selection was complicated by the fact that Fidel Castro was a potential witness. As a result, Cuban exiles professed an inability to judge Noriega fairly if Castro testified at the trial.[116]

Similarly, the Rodney King case furnishes an example of circumstances under which a nationally publicized incident led to a change of venue. King, a black motorist, was severely beaten by Los Angeles law enforcement officers in March of 1991. His beating was captured on home video by a witness who recorded the event, and the video was prominently and frequently displayed by the national media. In *Powell v. Superior Court*,[117] the appellate court ordered a change of venue in order to afford the defendants charged with assaulting Rodney King a fair trial. Although the potential jury pool in Los Angeles County was sufficiently large and diverse that a supposedly fair jury could have been selected, the court deemed it wise to change the venue. It noted that although the nature of modern communications limits the effectiveness of a change of venue, the political turmoil engendered by such a controversial case warrants a change of venue.[118] The political overtones in the case, moreover, are endemic to Los Angeles and not to any other community in the United States.

The *Powell* case is instructive in another context. Where a publicized case has aroused the political passions of the community, a fair trial may be impossible. The possibility of riots if a particular verdict is rendered casts serious doubts on the ability of the defendant to receive a fair trial.[119] Thus, the *Powell* court referred to the Miami case of Officer William Lozano, who was convicted of manslaughter of two black motorists. The Florida appellate court reversed

Lozano's conviction because the community was concerned about riots that could erupt if Lozano was acquitted.[120]

In less publicized cases, moreover, the effectiveness of a change of venue is more telling. For example, in *Mu'Min*, the defendant requested and could have been granted a change of venue. Given the exposure of the jurors to adverse publicity, Mu'Min could have profited from such a procedure. Indeed, a change of venue would have meant that Mu'Min's fate would not have been decided by jurors who read or saw accounts indicative of his guilt and were exposed to prejudicial inadmissible evidence.

It is true that a change of venue is regarded as an ineffective remedy because it interferes with a defendant's right to be tried where the crime occurred and because it frustrates the community's desire to decide the outcome of the case.[121] However, a defendant who seeks a change of venue necessarily waives his right to a trial in the community where the crime occurred. He does so in order to enhance the chances of receiving a fair jury. Given the accused's constitutional right to a fair trial, moreover, the community's interest in deciding the case ought to give way to the accused's higher stake. After all, a defendant's right to a fair trial by an impartial jury is constitutionally protected; a community's desire to resolve the accused's fate is not.

In determining whether a change of venue is warranted, trial courts should defer to a defendant's request when substantial pretrial publicity has infected prospective jurors. Where evidence reflects biases and preconceived opinions, courts must resolve doubts as to their ability to furnish the accused a trial by a fair and impartial jury in favor of the defendant. Prejudicial pretrial publicity reduces the chances a defendant will receive a fair trial. Trial courts ought to recognize that the evidence does not support the notion that voir dire is an effective mechanism for detecting juror bias. Accordingly, they must be more amenable to defendants' wishes for a change of venue in cases saturated with pretrial publicity regarding the accused's guilt.

One could object to this proposal on practical grounds because changes of venue are administratively inconvenient and tax an already overburdened criminal justice system. Nonetheless, this exception is unwarranted in light of the minuscule number of criminal cases that engender substantial pretrial publicity and thereby endanger the prospect of selecting an impartial jury.

CONCLUSION

The Supreme Court's flawed jurisprudence in the free press–fair trial area derives from its indifference to the disparate roles played by these two cherished freedoms. Fundamental fairness required in the criminal context dictates a more sensitive response than that generated by the Court. Freedom to report on criminal cases that concern and appeal to the community necessitates more care for the defendant's fair trial rights. Otherwise, the grim prospect raised by Justice Brennan, that is, "the sacrifice of Sixth Amendment rights on the altar of the First Amendment,"[122] could turn into reality.

NOTES

1. The Sixth Amendment stipulates that "In all criminal prosecutions, the accused shall enjoy the right to a speedy and public trial, by an impartial jury of the State and district wherein the crime shall have been committed," U.S. CONST. Amend. VI. The First Amendment provides, in pertinent part, that "Congress shall make no law . . . abridging the freedom of speech, or of the press," U.S. CONST. Amend. I.

2. *Nebraska Press Assn. v. Stuart*, 427 U.S. 539, 547 (1976).

3. Id. Chief Justice Burger writes that "Neither in the Constitution nor in contemporaneous writings do we find that the conflict between these two important rights was anticipated, yet it is inconceivable that the authors of the Constitution were unaware of the potential conflicts between the right to an unbiased jury and the guarantee of freedom of the press."

4. *In re Oliver*, 333 U.S. 257, 270–71 (1948). As the Court has remarked, "Public scrutiny of a criminal trial enhances the quality and safeguards the integrity of the factfinding process, with benefits to both the defendant and to society as a whole," *Globe Newspaper Co. v. Superior Court*, 457 U.S. 596, 606 (1982).

5. *Bridges v. California*, 314 U.S. 252, 260 (1941).

6. Powe, THE FOURTH ESTATE AND THE CONSTITUTION, 278 (1991).

7. Id. at 278–79.

8. *Estes v. Texas*, 381 U.S. 532, 540 (1965).

9. *Nebraska Press Assn. v. Stuart*, 427 U.S. at 561.

10. *See*, e.g., *Press Enterprise Co. v. Superior Court*, 464 U.S. 501, 508 (1984); *Richmond Newspapers, Inc. v. Virginia*, 448 U.S. 555, 564 (1980).

11. *Nebraska Press Assn. v. Stuart*, 427 U.S. at 612 (Brennan, J., concurring).

12. *See*, e.g., *Richmond Newspapers Inc. v. Virginia*, 448 U.S. at 569–71; *Press Enterprise Co. v. Superior Court*, 464 U.S. at 508.

13. *See* notes 6–7 and accompanying text.

14. *Reynolds v. United States*, 98 U.S. 145, 156 (1878).

15. *United States v. Burr*, 25 F.Cas. 49–51 (C.C.D. Va. 1807) (No. 14, 692g).

16. *See* Minow and Cate, *Who is an Impartial Juror in an Age of Mass Media*, 40 AMER. L. REV., 631, 635–36 (1991).

17. This was the standard fashioned by Chief Justice Marshall in the *Burr* case, *supra*, and followed by the Court in *Reynolds*. Subsequently, the modern Court followed that criterion in *Irvin v. Dowd*, 366 U.S. 717 (1961).

18. 427 U.S. 539 (1976).

19. Id. at 542–43.

20. Id. at 562–63.

21. Id. at 563–67.

22. Id. at 566–69.

23. Id. at 569.

24. 443 U.S. 368 (1979).

25. Id. at 372–75.

26. Id. at 379–88.

27. Id. at 392.

28. 448 U.S. 555 (1980).

29. Id. at 573–80. The plurality opinion in *Richmond* was written by Chief Justice Burger. The concurring opinions of the other justices concurred in the notion that the First Amendment and, derivatively, the Fourteenth Amendment, guaranteed public access to criminal trials. Justice Blackmun, who dissented in *Gannett*, found a right to access in the Sixth Amendment as well as in the First.

30. Id. at 587–94 (Brennan, J., concurring).

31. Id. at 559–61.

32. Minow and Cate, *supra* note 16, at 633. As the authors point out, "It is often impossible for a judge to control the publication of prejudicial information because, increasingly, the most dramatic revelations occur at the time of the crime itself, long before there is a trial, much less a judge selected to oversee the trial," id.

33. Id. at 580–81.

34. This position was taken by Chief Justice Burger and Justices White, Stevens, and Stewart.

35. 457 U.S. 596 (1982).

36. Id. at 606–07.

37. Id. at 610–11.

38. Id. at 607–08.

39. Id. at 599.

40. 464 U.S. 501 (1984).

41. Id. at 521 (Marshall, J., concurring).

42. Id. at 503.

43. The potentially embarrassing information which might dissuade a juror from being candid might involve a sexual attack on the juror or a member of the juror's family, id. at 512. In the *Globe* case, "overriding interest" was found wanting because the trial court failed to consider alternatives to closure, id. at 510–13.

44. As Justice Stevens pointed out in his concurring opinion, the defendant did not oppose the closure on his Sixth Amendment right to a public trial. Hence, the Court did not reach the issue whether selection of the jury was part of the trial for Sixth Amendment purposes, id. at 516 (Stevens, J., concurring).

45. 478 U.S. 1 (1986).

46. Cal. Penal Code Ann. Sec. 868 (1985) permits closure of preliminary hearings if the "exclusion of the public is necessary in order to protect the defendant's right to a fair and impartial trial."

47. *Press Enterprise Co. v. Superior Court*, 478 U.S. at 4–5.

48. Id. at 10–15.

49. *Richmond Newspaper Co. v. Virginia*, 448 U.S. at 570 (cited in *Press Enterprise II* at 13).

50. *Nebraska Press Assn. v. Stuart*, 427 U.S. at 588 (Brennan, J., concurring).

51. Id. at 612.

52. *See* part II, *infra*.

53. *See* part II, *infra*.

54. 98 U.S. 145 (1878).

55. *Burr, supra* note 15.

56. *Reynolds v. United States*, 98 U.S. at 155–56.

57. Id. at 156–57.

58. Id. at 156.
59. Id. at 155.
60. 366 U.S. 717 (1961).
61. Id. at 727.
62. Id. at 728.
63. Id. at 727–28.
64. Id. at 724–25 (quoting from *United States v. Wood*, 299 U.S. 123, 145–46 (1936)).
65. Id. at 724.
66. Id. at 723.
67. Minow and Cate, *supra* note 16, at 642–43.
68. 373 U.S. 723 (1963).
69. Id. at 724.
70. Id. at 726.
71. Id. at 727.
72. 421 U.S. 794 (1975).
73. Id. at 803.
74. Id. at 798–99. The Court paraded as examples of this circus atmosphere the trials in *Rideau, Irvin, Sheppard v. Maxwell*, 384 U.S. 333 (1966), and *Estes v. Texas*, 381 U.S. 532 (1965).
75. Id. at 799.
76. Id. at 800–02.
77. Id. at 802.
78. Id. at 803.
79. Id. at 806, n.1 (Brennan, J., dissenting).
80. Id. at 807.
81. 467 U.S. 1025 (1984).
82. Id. at 1026–27. The prosecution dismissed the rape charge prior to the second trial, id. at 1027.
83. Id. at 1029.
84. Id. at 1029–30.
85. *See* notes 60–67, *infra* and accompanying text.
86. Id. at 1033.
87. Id. at 1032.
88. *Murphy v. Florida*, 421 U.S. at 805.
89. Id. at 1045–46 (Stevens, J., dissenting).
90. *Murphy v. Florida*, 421 U.S. at 805.
91. *Coleman v. Kemp*, 778 F.2d 1487 (11th Cir. 1985), where the appellate court painstakingly detailed the adverse pretrial publicity, id. at 1491–1533.
92. *Smith v. Phillips*, 455 U.S. 209, 221–22 (1982) (O'Connor, J., concurring). *See* also Isaacson, *Fair Trial and Free Press: An Opportunity for Coexistence*, 29 STAN. L. REV. 561, 565 (1977).
93. 455 U.S. 209 (1982).
94. Id. at 220. Justice O'Connor posited in her concurring opinion circumstances under which "implied" bias would automatically attach: for example, if a juror is employed by the prosecution; if the juror is related to a trial participant or to a member of the criminal enterprise; or if the juror "was a witness or somehow involved in the criminal transaction," id. at 222 (O'Connor, J., concurring). Justice O'Connor also cited *Leonard*

v. United States, 378 U.S. 544 (1964) (per curiam), in which the Court held that prospective jurors who had heard the trial court announce the defendant's guilty verdict in the first trial should be automatically disqualified from sitting on a second trial on similar charges, id. at 223–24.

95. Id. at 216 (quoting from *Dennis v. United States*, 339 U.S. 162, 171–72 (1950)).

96. *Patton v. Yount*, 467 U.S. at 1030 (quoting from Judge Garth's concurring opinion in the court below).

97. Kerr, Kramer, Carroll and Alfini, *On the effectiveness of voir dire in criminal cases with prejudicial pretrial publicity: An empirical study*, 40 AMER. U. LAW REVIEW, 665, 671 (1991).

98. Minow and Cate, *supra* note 16, at 650–54.

99. Id. at 646–49. The Sixth Amendment provides in pertinent part that a defendant has a right to be tried before a ''jury in of the State and district wherein the crime shall have been committed,'' U.S. CONST. Amend. VI.

100. *Nebraska Press. Assn. v. Stuart*, 427 U.S. at 564.

101. 111 S.Ct. 1899 (1991).

102. Id. at 1908.

103. Id. at 1919 (Kennedy, J., dissenting).

104. Id. at 1902.

105. Id. at 1902. The questions posed by the trial court are open-textured; they are leading in the sense that civic-minded persons are apt to believe the correct response is to insist on impartiality and to deny the existence of fixed opinions about guilt or innocence. In fact, only one of the sixteen venirepersons who heard or read about the case admitted he could not be impartial. The questions read as follows:

> Would the information that you heard, received, or read from whatever source, would that information affect your partiality in this case?
>
> Is there anyone that would say what you've read, seen, heard, or whatever information you may have acquired from whatever the source would affect your impartiality so that you could not be impartial?
>
> Considering what the ladies and gentlemen who have answered in the affirmative have heard or read about the case, do you believe that you can enter the Jury box with an open mind and wait until the entire case is presented before reaching a fixed opinion or conclusion as to the guilt or innocence of the accused?
>
> . . . In view of everything that you've seen, heard, or read, or any information from whatever source that you've acquired about this case, is there anyone who believes that you could not become a Juror, enter the Jury box with an open mind and wait until the entire case is presented before reaching a fixed opinion or a conclusion as to the guilt or innocence of the accused? (Id.)

106. Id. at 1903.

107. Id. at 1905.

108. Id. The majority relies on *Murphy v. Florida* for this precept.

109. Id. at 1913–15 (Marshall, J., dissenting).

110. *United States v. Johnson*, 584 F.2d 148, 155 (6th Cir. 1978); *see* also *United States v. Blanton*, 719 F.2d 815, 835–38 (Kennedy, J., dissenting), *cert. denied*, 104 S.Ct. 1592 (1984).

111. *Mu'Min v. Virginia*, 111 S.Ct. at 1914–15, n.4 (Marshall, J., dissenting).

112. *Irvin v. Dowd*, 366 U.S. at 723.

113. Powe, *supra* note 6, at 104.

114. *See supra*.

115. *See supra*.

116. MIAMI HERALD, Sept. 7, 1991, at 2B. col. 3.

117. 283 Cal.Rptr. 777 (Cal.App. 2 Dist. 1991).

118. Id. at 784 (citations omitted). The court distinguished the *Manson* case in which the publicity arose from the nature of the crimes and not from political issues unique to Los Angeles.

119. Id. at 787–88.

120. Id. at 787 (citing *Lozano v. Florida* (June 25, 1991, 90–217)-So.2d-—[slip. opn. pp. 4–7]).

121. *See* note 99 *supra*, and accompanying text.

122. *Nebraska Press Assn. v. Stuart*, 427 U.S. at 612.

Conclusion

The Supreme Court has observed that "the Constitution recognizes an adversary system as the proper method of determining guilt."[1] Guaranteeing such an adversarial process is the Sixth Amendment to the Constitution. Essentially, the amendment allows the defendant to test the government's case and to present a defense through the means of a vigorous advocate. Further, the Sixth Amendment protects the defendant's liberty interests by giving her the right to a jury trial, thus blunting the potential abuse of either the "overzealous" prosecutor or the "biased" or complacent judge. All of these safeguards are designed to afford the accused a fighting chance against the organized power of the government.

Aside from this practical function, the amendment is emblematic of our criminal adversarial process. It symbolizes the commitment of the system to a fair process in which the defendant must be proven guilty beyond a reasonable doubt before he loses the most precious right in a democratic society, his freedom. Indeed, the criminal justice system is premised on the adversarial system of adjudication. The Sixth Amendment codifies the adversarial process by providing criminal defendants with the shield necessary to combat the prosecution: an attorney who advocates their cause and who tests the state's case through the crucible of cross-examination.

The Supreme Court's interpretation of the amendment has stripped it of much of its practical and symbolic function. The Court's result-driven jurisprudence has ignored the central role the amendment plays in the adversarial criminal system. It seems that the majority of the Court is comfortable with depriving defendants of their counsel of choice, with constraining the right of the defendant to confront his accusers, and with precluding the accused's prerogative to present a defense. Furthermore, the Court has done this in the name of furthering law enforcement objectives. What is remarkable is that the majority of the Court has candidly admitted in recent opinions that the real rationale behind the rulings is a crime-control ideology.[2]

Justice Stevens has rebuked his brethren for manifesting a preference for an inquisitorial system of justice.[3] The majority answered this criticism by noting that the adversarial system is distinguished from an inquisitorial one by the presence of an impartial judge who does not conduct the factual and legal investigation but permits the parties the right to do so.[4] Technically, the majority's assessment is correct. However, the spirit of Justice Stevens' remarks is quite to the point.

What the majority of the Supreme Court apparently prefers is not a true adversarial process. Rather, it is a *pseudo*-adversarial system in which one side has a decided advantage. The majority is not interested in discarding or dismembering the facade of the criminal adversarial process. Rather, its objective is to leave the elements of the system in place while ensuring the correct result: the defendant's conviction. The majority has successfully achieved its goals by partially depriving the accused of the means with which to combat the prosecution. Therefore, the system is supposedly intact while the scales are unevenly weighted in favor of the government.

One must ask whether the Court's attempts to "stack the deck" against criminal defendants is really necessary. Will the war against drugs be more successful now that those accused of major drug-related offenses will have to resort to public defenders or court-appointed counsel? I seriously doubt it. The crime-control ideology unabashedly proclaimed by the Court will have a negligible effect on crime. Unfortunately, it will have an adverse effect on the symbolic and pragmatic functions the Sixth Amendment serves in our system of adjudication.

A historian of our legal antecedents has acutely remarked that "the preeminent American nightmare, vivified by its revolutionary experience, is that a frenzied or tyrannical majority will reach out to [suppress] the 'rights and fundamental liberties' of citizens, and the Court will do nothing to resist this intrusion through the constitutional mechanisms available to it."[5] I am not sure whether a "frenzied" majority has agreed to divorce the Sixth Amendment from its crucial purpose in our adversary system of adjudication, but I believe that the majority of the Supreme Court ought to heed the warning contained in our revolutionary background.

NOTES

1. *Singer v. United States*, 380 U.S. 24, 36 (1965).
2. *See*, e.g., *McNeil v. Wisconsin*, 111 S.Ct. 2204 (1991); *Caplin and Drysdale v. United States*, 109 S.Ct. 2646 (1989).
3. *McNeil v. Wisconsin*, 111 S.Ct. 2204, 2214 (Stevens, J., dissenting).
4. Id. at 2210, n.2.
5. Stimson, THE AMERICAN REVOLUTION IN THE LAW: ANGLO-AMERICAN JURISPRUDENCE BEFORE JOHN MARSHALL, 146 (1990).

Bibliography

Alschuler, *The Supreme Court and the Jury: Voir Dire, Peremptory Challenges, and the Review of Jury Verdicts*, 56 U. CHICAGO L. REV. 153 (1989).

Amsterdam, *Speedy Criminal Trial: Rights and Remedies*, 27 STAN. L. REV. 525 (1975).

Arenella, *Rethinking the Functions of Criminal Procedure*, 72 GEO. L. J. 185 (1983).

Babcock, *Fair Play: Evidence Favorable to an Accused and Effective Assistance of Counsel*, 34 STAN. L. REV. 1133 (1982).

Baldwin, *Due Process and the Exclusionary Rule: Integrity and Justification*, 39 U. FLA. L. REV. 505 (1987).

Beany, W. THE RIGHT TO COUNSEL IN AMERICAN COURTS (1955).

Calo, *Joint Trials, Spillover Prejudice, and the Ineffectiveness of a Bare Limiting Instruction*, 9 AM. J. TRIAL ADVOC. 21 (1985).

Caplan, *Questioning Miranda*, 38 VAND. L. REV. 1417 (1985).

Casper, Benedict, & Perry, Juror Decision-Making, Attitudes, and the Hindsight Bias (American Bar Foundation Working Paper No. 8702, 1987).

Dawson, *Joint Trials of Defendants in Criminal Cases: An Analysis of Efficiencies and Prejudices*, 77 MICH. L. REV. 1379 (1979).

Di Perna, P. JURIES ON TRIAL (1984).

Doyel, *The Federal Speedy Trial Act: Stampede into Ambush*, 16 J. MARSHALL L. REV. 27 (1982).

Feely, M. COURT REFORM ON TRIAL (1983).

Frankel, PARTISAN JUSTICE (1980).

Frankel, *The Search for Truth: An Umpireal View*, 123 U. PA. L. REV. 1031 (1975).

Frankel, *From Private Rights to Public Justice*, 51 NYU L. REV. 516 (1976).

Freedman, *Client Confidences and Client Perjury: Some Unanswered Questions*, 136 U. PA. L. REV. 1939 (1988).

Freedman, UNDERSTANDING LAWYERS' ETHICS (1990).

Garcia, *Mental Sanity and Confessions: The Supreme Court's New Version of the Old "Voluntariness" Standard*, 21 AKRON L. REV. 275 (1988).

Garcia, *The Winding Path of* Bruton v. United States: *A Case of Doctrinal Inconsistency*, 26 AMER. CRIM L. REV. 401 (1988).

Garcia, *The Compulsory Process Clause and the "Sporting Theory of Justice": The Supreme Court Evens the Score*, 28 DUQ. L. REV. 619 (1990).

Garcia, *Speedy Trial, Swift Justice: Full-Fledged Right or "Second-Class Citizen"?*, 21 S. W. UNIV. L. REV. 31 (1992).

Gaynes, *Two Juries/One Trial: Panacea of Judicial Economy or Personification of Murphy's Law?*, 5 AM. J. TRIAL ADVOC. 285 (1981).

Genego, *The Future of Effective Counsel: Performance Standards and Competent Representation*, 22 AM. CRIM. L. REV. 181 (1984).

Genego, *The New Adversary*, 54 BROOKLYN L. REV. 781 (1988).

Godbold, *Speedy Trial—Major Surgery for a National Ill*, 24 ALA. L. REV. 265 (1972).

Goebel, J. 1 HISTORY OF THE SUPREME COURT OF THE UNITED STATES (1971).

Goldfarb, *When Judges Abandon Analogy: The Problem of Delay in Commencing Criminal Prosecutions*, 31 WILLIAM & MARY L. REV. 607 (1990).

Goldman, *Not so "Firmly Rooted": Exceptions to the Confrontation Clause*, 66 N.C.L. REV. 1 (1987).

Goldwasser, *Limiting a Criminal Defendant's Use of Peremptory Challenges: On Symmetry and the Jury in a Criminal Trial*, 102 HARV. L. REV. 808 (1989).

Goodpaster, *On the Theory of American Adversary Criminal Trial*, 78 J. CRIM. L. & CRIMINOLOGY 118 (1987).

Graham, *The Right to Confrontation and the Hearsay Rule; Sir Walter Raleigh Loses Another One*, 8 CRIM. L. BULL. 99 (1972).

Grano, *Implementing the Objectives of Procedural Reform: The Proposed Michigan Rules of Criminal Procedure—Part I*, 32 WAYNE L. REV. 1007 (1986).

Grano, Miranda v. Arizona *and the Legal Mind: Formalism's Triumph over Substance and Reason*, 24 AM. CRIM. L. REV. 243 (1986).

Green, *"Through a Glass, Darkly": How the Court Sees Motions to Disqualify Criminal Defense Lawyers*, 89 COLUM. L. REV. 1201 (1989).

Haddad, *Post-*Bruton *Developments: A Reconsideration of the Confrontation Rationale and a Proposal for a Due Process Evaluation of Limiting Instructions*, 18 AM. CRIM. L. REV. 1 (1980).

Hanley, *The Last Thirty Days*, 10 LITIGATION P. 10, Winter 1984.

Hazard, ETHICS IN THE PRACTICE OF LAW (1978).

Heller, F. THE SIXTH AMENDMENT TO THE CONSTITUTION OF THE UNITED STATES (1951).

Isaacson, *Fair Trial and Free Press: An Opportunity for Coexistence*, 29 STAN L. REV. 561 (1977).

Jonakait, *Restoring the Confrontation Clause to the Sixth Amendment*, 35 UCLA L. REV. 557 (1988).

Kalven, H., & H. Ziezel, THE AMERICAN JURY (1966).

Kamisar, Gideon v. Wainwright *a Quarter Century Later*, 10 PACE L. REV. 343 (1990).

Kamisar, *The* Gideon *Case 25 Years Later*, N.Y. TIMES, March 10, 1988 at A27, col.1.

Kaufman, *Does the Judge Have a Right to Qualified Counsel?*, 61 ABAJ 569 (1975).

Kaye, Gideon v. Wainwright: *A Lesson in the Obvious*, 10 PACE L. REV. 419 (1990).

Kerr, Kramer, Carroll & Alfini, *On the Effectiveness of Voir Dire in Criminal Cases with Prejudicial Pretrial Publicity: An Empirical Study*, 40 AMER. L. REV. 665 (1991).

Kirst, *The Procedural Dimension of the Confrontation Doctrine*, 66 NEB. L. REV. 485 (1987).

Krash & Lewis, *The History of* Gideon v. Wainwright, 10 PACE L. REV. 379 (1990).

Lafave, W., & J. Israel, CRIMINAL PROCEDURE (1985).

Landsman, S. THE ADVERSARY SYSTEM: A DESCRIPTION AND DEFENSE (1984).

Levy, ORIGINAL INTENT AND THE FRAMERS OF THE CONSTITUTION (1988).

Lilly, *Notes on the Confrontation Clause and* Ohio v. Roberts, 36 U. FLA. L. REV. 207 (1984).

Maclin, *Constructing Fourth Amendment Principles from the Government Perspective: Whose Amendment is it Anyway*, 25 AM. CRIM. L. REV. 669 (1987).

Marcus, *The Confrontation Clause and Co-defendant Confessions: The Drift from* Bruton *to* Parker v. Randolph, 1979 U. ILL. L. F. 559.

Margulies, *Resource Deprivation and the Right to Counsel*, 80 J. CRIM. L. & CRIMINOLOGY 673 (1989).

Massaro, *Peremptories or Peers? Rethinking Sixth Amendment Doctrine, Images, and Procedures*, 64 N. CAR. L. REV. 501 (1986).

Massaro, *The Dignity Value of Face-to-Face Confrontations*, 40 U. FLA. L. REV. 863 (1988).

McCormick, C., MCORMICK ON EVIDENCE (E. Cleary 3d ed. 1984).

McNamara, R. CONSTITUTIONAL LIMITATIONS ON CRIMINAL PROCEDURE (1972).

Miller, *The Adversary System: Dinosaur or Phoenix*, 69 MINN. L. REV. 1 (1984).

Minow and Cate, *Who is an Impartial Juror in an Age of Mass Media*, 40 AMER. L. REV. 631 (1991).

Misner, SPEEDY TRIAL—FEDERAL AND STATE PRACTICE (1983).

Note, *Inculpatory Statements Against Penal Interest and the Confrontation Clause*, 83 COLUM. L. REV. 159 (1983).

Note, Richardson v. Marsh: *Co-defendant Confessions and the Demise of Confrontation*, 101 HARV. L. REV. 1876 (1988).

Note, *Sixth Amendment—Confrontation and the Use of Interlocking Confessions at Joint Trial*, 78 J. CRIM. L. & CRIMINOLOGY 937 (1988).

Note, *Sixth Amendment—Limiting the Scope of* Bruton, 78 J. CRIM. L. & CRIMINOLOGY 984 (1988).

Packer, H. THE LIMITS OF THE CRIMINAL SANCTION (1968).

Partridge, A. LEGISLATIVE HISTORY OF TITLE I OF THE SPEEDY TRIAL ACT OF 1974 (1980).

Pizzi, Batson v. Kentucky: *Curing the Disease but Killing the Patient*, 1987 S. CT. REV. 97.

Posner, THE PROBLEMS OF JURISPRUDENCE (1990).

Powe, THE FOURTH ESTATE AND THE CONSTITUTION (1991).

Pound, *The Causes of Popular Dissatisfaction with the Administration of Justice*, 29 ABA REP. 395 (1906).

Rosenthal & Rice, *Whittling Away the Right to Counsel: The Supreme Court's New Approach to the Sixth Amendment*, 3 CRIM JUST. 2 (1989).

Saltzburg, *Lawyers, Clients, and the Adversary System*, 37 MERCER L. REV. 647 (1986).

Schwartz, *The Zeal of the Civil Advocate*, 1983 AM. B. FOUND. RES. J. 543.

Seidelson, *The Confrontation Clause, the Right Against Self-Incrimination, and the Supreme Court: A Critique and Some Modest Proposals*, 20 DUQ. L. REV. 429 (1982).

Silver, *Equality of Arms and the Adversarial Process*, 1990 WIS. L. REV. 1007.

Simon, *The Ideology of Advocacy: Procedural Justice and Professional Ethics*, 1978 WIS. L. REV. 29.

Steffen, *Truth as Second Fiddle: Reevaluating the Place of Truth in the Adversarial Trial Ensemble*, 1988 UTAH L. REV. 799.

Stimson, THE AMERICAN REVOLUTION IN THE LAW: ANGLO–AMERICAN JURISPRUDENCE BEFORE JOHN MARSHALL (1990).

Stuntz, *Waiving Rights in Criminal Procedure*, 75 VA. L. REV. 761 (1989).

Sward, *Values, Ideology, and the Evolution of the Adversary System*, 64 IND. L. J. 301 (1986).

Tribe, *Trial by Mathematics: Precision and Ritual in the Legal Process*, 84 HARV. L. REV. 1329 (1971).

Uviller, Barker v. Wingo: *Speedy Trial Gets a Fast Shuffle*, 72 COLUM. L. REV. 1376 (1972).

Weisberg, *Criminal Procedure Doctrine: Some Versions of the Skeptical*, 76 J. CRIM. L. & CRIMINOLOGY 832 (1985).

Westen, *Confrontation and Compulsory Process: A Unified Theory of Evidence for Criminal Cases*, 91 HARV. L. REV. 570 (1978).

Westen, *The Compulsory Process Clause*, 73 MICH. L. REV. 76 (1974).

White, *Evidentiary Privileges and the Defendant's Constitutional Right to Introduce Evidence*, 80 J. CRIM. L. & CRIMINOLOGY 377 (1989).

White, *Police Trickery in Inducing Confessions*, 127 U. PA. L. REV. 581 (1979).

Whitebread, C., & C. Slobogin, CRIMINAL PROCEDURE (2d ed. 1986).

Wolfram, MODERN LEGAL ETHICS (1986).

Zupancic, *Truth and Impartiality in Criminal Process*, 7 J. CONTEMP. L. 39 (1982).

Table of Cases

Index

About the Author

ALFREDO GARCIA teaches Criminal Law and Procedure at the St. Thomas University School of Law. He has served as an Assistant State Attorney in Florida and as a criminal defense attorney at both the state and federal levels. He has written frequently on the Sixth Amendment in professional journals.

www.ingramcontent.com/pod-product-compliance
Lightning Source LLC
LaVergne TN
LVHW011756200926
848484LV00003B/717
* 9 7 8 0 3 1 3 2 7 8 7 7 8 *